CW01368209

MEN IN THE MIDDLE

MEN IN THE MIDDLE

Searching for Masculinity in the 1950s

JAMES GILBERT

The University of Chicago Press / Chicago and London

James Gilbert is professor of history at the University of Maryland.

The University of Chicago Press, Chicago 60637
The University of Chicago Press, Ltd., London
© 2005 by The University of Chicago
All rights reserved. Published 2005
Printed in the United States of America
14 13 12 11 10 09 08 07 06 05   1 2 3 4 5
ISBN: 0–226–29324–6 (cloth)

Library of Congress Cataloging-in-Publication Data

Gilbert, James Burkhart.
    Men in the middle : searching for masculinity in the 1950s / James Gilbert.
        p. cm.
    Includes bibliographical references and index.
    ISBN 0-226-29324-6 (cloth : alk. paper)
        1. Men—United States—History—20th century. 2. Masculinity—United States—History—20th century. 3. Men in popular culture—United States—History—20th century. 4. Men—United States—Social conditions. I. Title.
    HQ1090.3.G55 2005
    305.31′0973′0904—dc22

                                                                            2004021636

♾ The paper used in this publication meets the minimum requirements of the American National Standard for Information Sciences–Permanence of Paper for Printed Library Materials, ANSI Z39.48–1992.

Contents

	Preface	ix
1	Introduction: Men in the Middle	1
2	Crisis and the History of Masculinity	15
3	Lonely Men: David Riesman and Character	34
4	A Feeling of Crisis: The 1950s	62
5	"Sex Is Sex": Alfred Kinsey and the Report That Shook the World	81
6	"My Answer": Billy Graham and Male Conversions	106
7	The Ozzie Show: Learning Companionate Fatherhood	135
8	Mendacity: Men, Lies, and *Cat on a Hot Tin Roof*	164
9	The Gender of High Culture	189
10	Getting Used to Women: Perspectives on Masculinity Crisis	215
	Notes	225
	Index	259

For Chip

Preface

Books begin several times and in many ways—in ideas that slowly emerge, in hunches that meander around interesting questions. They also often depend upon serendipity and chance. The initial idea for *Men in the Middle* came during a trip I made several years ago to the American Heritage Center at the University of Wyoming. Scheduled to give a talk at a conference, I arrived far too early. To occupy my time, the associate director of the center, Rick Ewig, suggested that I look over the holdings of the center. What caught my eye immediately was a description of the *Ozzie and Harriet* manuscripts. Looking at the list of scripts and story lines, I found titles that confounded my memories of the program and seemed to conflict with what I thought I knew about this and other TV situation comedies. The titles of the episodes alone suggested something much more complex. So I ordered several, although one in particular from the radio years seemed, more than anything else, to contradict the stereotypes that I thought had ruled the 1950s. This extraordinary and complicated episode about confused gender roles persuaded me to look further. I determined to come back and do a more thorough search. The results now constitute a chapter in the book that follows.

Books are also the products of communities. The archives and manuscript collections that I visited were always inviting and their curators were more than helpful. I especially wish to thank the Harvard University Archives, the University of Delaware Archives, the Princeton University Archives, the American Heritage Center at the University of Wyoming, the Kinsey Institute for Research in Sex, Gender, and Reproduction, the Billy Graham Center at Wheaton College, and the Harry Ransom Humanities Research Center at the University of Texas at Austin. I benefited from the marvelous general collection at the Library of Congress, as well as the friendly and pleasant surroundings of the Fondren Library at Rice University, where I did much of my writing. I am also grateful for the generous support provided by the University of Maryland General Research Board.

Beyond the institutions that facilitated my research and writing, there are many individuals who willingly listened to and criticized my ideas. To them I owe a special debt. They include my colleagues at Uppsala University in Sweden, especially Erik Åsard, the seminar at the Institute for Historical Studies at the University of Maryland, the historical seminar at the New School in New York City, the historical seminar at Catholic University, and the participants at the Tutzing Conference on American Gender History in Germany in 2004. Individuals who read parts of the manuscript or allowed me to try out ideas on them include Robyn Muncy, Sonya Michel, Gary Gerstle, Tim Meagher, Leo Ribuffo, Jackson Bryer, Eli Zaretsky, John Judis, Mark Micale, Larry Eskridge, and G. H. Rothschild. I am grateful to Beth Emmering for her research assistance. Angela Kurtz read the manuscript to untangle footnotes and unscramble syntax. More than almost anyone, Doug Mitchell should be credited with whatever virtues this work may have. He is the ideal editor as well as a constant friend.

1

Introduction: Men in the Middle

In 1948, shortly after reading about Alfred Kinsey's new book *Sexual Behavior in the Human Male*, a teenager from Texas wrote to the author, pleading for help. "I know there must be thousand[s] of young boys today who are in the same position and state of mind that I am in and have been for years, ever since I began to understand that life often is a 'hell on earth,'" he volunteered. As if to prompt the sexologist with an analysis, he continued, "I have a great inferiority complex that never gives me any rest." "I am an introvert," he added.[1]

Although he readily found facile psychological language to express his sense of isolation and awkwardness, the boy never did reveal to Kinsey his problem: just that being a boy and growing up was difficult and confusing and disorienting in what Garry Wills has called "John Wayne's America." As much of Kinsey's other correspondence reveals, and the intense interest in masculinity during the following decade underscores, the boy was not alone. Growing up in the 1950s, if not always absurd, as Paul Goodman described it, was nonetheless agitated by conflict and uncertainty, but above all, by a sense of rapid, puzzling change.[2]

There were and are many "1950s," a decade of American history that continues to evoke particularly vivid memories and strong opinions—my own included. It is the first era of American history to have a memory recorded by television, and the first to inspire nostalgic sitcoms about these pioneering days in the same medium. The yearning for such seductive times, with its inventive music, movies, dress, fashion, cars, and pop culture, has a distinctly youthful cast to it, as if this were an age of cultural adolescence, when society itself relentlessly focused on the joys and hardships and the inventive new ways of growing up to be American, white, and middle class. Encouraged by an obsessive attention to generational experience, whether in the sinister guise of juvenile delinquency or the sentimentalized fads of teenage romance, the 1950s have often appeared to be, primarily, about the perils and prospects of becoming an adult and particularly about growing up to be masculine or feminine.

There are, of course, a great many problems with such a picture, not the least of which is the notion of the decade itself as a useful historical construct. For what is sometimes remembered as characteristic of a broad period may have been true only briefly, if at all. And usually it is confined to a particular group. What most Americans "remember" about the 1950s probably happened, if at all, in two short periods: from after the war to around 1953 (the most intense period of the cold war) or between 1953 and 1957. This middle half-decade corresponds exactly with my own years in high school. I am, thus, doubly wary, as a historian writing with an uncertain memory about a period I lived through and necessarily reluctant to universalize my particular interpretation, and a participant alert to the possibility of distortion by the "happy days" industries of contemporary culture.

In fact, this book is written as something of an endeavor to discover the place of my own "fifties" in a larger and more complex context, especially within the sharp contour of conflicting definitions of gender. Almost always visible behind the depictions of those halcyon days of a culture coming of age were the nagging problems of growing up, of becoming a young man in a time of uncertain and changing concepts of masculinity—of celebrating and aspiring to the very roles that youth defined itself against. Indeed, in the 1950s, there was an enormous popular and professional literature on gender, either openly directed to concepts of masculinity or sometimes imbedded in discussions only thinly disguised by the invocation of the generic "man" when the subject was quite clearly just men—and white, middle-class men at that.

Most of that literature about adolescent and adult men was directed at or written about the special problems of middle-class men. Although there is a huge contemporary proscriptive/descriptive dialogue about femininity, that is not my topic except insofar as it highlights the conversation about masculinity. I believe that the 1950s were unusual (although not unique) for their relentless and self-conscious preoccupation with masculinity, in part because the period followed wartime self-confidence based upon the sacrifice and heroism of ordinary men. Historians have found concern and even the evidences of a "male panic"—intense uncertainties about masculine identity—in almost every era of American history. But the 1950s appear to hold a special place in this ongoing discussion largely because sociologists and historians began at that moment to define the basic notions of social character and to isolate masculinity as a subject for contemporary study within this new category. To them, history appeared to be a process of evolving psychological states and character types. Thus increased attention to the history of social character occurred in a context of considerable flux and concern about problems of gender identity.

Historians today use the term "male panic" to denote a time when men self-consciously rebel against real or imagined "feminization" developing within the workplace, public spheres, and/or domestic relationships. Since the end of the nineteenth century, the symptoms of this anxiety have usually been signaled by an outpouring of literature and expert advice about how to reconstitute masculinity on a new plane, to find or create new models of masculine vigor and assertion outside of, or in defiance of, threatening changes in work or family relationships. "Real masculinity" might be achieved through some sort of actual or (increasingly in the modern era) vicarious experience and emulation: warfare, sport, or identification with mythical heroes of literature, films, and other formats of popular culture. Certainly, such apprehensions and their cultural manifestations were typical of the 1950s. For example, they were mustered in the anxious "techno language" of atomic Armageddon as well as in the more benign parades of President Eisenhower's patriarchal platitudes. Often, a tough-guy masculinity was the source of language and metaphors in foreign policy discussions where clichés from western films served as descriptions of the strengths of American determination and the character of our response to threats. These publicly held assumptions about masculinity probably intensified the "lavender scare" that resulted in firing hundreds of suspected homosexuals in government service after 1950.[3] But what made this period so animated was, in fact, a real conflict between an assumed norm of masculinity and new forms of masculinity based upon notions of companionship and cooperation within the family and workplace. The absurdity of growing up in the 1950s was heightened by the reluctance—the downright opposition—of a great many cultural spokesmen to accept the changes occurring in American society. Often they interpreted such developments as a threat to masculinity. But at the same time there were dissenting, clear voices, proposing alternative constructions of gender that saw opportunity in those same changes. Somehow we have lost sight of these positive accents.[4]

In fact, the 1950s were host to a number of remarkable social and cultural transitions that became highly visible and often controversial during this era. Several of these also had implications for masculinity. While it is well known that a revived civil rights movement began its highly successful assault on legal obstacles to racial equality in this period, there were other quieter integrations that profoundly reshaped American society. One of these lowered the barriers erected to keep Catholics out of the mainstream of American society. This transformation was signaled vividly by the election of John F. Kennedy in 1960, a contest in which masculine vigor became the watchword of the candidate's identity. Another advance was the elimination of some of the corrosive elements of anti-Semitism, such as quotas in higher education. If nothing else, these transitions had the effect of creating the possibility for more diverse role models for middle-class Americans and for opening middle-class status to excluded others, even if African Americans gained entrance only at the margins.

Responses to other important social changes in the period greatly complicated the debates over masculinity. Indeed, at times, gender became the language invoked to explore the significance of these changes. By understanding the importance of this central metaphor, we can understand the 1950s from a new perspective. Broadly speaking, issues of masculinity linked discussions of conformity, mass consumption, and mass culture. Gender anxiety infiltrated this critical literature and redefined these subjects by providing immense energy and a seeming timeliness. A vast and widely read critical literature emerged around social and cultural conformity, the censure of suburban life, and the condemnation of mass culture. A fundamental element of each critique revealed fears of masculine decline. Indeed, worry about masculinity supplied more than just metaphors and arguments. It was sometimes the essential inspiration for the critique in the first place. To put this complex argument as simply as possible, the effects of conformity, suburban life, and mass culture were depicted as feminizing and debasing, and the proposed solution often lay in a renewal of traditional masculine vigor and individualism.

This gendering of modern mass culture, consumption, and conformity had older roots. There were many versions of this idea drawn from traditional descriptions of culture associated with women to the outright conclusion that modern culture was feminizing. For example, in his seminal critique of mass culture in 1953, the radical social and literary critic Dwight Macdonald declared that the audience for mass culture had become passive consumers. Borrowing from a resentful and stereotyped vocabulary describing women, this argument lamented that women were easily manipulated; they suffered infantile regression and engaged in a sentimental worship of motherhood. And the addict of mass culture was all this and more. Much earlier, Thorstein Veblen had argued something of the same thing about the relationship of women to leisure and consumption.

In his famous critique of the late nineteenth century, *Theory of the Leisure Class*, he wrote that a woman was "even required to consume largely and conspicuously—vicariously for her husband or other natural guardian. She is exempted, or debarred, from vulgarly useful employment."[5] She was passive and controlled.

And even before this, as Victoria de Grazia has demonstrated, marketable objects carried sexual connotations to such an extent that one could argue the adage "Consumption, thy name is woman." In fact, however, this gendering of consumption, she notes, came from long-standing divisions of labor and the separation of household and workplace into separate, gendered spheres.[6]

The contemporary import of this gendering of consumption and mass culture was related to the vast expansion of consumerism after World War II in the United States and the appearance of a new form of consumer society. There were many responses to this revolution, what Lizabeth Cohen deems the "Consumers' Republic." But most remarkable was the explosion of an acerbic and dismissive literature denouncing, on moral and economic grounds, the new expansion of consumerism, and with it, the gradual evolution—amounting to a moral revolution of sorts—toward acceptance of mass consumption as essential for social well-being. With a hefty rise in real, disposable income between the late 1940s and 1950s, American families spent their way into new lifestyles, in suburbs, new shopping malls, transported by bicolored and overdesigned automobiles. It was this remarkable increase in objects and their radical design that redefined economic, social, and psychological relationships—the substance of what Gary Cross calls the "All-Consuming Century." Inevitably, these developments in middle-class lifestyles provoked a critical literature deploring the decline of older values associated with work and individualism—and masculinity—and the rise of a feminized mass culture.[7]

The literature and speech that carried this critique was powerful and widespread, the stuff of best-seller lists, conferences, and magazine exposés. What made these negative assessments powerful and abiding was, in part, the serious purpose of the public intellectuals who articulated them and their penetrating and radical style. By public intellectual I refer to the scientists, theologians, academics, and political and social commentators who struggled to understand the profound changes in American society after World War II and who, at the moment, commanded considerable attention and prestige. In many cases, these public commentators sounded the alarm over what they discovered. They worried about the new emphasis in American culture on domesticity and the changes in the workplace toward larger white-collar bureaucracies. They sometimes even feared that the younger generation would be inadequate to the challenges of the cold war.[8] They proved to be especially suspicious of new techniques of socially and psychologically engineered cooperation. They worried about the impact of mass culture as it impinged through its very pervasiveness upon intellectual freedom and individual identity. They constructed a general critique of mass consumer society based upon an implicit contrast with the traditional American values of individualism and personal autonomy. And in high culture they often preferred a tough, hard-edged, and sometimes inaccessible modernism.

Sociologist C. Wright Mills, himself an important public intellectual, devoted a lengthy analysis to the nature of this outpouring of social criticism in modern American society. "The intellectual," he wrote, "ought to be the moral conscience of his society, at least with reference to the value of truth, for in the defining instance, that *is* his politics." Mills suggested that the function of the critic was, itself, being undermined by the same processes and powers that established the predominance of mass culture. But fellow radical Irving Howe disagreed. The role of the public intellectual, he wrote, had emerged even stronger after World War II, for "capitalism in its most recent stage has found an honored place for the intellectuals."[9]

Historian Richard Hofstadter agreed that the role of public intellectual in the 1950s was extraordinary. In one short paragraph, he managed to suggest how this group of writers had come to dominate American discourse and the distinctive tone they had lent this discussion:

In social criticism, professional jeremiads like Vance Packard become bestsellers; and more serious writers like C. Wright Mills, who compulsively asserted the most thoroughgoing repudiation of American life in its every aspect, are respectfully reviewed and eagerly read. David Riesman's *The Lonely Crowd*, which can be taken as a depressing account of what the American character has become, is the most widely read book in the history of sociology, and William H. Whyte's mordant analysis of *The Organization Man* is read everywhere by organization men.[10]

Public intellectuals operating either as independent writers or as academics published an array of widely read critical, analytical literature in the 1950s. Their focus repeatedly returned to the corrosive properties of the new mass culture and consumer society, and their consequences for postwar society. As this literature of hesitation and rejection etched its signature upon the decade, caricaturing American society as a world peopled by conformist and self-effacing "dads" unable to communicate with their sons and afraid to confront their bosses or their wives and "moms," it produced the impression that American society suffered as much as it enjoyed the fruits of prosperity. Yet here we must pause. For this literature obscured other voices that proposed, in one form or another, some sort of positive acceptance of that new world. Such accommodationist voices have been, by and large, missing from our accounts of the 1950s. But they were strong and credible at the time. Indeed, their acceptance of the world denounced elsewhere as "other directed," "conformist," or "mass" simply intensified the conflict between possibilities.

This book seeks to recover the lost debate among critics, cultural optimists, and dissenters in the 1950s, especially in the realm of gender, where their arguments cut deeply. Indeed, it is probably not possible to understand the arguments around gender in the 1950s—and the frequent invocation of panic and anxiety—without understanding the context of social criticism in which these arguments were generated. So I will try to reread some of the key sources of the 1950s, removing the language of panic and anxiety to uncover what lay beneath the repeated attacks on the new, mass-consumption society: an attempt to revive traditional notions of individualism and older models of masculinity—what Betty Friedan would later aptly name the "masculine mystique." This was, after all, a period populated by icons of military men, sports figures, and cowboy heroes. Even the ambiguous Beat writers declared their distaste for a listless and cloying domesticity when they drifted out onto the aimless open road. At the same time, there were voices that advised a less hostile reaction to changes in domestic and workplace arrangements or who defined change as possibility and opportunity.

Curiously, what I recall about the 1950s exactly fits the stereotype that now appears dubious to me: the horror of the suburbs (where I lived), the dread of conformity (that I embraced in its most lurid description), and the fear of being engulfed by a trivial mass culture (that I pretended to dislike). Looking at the sources has changed my mind and revealed my memories to be incomplete and limited. I intend to let these sources tell a far more complicated story.

This will not, however, be a complete story of the twists and turns of the conflict over masculinity that engulfed the period. Instead, it focuses on selected elements of contradictions that emerged during this time. In particular, I want to suggest why that young man from Texas might have felt conflicted about the masculine identity to which he aspired. Because, in fact, there was a conflict. So, for example, in our mental picture of the

1950s, we need to remember that portrayals of masculinity in the most pervasive of public arenas, the Hollywood film, ran from Marlon Brando to James Dean, to Rock Hudson, to Gary Cooper, and to John Wayne. Based upon their consumption of images from television, boys were equally attracted to donning a Davy Crockett coonskin cap and the garish pastels worn by Elvis Presley. This was never entirely John Wayne's world anymore than it ever belonged to Liberace. Despite widespread condemnation of mass culture, and the rich literature and sociology of suburban angst, millions of American men continued to aspire to buy a home and settle there with their wives and children.[11] And despite his best efforts, the brilliant critic Dwight Macdonald never convinced Americans to give up what he denounced as effeminate mass culture in favor of contemporary modernism in the arts—or even accept his association of masculinity with highbrow culture.

Must we then change our assumption that there was a single, prevailing, agreed-upon norm of masculinity during the decade? I believe that we must. Many writers and social critics acted as if there were just one standard–as if everyone knew what they were talking about. But do their references to an assumed uniform construct make it so? When we twist the lens of interpretation to get a closer look, what is revealed in this specimen is not only variety, but the contending shapes of gender that begin to look like the diversity expressed so famously in the next decades.

The essays that follow explore American masculinity in the 1950s from a variety of perspectives but with most attention given to those I call "men in the middle," that is, white, middle-class, middle Americans, living in the middle decade of the century, in the midst of a profound questioning of gender identities. They were, before anyone else, the subject matter of the discussion and the focus of concern. These essays seek to establish and explore two principal contentions. The first is the existence of a variety of possibilities available in the discourse about masculinity in public images and symbols. All of the figures considered here, whether real individuals, or fictions of one sort or another, were known through their existence in the public sphere. All of them were concerned with defining some sort of viable version of masculinity—although they might not have lingered on this terminology. All of them contributed to the presentation of different versions of masculinity that, by their mere presence in the public arena, offered distinct and differing models for behavior.

It follows, secondly, that the nature of what has sometimes been called a "male panic" seriously needs reevaluation. Certainly, literature of anxiety and discomfort over male identity was plentiful in this period. It is easy to find strident assertions about declining American masculinity. This clearly does constitute evidence for uneasiness about gender roles, but it is not necessarily indicative of anything so serious or pandemic as the word "panic" implies. What it surely suggests is the existence of an important cluster of writers and public figures who analyzed society in this way and who spoke in universal categories about a situation with which they had intimate familiarity. But it is just as plausible to argue that these same public figures were reacting with hostility to the changes that other men in society were quite happy to accept. The challenge for the historian is, therefore, to resist the seduction of generalizing from such brilliant literary sources. A similar case in point marks the end of the nineteenth century, which has often been depicted as the decisive moment in the definition of modern American social character. It is clear that educator G. Stanley Hall, philosopher William James, and President Theodore Roosevelt all deeply worried about issues of masculinity and went to strenuous lengths in their lives and writings to find some personal resolution to their doubts. Their works were widely read and they were popular and influential figures of their day. But their focus on masculinity is not, in itself, evidence of a general male panic in the first decade of the twentieth century, however much historians have been tempted to universalize an American mood of alienation and inadequacy from their compelling writings.[12]

Our story begins with a survey of the historical literature about male panic. This is crucial for a number of reasons, not least being the importance of this notion to current-day interpretations of the 1950s. What needs emphasis is the relationship of this notion of a masculinity crisis during the 1950s to the emergence of the historical discussion of character that was elaborated during the same decade. This new history of character became a persuasive model to depict both the past (1890s) and the contemporary 1950s as parallel times, with similar changes in psychological type and controversies over gender. Since a generation of powerful and prominent historians came of age in this latter period, it is crucial to speculate about the effects of this environment of character analysis and crisis upon their writings.

The most influential version of the new history of character was expounded by sociologist David Riesman, the subject of chapter 3. In some respects, Riesman is the central public intellectual of the 1950s. Above all, he is responsible for translating historical change into the evolution of character and psychological types. His surprise best seller, *The Lonely Crowd* (1950), stimulated a widespread and profound dialogue about conformity in the 1950s and introduced a persuasive account of the historical development of American character. Although not overtly, *The Lonely Crowd* also proposed a special version of American history told in terms of the transitions in male personality, the unacknowledged subject of his study. A key document in the discussion of masculinity in the 1950s, then, Riesman's work was seminal for many reasons, not the least because he put the evolution of character at the center of a vigorous critique of conformity, mass culture, and consumerism. Even if Riesman's arguments were sometimes misunderstood or misappropriated, as he often claimed, he provided the language for the discussion that seemed to fire public imagination. He also identified the end of the nineteenth century as the turning point in the transition in establishing the modern American character. Among American historians this assertion added to an already existing sense of that period as the defining moment in modern American society. Riesman supplied the language and character constructs to understand this process in a new way that upstaged other interpretations. In so doing, he promoted a serious albeit anxious historical critique of the personal costs (and opportunities) of modern mass society.

If Riesman provided a sophisticated and worrying account of the challenges faced by Americans, and particularly by American men, in adjusting to the modern world of mass culture, consumption, and middle-class work, there were powerful analogues to his work in more popular venues. The subject of chapter 4, this literature took the character, perhaps more aptly put, the caricature, of a journalistic assault on women. Such depictions depended upon the popular acceptance of a notion that men's prerogatives as well as their psychic well-being and identity were being challenged by overbearing and overpowerful women. Beginning with Philip Wylie's caustic *Generation of Vipers* (1942), a new literature of gender complaint found fault with men for accepting the feminization of American culture and criticized women for exercising hegemony over it. This remarkable outpouring was partly aimed at convincing women to give up full-time employment after a stint as replacement workers during the war and seek satisfaction and fulfillment at home and through marriage. In addition to becoming a postwar reflex, this was also an extended pep talk to men about pumping up their drive, energy, and ambition for encounters with a world that conspired to smooth the sharp edges competition and reduce individuality to styles of consumption—where the "self-made" man was transformed into the mass-produced man. Diagnoses of the problem "What's Wrong with the

American Male" became the preoccupation of public intellectuals, anthropologists, sociologists, and psychologists, as well as journalists and advice columnists. And the answer was discouragingly repetitive: American women.

Because this literature was so pervasive and convincing in invoking a contemporary crisis of masculinity, American historians living through that period, or registering its aftershocks, may have accepted the terms of this phenomenon as expressed. More important, many of them were convinced that a history of character, in which gender panic was sometimes an explicit feature, represented a persuasive way to retell the story of American social development. Thus, the 1950s became a crucial decade as subject *and* object in a major reformulation of American historiography, and this development in turn has continued to influence the writing of American history and gender history within it even today.

While David Riesman identified a history of fundamental character change in American history, Alfred Kinsey, the subject of chapter 5, believed he had discovered a sexual revolution in the contemporary behavior of American men. With the publication of his immense, innovative, and shocking study of sexual behavior of American males in 1948, Kinsey ignited a firestorm of controversy with his descriptions that started an equally strong backfire of criticism from public intellectuals, journalists, and professional psychologists and psychiatrists who sought to discredit his assertions. Kinsey's critics were always divided between those who said he was wrong and those who said he was wrong to reveal the male sexual practices he discovered. But Kinsey was also a revolutionary who sought not so much to alter practice directly as to change the way people talked about sex and understood it and thereby to transform both the act and the account. Kinsey thought that his surveys and statistics defined the way men really behaved. For its own good, he said, society ought to accept the fluidity of practice and the deviation from norms as the definition of normal itself. He believed that he had assembled powerful statistics to decouple sex acts from prevailing notions of normal masculinity.

Billy Graham, the subject of the next chapter, conceived of his era as a moment of profound crisis. But gender played a different role in his formulations of the problems in American culture. Convinced of the imminent probability of end-time for humanity, Graham preached immediate conversion and regeneration in a way that was deeply pessimistic yet fundamentally joyous. Like most Protestant evangelicals in American history, he also faced an endemic problem: the skewed gender ratios of his audiences and conversions. Given the potential passivity and fervent emotionalism in evangelical religion (and the common identification of such psychological states with women), Graham focused his attention on the moments of Christian rebirth that involved the most threatening expression of these off-putting and dangerous emotions. Although still attracting far more women than men through his ministry, Graham developed several remarkable measures designed to promote male conversion—indeed, to transform the process of conversion itself into an appealing male experience.

Contrast Graham's fiery speeches and tender invitations with the genial purgatory of sitcom America and the mythic figure of Ozzie Nelson, the baffled patriarch and companionate father of the radio and television series *The Adventures of Ozzie and Harriet*. This immensely popular and long-lived series, running from the 1940s through 1966, featured a central character whose weekly comic escapades surveyed the nagging problems of men adjusting to a confusing new world of women, children, and mass consumption. Thoroughly middle-class and middle American Ozzie spent each week learning the lessons of togetherness that he had forgotten from the week before: how to get along in the new environment of domesticity and companionate marriage.[13] Ozzie earnestly wanted to live up to the standards of this new world in which men and women were friends and lovers and children were pals, but he always failed—and therein lay the comedy. No doubt this bumbling persona helped endear him to the audience. He desired nothing more than to be a partner to his wife and a companion to his sons, but his preposterous and grandiose ideas about his role, his inappropriate devotion to patriarchal, elitist and "old-fashioned" values continually tripped him up. The end was inevitable. Ozzie learned his lesson, which he then promptly forgot, just in time for the next exploration in this gentle satire of the male mystique. His situation was the drama of the happy accommodation to "other-direction." Most remarkable, the series was preoccupied with the very questions that enthralled public intellectuals of the day: mass culture, consumerism, and conformity—except that Ozzie's weekly lesson was to get along in, not condemn, this brave new world.

Tennessee Williams also dramatized the contemporary family in his exploration of social and gender relations, but gentle satire was rarely, if ever, his mode of discourse. The most popular American playwright of the 1950s and the inspiration for more than a score of films, Williams wrote memorable characters of immense personality for the American stage. In *Cat on a Hot Tin Roof*, his most popular play (and film), Williams created a male lead, Brick Pollitt, whose sexual ambiguity set off a prolonged and profound examination of contemporary masculine roles: son, brother, father, and husband. In the various versions of the play (published and unpublished) and in the film made from the Broadway production, as the work shifts on an axis of changing emphasis, Williams tears away the masks and lies and self-deceptions that surround the expectations of masculinity. In the end, only lies, fiction, and performance itself seem to define the meaning of manhood.

My final essay on individuals returns the story of masculinity to its starting point: the perception of a crisis. Writer and critic Auguste Comte Spectorsky surveyed the world of letters in the late 1950s and despaired at his discovery—or better—at what he could *not* find, which was a thriving, masculine high culture. In accepting the managing editor position at *Playboy* magazine in 1956, Spectorsky brought sophisticated cultural tastes and contacts with highbrow periodicals like the *New Yorker* to Hugh Hefner's soft-core pornography. To Hefner, this veneer of high culture was an essential marker of the sophisticated lifestyle that the Bunny enterprises promoted. To Spectorsky, the endeavor had a somewhat different, more ambitious purpose: he hoped to remasculinize high culture. The account of his story concludes with a 1962 symposium in the magazine inspired by his friend Philip Wylie and devoted to explaining the decline of American masculinity. Marked by stale complaints, culled from a decade of worry, the symposium ended where the argument began, in irresolution, confusion, and name-calling. Perhaps this was the surest sign that the terms of an argument were ready to shift to a new configuration of gender concerns and responses.

The final chapter opens up the argument of the book in two respects. It suggests a different way to understand what has heretofore been deemed the recurring crisis of masculinity in American history. It identifies a historical process that appears to shed new light on this discussion of gender. It also briefly engages the problems of thinking about masculinity in our own very recent past.

Before embarking on this exploration, it should be emphasized that the subject of this book is not the measure of men's behavior in the 1950s. While there are implications to be drawn from the omnipresent public discussions about how men acted or should act, words do not necessarily represent conduct. Sometimes the public airing of issues such as gender identity carry the scent of cliché, making it seem as if everyone, everywhere was responding with the same degree of apprehension. Masculinity was, certainly, an issue for the 1950s. Some observers, particularly public intellectuals, worried deeply about it, and addressed it implicitly or explicitly. But other figures who participated in this general discourse about middle-class men saw different problems as well as opportunities. It is this broader discussion of possibilities that defines *Men in the Middle*.

2

Crisis and the History of Masculinity

The starting point for any discussion of masculinity must be the contingency of all sexual identity. Inevitably, the environment in which masculinity is expressed will have a profound affect upon its meaning. This suggests that the complex ideological, behavioral, and physical package that society designates as masculine (or feminine) must be viewed as socially constructed even when the actors in gender dramas are convinced that their roles are stable and natural. As R. W. Connell has put it, "Gender exists precisely to the extent that biology does *not* determine the social."[1]

But a socially constructed masculinity is nevertheless limited by and dependent upon biology as much as it is articulated in culture, social interaction, and imagination. Its raw materials are, first of all, primary and secondary sexual traits (their development and decline over a lifetime). Male identity is also, fundamentally, relational. It is defined in terms of its apparent opposite, such as femininity, or divided internally by developmental stages such as boyhood, manhood, and the androgyny of old age, or more recently characterized by its difference from homosexuality or the transgendered. None of these relations is absolute, and each can vary widely from culture to culture and historic period.

Masculinity has both a social and an individual face. What societies define as standards of male behavior, even in the most prescribed circumstances, have considerable play and offer varieties of potential roles. Some of these are intensely practical and almost universally accepted in the human community, such as marriage and, in many societies, patriarchy. Others, however, are more clearly ideological, and the stuff of imagination, derived from political expressions or cultural products, and particularly, in the twentieth century in the United States in the presentations of mass culture. In other words, they are manufactured role models available for emulation in the examples of celebrities, sports figures, and politicians, or fictitious characters and heroes. Of course any such model is also open to individual interpretation and appropriation. It is not surprising, then, that historians increasingly see such public characters in terms of social roles that shade and blend into each other. Add to this the different circumstances where masculinity is expressed—in domestic relations, leisure, work, in public and in politics, before audiences of male peers or women or children or strangers, and so on—and it is easy to find a great deal of variety. At one time or another, an individual may be called upon to play each of these different roles with their different emphases. Finally, given that masculinity has been increasingly defined in terms of mass culture and celebrity icons, there exists today an almost parallel universe for presentations of manliness that are unattainable for most individuals even if they are considered to be aspirational heroes.

Considering the apparently growing complexity of these roles, historians have increasingly written about "masculinity crisis" as a chronic problem. Usually this is considered a subset of larger, moral panics revolving around issues of race, religion, and culture that seem to recur throughout American history.[2] By masculinity crisis, historians refer to a moment when observers begin to notice that assumptions about masculinity and expected male behavior are being undercut by circumstance and social and psychological changes. The result appears to be a cyclical pattern of anxiety and worry, and then the development of new cultural forms to fill the spaces vacated by older behaviors that seem less suitable or attainable. No historical period seems to be better described in these terms than the 1950s.

While the mood of crisis has clearly recurred throughout American history, it has seemed most intense during and after the 1890s, when the transformation of work and patterns of urbanization made it difficult to enact an older ideology of individualism, self-reliance, and manliness. As work became more bureaucratized, service-oriented, and located in urban areas, it became inappropriate to express older models of masculinity derived from traditions of craft, agriculture, and small business. Throughout the twentieth century, at repeated intervals, the remaining pockets in which older concepts of masculinity still prevailed were further undercut, particularly in the 1940s and 1950s with the rise of the companionate, nuclear family, the entrance of women in large numbers into the workforce, and finally by the feminist movements beginning in the 1960s. During the most severe of these crises, the 1890s and the 1950s, concepts of masculinity were sometimes rebuilt around ideals of difference (a racially, gendered, or sexually oriented other), and in ways that, if only vicarious as in the emulation of celebrities or sports and war heroes, still reasserted some sort of male social dominance.

The historical literature of male crisis is rich and voluminous—so elaborate and thoughtful that I will let it stand for the major accepted narrative of gender development upon which my own work is a commentary, and, in some important respects, a disagreement. A survey of this literature also reveals the wide variety of commentaries on the history of masculinity in addition to the centrality of a notion of recurring crisis of male gender identity.

A great many of these works begin with the major shifts in American economic life, specifically in the way work is organized. For example, in his book *Manhood in the Making*, anthropologist David Gilmore sees masculinity as a problematic trait in modern society—acutely so in the United States. If, as he argues, there is a "strong connection between the social organization of production and the intensity of the male image," then fundamental social and economic change undoubtedly result in disruption and displacement. If, indeed, "the harsher the environment and the scarcer the resources, the more manhood is stressed as inspiration and goal," the reverse of this precept also seems true: the growing consumer society of the modern era evokes confusion and disorientation because its demands are mystifying or difficult to recognize. Is it possible that contemporary masculinity under stress, he asks, will become "simply autonomous mental projections or psychic fantasies writ large?"[3] Some form or another of this basic argument about the shifting tectonics of the economy and its psychic effects motivates much of the historical literature about gender relations in the twentieth century. In other words, the shift from production to consumption has disrupted the tight definition of manhood around work and individual initiative.

As much as anyone, E. Anthony Rotundo established the basic timeline and categorizations of masculinity history in his *American Manhood: Transformations in Masculinity from the Revolution to the Modern Era*. Rotundo identifies three characterological stages through which the history of masculinity has passed: communal manhood, self-made manhood, and passionate manhood.[4] Much of his account centers on the nineteenth- and the early twentieth-century transition from self-made manhood to passionate manhood, the more recent period a time when adolescence suddenly became a much written-about stage of development. Rotundo analyzes a host of new institutions, beliefs, and practices tied to the emergence of revised views of manhood in the early twentieth century. Like much of the literature in this field, this survey is heavily weighted toward middle-class masculinity and its articulation in social and cultural institutions, literature, and the workplace. What lies beneath the more modern transitions, Rotundo explains, is a dramatic change in the nature of work, with men moving into white-collar jobs, within burgeoning cities, into occupations defined by a new consumer economy. In each of these realms of work and consumption, older notions of boy and manhood became problematic. What emerged was a revised understanding and space for a masculinity that expressed itself within the expanding leisure and consumer worlds in terms of sports, pleasure, increased attention to the physical body, and ambition and social competition.

John D'Emilio and Estelle Freedman's *Intimate Matters; A History of Sexuality in America* discovers similar signposts of stress and change. Like most historians of gender, they tie changes in behavior to long-term economic and social change: the shift to white-collar work, advances in women's roles into the public sphere, various phases of sexual revolution, and modifications in the size and constitution of the family. In defining masculinity, they explore the growing importance of arguments about essentialism, supported by modern psychological definitions and theories. By essentialism they mean the belief in basic, universal attributes. Thus while masculinity became more socially and economically problematic, it was increasingly defined as a natural and inherent characteristic. One result of this thinking, they argue, was the creation of the category of homosexual, which, after the 1920s, came to represent an identifiable personality in medical literature and public speech, thus shifting a form of behavior from an act to a personality type, making it, in other words, an object against which "normal" masculinity could be defined.[5]

D'Emilio and Freedman approach the 1950s as a complex and contradictory era. While there was certainly conformity and uniformity, they argue, and a considerable degree of sexual and social repression, the sexual revolution that had begun three decades earlier in the 1920s continued apace and corroded the dominant conformist categories that stressed monogamy, sexual repression, and domestic ideology.[6] In this context, they argue, the poisonous flower of "homosexual panic" that blossomed in Washington during the early 1950s and led to purges of employees in the State Department as well as federal job discrimination appeared to reinforce the boundaries of heterosexual marriage. But these boundaries proved to be either porous or difficult to patrol. Not just homosexuality, but promiscuity, the new *Playboy* lifestyle (after 1953), eroticized racism (for example in the novels of Norman Mailer), and fears of female sexuality challenged the viability of white, middle-class companionate marriage.[7] The direction of change, they conclude, was inherently destructive to the stability of heterosexual marriage: "The logic of consumer capitalism pushed the erotic beyond the boundaries of the monogamous couple as entrepreneurs played with erotic impulses and affluent youth pursued their pleasures outside the marital bond."[8] Ironically, they find, just as categories of sanctioned gender relations hardened during the 1950s, prosperity, mobility, and urbanism made definitions of masculinity potentially more fluid.

Peter Filene emphasizes many of these same divisions, contradictions, and changes in gender identity in modern America. Out of the economic crisis of the 1890s and the transformation of white-collar work, he notes, came an ambivalent masculinity that celebrated a new activism expressed in novel forms of vicarious self-vindication: spectator sports, Boy Scouts, warfare (at least in the imagination), and nostalgia for frontier life. Unfortunately, World War I poured an icy bath over military romanticism, and the frontier closed down to all but the fictitious cowboys of novels and films. Another encroachment came in the 1920s when the "New Woman" proclaimed her sexual liberation. Add to this the somewhat greater commitment of men to family life and domesticity and widespread identification through the mass media with celebrities like Charles Lindbergh, who soared into solitary heroism. By the 1950s, the split between ideology and reality had widened as more women entered the workplace and the workplace itself was becoming feminized—that is, an office environment stressing cooperation, collective effort, and social skills.[9]

Michael Kimmel, in his *Manhood in America: A Cultural History*, finds the repeated invocation of male crisis to be an ongoing spur to developing new expressions of American masculinity. Manhood, he writes, is a "relentless test," a constant demand to prove to oneself and to convince other men of one's adequacy. Kimmel identifies several ideal types of manliness that appear and then dissolve throughout history—for example, the self-reliant man of the nineteenth century—and compounded with this, the new emphasis on physical virility and bodily well-being that emerged in the 1890s. Variations of such images of self-creation passed through a series of changes and challenges until the 1960s when, he argues, the attraction of this character type collapsed.

Kimmel's interesting and complex work weaves the story of self-made masculinity into a narrative studded with a variety of mass culture examples as his source material. But, as he notes, by the 1950s, men faced a dilemma of opposite demands: Could a tough guy also be gentle? Could cultural transition, growth, and development, as well as an era of appalling political conformity. We should be doubly cautious because this was the era when the basic historical narratives of male crisis and personality development were established—when the 1890s as well as the 1950s were identified as periods of profound shift in American character. As for essentialism, there are clearly limits in using this concept as well as its opposite—the social construction of masculinity. Certainly, categories like "masculine" are fluid, changing, evolving, and always performative. But by no stretch of imagination are they infinitely flexible or entirely constructed. That, by itself, would be a form of essentialism and a sort of apriorism, as ahistorical as the notion that masculinity always and everywhere is the same. As for the notion of masculinity crisis, it is crucial to turn to the 1890s, a period that contemporary historians have almost universally accepted as the anguished beginnings of modern masculinity. This survey will suggest how it is that the 1890s crisis of masculinity became the starting point for a discussion of modern manhood, and what is implied in that analysis.

In its modern guise the discussion of masculinity crisis as a cultural phenomenon began with historian John Higham's widely noted essay on the 1890s, "The Reorientation of American Culture," published in 1965. This seminal work accepted Frederick Jackson Turner's identification of the 1890s as a watershed period in American history but significantly reevaluated the nature of change during that period, more in line with the evolution of character described by David Riesman. Higham identified his task clearly. His subject was changing middle-class attitudes. And, while he did not focus on masculinity by name, looking rather to cultural change generally, his subject was, by default, changes in the culture and practices of manhood. Like most of his contemporary fellow historians of American civilization, he paid attention generally to those aspects of culture dominated by and focused on men even if he cast them as general cultural signifiers.[14]

Higham began his account of changes in male aspirations with the establishment of sports at Ivy League colleges and then broadened his scope to include a new interest in physical culture, Wild West fiction, and the analogous action-oriented philosophic pragmatism of intellectuals such as William James. Of course, the ubiquitous Theodore Roosevelt makes a cameo appearance plunking for the strenuous life. Compared to contemporary Europeans, he continues, Americans tended to be optimistic (despite counterexamples like the elegant pessimist, Henry Adams), and rarely developed the anxious gloom exhibited by writers such as the German Max Nordau, in his bleak book, *Degeneration* (1895). The reorientation of American culture, despite (or because of) its response to a newly routinized economic life, and spurred by the revolt of New Women against accepted domestic and social roles, still managed a largely positive response: "It was everywhere an urge to be young, masculine, and adventurous."[15]

Higham's insights and argument, if not always his optimism, became the template for much of the subsequent discussion of masculinity crisis in the 1890s. Curiously, however, one element of his essay was expanded while another was almost forgotten. The first is represented in the picture of Theodore Roosevelt, the self-made man: athlete, scholar, soldier, and cowboy president—the Everyman of modern masculinity. In much of the literature about the 1890s and thereafter, Roosevelt towers, buttressed by G. Stanley Hall, innovator in American education and psychology, and inventor of the modern notion of adolescence. Roosevelt, Hall, Owen Wister (author of *The Virginian*, the seminal western novel), William James, Harvard, Boston, the Ivy League, these in ever widening concentric circles, symbolized the expanding ripples of the new masculinity.

Perhaps it was the tenor of his time, but Higham, unlike many who followed in his footsteps, did not particularly emphasize crisis, nor did he view the new culture of masculinity as a patchwork of poultices and bandages wound around a collective wounded ego. For him, this new culture of masculinity was, by and large, optimistic, especially when compared to its morose and introspective European counterparts.

If Higham could still see reorientation rather than crisis as the mood of the 1890s, it is probably because he did not view masculinity itself as a problematic category. Certainly he was aware of and influenced by the extensive discussion of masculinity that took place in the 1950s in the guise of national character history, as well as the identification of the 1890s as a deeply troubled transition era by other writers. Perhaps he was influenced by the rapidly changing mores of the late 1960s when he wrote the essay. But he did not challenge the category of masculinity itself. That would come later under the impact of women's history and modern gender studies and, particularly, in the last decade's writing about sexual identities.

Unlike many historians who followed him, Higham found no reason to offer up a vocabulary of chaos, panic, and betrayal. Nevertheless, he did assume a developing bifurcation in American culture that split the demands of routinized work and family obligations from an ever more exclusively cultural vision of masculinity—what I shall call "spectatorship masculinity"—in which identity was formed (or imagined at least) around observation and emulation of masculine heroes in sport and public life, within the literary imagination, or through mass culture. It is precisely this separation that historians have stressed in their depictions of the 1890s as a cultural and psychological crisis. Finally, the narrow focus of Higham's article suggests the limitations of the argument. Most of his sources were located in the Northeast and confined to the biographies of a few key figures that made a public show of their anxious manliness.

In the last decade or so, historians have concluded that the modern version of masculinity as depicted in the 1890s is both problematic and troubled. David Savran's *Taking It Like a Man: White Masculinity, Masochism, and Contemporary American Culture* is an interesting case in point. Savran writes of the expanding importance of a dissident masculinity that has become "hegemonic in U.S. culture." This is the "victimized male," the "angry white male, the sensitive male, the male searching for the Wild Man within, the white supremacist, the spiritual male."[16] The origins of contemporary dilemmas of manhood that opened a space for such troubled souls, he concludes, found their beginnings in the marginalized and underground culture of the Progressive Era. By the 1970s, the wounded, sadomasochistic male hero, he argued, had emerged full-blown in popular culture.[17]

In their discussion of the turn-of-the-century crisis in masculinity, other historians have pushed back the origins of change into the Victorian age. In a fascinating study of secret rituals, fraternal organizations, and clubs, Mark Carnes suggests that the "fraternal ritual provided solace and psychological guidance during young men's troubled passage to manhood in Victorian America." Young men bore the burden of the anxieties of their fathers and grandfathers. Against the backdrop of an increasingly feminized and sentimental religion and a newly powerful domestic ideology in the early nineteenth century, these set-apart homosocial environments provided escape, solace, and comradeship.

Carnes concludes that this culture of clubiness declined by the late 1930s when changes in the family and economy created new gender and work relations. Now young men did not have to flee the family and domesticity; they could develop an identity through leisure and consumption. While Carnes recognizes many of the problems that engage other historians of the masculinity crisis in the 1890s, his emphasis on fraternal organizations appearing before the Civil War and extending well past the 1920s suggests a larger, coherent, and continuing mind-set for most American men, heightened at the turn of the century, perhaps, but a persisting history, not something unique to that transitional period.[18]

Another work that situates turn-of-the-century America within a larger narrative explanation is Kevin White's *The First Sexual Revolution: The Emergence of Male Heterosexuality in Modern America*. Extending Higham's categories, White emphasizes the "new man" that emerged from the unmet expectations of the Victorian era. As nineteenth-century reticence and repression broke up on the shoals of the new century, male identity embraced a number of changed tenets and values: primitivism, physical culture, new clothing styles, sexual fulfillment, the idea of personality, and a manliness defined in opposition to the newly recognized category of homosexuality. In due course, the new middle-class man adopted—or tried to—the cultural swagger of working-class men. As the historian writes, "In early twentieth-century America, men faced increasing expectations that they be young and sexually attractive, that primitivism be emphasized over gentlemanliness, that sexual expression be stressed over repression."[19]

Gail Bederman's *Manliness and Civilization* greatly enriches this chronicle of male crisis by focusing on two of the principle figures of late Victorian America and one of the most popular novels of the early twentieth century. Picking G. Stanley Hall and Theodore Roosevelt for her male protagonists, and Tarzan as their fictional counterpart, Bederman identifies a new way that was developed to resolve male ego problems like neurasthenia and anxiety by injecting primitivism into a celebration of civilization and racial superiority. Hall and Roosevelt—even Tarzan—were personalities defined by self-creation. In each case, their new manhood was achieved at the cost of casting others as inferior: women and nonwhite races. In the evolution of Western civilization, these figures sought the best of all possible worlds: a manhood constructed of virility, primitivism, and cultural superiority.[20]

By mixing the real with the imaginary, Bederman also reveals an ingredient of the unattainable existing within the new ideal of masculinity. This can be seen in comparing the lives of Roosevelt and Edgar Rice Burroughs (creator of Tarzan). Rare among men of the twentieth century, Roosevelt could enact the "bully" life and become soldier, cowboy, and big game hunter, even president of the United States. The very extravagance of his achievements made him a national hero, worthy of emulation although impossible to imitate. One of his most significant admirers was Edgar Rice Burroughs, author of some eighty or more adventure stories about white American males triumphing over the inhabitants of exotic settings: in the jungle, on Mars and Venus, and at the center of the earth. But Burroughs's real-life feats were a feeble caricature of Roosevelt's accomplishments. He failed to gain entrance to West Point and served only a short, unhappy time in the army. His application to join Roosevelt's "Rough Riders" for the glorious fight in the Spanish American war was rejected. He worked at a succession of businesses, none successful or satisfying. Finally, in 1911, he published his first novel, *A Princess of Mars*, in which his hero, by a cosmic leap of imagination, finds himself on the planet Mars. What follows in the novel is a series of rapid-fire adventures in which the hero, naked and unarmed except for his wit and crude weapons, survives to win the love of the most beautiful woman on the planet.

In this imaginative tale, Burroughs fled civilization, earth, society, and history in order to enact a pure sort of masculinity obviously unavailable in the real world except perhaps to the exceptional and fortunate man like Roosevelt. Perhaps because of his failures, he understood the allure of such imaginary characters for others of similar background and prospects. Thus he shaped the dreams of millions of boys and men who bought his books and who shared the limitations he had experienced. But these were fantasies, a form of spectator masculinity, and elements of an imaginary popular culture universe, not available models for real life. In fact, the fictional legends of Burroughs's heroes and Roosevelt's public persona were equally remote and unattainable, and that is perhaps the most important point about the role models established in the popular culture of that decade.[21]

Many historians have looked with dismay at these new aggressive ideals of masculinity developed at the turn of the century, and some among them have defined the response as a destructive sociopsychological pattern. This seemed particularly true for Europe but also characteristic of the United States. George L. Mosse, in his comparative study of modern masculinity, found a deep crisis of confidence in Europe, particularly Germany, over the public agitation for women's rights and the growing visibility of homosexuality. The defensive reaction—to claim difference as the key to male identity—opened up a martial route to manliness. In effect, then, he sees the turn-of-the-century response as one that attempted (successfully in some instances) to make distinctions between men and women and between heterosexual and homosexual men more rigid and obvious with the negative consequences of an aggressive militarism.[22]

American ideals of masculinity, however, also marched to a more peaceful tune. R. Marie Griffith, in a fascinating cameo look at "Apostles of Abstinence: Fasting and Masculinity during the Progressive Era," finds such central figures as Bernarr Macfadden, and Edward Hook Dewey before him, pushing masculine self-control over the brink into obsession. Dewey and then Macfadden, she concludes, advised fasting as an extreme means of bodily self-control. The idea was to exert manly self-restraint as a means to virility and success even to the point of controlling bodily functions. In fact, control over diet and exercise could be seen as a principal area remaining under individual control among a whole range of nineteenth-century strategies once assumed to promote social success and achievement.[23] Self-discipline of the body seemed to reassert individuality in an age of increasing social control.

Of course the excessive preoccupation with order and self-control suggested a fear of rising social and cultural disorder. Jeffrey P. Hartover, in his fascinating article on the Boy Scouts, attributes the popularity of the organization as well as burgeoning sports enthusiasm, to deep-seated changes in work patterns and the rise of urban living. "The supporters of the Scout movement," he wrote, "those who gave their time, money, and public approval, believed that changes in work, the family, and adolescent life threatened the development of manliness in boys and its expression in men."[24]

Because of the importance historians have accorded to Harvard men such as Roosevelt, William James, and the western novelist Owen Wister, it is not surprising (because it is in some respects intellectually redundant) to find one of the most convincing and exhaustive studies of the era's masculinity crisis in a work by Kim Townsend, *Manhood at Harvard*. This study makes clear the seminal role of Harvard in defining the notion of masculinity crisis in the late nineteenth century. Within the walls of this influential institution, a fraternity of worried men imagined and then, as much as they could, acted out the creed of a new, rough order of manliness. Harvard, from the office of President Eliot to the athletic playing fields, to the psychology laboratory of William James, to the classrooms, and enlarged by its illustrious alumni such as Wister, who wrote about roughnecks and cowboys, and Roosevelt, who bullied his way into politics, was clearly a compass point of this reorientation of gender ideals. For Eliot, the revolution in higher education that he brought to Harvard was coequal and equivalent to a new prototype of American manliness.

The impulse for this attention to gender came, the author argues, from a variety of sources: a sense of malaise and crisis following the Civil War, and the very specific experiences of key figures like James, Wister, and Roosevelt, all of whom reacted with ambiguity and uneasiness to the shifting cultural stimulations of their society. But a somewhat understated, equally crucial point of this essay is Townsend's discovery of alternative meanings for manhood that appeared simultaneously at Harvard. If you muffled the shrill voice of Theodore Roosevelt and his cohort, you might overhear different voices in the Yard speaking in less extravagant tones: W. E. B. Du Bois, Van Wyck Brooks, and, ultimately, James Lowell, the president after Eliot, who deflated the overblown manhood rhetoric of the college.[25]

Pursuing these less strident expressions about manhood in the 1890s, Margaret Marsh, looking at the same period in her essay on men and domesticity, challenges the notion of male panic, and proposes, instead, that historians consider a new model of "masculine domesticity" that began appearing in contemporary literature and in popular journals. Presaging the 1950s with its discussion of suburbs and middle-class gender roles, this expanding literature urged men to help around the house and learn the important tasks of child-rearing, especially for sons. While this advice did not necessarily imply feminism—any more than the domestic ideology or companionate marriage of the 1950s did—it did suggest that masculinity could be enacted in the home, not just through the emulation of distant heroes or in a vicarious strenuous life.[26]

Other commentators have recently questioned the whole notion of a male crisis in the 1890s. Mary Chapman and Glenn Hendler, in their collection of essays on sentimentalism, emotion, and male writers, conclude that "American masculinity has always been in crisis, in the sense of being constantly engaged in its own redefinition." Their argument aims to rehabilitate such attributes as sentiment as an important and common male emotional response in traditional figures such as Melville and Cooper, and other nineteenth-century writers who sympathetically portrayed dying children and the suffering of marginal figures. In other words, traditional literary figures noted for their portrayal of archetypal male heroes embraced a strong element of emotionalism previously identified principally with female writers.[27] And in his book *Modernism and Masculinity*, Gerald Izenberg suggests that the notion of a crisis has been derived largely from sources confined to literature and the arts. It is, therefore, inferred about American men rather than demonstrated, making the argument circular at best. What was, he asks, the "actual impact on the consciousness of middle-class businessmen and professionals"? The only real evidence, he concludes, is inferential.[28]

Compared to the work on the 1890s, the historiography of masculinity in the 1950s is doubly complicated. It is sometimes described as a second act of modernity—the next crisis in the development of modern masculinity following the first grave outbreak in the Progressive Era. It should be stressed at the outset, however, that some of the assumptions about the 1890s crisis were themselves developed in the 1950s, as a response to changes in that decade. In this respect, the subject and object of study have been combined and projected upon each other. Nineteen-fifties cultural politics were busy with worry about the American male and about gender relationships generally. Thus, the personal experience of historians who wrote or grew up in this period has colored their interpretations of the past. To cite one powerful and influential example, one of the participants in the public dialogue about masculinity of the 1950s, historian Arthur M. Schlesinger, Jr., also became a leading chronicler of twentieth-century America.[29]

The notion of a second male identity crisis in the 1950s (if not a third)[30] configures much of the discussion of culture in this important decade. The outlines of this argument have been firmly in place since the 1980s, although its appearance debuted earlier, in the 1950s itself. Barbara Ehrenreich's *The Hearts of Men*, published in 1983, and somewhat later, Elaine May's very influential *Homeward Bound*, sketched the basic elements of gender history in which masculinity crisis played a crucial role. Linking popular culture and gender stereotypes, they singled out the important, prevailing ideology of family and domesticity as the conventional home-front standard and victory in the cold war as the external strategy of American society. May's argument focuses far more upon female domesticity, but the effects of 1950s social attitudes about masculinity are readily apparent in her work. And Ehrenreich's emphasis upon the fear of homosexuality, engendered by public intellectuals, psychologists, and politicians keen to promote the institution of marriage, suggests a key component of the ideology. For both authors, this dogma was also both fragile and ultimately untenable as well as limiting and oppressive.[31]

David Halberstam's portrayal of the 1950s is a compendium of complex and interesting insights, particularly into the popular culture of the era, notably its films and television programs. Like other observers, he looks beneath the placid surfaces of domesticity and sanctioned social and gender roles of a world that wanted to define itself as a middle-class utopia. This was an orderly, prosperous and conservative period, he notes, but one pregnant with the social and cultural revolution which would make the following ten years both different and profoundly unstable. It could be argued then that the turbulent social and cultural explosions of the 1960s were primed in the previous decade.[32]

Recent studies of the 1950s have accentuated the underside and the contradictions to the master narratives of male panic and repressive conformity. The book of essays edited by Joanne Meyerowitz, *Not June Cleaver: Women and Gender in Postwar America, 1945–1960* (1994), does not reject the centrality of gender issues in the 1950s, but she does argue for a more complex and contradictory picture of the terrain of struggle. Another edited work, by Joel Foreman, *The Other Fifties: Interrogating Midcentury American Icons* (1997), suggests that the accepted liberal/conservative dichotomy formed around popular culture issues deserves considerable revision.[33]

Steven Cohan's study of masculinity and the movies carries this notion much further to argue that the taut surface agreement about masculinity in the 1950s could not, in fact, accommodate the contradictory elements that roiled that culture from below. While accepting the notion of a masculinity crisis, he does not see any single response as pervasive or predominant, a point that becomes clear in his consideration of leading films. In fact, he argues, a powerful opposing masculinity in the shape of the "Playboy lifestyle" directly assaulted the celebration of domestic bliss, faithfulness, and monogamy.[34]

A significant part of Cohan's discussion hinges on the role of homosexuality as a foil to heterosexual masculinity. Robert J. Corber's *Homosexuality in Cold War America* likewise focuses on the relationship between the homosexual panic of the early 1950s and the notion of male crisis during the same years. Given the huge government investment in a consumption-based domesticity that was situated physically in middle-class suburbs, and the equally significant psychological investment in marriage and a corporate economy with its bureaucratic work styles, homosexuality could plausibly seem to be a potent disruption to the stability of heterosexual marriage.[35] If, as Jonathan Katz has argued in *The Invention of Heterosexuality*, the contemporary categories of gender essentialism were the invention of late nineteenth-century psychology, then the period shortly before their destabilization in the 1960s was an important prelude to their demise.[36]

Reading through this literature it becomes apparent that the recurring efforts to refurbish the house of male supremacy and traditional masculinity have increasingly depended upon the projection of this idealized identity into a popular culture world populated by fictional idols, charismatic leaders, and celebrities. As historian Neil Gabler writes, life has become a movie in modern America.[37] The period from the 1890s up to World War I saw the creation of the cowboy myth, the Tarzan novels, and the heroic escapades of Teddy Roosevelt. The wartime exploits of John F. Kennedy were a modern version of the same heroism. But, for all but a tiny minority of Americans, it has not been possible to enact these exhilarating experiences on the frontier or in the jungle or in warfare or on Mars or trips to the moon. And Roosevelt and Kennedy were only the exceptions that proved the rule. In fact, society developed elaborate and vicarious ways (halfway institutions) to participate in heroic masculinity from a distance: spectator sports, physical culture, Boy Scouting, dude ranching, fan clubs of celebrities, and political movements devoted to charismatic leaders. While some of the older proofs of masculinity were also available in the military and in working-class labor, by and large there existed a yawning gulf between what American culture defined as ideal masculine behavior (in whatever exotic environment made its expression plausible) and the mundane lives of men at home, within the family, or at work.

James Thurber's wonderful story, "The Secret Life of Walter Mitty," published in 1939 and made into a film in 1947, sardonically captures the dynamic of this spectator masculinity and its cultural operation. Mitty, a henpecked, authority-shy male, oppressed by overpowering women and unredeeming work, daydreams his way into imaginary gallantry. He imagines himself as the intrepid hero: the ship commander, the brilliant physician, the tough guy on trial for murder, the courageous bomber pilot, the nonchalant soldier calmly facing his last moments before a firing squad. But nothing among this repertoire of film and literary fantasies can prevent his wife from breaking his reverie and barking orders at him like a drill sergeant. Nothing raises his esteem in the chance encounters with authority figures. And, at any sign of independence, his wife calls for doctors to administer strong medicine.

In Thurber's world of bedlam and role reversals, peopled with stout, sarcastic women, droopy dogs, and sorry men, heroic, self-confident masculinity can exist only as a figment of imagination. Yet, Thurber, for all his humor, made the key point about such fictional sources of masculinity: only the movies got it right. Movies made the man. Quite literally, they projected a momentary, accessible masculinity and offered a chance for imaginary emulation, the possibility, in other words, to live on two mental tiers: one dreaming about being someone of consequence, and the other bent and obliging under the yoke of small, everyday tyrannies.[38]

Some historians have considered these cultural daydreams to constitute the essential qualities of modern masculinity, arguing that masculinity was increasingly associated with violent, escapist, and heroically individualistic models in popular culture. But it is not clear to me that spectatorship masculinity is anything more than what it seems: fanciful. It is unreasonable to assume that most men misjudged the distance between their lives and this imagined heroism.

But one conclusion seems inevitable. To see masculinity as an aspect of a gender system in crisis is, in part, to inhabit the culture of the modern world, for that sense of crisis has developed and increased over time since the end of the nineteenth century. In some respects gender malaise was deemed a national calamity during the 1950s and projected backwards into a reinterpretation of American history. It found innumerable expressions, first in the attack on powerful, emasculating mothers and women, then in a critical literature deploring humiliating corporate work, fears of spies and homosexuals in government, distrust of youth and worries about juvenile delinquency, and a tense film culture which lionized war heroes, misfits, cowboys, and wandering poets. At the same time, the 1950s was the first time that the idea of the gender crisis really found a name. It was then that a search for the origins of the crisis became a preoccupation of sociologists and historians.

But is this notion of gender panic or crisis finally a useful term for historians? Or does it inevitably risk stereotype or exaggeration? It is easy to find repeated expressions of worry about declining masculinity throughout the hundred years of the twentieth century, and historians have done so. But it is nevertheless appropriate to ask what these expressions in journals, literature, academic writing, and in the mass media had to do with practical, day-to-day life. It is meaningful, beyond any doubt, that millions of men (and boys) read Tarzan stories and Superman comic strips, or studied baseball box scores while hurtling along in fetid, hot subway cars and buses to work they were thought to despise and then back again to domestic ties that bound and chafed. But did they—or better, how did they—integrate imagination with the mundane? How did they perform that emulation of these fictional characters and celebrities? And did those figures represent the masculinity that historians have ascribed to them? Have we read the sources correctly? Have we chosen representative examples? Certainly it is possible to find panicked, anxious, and belligerent maleness everywhere in cultural production, from pulp-fiction writers, to social science experts, to billboard advertisements, even in the arch reproaches of New York intellectuals against mass culture. But it is also possible to find contrary expressions with almost the same frequency. To pose the question somewhat differently, but in the context of popular symbols in the film history of the 1950s, which is a better guide to masculine ideology of the period: John Wayne or Tennessee Williams? Or have we just got the question wrong?

Added to this complication of generalization is the problem of defining masculinity during the 1950s in the larger context of variations in social class, race, and ethnicity. The conversation about masculinity in this period was often narrowly focused. Observers at the time (and subsequently) generally paid scant attention to class, racial, and ethnic differences, and they defined the problem largely in terms of middle-class habits and possibilities. This exclusivity has allowed for a certain centering of attention and, sometimes, by implication, it has suggested that the excluded men (working class or black) commanded a more enviable masculinity. But, for the historian, this concentration has at least the virtue of consistency, for the mainstream conversation about masculinity throughout the first half of the twentieth century has regularly focused on white, middle-class men and their gender identity problems and scarcely on anyone else.

Like other narratives about masculinity, this book will consider some of the public images of masculinity offered to white middle-class men during the 1950s. Unlike the advocates of male panic and gender crisis interpretation, however, I hope to lift the discussion beyond these categories, to show that by and large, middle-class men during the decade had a rich and often contradictory range of images and personality aspirations available to them in public culture where we have asserted their absence—models to emulate who were not just cowboys, war heroes, Marlboro men, or athletes. What is striking about conventional celebrities and fictional characters is how utterly and almost self-consciously inappropriate they are to the realities of modern living. Once we pull aside the wizard's curtain, we can discover a rich alternative set of popular images that could be just as appealing as any escapist hero. There were many men who did not agree with the Torquemadas of the day who led the inquisition into masculinity in crisis. As middle-class men struggled with the issues of masculinity, inevitably they overheard the anxious public discussion about their conflicted lives. But they were also familiar with a wide variety of useful and ingenious alternative models. These examples are my subjects, and the complex encounters with masculinity of the men who proposed them are my focus.

3

Lonely Men: David Riesman and Character

America constantly outdistances its interpreters.—David Riesman

David Riesman's *The Lonely Crowd* was an unexpected best seller, a small miracle of publishing, and an essay that gripped the imagination of a major portion of the reading public in the 1950s. It was also, as Riesman well understood and often said, badly misinterpreted and put to the service of a schematized critique of American society that the author repeatedly tried to amend. There was certainly something about that title. It is difficult to imagine the amazing success of such a dense text had it been called "A Jury of Our Peers," or "A Change of Signals," or, even worse, "The Peers in Their Power: Changing Modes of Conformity in American Life" or "The Continental Pueblo"—all titles that he considered right down to the last moments before the book went to press.[1] Beyond its fortunate title, Riesman's book spoke directly and early to a concern that grew exponentially during the 1950s: uneasiness with the advent of mass society and its challenges to the character of man. *The Lonely Crowd* articulated that worry in a way that made it the founding text in a school of sociological critique that focused on conformity, mass culture, and consumerism. In language tinged with regret but subtle with qualification, Riesman sketched a new history of American character that seemed to challenge the very possibility of achieving selfhood in modern society.

David Riesman was only one of many public intellectuals who detected a broad transformation in American institutions following World War II, but he was probably the most influential. As one writer in 1972 put it, *The Lonely Crowd* was the first "quality" paperback to garner a popular audience. It "can be said to have made sociology 'popular' being the first of several '50s books, of varying merit, that set middle-class America on a binge of self-scrutiny."[2] First among such critics as William H. Whyte,

Vance Packard, Margaret Mead, C. Wright Mills, Reinhold Niebuhr, and a host of other important public intellectuals and their popularizers, Riesman identified the shifting stages of American historical development and, most important, provided a compelling vocabulary to understand the transitions to the contemporary world. Above all, it was his choice of words that launched his ideas. His book divided Western history into three stages marked by differences in population growth, although almost no one paid much attention to this explanatory factor except to criticize it. What attracted readers were the labels he attached to characterological types, or "directions" as he called them that emerged with each new stage of human history. "Tradition-direction" appeared first, then "inner-direction" with the advent of capitalism, and then "other-direction" in contemporary America. And, finally, Riesman believed he could detect the outlines of a fourth direction—"autonomy"—which he anticipated would combine some of the better elements of the latter two stages.

Although Riesman stated on many occasions that he did not favor the dynamic "inner-direction" associated with nineteenth-century capitalism, most readers understood him to favor exactly that, and so interpreted the descriptions of other-direction as a critique of present-day conformity. They were attracted by his description of the self-made, inner-directed man, the entrepreneur, the frontier farmer, and the small businessman who made the nineteenth century a period for dynamic self-expression. On the other hand, they reacted negatively to his picture of the other-directed personalities of corporate conformists and suburban commuters who took their cues from mass culture and the opinions of others. As he wrote in the introduction to the French edition of the book, "The very title of the book and the terms 'inner-direction' and 'other-direction' helped tilt matters this way.... Readers naturally satirized the evils they are familiar with, and have come to prefer our nostalgic picture of the inner-directed cowboy to our all too realistic picture of the other-directed organization man."[3] Yet when Yale University Press chose its marketing strategy for the book, it selected a picture to illustrate the content of the book that promoted this interpretation. "We used that photography in *Life* you may remember," wrote a Yale marketing representative to Riesman, "of the gloomy and terrified-looking people who were only waiting for a traffic light to change to show the salesmen what a lonely crowd looked like."[4] It is difficult to blame readers if they misunderstood this visual cue and the author apparently offered no objection to its use.

If the tone and circumstances of Riesman's critique lent themselves to exaggeration, if, in fact, he was misunderstood, it was, he realized, partly his own fault. He admitted this many times. In a letter in 1963, for example, he wrote, "The misunderstandings of *The Lonely Crowd*, partly I think my own fault, rise to some degree because of a tendency to talk too much about America as a whole and about its more visible segments such as big corporations, new suburbs, etc." Or, more candidly, he worried lest readers conclude that "all the qualities that go together with other-direction are negative, including empathy, while all that goes together with inner-direction (including often enough insensitivity to others) is valuable." Or as Eric Larabee put it (more clearly), "the penalty paid by any new set of categories is to become a parlor game—after which its creator is helpless to insist, and will protest in vain, that putting people in pigeon holes was not his objective."[5]

Riesman's book exposed a raw nerve of concern about modern society, but its reception was determined as much by a preexisting, vague, but growing worry about the institutions of mass culture, consumption, and abundance. *The Lonely Crowd* identified social typologies that appeared to make obvious good sense following the advent of postwar consumer lifestyles. The book described an emerging stage of history in which human character changed in response to working in large, impersonal, and bureaucratic institutions. And these hypotheses appeared to have immediate, practical application. As one enthusiastic correspondent noted in a letter to Riesman, he had just moved from a small town to the city. "I have always been inner directed," he declared, "and must now become other directed due to having to work for other men. It is not easy to do this but in a survival situation of one's employment life one must learn the reasons why one is not like other people and try to get to be like they are."

Other-direction seemed just as apt a description of changes in the spheres of family and community life. "Of course we are all becoming regimented, indeed we seem to be striving to be all alike," wrote a woman from Michigan. "As you say in your book, there are labels to show what we stand for, what group we are in—the Cadillac, the mink coat, the ranch house, the convertible, the trip to Florida."[6] What is immensely revealing, and characteristic in these two letters, is the gendered response to his categories, with men identifying problems at work and women with consumption.

Riesman's potent descriptive vocabulary quickly entered the emerging discussion of postwar American lifestyles, engaging this conversation on a number of levels. It became a popular tag line for *New Yorker* cartoons and the subject of worried commentaries about the decline of the self-made man in mass circulation magazines. Indeed, Riesman achieved a rare distinction for any academic: his face on the cover of *Time* magazine in 1954. But perhaps the most interesting use of the book was in earnest public forums, discussions sponsored by churches, libraries, and public schools about the changing nature of American civilization. It provoked inquiries of a deep moral and political nature. The discussion in St. Albans, Vermont, in 1956 appears to be typical. As the adult services librarian from Montpelier wrote to the author, *The Lonely Crowd* had been the basis for discussions sponsored by the American Library Association. "The people," he noted, "seemed disturbed at the idea of 'other-directedness.' It went against the grain and yet when they began to examine themselves and their neighbors, they were astonished to see the 'symptoms' close to home."[7]

Despite his reticence to admit it, Riesman sometimes deployed his categories in a similar manner. Discussing the application of his classifications to religion, Riesman wrote to a correspondent in 1953 that he had recently analyzed Protestant church services in Kansas City. His evidence, he noted, showed "that the sermon purveys 'other-directed' attitudes while the Men's Bible classes are reservoirs of older, 'inner-directed' values—the amalgam tends to make the church attractive." If it made the church attractive, it did so implicitly (although Riesman did not emphasize it) because it addressed audiences with very different gender messages. This suggested an analysis that Riesman did not explicitly pursue, but that nonetheless occupied the core of his sociological analysis. In his evolutionary schema of American character, he had created typologies that spoke primarily to the experiences of men in history; he had depicted the contemporary world—other-direction—as a situation that particularly threatened American masculinity.[8] His lonely crowd was principally an assembly of vulnerable men described in words that launched a signal of distress over the feminizing changes in modern culture.

Born into a distinguished academic Jewish family, David Riesman was an unlikely celebrity. His father was a professor of clinical medicine at the University of Pennsylvania. His mother had completed a degree at Bryn Mawr College and, while she passed up a potential academic career, she was an active intellectual, and, as he noted, "a skeptic to the point of cynicism." If this family situation encouraged a rarified intellectual environment at home, Riesman grew up with a respect for the intellectuality of his parents as well as rebellious streak against it, particularly his mother's persistent emphasis upon the "first-rate." Without doubt, one of the early influences on his development was psychology and, in particular, psychoanalysis. This too he associated with his mother, who was analyzed by the well-known Freudian Karen Horney.[9] After four years at Harvard exploring a variety of subjects (although not sociology), he entered the law school there. He attracted considerable attention, and Felix Frankfurter selected him to clerk for Justice Louis Brandeis. Undoubtedly he could have found some position in the New Deal during these early years of the Roosevelt administration, but chose instead to teach at the University of Buffalo Law School. While there, he met Reuel Denney, later one of his collaborators in *The Lonely Crowd*. But perhaps the most important step was—with his mother's urging—to undertake psychoanalysis with Erich Fromm in 1939. Commuting to New York City every other weekend, he met with Fromm, who helped him free himself from his parents' "verdicts on me." But much more important, he met a man whose works deeply influenced his thinking and laid the basis for his most important sociological work.[10]

Riesman drifted into sociology because he found the law less interesting and too narrow. After three years at Buffalo, he accepted a fellowship at Columbia Law School but actually began there an intensive study of sociology and social research. He also continued his psychoanalysis and attended seminars for psychoanalysts in training conducted by Fromm and Harry Stack Sullivan. Then, on the basis of a published article on civil liberties, he received an invitation to teach at the University of Chicago in the social sciences division. He moved with his family to Chicago and took up a hectic life of study and lectures and reading, especially, the works of Tocqueville and Weber and Freud. In the course of his years in Hyde Park, he brought Reuel Denney to Chicago to teach with him, and, together, they began research in American popular culture. In 1947, Riesman went to Yale for two years on a part-time research appointment with the Committee on National Policy. He also recruited Nathan Glazer to work on a developing survey project on American politics. The questionnaires they circulated became the basis for *The Lonely Crowd* and the sequel, *Faces in the Crowd*, published in 1952. Back in Chicago full time in 1949, he continued to work with Denney and Glazer on the project that eventually became his most important and influential work.[11]

There are a number of significant elements of this background that clarify the shape and content of the most celebrated sociological work of the decade. Without formal training in sociology, he missed the structural emphasis of Talcott Parsons and the behaviorism of John Watson and B. F. Skinner, all in vogue at that time. Instead, he tended to rely on his own reading in grand European theoretical works as well as the important

American survey literature such as Robert and Helen Lynd's "Middletown" studies. Like many intellectuals in the late 1930s and early 1940s he was keen to transfer the insights of psychoanalysis to sociology and political science, and his own direct experience with analysis under Fromm is strongly apparent in his work. His interest and faith in questionnaires was also significant for he believed, as many sociologists did in the 1940s and 1950s, that this method could dependably recover underlying assumptions and constructs of social character.

The genesis of *Lonely Crowd* is a crowded site of differing influences and intentions. In the late 1940s, Riesman was actually working on two major projects: an analysis of political apathy in the United States and a study that sought to apply psychoanalysis to social behavior and organization. Gradually, both projects shifted in focus. The political apathy study evolved into a wider survey of character typologies in American history, and the Freudian project became the basis for several articles published in the early 1950s. But, in a sense, both projects are intertwined in *The Lonely Crowd*. It is not surprising, then, that the eminent psychologist Bruno Bettelheim wrote of this book that it was "a major contribution toward filling" the gap between Freudianism and social models of behavior. That was Riesman's intent.[12]

Character study in the United States before the appearance of *The Lonely Crowd* was divided into several currents, most of which related to events in the 1930s and World War II. Many had a comparative or international element. Although Riesman insisted that his work not be lumped with some of the more chauvinistic contemporary depictions of American character, *The Lonely Crowd* nonetheless belonged to that broad and very popular genre of typology studies. In fact, when Michael McGiffert assembled a bibliography of writings on American character in 1963 for *American Quarterly*, he cited Riesman more than any other author.[13]

There were several roots of this important intellectual movement in the American university that sought, under the duress of the depression, war, and cold war, to redefine the essence of the American experience. One was the Tocqueville revival that emerged in the 1930s and became a huge interest by the early 1950s. Serious attention to Alexis de Tocqueville and his seminal study of American institutions began with George Wilson Pierson's *Tocqueville and Beaumont in America*, published in 1938 by Oxford University Press. New editions of Tocqueville's *Democracy in America* appeared in 1945 (Knopf), 1947 (Oxford), 1951 (Henry Regnery), 1954 (Vintage), and 1956 (New American Library) until it appeared that almost every major press wanted to publish its own version. As

Riesman later acknowledged, the "climate of social science within which the authors of *The Lonely Crowd* were working can be illustrated by our own and many of our colleagues' fascination with Tocqueville's *Democracy in America*." He believed that this was entirely appropriate. Writing to historian Andrew Hacker in 1958, he declared, "We are closer to Tocqueville's time now than in the post–Civil war period."[14] This revival focused, among other things, on the French aristocrat's understanding of democracy, his picture of American culture, his discussion of the "tyranny of the majority," and his portrayal of America's unique and exemplary historical role. Certainly Tocqueville's depiction of American exceptionalism was not unusual in this emerging literature of character; indeed, American singularity represented a principal assumption in most of the important books and articles published in this genre.[15]

A further important model for character studies came directly from the experience of World War II and the activities of such important anthropologists as Margaret Mead, who studied the distinctions between cultures as a way of furthering America's war aims. Mead's comparative orientation defined such books as her *And Keep Your Powder Dry*, published in 1942. As she later recalled, the purpose of her work for the military was to "obtain rapid information about the expected behavior of enemies and allies." In this book, Mead's reference to American traits such as democracy, efficiency, mobility, and so on seemed a list of specific advantages in wartime. But her writings had a far greater and longer influence than on immediate policy—attracting the attention of Riesman, for example. The two became friends and mutual critics while he was at Columbia.[16]

Wartime studies, such as Mead's and Geoffrey Gorer's postconflict *American People: A Study in National Character* (1948), were part of a much larger quest, influenced both by the war experience and then by the cold war, to define and defend American civilization. In some cases, such material was summarized and given to soldiers occupying Japan and Germany. But the new breakaway academic field of American studies pursued this inquiry as its central focus for a decade. Even such mainline American historians as Henry Steele Commager, for example, in his *The American Mind* (1950), assumed that there was a "distinctively American way of thought, character, and conduct." He was, if anything, typical in this undertaking, and American historiography resounded with titles that celebrated the virtues of American civilization.[17]

But the most extensive and complex articulation of this school of thought came in the American studies movement that began in the early

1930s at Harvard and Yale. Devoted to the joint study of American literature and history, the movement spread slowly to several elite academic institutions by the end of the decade, and then became a full-fledged academic movement after World War II with the appearance of the *American Quarterly*, as well as several thriving doctoral programs at institutions such as the University of Minnesota. As a companion to historical studies that celebrated an American exceptionalism, the scholarship produced in American studies was a major enterprise in the revival of important, but neglected, American male writers and philosophers. And, in its early years, the *Quarterly* became a leading journal for public intellectuals, featuring writers such as David Riesman, who often appeared as author or the subject of articles, and where his analysis of character received a major airing.[18]

If Riesman's *Lonely Crowd* does not precisely fit the category of American character history, the sociologist was, nonetheless, a central figure of the larger movement to rediscover the wellsprings of American civilization, and his works proved to have an extraordinary impact on redefining what historians and other observers of American culture had to say. His greatest influence lay in his challenge to prevailing economic and political interpretations of American history. In part this remarkable influence came because Riesman incorporated sociology and Freudian psychology as well as extrapolated Marxist categories into his reinterpretation of changing character types in America history. This secured him both a wider, more diverse audience and a more profound impact. At the same time it also refined a vocabulary of categories associated with a variety of assumptions about masculine and feminine cultural traits.

In many ways, Erich Fromm was the most important influence on Riesman's early work, especially because of the remarkable book the psychologist produced in 1941, *Escape from Freedom*. Fromm was a maverick member of the Frankfurt school of intellectuals who fled Nazi Germany and took refuge in the United States before World War II. Collectively, their influence on American ideas was profound. Their critique of capitalism, developed to explain the rise of Fascism, spotlighted the perils and distortions of mass culture and mass persuasion. They depicted the mass culture of capitalism as a flawed and manipulative system, open to abuse, corruption, and exploitation. While such men as Adorno, Marcuse, Horkheimer, and Fromm were all neo-Marxists to one degree or another, their engagement with class analysis was not nearly so influential in the 1950s as their belief in the ominous potential of mass persuasion and mass culture.[19]

Once in the United States, Fromm increasingly emphasized the enterprise of reconciling Freud and Marx into a social psychology based upon the relationship between personality and production. In *Escape from Freedom* he created a model that read history backward from the Third Reich to explain the appearance of modern totalitarianism. He proposed a scheme of changing character types that emerged historically in response to profound changes in modes of production. As he defined it, "Social character materializes external necessities and thus harnesses human energy for the task of a given economic and social system." In this manner the dominant social forms of a society were reproduced within the character of each individual.

Fromm found three principal historical structures, or "orientations" as he called them, in the evolution of social character. The first, he named "Medieval." He associated this form with stasis and stability and social integration—where every member of society belonged within a carefully structured and interconnected system of identities. The second he called "Protestant," symbolized in the works of Luther and Calvin, who articulated the contradictory new capitalist modes of freedom and disorder and creativity. Religion, he wrote, allowed men to escape the consequences of the breakdown of the integrated institutions of Medieval society, but substituted for them an alienating individualism. The third stage Fromm named the "Marketing Orientation," by which he meant modern society where personality, itself, had become a commodity. Human qualities were determined by the market, but in a fashion that seemed to deny individuality. The result was a conformity that in Germany had provoked an escape into the fanatical redoubt of Fascism. In the United States, this process created "compulsive conforming," with the individual become increasingly helpless and insecure and alienated. Although in the end Fromm glimpsed a hopeful resolution in the possibility of a more integrated personality, it was, by and large, a hard-hitting, even bleak, work.[20]

There is no doubt that Riesman considered Fromm and Mead his mentors. In 1949, well into the writing of *The Lonely Crowd,* he sent his manuscript to Mead for her comments. While she was full of praise for the work, she also proposed a more comparative and anthropological approach. The South Pacific material she had collected on population and culture was "a real laboratory for your theory," she concluded. If Riesman did not exactly accept this suggestion, he nonetheless looked to Mead as a vital intellectual, someone who had made it possible to link anthropology and the description of character to sciences like biology and psychoanalytic psychology. In effect, she did for anthropology what Riesman, himself, attempted in sociology. As she put it in 1951, "We are thus carried one step further toward considering the whole, toward placing man-in-society with a long social history and man-as-a-mammal with a long biological history in one frame of reference."[21]

Riesman's affinity for Tocqueville was also apparent. In lecture material in 1962, for example, Riesman noted the enormous contemporary popularity of Tocqueville. This, he explained, was partly because the Frenchman offered a countervailing theory to Marxism, stressing a liberal answer to the problems of freedom and poverty. But there was much more to his usefulness than anti-Communism. In a fascinating article for the *American Quarterly* in 1953 on psychological types and national character, Riesman invoked Tocqueville as a timely prophet for the contemporary world. America, he wrote, could benefit from close attention to his writings because of the similarities between the current world and the nineteenth century.[22]

Riesman's relationship to the enterprise of national character literature was more complicated. One should be cautious. The idea of national character, he wrote, could take a dangerous turn. Social scientists should be aware of the impact of their discoveries and the use of their terms—just as theoretical physicists "are compelled by the atom bomb into a sudden consciousness of human chain reactions." But national character also had its uses, particularly the variant developed by Mead, Ruth Benedict, and Geoffrey Gorer during World War II. But Riesman parted company from the celebrationists and cold war warriors with his interest in identifying the universal and cross-cultural elements of personality. Thus, he could isolate specific American characteristics, but there were also elements of personality that derived from the most basic and universal human drives discovered by Freud. The difficulty for Riesman as a researcher and theorist came in reconciling individual personalities revealed by personality tests with historically conditioned character types like "other-direction" that might eventually be found in other cultures.[23]

Riesman's preliminary thoughts about the project that eventually became *The Lonely Crowd* focused on the problem of political apathy in the United States. Riesman's account of his original intentions came in early 1948 in an interim report to the National Policy Committee at Yale that was sponsoring his work. The inquiry into political apathy would, he noted, simultaneously be a study of the effects of mass culture. Did the media create apathy? Did they engender conformity? But as they analyzed apathy, Riesman and his colleagues had moved quickly beyond the position that blamed mass culture for creating political alienation. Instead, his outline of study indicated that he had isolated several varieties of apathy and that each related to character structure. Toward the end of this progress report, he related apathy in one form or another to each of the various forms of societies: traditional (Medieval and precapitalist), Protestant (high capitalism) and Marketing—categories obviously borrowed directly from Fromm. It is also clear in this draft that the third form of society—Marketing—was the origin of a character type that led to contemporary political apathy. A different "autonomous wing" existed, he thought, but it suffered from the difficulty of not knowing how or how far to defy conformity. In the end, the authors hoped to find a way to link mass communications policy creatively to "historically-derived character types" and "get some sense of what is happening and what the future holds."[24]

At this early point, somewhere around four or five months into the project, Riesman and his colleagues had defined the subject of their study in a way that reversed the priorities of the final version of *The Lonely Crowd*. If political apathy was, originally, the subject of their inquiry and the purpose of their surveys and questionnaires, it would fast become merely one element in the larger discussion of character types and their historical significance. And in this very early version it is quite clear that their interviews turned up peculiar responses to questions about political behavior and that Riesman was already categorizing these in terms of historic shifts in personality type.

Only a month later, the emphasis had shifted dramatically, and the basic form of the book began to emerge. The influence of Fromm was never more obvious than in early drafts of chapters for *The Lonely Crowd* that Riesman and his co-researchers put together as a report on their ideas for their next presentation to the Yale Seminar. This May 1948 version expanded on Fromm's notion that character structure was an organization of personality responsive to a given social and economic structure. To this notion they added Erik Erikson's theories of child training, to explain how "culture imperatives are imbedded in the social character." Most striking, however, was their explicit borrowing of Fromm's categories of character typologies. There were, they wrote, three, including the "Hedonist, Protestant, and Marketing." These corresponded exactly to Fromm's concepts and in the latter two cases even borrowed his terminology. The problem in using these categories, they found, however, was the difficulty caused by the invocation of terms that seemed largely historical. To make it possible to explain the persistence of certain older traits in the present, they changed the labels of personality types into the more timeless terms:

"traditional," "conscience-direction," and "other-direction."[25] The latter two, conscience- and other-direction, suggested the way individual adjustment occurred, not when. In other words, it made the categories both historical and universal. Through child rearing and social interaction, individuals in the period of relatively open-ended capitalism (conscience-direction) were endowed with an inner gyroscope, implanted as a kind of social conscience that allowed them to function in a society with relatively little external regulation. In the other-directed world of the present, however, the individual was more likely to possess a kind of radar, a social scanning ability to detect the demands and desires of others and so respond to them. In the increasingly administrative and bureaucratic postwar world, the individual required "neither such zeal nor such independence" as was demanded in the nineteenth century. He now needed to fit into a "personality market."

Of course, individuals could resist or even fail at such adjustments and could thereby suffer from anomie and alienation. But, by and large, most individuals could make the adaptations necessary to survive in this world. What made the modern world so remarkable and perilous, however, were the incipient damage and anxiety brought about even by perfectly healthy adjustment to the other-directed world. This was particularly visible in the effects of mass culture. In America, "as people become increasingly permeable to the words and images of the mass media, they become increasingly opaque to themselves." In a curious way, the classes that succeeded the best socially could be defined as neurotic. Thus, anxiety might be a symptom of successful adjustment to other-direction.[26]

If adjustment to contemporary society sometimes implied a sort of social neurosis, there was, nonetheless, considerable hope, because other observers understood the problem in like fashion. The authors noted that they found similar writing about American culture in "current criticisms" and even in Tocqueville a century earlier. But, "the critics often stop at this point and fail to see the great human achievement of those individuals who are able to become autonomous at the present time." Unlike in the published version of *The Lonely Crowd*, the truly autonomous person within the other-oriented world was not the harbinger of a new form of character, but at this point was still considered an exception. Indeed, in the Marketing society, the autonomous person, as they wrote, "threatens the whole shaky mode of adaptation." Often he was either tuned out or isolated. The best existing model for resolving the problems of autonomy, they wrote, could be found in literature, in the characters of Tolstoy or in the essays of John Stuart Mill or the novels of Sartre.[27]

Up to this point, the purpose of the study was still focused on the causes of political apathy, and characterological categories were invoked to understand political attitudes. The most active and energetic participants in politics—the "non-apathetic"—came from the ranks of either "autonomous" elements in America or surviving "Puritans of high position and comparative flexibility." In their interviews, Riesman and Glazer noted that the most politically active members of society came from such groups. Less autonomous, apathetic individuals tended to be either adjusted Market personalities or indignant or incompetent "anomic" personalities. The attitudes of these latter two groups were enforced, although not created, by the mass media. In fact, the mass media worked in two ways: they enhanced the conformity of the apathetic yet they could stimulate "the autonomous person to elevate his own taste above prevailing standards." Riesman put this notion forcefully in a letter to Reuel Denney in March 1949. The separation of mass culture from high culture, he argued, was a positive development: "I am opposed to the current of thinking both in social science and in humanities which looks with gloom on the alienation of the writer and artist. I see this alienism as the condition of advance."[28]

When *The Lonely Crowd* appeared, "character" had trumped "apathy" and politics as the focus of the study. In a memo on the project in early 1949, Riesman had already made extraordinary claims for his insights. "We may even suggest that," he wrote, "while the class struggle is a thing of the past in the advanced industrial countries and especially in America, the *characterological* struggle—the struggle between the autonomous few and the non-autonomous many—is only beginning."[29] In other words, his work would announce a wholly new and radical way of understanding society and culture rather than a limited explanation of political behavior. Indeed, his book suggested nothing less than a systematic reevaluation of American history, conceptualized in a framework of transitions of character. What made it even more compelling was its potential for understanding the most serious questions of the 1950s: how to remain an individual—how to be a man in an increasingly feminized world of mass culture, consumption, and conformity.

By the date of its publication in 1950, *The Lonely Crowd* had passed through many transitions and absorbed a great deal of advice and suggestion. From the outset it was a collaborative work based upon multiple sources: interviews, Freudian psychology, Erich Fromm's study of character types, mass media studies, and anthropology. It glistened with notions that reflected upon the growing literature on American character and added to a rising critique of conformity and mass society. There were clear traces of the ideas about consumption developed by Thorstein Veblen, the maverick sociologist whose writings Riesman studied and admired. It sounded with echoes of American historian Frederick Jackson Turner and Alexis de Tocqueville and the Frankfurt school of neo-Marxism. It borrowed ideas about ideal social types from the German sociologist Max Weber. It proposed a way of thinking about contemporary society that linked psychoanalysis to sociology to social criticism. It outlined a new grand narrative of American history whose intent was to enlighten and change the world of the 1950s. It was a book about doubt and hope that related the development of economic and social structure to the evolution of the individual personality. And it was, like almost all of the important popular sociology of the day, the story of society told around the problems of men. Riesman, in other words, focused this variously sourced book—a study of quite remarkable erudition and breadth—upon the dilemmas of modern men and besieged masculinity. In this respect, he simultaneously narrowed the work to what made modern men "lonely."

The initial hardbound version, with its last-minute and fortuitous title change and countless revisions and transformations, was a dense, diffuse, and exhaustive look at the evolution of American character—hardly the prescription for a best seller. Reviewed widely and favorably, the book found its huge popular audience only after the appearance of the somewhat shortened 1953 paperback edition. That version brought fame to its author, who became one of the most sought-after public intellectuals of the postwar period, and it gave immortality to his metaphors. "Inner-directed" and "other-directed" entered the American vocabulary as terms that resonated with the meanings he ascribed to them as well as meanings modified by the popular understanding of the work.

The argument of the book when it appeared had been distilled to a revelation of character types; issues of political apathy are scarcely visible in the index, although there remains one long section on politics and character. The initial part of the book, which defines the various types of character, ascribes them to shifts in population growth. But the heart of the work relates to the formation of each character type and the forces that shape and perpetuate it. Although some attention is paid to the phase of tradition direction, the focus shifts quickly to inner- and then other-direction.

In his analysis, Riesman begins each stage by looking first at the role of the family in reproducing prevailing character norms on each individual, then teachers, peer groups, and finally the mass media. The most effective and enthusiastically written portions of the book are the comparison of inner- and other-direction and, then (separated by a long section on politics), the discussion of other-direction and autonomy.

Although Riesman claimed that he was not overtly praising inner-direction, and that other-direction had many elements that could be folded into a new autonomous personality, his language inspired misinterpretation. Inner-direction, whatever the costs and disabilities he ascribed to it, sounded like traditional American individualism and entrepreneurial competence. Other-direction, described as lonely, superficial, over personalized, and manipulative, sounded very much like the worst elements of mass society assailed by contemporary critics. Because Riesman chose words to describe these character types that trailed ideological and gendered meanings, the book, in certain respects, argued against itself. It was widely understood to be a critique of the excesses of other-direction, conformity, and mass society. And, it would be difficult to miss the power of the last words in the book: "The idea that men are created free and equal is both true and misleading: men are created different; they lose their social freedom and their individual autonomy in seeking to become like each other."[30] As Dennis Wrong summed up the reception of the book, most reviewers believed the author was "really deploring the ascendance of the 'other-directed' man with his flabby conformist outlook and his pathetic readiness to surrender his individuality in the name of 'adjustment' or 'teamwork.'" And on occasion, Riesman revealed the same hesitations about contemporary society that his pessimistic readers discovered in his work. For example, in an essay entitled "The Saving Remnant," he argued that the "newly reached horizons of leisure and consumption made possible by our economic abundance have not been as exhilarating for the individual as the realized horizons of work and production proved to be for many in the age of expanding horizons."[31]

Riesman found the defining qualities of his character types partly from his reading, from his own experience ("It should be emphasized that this book is based on our experiences of living in America"), and, of course, from the interviews he and his colleagues conducted. During these sessions he began to notice a key form of behavior that would help articulate the distinction between inner- and other-direction. This was the feeling that American institutions appeared to require "the lubrication of human friendliness from a great many participants, especially in the expanding white-collar and service occupations." The smile, friendliness, and the desire to please all seemed to characterize the new, other-directed individual.[32] This sort of insight, this attention to the physical attributes of interaction, he insisted, was not just criticism of conformity but an observation that illustrated the potential of social psychology.

Riesman also raised two very profound issues that confronted his age. The first was economic abundance and its consequences. Whatever its new affluence, it is difficult from a later perspective to think of the early 1950s as particularly flush, yet all the indications of coming prosperity were present. Riesman, like many other writers of the period, tried to predict the effects of this prosperity and, indeed, considered them to be a major challenge in defining the new, postwar society. He understood that abundance changed everything, redefining work and opening up a new "frontier" of consumption. As he put it in an essay two years later, leisure had replaced work in essential ways as an organizing principle of society. "In a society in which competence in work is no longer a self-evident requirement either for individual or for social advance," he wrote, "competence in leisure may have to take over much of the justificatory quality previously found in work." In other words an ethic of consumption had replaced the work ethic. A corollary problem also derived from mass society. Contemporary culture, characterized by large, bureaucratic institutions and mass media, demanded skills for getting along rather than strategies for getting ahead. Thus, the very successes of affluence and economic and cultural integration presented serious challenges. The shaping power of these two interwoven trends was, he argued, enormous, and *The Lonely Crowd* is perceptive for its ability to chart the consequences for behavior that they engendered.[33]

The Lonely Crowd also profoundly challenged thinking about American history. It divided national history into three stages, linking social and economic change to shifts in personality adjustment. The two most important phases were, of course, inner- and then other-direction, the first describing an individualist capitalism characterized by the predominance of production, and the more recent one, a period of large corporations and institutions dependent upon consumption. What happened in the workplace, the authors wrote, also transformed the home and impacted the personality. Not surprisingly, these important periods coincided with what American historians had already isolated as occasions of transition: the beginnings of Victorian America and the abrupt shift to corporate capitalism at the end of the nineteenth century. In dramatic fashion, Riesman reworked the insights of such writers as Frederick Jackson Turner into a discussion not of the frontier in American history and American democracy, but of character formation relating to new economic and social institutions of abundance. Far more than Turner imagined, Riesman's picture of American development stressed abundance, consumerism, and mass institutions. This was no critique aimed at superficiality, but a profound insight into the nature of modern institutions and the shift to a world of consumption—the Market society in Fromm's original terminology.

David Potter, one of the historians most influenced by Riesman, used the sociologist's focus on abundance to propose nothing less than a revision in the prevailing narrative of American history. The profession had once almost uniformly believed in a national character, he wrote, and, in particular, had accepted Turner's emphasis upon the moving frontier of opportunity and free land as the salient fact of American exceptionalism. However, he wrote, Turner was actually writing about abundance and plenty, not just open spaces. Looking at the transformation of modern America in this way, he concluded, would allow for a revision of national character studies in the direction of social science, incorporating insights by the likes of Riesman, Mead, and Horney.[34]

In fact, however, it was Potter's short essay in the obscure journal the *Stetson University Bulletin* in 1962 that offered the most profound consideration of national character studies and, in particular, uncovered the unstated premises of *The Lonely Crowd*. Potter declared what was so obvious that, like Poe's "Purloined Letter," it had escaped scrutiny. "Our social generalization is mostly in masculine terms," he wrote. Speaking of "mankind" seems to include both men and women, he concluded, but "when we speak of womankind, we mean the ladies, God bless them." In other words, "man" indicated generalized humanity and "woman" meant a specific exception. This gendered language was, he argued, typical of almost all writing about American history. Turner, for example, in defining the individualism evoked by the frontier, certainly did not mean to include women. Neither his language nor his descriptions could be read this way. Women certainly lived on the frontier (some women at least), but their experience was not likely to be the same as that of Davy Crockett or Kit Carson or other visible heroes of American history. Women were neither free nor individualistic in terms of the economy or politics in the nineteenth century; they were first and foremost women. Their lives were far more likely to be circumscribed by constant gender considerations even in changing physical settings. Engaged in domestic production, childbirth, childcare, family relationships, schools, and religion, they were less affected by the challenges that Turner celebrated and generalized.[35]

Potter particularly focused his attention to gender on *The Lonely Crowd* and its concepts of changing character and its relationship to work. Did Riesman, he asked, ever even intend for his typologies to refer to women?

Did it make any sense to describe women as inner-directed during the nineteenth century? Had they not always possessed the "radar screen" of other-direction to aid them in anticipating and conforming to the demands of others? Were they not always part of a group, and almost never individual entrepreneurs? Were they not quicker to conform "to the expectations of a group of other women than men are to a group of other men?" Was it not true, he asked finally, that history affected men and women differently because of their distinct positions within the family and in larger society? One could, he concluded, argue that the toxic effects of alienating work in the twentieth century had not affected most women, who instead found their occupation as housekeeper and mother greatly eased by labor-saving devices.[36]

Potter's essay ends with an ambivalent view of American womanhood, which he pictured as liberated and constrained, self-centered and generous, free and frustrated. But the larger point was a brilliant one and merited a far more important venue than the obscure publication where he placed his essay. Potter had offered the profound criticism that history and social science ignored gender in their descriptions of American character and, in doing so, excised a huge part of the story. In effect, he said, they had gotten it all wrong.

Potter's argument about exclusion certainly applies to the emerging national character literature of the 1950s that centered on ideas of American exceptionalism, formed around an emerging mythos of typical characters and traits, and a canon of male writers. And it was clearly and profoundly true of *The Lonely Crowd,* which can best be understood as a discussion of changes in male culture throughout American history—in fact, as an implicit warning that men were becoming like women, which is to say, other-directed. Riesman's response to this possibility is fascinating, if vague. He spoke many times about the book, discussing changes he should like to make to prevent misinterpretations of his concepts of inner- and other-direction. He also grappled, on occasion, with the problem of women, although he did not ever recognize the degree to which his book reconstructed history and personality in terms of changing modes of masculinity. Not that he was unsympathetic to women. Indeed, in the section on autonomy, he sympathetically portrayed the social and intellectual isolation of suburban wives. But his views were not particularly enlightened, either. As he told an audience at Bennington College in 1956, the "feminist stance," the "bluestocking," had pretty much faded in the present era. He also agreed with Margaret Mead that feminism could be a "subtle form of male dominance" because it trivialized motherhood. So, women should be educated for the "contingencies of life," but not necessarily a career.[37]

Once, in 1967, Riesman very briefly addressed possible gender differences in his essay "American Character in the Twentieth Century." Then, twice, late in life, he commented on the role of women in contemporary society. Writing in 1990 he confessed that of all the changes in society that "surprised me I would place the contemporary woman's movements first, with their impact on older and younger age cohorts." Then in 1992, he noted, "I had no anticipation of the strength of the women's movements that erupted as an outgrowth of, and in considerable measure a reaction against, the male dominated student protests and the counterculture of the 1960s."[38] Indeed, the sociologist had once congratulated his team on their inclusion of a special section on women in *The Lonely Crowd*, but he did not recognize, beyond this point, the lopsided degree to which his study was aimed at the experience of men and told from their perspective.[39] Certainly, he did not invent the male perspective of American history—far from it. But when he proposed his radical new revision, he dressed the masculine point of view in the new garb of character.

When Riesman and Nathan Glazer published *Faces in the Crowd: Individual Studies in Character and Politics* in 1952, they presented, in depth, some of the interviews they had conducted as a part of the original study for *The Lonely Crowd*. Their survey was not statistically representative, they argued, but conducted to reveal structures of character. This, they said, justified the unrepresentative sample of their interviews. In fact, the book made no pretence to being comprehensive. For example, they selected 21 extended portraits to present out of the 180 interviews they conducted. Of these, 14 were of men and 7 of women. But the most interesting proposition is their justification for this bias. Since he and his collaborators were interested in developing a typology and a method of interpreting interviews, Riesman wrote, "we were not worried by the fact that we had many more Jews and Negroes than their numerical proportion in the population, more men than women, more young than old, more from the upper than from the lower social strata, more from the East than from the West and South." Their choices, they contended, would provide them with a "sifted embodiment of American culture." A positive benefit of this homogeneity made it possible to reduce distinctions into a single character type. It eliminated any effort to measure differences within a group or category.[40] Riesman appeared to be well aware that he was exaggerating the coherence of his essential types and suggesting some real existence of ideal categories "in nature." He also admitted that any group might share certain characteristics with others: Frenchmen are like and unlike Americans. Every individual, he wrote, in a very curious passage, was "an entire stock company." Thus, as men, he continued, "we contain the 'part' or 'role' of the women with whom we interact, and vice versa— and not only in those collegiate or army shows in which we put on bras, use pillows for breasts, and wear lipstick in a mock-denial that there is anything womanly about us." The most important conclusion to be drawn from this embarrassing passage is simply to emphasize how resolutely masculine was his point of view—and how uncomfortable he revealed himself to be when attempting to include women.[41]

Yet in one instance, at least, Riesman proved quite capable of exploring gender issues in a sensitive fashion. In his interpretation of Thorstein Veblen, published in 1953, the sociologist examined the consequences of what he suspected were Veblen's feelings of inadequate masculinity. This vulnerability, Riesman concluded, led the early sociologist to turn his withering satire against the extravagant masculine elements in contemporary civilization. In fact, Veblen argued that women had been consistently exploited and oppressed throughout history, even in the more liberated 1890s when they were persuaded to flaunt in dress and social manner the vulgar accomplishments of the Captains of Industry. Riesman believed that Veblen's psychological compensation led him to defend "the peaceable types who throughout history had been overcome by masculine force and fraud." The result was a vantage point that the great turn-of-the-century thinker transformed into the savage irony of *Theory of the Leisure Classes*. This iconoclastic work, concluded Riesman, pitted feminine against masculine, a passive acceptance against protest—and paid tribute to the former. As for his revival in popularity during the 1950s, Riesman believed that Veblen had prefigured the intellectual's "failure and despondency," a popular theme of the age.[42]

Riesman's foray into gender analysis, unusual in his writings, remains fundamentally consistent with his understanding of male and female cultural attributes. In his schema, masculine generally meant self-reliant, aggressive, and socially effective; feminine meant passive, exploited, peaceful. In some respects, these divisions coincided with his characterizations of inner- and other-direction. Furthermore, they revealed his penchant for popular psychological analysis that used sexual divisions, feelings of inadequacy, and compensation as tools of analysis. It is also hard to believe that Riesman did not, in some sense, think that this sort of explanation undercut the validity of Veblen's attacks on nineteenth-century capitalism. To accuse him of hiding behind masculine science and objectivity, to picture him as a scholar who "involutes what he has to say in ceremonial linguistic panoply"—like a tough cowboy who wears embroidered shirts—could hardly be considered a neutral way to represent him to the early 1950s. In effect, he had construed the sociologist's sensitivity to women to be the result of compromised masculinity.[43]

In presenting the story of American character as a male declension narrative, Riesman imbedded multiple allusions to the growing fear in contemporary society of the feminization of contemporary men—especially middle-class men—in his analysis. This occurred primarily through descriptions of the culture of other-directedness contrasted to the implicit higher valuation of entrepreneurial individualism and production, either in its inner-directed or autonomous guises. Because American culture assigned separate and opposing values to the behaviors he described, his utilization of contemporary words inevitably skewed his argument and linked his ideas to contemporary, often negative, evaluations of aspects of modern culture.

These worries described three developments, each of which defined a portion of the culture wars of the 1940s and 1950s. The first was the opposition between high and mass culture. The second was the supercharged significance assigned to the concepts of production and consumption. The third was an opposition between individualism and mass society. In each of these cases, public intellectuals and cultural critics praised the first and disparaged the second. It appeared to a great many writers that individualism, a production ethic, and high culture (or tradition) were being challenged everywhere by the new and debased values of mass society, consumption, and mass culture. And what lay just beneath the surface of this sometimes strident evaluation was the identification of the new mass society with women and feminization.[44] By invoking a discourse that had come to identify mass consumer society with women, and by adding his own vivid terminology to explain this phenomenon, Riesman implicitly wrote the history of character as a story of the decline of masculinity. He ended with hopes for the rise of a new, reborn, autonomous man. But his words to this purpose were not nearly as convincing as was his critique, and the book earned its extraordinary reputation precisely because of the power of its sober picture of a mass society of conforming men. If such a crowd were defined as female, then any man might feel lonely in it, for the once-cherished values of individuality and productivity seemed no longer valid.

In two compelling portraits, Riesman demonstrated the key role played by women in the socialization of other-direction. *The Lonely Crowd* disclosed the power of feminization both in teaching a social ethic of getting along and in the transformation of the workplace according to new bureaucratic standards. Schoolchildren learned the virtue of conformity in the classroom through stories that reinforced other-directed behavior. Riesman found a representative example in the Little Golden Books series for beginning readers. The story, "Tootle the Engine," depicted a train that refused to stay on the tracks, choosing instead to wander where it wished. Despite warnings, "he" (the engine) refuses to confine himself to the railway. Finally, the whole town pitches in by placing red warning flags everywhere except on the tracks. Tootle gives in, happily, and returns to the roundhouse, with promises that he will grow up to be a streamliner. As is always the case, Riesman's understanding of this story is complex, but this was precisely the sort of material that persuaded readers that he was denouncing the predominance of the feminized group.[45]

Even the presentation is gender coded in this example: the teacher is clearly a woman and the train (he) is masculine. Riesman goes on to say, "The teacher's role in this situation is often that of opinion leader. She is the spreader of the messages concerning taste that come from the progressive urban centers." In their classrooms, children "are supposed to learn democracy by underplaying the skills of intellect and overplaying the skills of gregariousness." Riesman then explicitly links this learning environment with another principal setting that demands suppression of individualism: the modern workplace. There was a "curious resemblance," he concluded, between the modern schoolroom with its progressive education and "the role of the industrial relations department in a modern factory." Here, too, an ethic of "cooperation between men and men and between men and management" prevailed, while the demand for technical skills and initiative had apparently diminished. Thus, the other-directed child "is taught at school to take his place in a society where the concern of the group is less with what it produces than with its internal group relations, its morale." What Riesman does not mention in this passage, although he presumably was aware of it, was the growing female predominance in the profession of personnel management, the very corporate division that used controversial aptitude and personality tests to promote an other-directed personality and the ethic of pleasing others (the number of personnel workers doubled in the 1950s).[46] As one historian has recently noted, "From its inception in the years just before World War I, personnel theory was dominated by college-trained women." Thus, *The Lonely Crowd* needs to be understood as a sophisticated, if unwitting, summary of gender attitudes focused around the issue of character formation.

Although the authors do not clearly and consistently differentiate between men and women in their discussions, it is certain that the subject of most character descriptions is male. By utilizing disparaging language to depict other-direction with its manipulative, peer-oriented effects on character, the book evoked a highly gendered and schematized value system. By identifying women as the teachers, supervisors, and facilitators of these attitudes, they implied that other-direction meant feminization. And, perhaps if it had not done so, if the book had discouraged such a reading, it might not have enjoyed the considerable success it did.[47]

Riesman was joined in his enterprise of modern character analysis by a host of like-minded critics whose works deepened and sometimes redirected his work. Indeed, the atmosphere of public discourse in the 1950s crackled with sharp sallies against the decline of an individualist ethic and the rise of group think. As Riesman's close friend Columbia historian Richard Hofstadter wrote, the shift from individualism to the socialized personality, from production to consumption, from manipulation of things to administration of people had touched off a broad discussion, with "overtones of distress and concern, anxiety about the implications of this change." It had, he noted, made many of his friends nostalgic for the "inner-directed man that they may never have known."[48]

Perhaps the most important of these colleagues was William H. Whyte, whose 1956 book *The Organization Man* refocused Riesman's insights on modern character on the suburbs and the men who commuted from these bedroom communities to the new work environments of modern corporations.[49] In a 1958 collection, Riesman joined Whyte and a chorus of other critics of the suburbs with an essay published under the auspices of the Center for the Study of Leisure at the University of Chicago, which he had helped establish. While his ideas here represented an extension of *The Lonely Crowd*, concentrating on one particular environment, Riesman invoked many of the general criticisms of other-direction to analyze this new world. The title said it all: "The Suburban Sadness." But the "sadness" was actually Riesman's, uneasy as he was about the growth of suburban lifestyles and their displacement of urban orientations. The result was a "loss of certain kinds of diversity, complexity, and texture." In the new world of consumption-orientation, decentralization, and "familism" (domesticity), there was a kind of "pervasive low-keyed unpleasure" identified elsewhere by Erich Fromm and Percival and Paul Goodman. In a world where work had lost its traditional meaning, replaced by an emphasis on leisure and consumption, Riesman found from asking several hundred college students, that most of them hoped to find mates whom "we might call station-wagon types: educated, companionable, civic-minded, and profoundly domestic." While this prospect was far from desperate given the potential to invent outlets for creativity and ingenuity in this new suburban environment, the impression communicated by this piece (with its disparaging metaphor of the presumably female "station-wagon type") was a deeply critical perspective on the major trends of consumption and peer-oriented work and leisure.[50]

What the public made of the growing tide of works depicting a decline from traditional American character—and descriptions of a changeover to a new personality type—is probably simpler and more pessimistic, and certainly more conservative, than most of its creators intended. It appeared to many readers that Riesman's works were coded in the kind of conservative, back-to-basics language that he himself vociferously rejected. The popular reading of *The Lonely Crowd* in reviews and magazine articles often stressed a decline of individualism and a need to break through the fog of conformity and stale suburban life. In an ideological world that still valued production over consumption, elite culture over mass, individualism over collectivism, and male "values" over female "virtues," the emerging pattern of social criticism had a confusing political caste to it. In this light, *The Lonely Crowd* can be read as one of the origins of modern neoconservatism, and some of the most important public intellectuals in that emerging tradition were early participants in the critique of 1950s mass society. Seymour Martin Lipset believed he detected this conservative political slant in both Riesman and Whyte, linking them to the aristocratic ideals of Alexis de Tocqueville. While they "would deny that their works contain conservative value preferences, and insist that they are simply analyzing changes . . . it seems fairly evident that, like the more elitist travelers of the nineteenth century, they dislike many of the dominant trends." But during the 1950s, the deeper political overtones were not generally audible and *The Lonely Crowd* as well as similar literature was often understood to be a radical critique of society.[51]

One sign of Riesman's discomfort with his interpreters and their desire to catalogue him was his frequent dialogue with *The Lonely Crowd* itself and his comments on what he might have done to prevent misunderstanding. This ranged from his growing wariness about a title that seemed to announce a diatribe against modern American society to alternative words he could have chosen for his character types. He found allies in this search to assert his original intent. For example, fellow sociologist Lipset wrote that "vulgarizations of the theses of Riesman and Whyte have been published in many magazines and cited at P.T.A. meetings all over the country where outraged middle-class parents demand a return to 'old-fashioned' methods of teaching."[52] As if this feminized location in itself proved the invidious distortion of sophisticated ideas!

Of course, there were also many critics who denied Riesman's worries about changing American character, from *Time* magazine, which defended the health of individualism and said that *The Lonely Crowd* presented a "typological menagerie," to philosopher Will Herberg, who accepted some of the categories of the book, but faulted the sociologist for his failure to propose change through the transcendence of worldly concerns.[53] Historians greeted the book with a measure of enthusiasm and skepticism. David Potter's 1954 work, *People of Plenty*, of course, commended Riesman, Mead, and others for revising the terms of national character studies. Although he glossed over Riesman's critique of contemporary society, Potter noted that he had "described the consumer personality with notable insight." What really mattered to Potter however, was the defining characteristic of American life—its abundance—hence the need to study the effects of plenty on national development. Carl Degler's evaluation, "The Sociologist as Historian," scrutinized Riesman's method and criticized its specifics. Degler found that the historical transitions upon which inner- and other-direction were purportedly based did not bear up under examination. Comparing the nineteenth and twentieth centuries, one did not find distinct differences in personality. In fact, Degler argued, other-direction clearly existed in Tocqueville's age and was "the dominant element in our national character through most of our history." Riesman correctly stressed a transition between different eras of production and consumption, but even here the changes were not as clear-cut as he believed. But one could (and should) retain what was Riesman's most salient insight: there was such a thing as an American character and it was other-directed.[54]

Such reactions, beyond a defense of academic turf, suggest the conditions under which Riesman's notions of national character entered American historiography in the 1950s. Even if some historians faulted his knowledge of the periods he described, the basic structure of character history could be salvaged and put to use. This was particularly crucial to a decade of thinkers who were growing skeptical of traditional economic explanations of history. Several of Riesman's most important ideas either reinforced prevailing notions among American historians or suggested new ways of looking at the past. Heading this list would be his assessment of abundance in American society and its effects upon the American character. Furthermore, Riesman's description of other-direction had considerable resonance. Finally, and most important, there was his description of a shift in American history from production to consumption from the end of the nineteenth century onward as an organizing principle of the economy, society, and individual psychology. This insight became a major premise of historians during the decades that followed.

Even economic historians could fruitfully adopt Riesman's categories. As Theodore Levitt wrote in 1956 in his essay "The Lonely Crowd and the Economic Man," the sociologist's notions challenged economists to rethink the nature and function of the model "economic man" and his function in a creative economy. After admitting that the "newly emerging other-directed society seems offhand to impose the torpor of conformity" on the economy, Levitt claimed he had discovered the saving remnant of inner-direction, enough at least to continue to drive the American economy and salvage the concept of economic man as the centerpiece of economic theory. The "strong will survive," he wrote hopefully, made even more vigorous by their clash with conformity.[55]

One of Riesman's closest academic friends, Richard Hofstadter at Columbia University, particularly acknowledged his influence. Shortly after *The Lonely Crowd* appeared, he wrote the author, "I want to tell you how much *The Lonely Crowd* has meant to me . . . I can only say that it has already affected me profoundly." In turn, Riesman supported some of Hofstadter's students by promoting their books and working to find them employment. For example, in 1957, he wrote recommendations for students Eric McKittrick and Stanley Elkins, who were innovators in applying the social sciences to historical research. Others recognized Riesman's relevance to the history profession. Thus, Reuel Denney wrote to him in 1968: "You are probably too modest in the claims that you make for your influence on what questions American historians of the 19th Century now ask themselves." He went on to list historians who used Riesman's insights, including Hofstadter.[56]

Riesman's notions have lingered at the center of historical writing since the 1950s, although the sociologist is not solely responsible for their shape and evolution. He also conveyed to historians a tone of censure and a persistent vocabulary of criticism and ambiguity. Other-direction, the decline of individualism, the advent of mass culture, the rise of the suburb, and consumerism have often been identified by historians as negative developments in American civilization.[57] But in some respects the most important legacy of Riesman to the history profession was the degree to which his work strengthened gendered values as an undercurrent of historical narrative. In the end, Riesman substituted an account of implicit masculinity crisis for the principle contours of American history.

To many sociologists and public intellectuals Riesman remained the key figure in 1950s social criticism and the source of a new school of analysis. E. Digby Baltzell placed him at the center of a large and largely depressing literature criticizing the quality of America's postwar culture, citing books like *The Lonely Crowd*, *The Organization Man*, and *The Exurbanites* as examples. In fact, he wrote, this school had been so persuasive that ideal types and character categories had become "firmly fixed in the jargon of social science and in the minds of most modern social critics." Or as historian Cushing Strout said of *The Lonely Crowd* in 1964, "we can no longer look at our own time without reference to its categories."[58]

If Riesman had any disappointment in his success it was undoubtedly the failure of readers and critics to take seriously his chapters on the autonomous personality. In this last section of the book, the sociologist proposed ways to transform work and consumption and leisure through such devices as hobbies and competent craftsmanship. Instruction in leisure, the upgrading of mass culture, and avocational counseling by art teachers, interior decorators, and even salespeople might help rescue the individual with "overindustrialized elements in himself and his environment that constitute a threat to his humanity." But the unfocused and piecemeal presentation of this section diminished its potential appeal.[59]

If not all academic or professional intellectuals accepted his descriptions of society, Riesman, himself, recognized that the book had made it to the best-seller list because of popular enthusiasm for its ideas—for the common sense it affirmed as much as for what it invented. He noted it had "in some measure entered the picture many Americans—and some readers in other countries—have of ourselves, both past and present."[60] It also became a text about nonconformity, a tract seeming to celebrate an earlier, freer time. It lent itself to parlor games and amateur psychology. The book portrayed American history in terms of stages of consciousness, not quite Freudian in nature, but close enough to appear scientific in its orientation to human psychology. It borrowed from a host of works by American historians, familiar travelers' accounts, anthropology, literature, sociology, philosophy, economics, suburban studies, and the Frankfurt-school criticism of mass culture. It injected a diluted Marxism into the mainstream of American social science. No doubt its success surprised Riesman and the Yale press, but perhaps eventually he understood why. His continued interest in tinkering with titles and terminology suggests that he suspected what had happened—what really explained his success. The book articulated, better than almost any document of the age, the ambiguous and divided feelings that middle-class Americans and opinion leaders evinced toward the new mass society of work, consumption, and domesticity that began to emerge with remarkable force after the war. As Kenneth Kenistan put it, *The Lonely Crowd* captured something "quintessential about America at the time."[61] Its success rested not in its scientific validity so much as in the plausibility of the familiar—in the sociologist's ability to give substance and coherence to, and to name an emerging critique of modern society. David Riesman was the reluctant prophet of the new man in this purportedly feminized modern world of togetherness, suburbs, personnel manipulation, and mass culture. He made it plausible to believe that the nature of social evolution itself had ended up where public intellectuals feared: in a debased mass culture. As much as anyone in the 1950s, he promoted a view of character and culture in crisis, and his terms became the familiar terminology of that discussion. Yet he retained considerable optimism about the future of a new, autonomous self that might emerge dialectically out of previous character types. In the final analysis, Riesman seemed to want it both ways.

4

A Feeling of Crisis: The 1950s

We are drifting toward a social structure made up of he-women and she-men.
—Dr. Irene Josselyn

If David Riesman constructed an American history of character that lent itself to growing alarm over the state of contemporary manhood, his subtlety and hesitations disappeared in popular works that simplified and vulgarized his findings, or that simply substituted misogyny for social insight. Whether men actually suffered an identity crisis—or crises—during the 1950s, there were many observers who strongly believed that Riesman's lonely men were afflicted by an increasingly feminized world. Arthur M. Schlesinger, Jr., is a representative of this chorus of prophets, although he was neither the most original nor the most influential writer to lament the passing of a chiseled model of American masculinity. But, as a historian who lionized John Kennedy in the 1960s and depicted him and Lyndon Johnson as twin pillars of political manhood (struggling against a feminized, "other-directed" Richard Nixon), his observations during the era and about its history—his considerable efforts to establish political virility as the coin of the realm—magnify the significance of his account.[1]

Writing for *Look* magazine in 1958 on "The Crisis of American Masculinity," Schlesinger worried about ambiguity of the contemporary male role; it had, apparently, "lost its rugged clarity of outline." This blurring of images into a softer domesticated version could be detected in a wide variety of striking examples found in popular culture: in the media craze over Christine Jorgensen's sex change operation, in plays like *Compulsion* and *Tea and Sympathy*, and in dubious and louche films like *Cat on a Hot Tin Roof* and *Look Back in Anger*. The historian made no bones about it: gender confusion led to heightened worries about homosexuality if not its actual increase.

Schlesinger served up his diagnosis from a menu of causes that by 1958 had become a standard bill of fare: aggressive women, the fluid uncertainties of modern society, the cost in esteem of adjusting to centralization, and modern bureaucratic control of the workplace. Other commentators before him had popularized a vocabulary of critical terms to describe the same problems: the lonely crowd, organization men, the togetherness ethic, and other unsavory depictions. Schlesinger did not propose to turn back the clock to some dusty patriarchy, but suggested, instead, "a new belief in apartness." A man had to think of himself, not the group, to value and nourish his spontaneous individuality. If not exactly an individualized version of the "New Frontier" (advocated as a political slogan by John Kennedy a few years later), this argument did, in fact, resonate with a similar aura of traditions plucked from the heroic moments of American history. Schlesinger deplored mass culture; he called for a reinvigoration of the arts and a commitment to a newly aggressive liberal politics as a buttress of manhood.[2]

The capacious perhaps, but vague, terms of the historian's remedy might seem inconsequential compared to the scope of the problems he conjured up, but this is understandable. It is, after all, difficult if not inconceivable to provoke a national revolution in self-esteem with one short magazine article that was, itself, high in negative descriptions. Perhaps this is why Schlesinger ended on a note of worry, revisiting the troubled analysis of the beginning: "If we want to have *men* [his italics] again in our theaters and our films and our novels—not to speak of in our classrooms, our business offices, and our homes—we must first have a society which encourages each of its members to have a distinct identity."[3]

There is much of interest in this article: the implication that conformity is emasculating and that modern mass society is feminizing, for example. Of interest too is the author's manner of picking out invidious mass culture symbols to epitomize his era: a Tennessee Williams film to exemplify contemporary decline, and the early American writer James Fenimore Cooper to represent lost standards of masculinity and traditional heroism. The importance of such literary and popular culture figures and their metaphoric incarnations is not something that Schlesinger invented. The age was full of dire warnings portrayed in symbols drawn from examples in the mass media and literary history, as if a shocking film or a frontier tale could represent a whole society. As a historian, he might have been suspicious of what these cultural examples actually represented, so much the more because his prestige as a public intellectual augmented the influence of his words.

Without a clear sense of masculinity—as a cultural essence—Schlesinger might not have worried about the 1950s in just this way. Absent an agreed-upon cultural division between gendered mannerisms, tastes, and activities, absent an accepted symbolism of male and female throughout society, dividing not just behavior, but even objects and words into tints of pink or blue, such worries could not have existed. Thus neither Schlesinger nor others in the large chorus of disapproving commentators would have found much to complain about if they were not certain what the ideal American male had been historically and ought to be in contemporary society. As Joseph Peck wrote in his contemporary 1958 study, *All About Men*, "Times and customs change, but human nature is pretty constant."[4] But what if, as the defensive tone of Schlesinger's analysis seemed to suggest, the constant was actually contingent? What if the most stable symbolic systems—those of personal identity—were in flux?

This possibility of historical contingency was certainly not apparent everywhere. A remarkable analysis published in the late 1940s reveals the extent to which the popular gendered code had made its way into the social science of the era. Harvard anthropologist Carl C. Seltzer, in the article "The Relationship between the Masculine Component and Personality," tabulated the correspondence between body type and personal affect. The author reveals his assumptions early on: "It is a common observation that the male body build varies from an angular, rough-surfaced, narrow-hipped, well-muscled, masculine type to the rounder, softer, broad-hipped, less-well muscled feminine type." The stronger the physical "masculine component," he discovered, the more likely the individual would also exhibit "masculine" personality traits. Continuing to divide men according to inclinations to the more masculine or more feminine range, Seltzer found that one extreme tended toward weakness, indecisiveness, the arts, and the feminine, whereas the other exhibited strength and vitality—the more masculine. There was, he concluded, an obvious physical-psychological continuity. Men who looked masculine were just that: masculine. If this conclusion was based upon an arbitrary and culturally determined common sense, that hardly reduces its significance. For the point is not that this was bad social science, but that, in certain respects, it was quite good social intelligence, well attuned to measure prevailing beliefs and customs because it took the assumed knowledge of the age as its standard of evaluation.[5]

There was nothing unique or surprising about this approach. Elizabeth Lunbeck's very interesting study of what she calls "the psychiatric persuasion" traces the profound shifts in modern America intensified by the acceptance of a psychiatric, therapeutic model for culture and gender. As she demonstrates, this model was clearly in place by the 1950s with its definitions of masculinity, its descriptions of homosexuality, and its deep concern about the problems of adolescence. All of these assumptions reinforced the division of culture into gendered realms. As Joseph Pleck has written, this made the "maintenance of masculinity the dominant feature of Freudian thought" in American culture. It stressed developmental normality and offered psychiatry as treatment for those who did not quite attain the masculine (or feminine) norm. This was precisely the nature of the advice, for example, proffered by Abram Kardiner, professor of clinical psychiatry at Columbia University. In 1955, he wrote, "The social significance of homosexuality is, then, a complex subject, as well as an alarming one. It reaches deep into the social distresses of our time." It represented a failure of individual development, a stunted personality, and a revolt against the responsibilities of manhood. The homosexual, like the weaker male primate in a violent confrontation, took on a cringing female role when faced with a stronger opponent.[6] Quite clearly, this sort of psychiatric analysis, together with other forms of social science, bolstered prevailing cultural stereotypes about gender.

Worry about masculine identity thus had its origins partially in the desire to maintain clear cultural and social distinctions between men and women and in the belief in the historical certainty and efficacy of such distinctions. The past could be imagined as a gendered utopia. Moderation of severe and opposing gender typologies during the 1950s might have been possible (indeed changes were rapidly occurring), but only a few popular commentators at the time promoted complexity over clear distinctions. Few wanted to relinquish the comfort of their worry or the easy explanation apparently favored by a public that masculinity must be in decline.[7]

In a characteristic what-is-wrong-with-our-men symposium in 1957, *Cosmopolitan* magazine identified several familiar problems of modern masculinity. To the prolific free-lance journalist Richard Gehman the disappearance of gender distinctions in modern America was a striking and dangerous development to be deplored. Men now cooked, cleaned, and washed dishes. But this was no cause for celebrating equality; indeed, the opposite response was more appropriate. "So, what man can now say he is not a menial?" he concluded. At the same time as women became more aggressive and powerful, invading male precincts like the upper echelons of business organizations and exclusive clubs, men were being feminized by adopting fashion, beauty treatments, wearing girdles, and frequenting beauty parlors. Not much was being done to stem this creeping cultural androgyny, although one very encouraging sign to the author was the creation of a special United Airlines "executive" flight linking Chicago and New York. Male-only customers could unwind on the flight in "a shirtsleeve atmosphere," don slippers, down a drink," and eat a "three-ounce steak cooked to order."[8]

Gehman's flip pessimism and exaggerated warnings capture the tone of a great deal of this literature in the 1950s wherein author after author tries to outdo his predecessors with horrifying examples of male oppression and gender-bending behavior. But such diatribes are instructive, for they suggest that editors and publishers widely believed in an eager reading audience that shared the authors' assumption that there were clear-cut male and female cultures in the United States under assault. Perhaps this was a continuing reaction to the war experience that substituted women for men in countless civilian positions. But there was also an amplified worry about the relationship of gender to consumption. Such readers would, it was assumed, understand that even consumer objects had essential gender identities. Everyone knew, Gehman could assume, that certain objects symbolized the male and female, so to cross over and use an inappropriate item constituted a serious transgression and an occasion to be concerned about the future of society itself.

There was a linguistic and social equivalent of this apparent division among physical objects and consumer items. In the 1950s, when social critics and public intellectuals wrote about society, they almost universally referred to "man" or "men," and in most cases actually meant male and not female. Man, in *The Lonely Crowd*, for example, was clearly the measure of the social order. So, too, in many works, "man" meant essential and representative, while female implied frivolous or inessential or marginal. This division gave a curious twist to some of the deepest and most radical discussions of American society in the 1950s and salted social criticism with the distinct flavor of misogyny. The terms "masculine" and "feminine" also carried inherent implications of positive and negative. Thus, mass culture, consumerism, and suburbia were often portrayed as soft, manipulative, seductive, feminine, and weak, while the remedy for contemporary cultural ills lay in the assertion of vigor, criticism, energy, authority, and a whole range of attributes associated with traditional male individualism—the sort of division Riesman implied in his descriptions of inner- and other-direction.

What were the consequences of such thinking? The popular diagnosis/prognosis of male weakness fell into three worrisome categories.

The first was the charge that women had either actually usurped male roles or aggrandized their traditional vocation of motherhood into the inflated and potent figure of "Mom." By whatever means, guile or competition, they had become the dominant sex within the family. In a kind of Freudian nightmare, Moms seized the initiative in raising sons and in doing so, refused to allow them to mature, resulting in a variety of aberrant behaviors. The second fear focused on weak or distant fathers who appeared to be raising sons whose stunted psychological growth froze their development at a perilous, immature point. This decline of paternal authority, it was charged, could explain the increase in homosexuality and juvenile delinquency that many observers believed they had detected. And, finally, the traditions of masculinity could be distorted with fatal consequences. American men, it was charged, were literally working themselves to death in meaningless jobs for the sake of career and maintaining family consumption.

If anything, popular culture reproduced and simplified such assumptions. Without these clear-cut gender ideals and commonly accepted male and female identities, the novels of Ayn Rand would never have gained their surprising currency. Well before the decade began, Rand announced the major theme in the 1950s discussion of masculinity: its incipient decline. Rand gave the problem of male panic such a violent and perverse twist, that it was scarcely apparent that her mirror of America also refracted into the writings of many liberal intellectuals who followed her. Her 1943 novel *The Fountainhead* revealed a series of themes that anticipated the coming critique of American masculinity across the political spectrum. This was probably one of the oddest successes of American letters. The novel is ponderous with stiff conversation and deadly dull descriptions. The motivations of its main characters are preposterous and have to be explained with raw chunks of political philosophy. Yet the book had an extraordinary half-life after exploding onto the best-seller list, eventually selling more than four million copies, and it transformed Rand into the unlikely leader of a national political-intellectual faction.

The main character was based very loosely on Frank Lloyd Wright, who, at the time, was uttering self-indulgent condemnations of American architecture and social life to anyone who would pay to be insulted.[9] The novel incorporated mythologies about Wright's life: the thwarted genius, absolution by artistic achievement, and the utter depravity of tradition and compromise. Howard Roark (the Wright figure in the book) is a paragon of genius and masculinity, the two being inseparable in his case. Entirely self-absorbed, he breaks the fundamental rules of social discourse and morality and also flouts architectural tradition. He takes what he wants—a beautiful woman, Dominique Francon—in a notoriously vulgar rape/love scene. ("One gesture of tenderness from him—and she would have remained cold, untouched by the thing done to her body. But the act of a master taking shameful, contemptuous possession of her was the kind of rapture she had wanted.")

Rand also gives Roark license to destroy what he disapproves. Later in the novel, he blows up a housing project he had designed, but which was modified during its construction to create softer lines with more traditional embellishments. This was a defiant act that the architect defended successfully before a jury. Yet this was hardly a reason for optimism. Roark was only one man in a world of diminutive projects and compromised people. As one character despairs in the end, "The age of the skyscraper is gone. This is the age of the housing project! Which is always a prelude to the age of the cave."[10] How short a distance from this utterance to the disparaging attacks on Levittown by public intellectuals a decade later!

The liberal intellectuals largely responsible for constructing the negative image of a conformist 1950s, of men trapped within the pall of domesticity and assaulted by mass culture, certainly did not advocate rape and arson for social solutions. Rand drove their argument (even before they made it) ad absurdum. Yet there is an important continuity in the picture of masculinity-in-crisis that she announced. She made two arguments with a force and clarity few could surpass: the first was the prior existence of an American masculinity defined through arduous struggle against an unfriendly, even hostile environment. Rapid social and economic change was rendering this sort of individualism obsolete and even dangerous to the emerging order. The traditional male, the builder, innovator, conqueror, had become a social outcast almost by definition. Her second innovation was to link genius and masculinity, the mental and the physical, high art with strength and muscles. Even critic Dwight Macdonald, for all his celebration of bare-chested avant-garde literature, could not improve on this version of the macho-intellectual.

If Ayn Rand's clarion call for a new individualism somehow missed the higher registers of many liberal social commentators who generally dismissed or ignored it, it was left to Philip Wylie in 1942 in his book *Generation of Vipers* to announce and denounce the precarious modern world of emasculating and overbearing Moms in terms no one could dismiss as mere fiction or a conservative masquerade. Reading this anguished and wounded book today, it is almost impossible to conjure up the terrifying behemoth of unruly womanhood that so frightened Wylie.

Even James Thurber's contemporary, cartoon Amazons in the *New Yorker* were only dowdy, comic figures. Yet, by 1955, Wylie's diatribe had sold 180,000 copies and, tellingly, the author had stirred up 60,000 letters in response.

Wylie blamed the debased culture of modern America with its excessive consumerism, bureaucracy, and political apathy on the controlling influence of modern woman, who, he claimed, managed the politics, economy, and emotions of the nation. No surprise then at the inevitable decline of true masculinity and individualism and an increase in servility and homosexuality. In a later edition he even blamed Moms for McCarthy and Liberace.[11] Women, he declared, suffered from a Cinderella complex, a social psychosis that encouraged them in unreal expectations. The result was pampered, demanding, and all-powerful women—Moms with a vengeful urge to express their frustrations by wreaking vengeance on men.

Despite this breathtakingly distorted view of woman's position in American society—itself better characterized by segregation, patriarchy, and inequality—Wylie's harsh analysis announced the 1950s in two important ways. The first was his overt use of Freud and Jung, particularly Jung, to identify the archetypal human characters that he invoked: the hero, the dual woman (good-bad), the wise old man, the Cinderella, and so on. Since he believed that recourse to physical science and religion failed to explicate the problems of contemporary society, it was now psychology's turn, and the new mental sciences offered something better and more appropriate, he believed. Certainly Wylie was not the first to summon Freud or Jung to the analysis of popular culture, but his effort to place both psychologists in the service of social commentary became a much-repeated recourse in the 1950s, particularly in discussing issues of gender.

The second relevant proposition of *Generation of Vipers* came through its focus on gender relations and the masculinity crisis. Wylie had said something important about his generation. Holding his nose in disgust, he sneered at changes he feared would sweep through the 1950s and beyond. To him, the developing multiplicity of male social and cultural roles presented a crisis of inestimable severity. And these were real changes that Wylie and a legion of social commentators who followed him were talking about. There were significant shifts in domestic relationships that by and large they deplored and which challenged what they believed to be fundamental and gender-specific male American values like individualism, self-reliance, genius, and responsibility. The new ways of enacting manhood, expressed through domesticity, organization, bureaucracy, and "togetherness"—that most notorious of verbal corruptions of the era—offered a confusing array of social possibilities to American men that would make them lose sight of the fundamental one they were called upon by nature and necessity to play.

Historian James Truslow Adams in his 1943 book, *The American*, wrote a more tempered version of much the same conclusion. Americans, he concluded, worshipped at two shrines: the flag and woman. Placing women on a pedestal caused a corresponding decline of manhood. Man had relinquished influence in the home, and in social and cultural life. He ceded, he yielded, he gave up, until woman became an "impossible eminence."[12] Thus the subtle prison of admiration and privilege debased the men who confined women within it.

Such arguments quickly made their way down the publishing food chain. In 1949, the *Reader's Digest* printed a symposium that can best be described as the public airing of squabbles between husbands and wives. One author asked, "Should Your Wife Be Fired?" Another compiled a list of seven faults that explained "What's Wrong with American Women?" (including the charge that women were spoiled, aggressive, restless, bored, unhappy, and unfeminine).[13] In the same issue, Ramona Barth invoked the most august of literary classics for her comments on uncontrollable women. "If you would make women less aggressive, give us aggressive men whose real masculinity allows women to bask and glory in their true femininity." True since Shakespeare's time, "every shrew needs and wants to be tamed. She acts as she does, twittering, nagging, screaming, in subconscious rebellion at living with a pantywaist."[14]

As much as anything, the fear of changing places drove much of the discussion of masculine decline. Russell Lynes, a best-selling social commentator and quote-*meister* of the 1950s, put the problem this way: We have "shuffled the functions of men and women in the most contrary way, not that it has become difficult to tell which is which, but it has become increasingly difficult to tell who does what and why . . . men have taken over women's work and women have taken over men's."[15]

While experts seemed to be divided over their evaluation of the interchangeable parts of male and female roles within the family, depictions of this situation often stressed the ridiculous and dangerous elements of gender confusion. A case in point is the report for the *New York Times Magazine* of a 1957 conference on "The Man in the Family" held by the Child Study Association of America. Entitled "Trousered Mothers and Dishwashing Dads," the piece duly reported several divergent opinions on the issue of men taking on more housework and childcare. But the sensational opening of the article, reporting the speech of Professor Otto Klineberg of Columbia University, set the tone for what followed and pitched the whole discussion into a slough of worry. Klineberg recounted that while he was preparing his talk for the conference, his seventeen-year-old son asked him the subject. When he heard it was the place of men in the home, the son retorted sarcastically, "The way things are going now you could just turn in a blank page." The article proceeded, then, to list worrisome developments, especially the lack of clear differentiation between the dress and activities of young boys and girls, warning of the possible negative outcomes. The end, of course, might not be so bleak at all, the reporter suggested, because older divisions of male and female had been based on useless stereotypes. But the journalistic temptation to emphasize a masculinity crisis controlled both the report and the argument.[16]

Although extended discussions of Momism and the historically anomalous power of modern American women had many participants and devoted experts, Margaret Mead, in 1957, evoked what came to be the accepted wisdom about the proposition and its cause: frustrated women. To the anthropologist, the problem was inherently reciprocal. American women, she wrote, could vote, hold jobs, attend universities, but they had opted for the shelter (and limitations) of the home. Domesticity set an equally tender trap for men. And men, being the barometer of civilization, had become as weak and conformist as the women they confined in the home. Unwilling to take risks, to pursue a true career that might contribute to the quality of national life, they chose security, safety, and home. For what, she asked, "So that they can die—as embittered young men say over their beer—five years earlier and leave their wives to the ineffable delights of well-heeled widowhood."[17] Almost a decade earlier, she had predicted that antagonisms between the sexes would be most noticeable in the middle classes because that is where it was easiest "for women to excel and where men find themselves most fenced in." Ayn Rand and Philip Wylie might not have been so judicious or sympathetic in their attitudes to gender roles, but their analysis of masculine weakness wasn't really much different from Mead's.

Momism, then, appeared to be a symptom of severe gender disorder affecting men as well as women. It seemed to stem, as writer Helen Mayer Hacker explained, from contradictory social signals that distorted domestic and business life. "Men are now expected to demonstrate the manipulative skill in interpersonal relations formerly reserved for women under the headings of intuition, charm, tact, coquetry, womanly wiles, et cetera.

They are asked to bring patience, understanding, gentleness to their human dealings." Yet at the same time, society insisted that they show strength and solidity to women.[18] At work and at home, they were asked to be inner- and other-directed at the same time.

Warren Susman has perceptively called the 1950s the "Age of Erik Erikson," by which he meant that the much-discussed problems of character and national identity were psychologically "redefined as that of personal identity." Erikson's *Childhood and Society*, published in 1950, evoked in psychological terms many of the arguments that fueled public concern over the effect of weak or absent fathers on the development of their sons. For Erikson, the ego operating in a social context was the principal focus of analysis. Immediately, however, a problem loomed, for the formation of identity in America, he argued, was a particularly difficult and perilous undertaking. In part, this vulnerability stemmed from those social processes that defined character. American history had divided experience in two, with a burgeoning activist frontier world reserving a more stationary, sedentary society for those who remained at home, in other words a characteristically male and female separation. In the modern world, this division also translated into the opposition between individualism and conformity. Clearly, modern America made contradictory demands on the individual man to operate with equal energy in both realms, active and sedentary.

The problem of Momism in the present day, he continued, could be traced back to its historic roots in frontier life and in rampant "bossism," its corollary, which developed with industrialization. By bossism, he meant the transformation of corporate work according to the newly instituted bureaucratic and manipulative management principles, a kind of corporate paternalism that infantilized employees. His conclusion was not, to say the least, optimistic: "As we consider what consequences must arise from the particular dangers threatening the emotional state of the nation, our attention is drawn to Momism and bossism, the two trends which have usurped the place of paternalism: Momism in alliance with the autocratic rigor of a new continent, and bossism with the autocracy of the machine."

The resulting gender confusion circulated through the family, making for a difficult adolescence because families were distorted by Momism and men oppressed by bossism. Mothers were cold, aloof, and punitive; fathers shy and guarded at home. "'Mother,'" wrote Erikson, "became 'Mom' only when Father became 'Pop' under the impact of the identical historical discontinuities. For, if you come down to it, Momism is only misplaced paternalism. American mothers stepped into the role of the grandfathers as the fathers abdicated their dominant place in the family, the field of education, and in cultural life." No wonder, he lamented, in "case after case" psychiatrists found that mental patients could point to a cold, domineering, rejecting mother.[19]

Erikson's identity psychology is important for two principal reasons. First, he provided expert testimony to the assertion that American women had become "Mom's" and affirmed the invidious description that went along with this picture of deformed feminism. Second, he lent support to the notion of continuity between individual psychology and cultural pathology, creating a sort of social-psychology which also doubled as cultural criticism.[20]

Some of the same suppositions structured the much-read *Organization Man* by William H. White, Jr., in 1956. Together with countless variations of the same charge that business had introduced an alien concept into its midst akin to Momism, Whyte deplored the decline of individualism and a rise of "collectivism." Men of the American middle class had left home spiritually and physically, "to take the vows of organization life, and it is they who are the mind and soul of our great self-perpetuating institutions."[21] A noteworthy axiom of this argument came from the tendency of writers like Whyte to see changes in business ethics as a form of feminization of the workplace, demanding that men develop the skills of getting along and compromise that were traditionally associated with women and domesticity.

Much of this social psychology found its way into popular expressions, so much so that by the end of the 1950s, it passed for common knowledge. *Look* magazine was only one of several periodicals preoccupied with male crisis in the 1950s, but its survey of the decade's arguments published in 1957 in the magazine and again in 1958 as a book can stand for much of the common wisdom of the era. The editors, in announcing their series on the "Decline of the American Male," had no difficulty finding illustrations in the best current informed opinion to support their point. Indeed, the series is remarkable for the attention paid to the literature of warnings pronounced by public intellectuals and experts.

Like so many other efforts along these lines, the series began with an appalling description of male withdrawal and irrelevance. It ended up with a call to burst the bondage of conformity. Structured in the form of a prophecy, the argument called upon men to reject the impending future and initiate a moral and cultural revolution that would restore masculinity and femininity to their true (if updated) and distinct natures.

"Scientists who study human behavior," wrote military historian and journalist J. Robert Moskin in the lead article, "fear that the American male is now dominated by the American female. These scientists worry that in the years since the end of World War II, he has changed radically and dangerously." He was "no longer the masculine, strong-minded man who pioneered the continent and built America's greatness."[22]

Moskin also revisited the arguments that Wylie had popularized more than a decade earlier. Female dominance came from a feminist revolution that deprived men of their power and thus compromised the historic mission of American masculinity, which was to conquer a continent. Quoting anthropologists Mead and Geoffrey Gorer, Moskin asserted that women had increased their power and ascendancy in just those areas where men were now likely to spend most of their time: in the home and participating in the consumer world. By prevailing in these two related spheres, women were just stuffing more trophies onto their already crowded shelf of stolen powers. They had previously won the battle to control sexual relations with their partners. And now culture, too. Anxious, passive men were the inevitable product of this series of reversals. As Moskin noted, "Social scientist David Riesman warns that today 'boys can be boys only from six to ten years of age. Beyond those years, a boy is unsure of his maleness.'"[23]

So much the worse for the sons raised in this bewildering world. By the late 1950s, if not before, a stereotype based upon such theories had been created in the contemporary print media, seconded by countless Hollywood films that portrayed power-hungry women and retiring, shy fathers, a stereotype of the gender crisis in America which singled out men as the victims and often blamed women for the ravages of ambiguity and anxiety sweeping the nation. And the sons were the ones who suffered most from the absence of an acceptable role model of either gender.

Momism seemed to play a particularly strong role in the terrible childhood dislocations engendered by the masculinity crisis, particularly in its early stages. Striking adolescents with particular force, the gender confusion provoked by weak fathers and aggressive women created two virulent strains of male personality disorder that perplexed the 1950s: the homosexual and the juvenile delinquent.

An early book by Edward A. Strecker, *Their Mothers' Sons: The Psychiatrist Examines an American Problem,* laid down the guidelines of this argument about wayward youth, and clearly blamed assertive women for the misbehavior of their children. In some respects, this attack on Momism was merely a rehash of Wylie, with the argument stretched out on a Freudian couch. But Strecker was more concerned, even than Wylie, with measuring the effects of the overpowerful, ungiving mother on her sons, whom she transformed into simpering homosexuals or delinquent monsters. Strecker even added Stalin, Mussolini, and Hitler to his list of the victims of Momism. There was a persuasiveness to this argument encouraged by the accusation that appeared everywhere in the 1950s: women had purloined fatherhood with the result of terrible loss and confusion for their sons.[24] As psychiatrist John Cavanagh warned the Catholic Family Life Conference in 1956, there were terrible "dangers resulting from the abdication of male authority—particularly the 'feminizing' of sons."[25]

Even Paul Goodman incorporated a version of such ideas into *Growing Up Absurd*, his critical but much more sympathetic account of adolescence published in 1960. Unlike many critics of the American family and gender system, Goodman developed a more radical analysis. He even praised the then-evident cracks in the gender phalanx opened up by the young Beat writers like Jack Kerouac and Allen Ginsberg and their less literate, but rebellious cousins, the juvenile delinquents. Such figures were not something to worry about or to occasion a blanket condemnation of contemporary culture, he wrote; the appearance of rebellion was actually a reason to celebrate. At the same time, however, Goodman's analysis rested upon some very familiar premises: the cloying, dysfunctional family and confused gender roles agitated by an economic and political system that was overorganized and antiindividualist. As he bluntly put it, "our present organized system of society does not want men."[26]

Goodman's and other analyses of the masculinity crisis suggest the importance of the homosexual and juvenile delinquent as the sometimes related symbols of the gender crisis. If mainstream commentators invoked these two despised and feared images with the assurance that most Americans would immediately recoil, there were others, like Goodman himself, who believed that their marginal status gave them a particular and important insight into the disorders of masculinity itself. As the character against whom normal masculinity could be defined, the homosexual was seen as a mirror for contemporary masculinity. But this mirror reflected both ways. Looking back on the decade, historian Robert J. Corber, in *Homosexuality in Cold War America*, for example, argues much the same proposition: that such intellectuals as Tennessee Williams, James Baldwin, Gore Vidal, and others had turned the tables. As the reviled other, they were in a position to recognize the linkage between a virulent masculinity and the ideology of cold war consensus.[27]

If homosexuality was both the clinical symptom and cultural image of the father's failure and the mother's overweening power, that is, the most serious social pathology of masculinity crisis, then the widely discussed sex-change operation of former soldier Christine Jorgensen in 1952, from male to female, vividly challenged the biological stability of gender and gender definitions by introducing the possibility of transsexuality. Most fundamentally, the case of Jorgensen and the huge public discussion around her transition suggested the prospect of a radical rupture between biology and sociology, between organic sexual characteristics and psychological identity in a way that reverberated through some of the decade's most controversial cultural productions. The recognition of ambiguity as well as the increasing visibility of new categories of sexual identity like transgendered and transsexual, profoundly destabilized the assumed continuities of biology and personality upon which the gender crisis and its most facile resolution rested.[28] If men were fast becoming feminized in the 1950s, the case of Jorgensen luridly posed the possibility that they could actually become women via the scalpel and hormone therapy.

Given the prevalence of male crisis as a topic in the mass media, it is no surprise to find a popular film like *Rebel Without a Cause* (1955) replaying almost all of these ideas as accepted truth. The film itself is a study in ambiguity and contradiction because it contains obvious allusions to so many of these notions jumbled together. The main character, Jim, is, and yet, isn't, a juvenile delinquent. He is and he isn't a homosexual. What he *is*, however, is an enormously sympathetic, attractive, and compelling movie hero who softened the picture of depraved youth by making this figure both attractive and sharply critical of stereotyped male roles. At the same time, there is a terrifying portrayal of Momism in the character of the father figure (played by Jim Backus), who wears an apron in most of the shots taken within the home and meekly follows the orders of his angry wife goaded by an even angrier mother-in-law. The movie itself is a critique of Momism, an invocation of the argument that weak fathers create wayward sons and provoke sexual disorientation. The one (almost) openly gay character, Plato, has neither mother nor father. Yet the film is also a celebration of adolescent anxiety and uncertainty and a blunt critique of mainstream society. It is, in a word, eclectic and contradictory in its premises, but rich in voicing alternative interpretations of ongoing ideas of a masculinity crisis prevalent in the 1950s.

The ambiguous position of homosexuals (and delinquents) in the male crisis literature and its popular culture portrayals underscores the importance of sexuality and sexual dysfunction to the whole picture of male crisis. Most commentators assumed there to be a seamless web linking the private and personal to the cultural, social, political, and psychological realms. The disruption of a single strand in this weave could weaken everything along the line and threaten the stability of the whole fabric. This argument was repeated over and over during the decade as various flaws in the masculinity superstructure came under scrutiny. Momism, bossism, conformity, the adolescent rebellion, and homosexuality were threatening because they supposedly endangered the family itself. Talcott Parsons, one of the leading American sociologists of the day, put the proposition as bluntly as his abstract language would allow. In a jointly authored text *Family, Socialization, and Interaction Process*, he wrote, "Homosexuality is a mode of structuring human relationships which is radically in conflict with the place of the nuclear family in the social structure and in the socialization of the child."[29] In other words, homosexuality threatened both individual and family.

This provocative discussion of gender played against the conspicuous background of sexual revolution. In many respects, for men at least, the sexual revolution had already begun by the 1950s. Patterns of sexual behavior in both men and women had, as sexologist Alfred Kinsey discovered, changed rapidly, particularly after World War I. But popular discourse rarely recognized this subterranean revolution until it became insistently visible with the publication of Kinsey's two surveys of male and female sexual behavior in 1948 and 1953. In some respects, it took Hugh Hefner and *Playboy* magazine to demonstrate the potential of these findings. Hefner's magazine, which celebrated and exemplified the "Playboy philosophy," captured a huge amount of attention in the late 1950s and early 1960s.[30] It advertised an alternative male sexual ethic offered up as traditional and virile, but existing outside and beyond marriage and middle-class norms.

Hefner's genius was to recognize that sex could be sold overtly and aboveboard as an item of modern consumption. This did not mean that he published hard-core pornography or encouraged prostitution—two traditional forms of commodified sex. Compared to contemporary cheesecake publications, the photos and cartoons in his journal were tame and demure. What he did do, however, was make sex another consumer object associated with other leisure pastimes and personal consumer products, almost a coffee table commodity. Denuding sexuality of moral and ethical constraint, he dressed it back up with new elements of a sophisticated masculine lifestyle: fine wines, clothing, vacations, good literature, and a connoisseur's appreciation of good art, food, music, and literature promoted by his editor Auguste Comte Spectorsky. In other words, he masculinized consumption by linking it to unmarried heterosexual sex. Issues like Momism were, thus, beside the point to the new bachelor masculinity that *Playboy* promoted even if the magazine often railed against them.[31]

There were some, however, who believed that the Playboy philosophy only exacerbated the masculinity crisis. Theologian Harvey Cox's short survey in *Christianity and Crisis* published in 1961 neatly summarized this analysis and argument. First of all, Cox identified the magazine as overtly middle-class, presuming to appeal to men in "college dormitories and suburban rumpus rooms." *Playboy*, he continued, spoke directly to the ongoing masculinity crisis, which itself had "at its roots a deep-set fear of sex." Certainly this accusation had been a subterranean element of much of the male crisis literature of the 1950s (particularly in its accusations of female sexual assertiveness), but Cox made the argument clearly and overtly. Invoking the always-powerful notion that mass culture manipulated and damaged—that it commodified and cheapened life—the theologian argued that Playboy sex wasn't sex at all, because it was so narcissistic and (by implication) adolescent. "It is precisely because these magazines are antisexual," he wrote, "that they deserve the most searching kind of theological criticism. They foster a heretical doctrine of man, one at radical variance with the Biblical view. For *Playboy*'s man, others, especially women—are *for* him." For Cox, Hefner's sexual revolution, even at its most extreme, was only a sad form of masturbation. The masculinity crisis was not resolved, he believed, by retreating from sexuality into solitary onanism. Indeed, it was only exacerbated.[32]

Beyond Momism and the perilous variation in masculine roles that appeared around the edges of the mainstream in the 1950, a different sort of exacerbating element of masculinity crisis was the much-discussed precarious physical health of American men. Ironically, however, in the guise of health advice, experts proposed a softer, not tougher, version of manliness. Amram Scheinfeld, an expert in heredity and sexuality, wrote in his 1957 contribution to the *Cosmopolitan* symposium on men that excessive masculinity was affecting health. "The practice of manliness has become a lethal curse," he said bluntly. Traditional manliness associated with hard work, vigorous play, competition, and self-promotion resulted in a short life in modern society. There was, he concluded, the need for a new masculinity that prized "mental and moral courage over physical daring and bravado." Such a repudiation of the strenuous life demanded a revolution of culture itself. Qualities like human warmth and kindness were not feminine, he argued, but "evidence of an advanced state of civilization."[33]

There was ample warning that too much hard work caused physical problems for men. Almost every observer of the subject stressed that a man's lifespan was considerably shorter than a woman's. In his article for *Today's Health*, Dr. Lemuel McGee, medical director for Hercules Powder Company, wrote that adherence to manly stereotypes inflicted an early death. The cult of manliness, he said bluntly, shortened life through stress and the failure to achieve a physical and emotional balance. A good share of happiness, noncompetitive exercise, and spontaneous play were crucial for men who otherwise would turn every endeavor into self-discipline and rivalry.[34]

Hannah Lees, writing in 1956 for the *Saturday Evening Post*, agreed with the observation about men's precarious lives, but differed in her diagnosis. In fact, she chose to respond directly to McGee. She repeated the familiar canard that "men are the weaker sex." Suffering from heart attacks, higher cancer rates, and ulcers, they continued to work hard in later life when women were able to relax. Did this mean that competition was to blame? Unfortunately, the answer she gave was yes and no. Yes, it was a cause of stress, emotional problems, and perhaps disease. And no because only women could help out. "Men, are always going to think it is sissy to ease up," she wrote, "unless we change their minds."[35] But even here, the solution was not clear-cut, for Lees advised manipulating men, and for women to take the lead in changing their minds as a way out of deadly competitiveness.

Even this brief view of the notion of masculinity crisis in the 1950s seen in some of the literature, popular culture, and commentary of the decade suggests the pervasiveness of the idea and the tenacity of the argument that women were at fault or at least deeply implicated in creating the problem. In effect, not much new had been added to Wylie's notions, although many of them were extended and elaborated. The revolution in gender relations that appeared to be occurring had struck first at men, tainting them with a sense of malaise and inadequacy. They were pulled in multiple directions by expert advice that told them to ease up and buckle down, to reassert their masculinity and reestablish individualistic values or take it easy and enjoy leisure and consumption. They were advised to be masculine role models for their sons. At the same time, they were told to be companions to their wives and children and strive for "togetherness" at home, in the community and at work. As Otis Wiese wrote in an article for *McCall's* in 1954, men, women, and children had embarked together on a new life of leisure, comfort, and mutual enjoyment "as a family sharing a common experience." For him, women's liberation from drudgery, her new world of leisure and consumption, presented an opportunity to share the new economic and psychological bounty with men.[36] It might be argued that beneath the surface of very loud complaints about men and masculinity, and laments about decline, the real issue was mass society itself and the widespread hesitations about what it meant to be a man in the consumer world where women had already staked a claim. The proclamation of crisis was just one response to the turmoil on the new suburban frontier.

This season of blaming women would be all but forgotten by the mid-1960s with the upheavals associated with the rise of feminism. But once again, in the 1980s and 1990s strong echoes describing a male crisis could be heard. Most important to remember, however difficult it is to believe the proposition, was that many Americans, evaluating the lives of the middle class in the 1950s, believed that women had already come too far and traveled along the wrong road at that, gaining unwarranted power in the home, over consumption, and threatening to revolutionize the workplace, and their men suffered gravely for it.

Yet anxiety about American manhood represents only one reaction to the immense changes occurring in postwar society. And not everyone responded by blaming women or organizations or transformations in the historic American character. In fact there were other strong voices that rejected the notion of crisis even as they grappled with the immense changes in the decade. They viewed the challenge of gender identity in a different light. It is time, now, to listen to some of their reflections.

5

"Sex Is Sex": Alfred Kinsey and the Report That Shook the World

In December 1995, Representative Steve Stockman of Texas introduced HR 2749, cosponsored by forty-one other members, calling for an investigation of Alfred Kinsey's research into human sexual behavior. Coming almost fifty years after the Indiana University entomologist published his famous *Sexual Behavior in the Human Male*, this would indeed seem to be a very distant aftershock. And his charge against Kinsey reflected an obsession of our own era: the molestation of children. Kinsey was accused of countenancing sex with minors as well as a variety of other perversions. This was a long-familiar charge with some new twists.[1]

Kinsey's reputation sank even further a couple of years later with the publication of biographical material revealing Kinsey's bisexuality and the unusual sexual practices of his previously silent family, his assistants, and their wives.[2] But when his original study burst into print in 1948—to become one of the densest, if not longest, best sellers in American history—Kinsey was known, if to a select group, only as the world's leading expert on the gall wasp. Here was a biologist who turned to the study of sexual behavior, as he recounted it, when he discovered the astonishing ignorance of his students about such matters while teaching a course on marriage. The resulting book fundamentally challenged everything that Americans believed (or admitted) they knew about sexuality. Spread through relentless charts and statistics, Kinsey recorded the incidence of intercourse and the different objects of sexual interest, as well as class variations. As he did so, he purposely undermined the premises of existing sexual identity, making the concept of normalcy, itself, an incomprehensible and confusing standard.

In 1948, knowledge of sexual practices in the United States existed in a number of guises, available to different audiences, making it uneven at best. What constituted scientific knowledge was based generally upon the researches and theories of Freud, Havelock Ellis, Richard Freiherr von Kraft-Ebbing, Robert L. Dickinson, Lewis Terman, Margaret Mead, and others. Some of this discussion had been, in a sense, rediscovered or reinvented from earlier publications, such as the insights of Havelock Ellis into autoeroticism and homosexuality. There were also important works that appeared around this time, such as Wilhelm Reich's *The Sexual Revolution*, published in the United States in 1945, as well as a few pioneering works on homosexuality.[3]

Despite the uneven quality of this work, in the 1940s the doors of research into sexuality had opened significantly, even if Kinsey in his publications sometimes acted as if he were the first pioneer to cross over the scientific threshold into a vacant space. There was even a burgeoning literature on marriage and sexual fulfillment within matrimony stressing the importance of female satisfaction that began to appear in popular magazines at the time. Since the early 1920s, the Committee for Research in Problems of Sex, under Robert Yerkes, and part of the National Research Council, had pushed into the field of sexual behavior studies. It was nevertheless correct that Kinsey's was the first truly massive study of sexual behavior in America, and it certainly achieved the broadest audience of any survey up through the 1950s.[4] It would also prove to have abiding implications for the contemporary discussion of masculinity and its relationship to sex.

When it first appeared, many scientists, doctors, and psychologists worldwide, including the American experts in this group of sex researchers, disagreed fundamentally among themselves even as to the legitimate subject matter and means to study, although, by the 1940s, the Freudian model was gaining importance, particularly in the United States. Based as this was on notions of sexual maturation and heterosexual intercourse, Freudianism in its American guise exercised a powerful sway in the psychological community and, perhaps more important, flourished in simplified translation as a model explanation of sexual conduct pumping through the heart of popular culture. Throughout the postwar era, one could find an abridged version of Freudianism outlined for popular consumption in Dr. Spock's enormously popular *Baby and Child Care* book, the films of Alfred Hitchcock, in novels, cartoons, and serious studies of juvenile delinquency and other antisocial behaviors. While Freud certainly had legitimated the discussion of sexuality, he and his followers (particularly in their American incarnation) recast this frankness into a narrative of normal and abnormal development. These were some of the assumptions that Kinsey encountered and challenged.[5]

A different line of scientific inquiry into sexual behavior had marked the Lewis M. Terman and Catherine Cox Miles 1936 study *Sex and Personality* and Carl C. Seltzer's *The Relationship between the Masculine Component and Personality*, published shortly after Kinsey. These were similar attitudinal/questionnaire studies that both assumed and sought to demonstrate continuities between masculine types apparent in physical appearance, mental stability, a healthy interest in sports and technology, and so on. Both of these studies presumed the relationship between culturally acceptable gender characteristics and sexual behavior. And they both pathologized homosexuality as an excess of the feminine, seeing it as a perversion against which the normal might be defined.[6]

Even though written earlier, the Terman and Miles study provided a relatively sophisticated description of this essentialist view of masculinity. In their important book, sponsored by the National Research Council (the same body that later funded Kinsey), Terman and Miles developed a questionnaire that measured masculine propensities by tabulating responses to a battery of preference and association tests. While many of their findings were subtly presented and contradicted stereotypic views of masculinity, others reinforced existing cultural prejudices: for example, that academically successful males scored low in masculine traits while college athletes were much higher. Quite clearly, the researchers were at the mercy of their redundant questions, which mistook contemporary cultural assumptions for objective standards. At the same time, their conclusions about the continuity of culturally defined masculinity and essential male identity gained legitimacy precisely because they confirmed popular wisdom.[7]

The landscape of more public knowledge about sexuality that Kinsey entered in 1948 was dappled with ignorance, mapped by unenforceable and obscure laws, and haunted by interlocking religious and moral prohibitions. In some respects this might appear to be counterintuitive. During the 1920s and early 1930s, public discourse on sexuality had opened up somewhat both in the United States and Europe. But by the end of the Depression years and during World War II a new reticence was initiated that extended into the early 1950s even as scientific exploration of sexuality became more acceptable. At this time, all three major American religions, to one extent or another, condemned extramarital sex. Discussion of masturbation was confused by punitive fictions. (Kinsey tried unsuccessfully to persuade the Boy Scouts to remove warnings against the health and moral risks of masturbation from some of their publications, for example.) During the 1930s, when Kinsey undertook his study of sexuality, one of the most widely read experts on masculinity was Bernarr Macfadden, whose publishing empire was then at its height. Macfadden's influence was in many respects contradictory. While he denounced prudery and celebrated the male physique, he nonetheless inveighed against the corrosive moral and health risks of masturbation and nonmarital sex.[8]

In part reflecting the power of enduring moral strictures, there existed a patchwork of local and state regulations outlawing pornography, sodomy (inconsistently defined), incest, rape, homosexuality, bestiality, prostitution, and adultery. Some of the punishments could be draconian, some mild, depending on the jurisdiction, with some penalizing one sex partner and not the other, but almost all of them were unenforceable and almost universally flouted. In addition to these religious and legal proscriptions, there were widely held misunderstandings about the nature of the sex act itself, reproduction, and the physiology of the orgasm.[9] At the same time, there were clearly movements toward greater liberalism. But without the benefit of historical hindsight, the times could have appeared either progressive or repressive to anyone, such as Kinsey, living through them.

Public discussion of sexuality, when it occurred, frequently consisted of euphemisms obscured by sly winks and innuendos or technical obscurity. Kinsey himself chose to characterize the moment as one of extreme repression and conservatism. Yet when conducting the thousands of interviews that constitute the raw material for his book, he often found it impossible not to be blunt, and he discovered that his subjects responded in kind. Moreover, a great many of the letters sent to Kinsey after the *Male* volume appeared contained frank and honest descriptions of sexual behavior and a rich vocabulary of terms to describe various sex acts. But the most important word (and concept) in the public and private discourse about sex was *normal*.[10] This suggested a single standard and the existence of an accepted and widely recognized model for behavior. Yet here Kinsey found anything but the stable pattern suggested by this term. Men, he discovered, engaged in sexual activity with themselves, male partners, animals, prostitutes, and mistresses, as well as with their wives. All of these objects he insisted upon calling "outlets," thereby discouraging any qualitative differentiation between them. With this unmistakable assault upon the vocabulary of normalcy Kinsey aimed to change the stories that Americans told themselves about sex and about being male in America. He hoped individuals would find a new way to talk about their own experiences. In doing so he suggested that masculinity as identity was only loosely connected to sexual practice. His purpose was to portray the yawning gap between ideology and behavior—to establish the fiction of the norm—and so liberate the sex act from guilt, moralistic condemnation, misunderstanding, and the harsh criminal codes that succeeded only in transforming almost every American into a potential sex offender.[11]

The appearance of *Sexual Behavior in the Human Male* in early 1948 represented one of the great publishing events in the history of American science. There is every reason to believe that Kinsey anticipated a powerful reaction, for he attempted to control and shape public response by careful surveillance of publicity and rigorous limitation of access to the Indiana University research institute by reporters. Nor was he modest about his accomplishment. The measure of his self-regard and ambition is suggested by his identification with Charles Darwin. His early and influential book on the gall wasp was titled (to recall Darwin's great book), *The Gall Wasp Genus Cynips: A Study in the Origin of Species* (1930).[12] If Kinsey flattered himself with the implicit comparison to fellow biologist Darwin, there is also no doubt that he believed his sex research would have a similar revolutionary effect on science as Darwin's research had for the story of species differentiation and evolution: the liberation from an old and unscientific story.

Kinsey also insisted upon an established publisher for his work, the W. B. Sanders Company, a respected medical publisher in Philadelphia. The venture flew all the flags of moderation and respectability. Kinsey's work was housed at Indiana University, located in a bedrock state of traditional values and attitudes. He secured financial support from the prestigious National Research Council and its Committee for Research in Problems of Sex funded by the Rockefeller Foundation.[13] And Kinsey brought his not unsubstantial scientific reputation as the world's leading expert on the gall wasp to the project. His taxonomy of these insect species (scores were named after him) was probably unmatched in sheer volume in modern biology.

Almost immediately, *Male Behavior* made the best-seller list, with 40,000 copies of the hardback volume sold just two weeks after the official publication date of January 6, and 200,000 in the first two months. The volume was exhaustively reviewed, and often favorably so, in much of the popular press and in scientific journals. Editions quickly appeared in French, Swedish, and Italian as well as a special separate publication for Great Britain.[14] This initial enthusiastic response rested, no doubt, upon some surprising and graphic assertions, most of them quite literally presented in graph form. Most remarked upon were Kinsey's discovery of the surprisingly large incidence of homosexual behavior, rampant masturbation, and widespread extramarital sex. It was next to impossible to miss his tone of celebration in the presentation of these figures. Almost every section, once it established the incidence of practice and its variations, divided behavior by social class, religion, and education. Throughout, the volume resounded with an obvious conclusion: the behavior of American men contradicted legal codes and moral precepts. It followed by implication that attempts to control behavior were misguided, punitive, and obviously ineffective.

Much of the early attention to the report quite appropriately focused on selected and controversial findings, or perhaps more accurately, on the way Kinsey defined sex itself. Kinsey chose the orgasm as the measure of all sexual behavior. Behavior, in turn, became the definition of sexuality. Using these criteria, Kinsey calculated that 37 percent of his male subjects had experienced orgasm at one time with another man. For married men, the percentage of orgasms achieved with their wives represented only 85 percent of their total outlets. The remaining 15 percent were with other women, men, through masturbation, or in nocturnal emissions. Certain class differences were also readily apparent in his figures. Lower mean (income) level males practiced masturbation less, had heterosexual orgasm earlier, went to prostitutes more frequently, but had fewer extramarital experiences. Among the populations Kinsey studied, the least and the most educated groups had considerable toleration of homosexuality, whereas people in the middle exhibited less. Among boys and men living on farms, he found a measurable incidence of using animals as sex outlets. At the same time, he discovered that a high degree of religious devotion, especially among Catholics, affected sexual behavior. Nevertheless, he estimated that over the course of a lifetime, the average man experienced about half of his orgasms in socially disapproved or illegal circumstances.[15]

All or parts of this (incomplete) catalog of findings shocked and intrigued reviewers and commentators, and certain patterns, such as the incidence of homosexual behavior and extramarital sex, became the bases for sensational headlines. And few missed Kinsey's purpose or the tone of his work. In effect, he argued, taxonomy was destiny: men were how they acted and how they acted depended upon time, class, situation, opportunity, education level, religious belief, and inclination. Variety, not majority behavior, was the best way to represent human sexual conduct. The "normal" was neither the average nor the median, nor even the ideal, but should be redefined as the entire range of experience itself. As he explained it, "modern taxonomy is the product of an increasing awareness among biologists of the uniqueness of individuals and of the wide range of variation which may occur in any population of individuals."[16]

Following this standard, Kinsey arranged his material to demonstrate and emphasize diversity, extremes, and variation rather than to depict means and averages, which he might just as well have done. In fact, he eliminated the equation between what most people did and any social or religious norms of behavior. Dismissing previous attempts to understand sexual activity, he wrote that his study would "provide the bases for sounder generalizations about sexual behavior of certain groups and someday, even of our American population as a whole."[17] The implications of such generalizations, he wrote, would have a huge impact on defining new social policy. "The publicly pretended code of morals," he wrote, "our social organization, our marriage customs, our sex laws, our educational and religious systems are based upon an assumption that all individuals are much alike sexually and that it is an equally simple matter for all of them to confine their behavior to a single pattern which the mores dictate."[18] The sexologist could barely conceal his contempt for such beliefs, nor his delight in uncovering galaxies of exceptions in this expansive universe of sexual outlets.

These revolutionary assertions were depicted in the decisions Kinsey made about organizing and presenting his findings. In the first place, he made a fundamental choice to publish his findings on men and women separately. This was a profound and purposeful move, for it implicitly banished the assumption that sexuality was necessarily heterosexual or even relational. This maneuver would have profound implications for his definition of masculinity. By specifying women as only one possible outlet among many, Kinsey challenged the notion that healthy sexual behavior meant intercourse in marriage, or heterosexual intercourse, or even intercourse at all. In fact, he redefined marriage as the institutional setting for just one form of sexual behavior. (In his later book, *Sexual Behavior in the Human Female* [1953], Kinsey shocked many commentators with his assertion that women did not require a male partner to achieve orgasm.) Kinsey's depiction of sexual behavior resembled an elaborate taxonomy of species. He grouped sums of orgasms—the common denominator of sexual behavior—into clusters of outlets in 162 tables and 173 graphs. His famous H-scale chart of hetero-homosexual behavior is the best illustration of how he thought about this as a visual presentation, as a sort of statistical hieroglyph. Kinsey identified seven categories on a scale that ranged from "exclusively heterosexual" to "exclusively homosexual" with five mixed categories in between. The obvious implication, particularly because this scale was presented with seven equal divisions, was that essentialist notions of heterosexuality and homosexuality were actually just the limits in a continuous series of related categories. Perhaps it is no accident that he assigned a null (or zero) to represent the possibility of exclusive heterosexuality. Most significantly, however, with this depiction Kinsey normalized homosexual behavior by placing it on the same graph as heterosexuality rather than assigning it a unique category. And if such visual symbolizations can be seen as revealing his underlying argument, the H-scale chart, by representing each tendency as equal in size and shape, suggests that they are equal numerically, which they are not, and that, in turn, most men were neither entirely homosexual or heterosexual, but somewhere in between, which was also not born out by his statistics.

Perhaps more disturbing to readers was his side-by-side depiction of sources of orgasms by age group. Here, on the same graph, he placed masturbation, nocturnal emissions, petting to climax, intercourse (this last divided into premarital, marital, extramarital), prostitutes, homosexual outlet, and animal contact. In presenting this broad scope of behavior, there were no judgments to be made, except the implicit one that all behavior was more or less equivalent. And if anyone missed the moral of the story, Kinsey later declared explicitly that any attempt to thwart specific varieties of sexual behavior was doomed to failure and could be psychologically destructive.[19] There were many other controversial conclusions, such as his contention that children sometimes enjoyed sexual acts. With this assertion, he challenged Freud by suggesting that childhood sexual encounters were sometimes real, not just the symbolic psychic dramas of Oedipus and Electra.

These were the conclusions that preoccupied the majority of reviewers and commentators who debated the meaning of Kinsey's findings. Although this conversation did not reach the strident pitch surrounding the volume on the human female published five years later, it was a disconcerting as well as titillating source of ideas for public discussion. Like so many other new ideas, Kinsey's findings were lampooned in *New Yorker* cartoons and provided a never-exhausted source of allusions for stand-up comedians, songs, and topics for sermons. As comedian Danny Kaye noted, the Kinsey Report joined flying saucers, the atom bomb, and Rita Hayworth as the target of humor in 1950.[20] Rather quickly, Kinsey's name itself became synonymous with sex. For a public made uneasy by prudery, yet transfixed by sexual innuendo, it was probably Kinsey's legitimizing of sex discussion, rather than his specific findings, that preoccupied much of the public discourse around his work. No doubt this notoriety inspired the aging Mae West to telegraph the scientist, inviting him up to her hotel room, in an effort to trade off his reputation. And no wonder that *Time* magazine put Kinsey on its cover. Not without reason did the mere mention of his last name inspire nervous laughter.[21]

Much of the public reception to the Kinsey Report focused on sensational aspects of his findings, making his a household name. Nonetheless, there were many who took his work very seriously. Kinsey was invited to address a number of scientific groups and he appeared on numerous college campuses. Perhaps the high point of public attention came in February 1949, when the scientist addressed nine thousand students at Berkeley.[22] But Kinsey's most critical (in both senses of the word) audience included psychologists, statisticians, and public intellectuals who wrestled with his revolutionary definitions of sexuality and male identity.

Almost immediately, some of these critics raised questions about the method and accuracy of his findings. The first focus was his selection of subjects to be interviewed. Kinsey explicitly rejected the technique of random sampling, citing a number of objections, such as the certain high number of refusals one could expect given such a delicate subject. In other words, he denied the possibility of randomness in exploring intimate matters. Instead, he targeted whole small populations and attempted to interview every member of a specific group (a fraternity, for example, or a prison population). As Jack Kerouac wrote in *On the Road*, "Kinsey spent a lot of time in Ritzy's Bar interviewing some of the boys." About one quarter of his results were based on such samples. In addition, he sought out special populations: prisoners, homosexuals, and so on. In some instances, he declined to report specifically on the behavior of groups such as African Americans, claiming he had insufficient numbers for generalization. Critics also noted that his subjects were more likely to be middle class than representative of the general population.[23]

A second large methodological dispute surfaced around the reliability of the interview itself. Kinsey developed his technique for soliciting answers based upon the assumption that everyone had a sexual story to tell and could remember it accurately. Thus, he assumed as much as he asked and strongly conveyed this expectation to his subject. Defending this technique, his assistant Wardell Pomeroy explained that this interview environment was the key to inspiring confidence. In his book discussing the taking of sex histories, Pomeroy wrote, "The definitive statement concerning normality is that there isn't anything that can be called 'normal' or 'abnormal'; it is a meaningless concept. This idea needs to be understood by the interviewer and conveyed to the respondent."[24] Kinsey sought to project interest and sympathy rather than judgment or even neutrality.

To disguise the process of recording and avoid the distraction of scratching pens and rustling papers, he developed a numerical coding system understandable only to himself and his close assistants (no looking over the shoulder at answers). Those few of his colleagues whom he allowed to conduct interviews were trained rigorously in his techniques.

Not surprisingly, a number of statisticians and psychologists questioned both elements of this method. Lewis Terman, much cited and frequently criticized in the volume, rejected Kinsey's findings on several grounds. The subjects were not randomly chosen nor were they typical, he noted. Nor could memories be trusted, he wrote. Terman liberally sprinkled his assessment with the words "ruthless" and "reckless" to describe Kinsey. Kinsey was "ruthless" in his use of language in his book and his frankness threatened to destroy public inhibitions that blocked dangerous and immoral behavior. There were "recklessly" worded evaluations suggesting a defense of "uninhibited sexual activity." In fact, however, Terman saw quite clearly that science was not really the issue. Kinsey's charts and graphs could be read—as he recognized they were intended to be—as illustrations in a moral tract that insisted that "sex drives as forces of nature will (and should) find their outlet regardless of measures taken to curb them." In other words, by emphasizing behavior and presenting a numerical definition of sexuality according to frequency, Kinsey underplayed the topics that had most preoccupied sex literature and research up to that point: venereal disease, pregnancy, and divorce, that is to say, the consequences of behavior. But neither Terman nor most other critical observers noticed that Kinsey's own charts, if construed over an average lifetime, actually demonstrated a sexual development over time wherein most men eventually achieved "mature" heterosexual behavior in later life. In other words, he demonstrated that sexual experimentation was largely associated with youth before sexual and gender identities had hardened.[25]

Another negative evaluation of the Kinsey group methods came in the *Journal of the American Statistical Association* in 1949. In his astute critique, W. Allen Wallis of the University of Chicago suggested that the study was not really about behavior at all, but rather, articulated Kinsey's preoccupation with morality. The author, he concluded, "is at heart a social reformer." Wallis criticized the size and composition of the sample (he preferred random sampling), and, in general, deplored the lack of accepted statistical procedures. He also disparaged many of the tables and graphs as meaningless. All of these propositions he followed with eleven pages of small-print notes listing, in detail, the statistical errors and methodological problems he believed damaged the reliability of the study.[26]

Statistical accuracy aside—and, in fact, such problems did not ultimately undermine the impact of the report—much of the criticism focused on the absent concepts of traditional morality, normality, and gender identity. *Reader's Digest* editor Fulton Oursler solicited mostly negative commentary from a number of public figures and published a compilation of their squibs. "Famous author" Norman Angell contended that Victorian values had proven effective; repression had made people happy. The Protestant pastor Norman Vincent Peale defended the social utility of maintaining a concept of abnormality as a means of policing behavior. FBI director J. Edgar Hoover worried that without a concept of normal and abnormal, "those who would destroy our civilization" would applaud a decline in "our way of life." Even Jackie Robinson pinch-hit for normalized sex as a form of "moral restraint" that acted as a powerful sublimation of energy that could be tapped for success in athletics and other productive enterprises.[27]

Beyond such expected retorts, there were two other groups that deeply deplored Kinsey's results: religious and secular moralists, and psychologists. These ranged from figures such as the young evangelist Billy Graham to the eminent liberal theologian Reinhold Niebuhr, both of whom denounced the book. Graham pointedly criticized Kinsey several times, linking him to rampant immorality, the cold war, and the decline of the family, hinting that such ideas weakened America in the face of Communism. Indeed, it was rare for any religious leader or spokesman to find much good in Kinsey's work, except those few who bruited his discovery that religious people were likely to be somewhat more inhibited in their choice of outlets. More typical however was the extreme hostility of the Catholic Church. Monsignor Maurice S. Sheehy of Catholic University in Washington, D.C., was blunt about his misgivings: Kinsey's book was "the most anti-religious book of our times," he wrote. The National Council of Catholic Women linked him to "morally degrading motion pictures" and birth control.[28]

Anthropologist Margaret Mead, widely known as an advocate of liberalized attitudes and theories of the cultural variability of sexual roles, someone who published her own important work on gender in 1949, worried that circulating Kinsey's findings might increase those sexual activities of American men "which are without any meaning." Geoffrey Gorer, friend of Mead and a well-known writer on American character, deplored the whole phenomenon—the huge success of "a dull and turgid book" that transformed sex into a consumer item. And columnist Dorothy Thompson rehearsed a popular version of Freudianism in her critique. Kinsey, she wrote, was justifying sexual licentiousness that is "a regression to infantilism where the erotic life is neither *centered* nor sublimated."[29]

Such moral objections were forcefully combined with criticisms of Kinsey's methodology in a stinging attack by the liberal critic and New York intellectual Lionel Trilling. To Trilling, the grievous fault committed by Kinsey ultimately reinforced the generic error of science itself with its obsessive and normative counting of things. He had no argument with Kinsey's measurements or even with his conclusions, which came as no shock to him. So, if there were no surprises in the book, what was the problem? Trilling accurately read Kinsey's intent to substitute behavior for morality, and to disrupt accepted definitions of gender, and he rejected this move completely. *Is* must never mean *ought*, he reminded his readers in a pithy formulation. The substitution of measures of frequency for judgment of values was specious and dangerous. This had always been the fatal flaw, he wrote, of all naturalistic philosophy stretching back to the Roman philosopher Lucretius. Kinsey had merely fallen into the rusty old trap of supposing that anything natural was also normal and good.[30]

The second pillar of Trilling's critique amounted to a passionate defense of Freudian psychology as a system of thought that mediated between science and philosophy. Trilling made this argument for several reasons. He recognized the dismissal of Freudian analysis in Kinsey's denial of the concept of normal. In defense of Freud, he praised the psychoanalyst's vision of a poetic definition of human psychology in place of a mechanistic one. To him, Freudian psychology was "exactly the stuff upon which the poet has always exercised his art." Where Kinsey found that children actually engaged in sex acts, Trilling, following Freud, insisted upon seeing a psychological struggle with desire that led to mental maturity. Such a difference in vision defined the difference between humanism and a barren and reductive modern science.[31]

Finally, Trilling confronted the centrality of homosexual behavior in the report. The critic pronounced himself dubious that psychiatrists would ever redefine such behavior as normal. In other words it would always exist as the defining opposition to male identity. For society to accept any profound revision, he concluded, it would have to change dramatically from the contemporary world, and he did not anticipate such a development.[32]

Trilling's spirited defense of normality is characteristic of the most profound critiques pronounced against Kinsey's works. There is no doubt that the sexologist was deeply disappointed, even though he must have anticipated that his assaults on accepted morality would arouse hostility. But there exists another audience that read his book differently, and it is probable that this group is the one with which he ultimately identified. These included the thousands of readers of the book who wrote to the Kinsey Institute in Indiana and the many more who shared the problems of these letter writers, if not their penchant for communication. Kinsey's attention to these letters was instructive and remarkable. He read and answered all of them until his health failed in the mid-1950s. This correspondence revealed to Kinsey how this audience read his work, but more important, it allowed him, in his responses, to issue instructions about how to intepret and implement his findings about the meaning of male behavior he had discovered.

Even a cursory examination of these letters reveals that Kinsey's book attracted thousands of Americans who were troubled about their own, their partner's, or their children's sexuality. A great many of them focused on two related social standards: normality and respectability. Many writers also, at one point or another, asked if their problem was typical of others that Kinsey encountered. Were they alone, they wanted to know? Were they normal?

Generally, the query related to some form of socially disapproved behavior. For example, a correspondent from Ohio announced in 1948 that she had just finished reading the *Male* volume. After several paragraphs reassuring the doctor that she was herself a mild nonconformist and a very educated person as well, she praised his work, saying that it validated her own experience. Then she finished with two fascinating, and common, ideas. "My husband," she wrote, "is extremely grateful at having "his own experiences and observations confirmed, and at being able to show 'proof' to women in general and his wife in particular." Although proof of what behavior is left unmentioned, the woman continued that she would be happy to supply Kinsey with her own sexual history.[33]

Another genre of letters asked Kinsey's advice about nonstandard sexual practices. One correspondent, for example, worried about a clash between her self-esteem, her husband's high standing in his profession, and the surprising sexual demands he made upon her. "To put it plainly [as plainly as she could allow herself], he likes to enjoy what he calls 'French' kisses, and to kiss feminine regions in this manner, and he also likes to have intercourse 'through the mouth.' . . . What I want to know is, is this customary among men, and *IS IT RIGHT*?" (her emphasis). Kinsey's usual response to such letters was to refer the reader to one of the many charts in his book so that he or she could locate him or herself in the continuity of experience. Or he simply restated the implicit message of the charts: that almost anything was a perfectly acceptable practice because it could be found in the wide repertoire of behavior he had discovered.

To queries about homosexuality—and there were many—Kinsey was sympathetic and reassuring. In an anguished letter in 1951, for example, a woman recounted that her son had returned home from air force duty to announce that he was a homosexual. "He believes he was born this way and that there is positively no chance that he can change." Because of the disgrace he might bring to the family, he declared his intention never to write, or call, or visit again: "We are to consider him dead." Kinsey replied that in his estimation society was suffering the problem, not her son: "It is very important that one learn to accept himself and to adjust his life in accordance." After recommending a "sympathetic" psychiatrist in the area, he warned that it would be a mistake to consult anyone who might "try to get him to accept a heterosexual pattern if he is primarily homosexual."

Of course some of the correspondents were desperate. An adolescent who called himself one of the "children of loneliness" sent a handwritten note from the isolation of a North Carolina tobacco farm. He confessed that he was attracted to other males, and had so far, but with increasing difficulty, resisted. But now he had reached the breaking point, and he had made himself sick with worry. Wanting to give in to these impulses and, at the same time, hoping to be cured, he assured Kinsey that his whole family "are respectable and have a good character." But, he lamented, "I am a young, helpless, *lost boy*."

Kinsey's response to this poignant plea was helpful and nonjudgmental. Not knowing the boy's whole sexual history, he confessed he could not give precise advice or make a diagnosis, although he did suggest a visit to the Duke University psychiatric clinic. But in this case (as elsewhere), Kinsey went much further. He suggested, first, that the boy might just be afraid of girls or unfamiliar with them. This was one of his interpretations of the origins of homosexuality. Whatever the causes, he warned, "One of the worst things that can happen to a person is to have them feel that they are abnormal and different from other persons. You must not feel that for that is probably not true." And then, remarkably, he added that should the boy be unable to find a psychiatrist, "write me again and we will see if there is any possibility of our getting together sometime when I may be traveling in your part of the country." On occasion, this proposition actually resulted in a visit where Kinsey took the sexual history of the correspondent. Such activity implied a therapeutic intervention for which Kinsey had no training but which was certainly implicit in the entire book and potentially present in his interviews.

Some writers conflated respectability with normality and the public with the private. In several instances, correspondents worried that private actions would somehow betray their public standing. As one man wrote in 1953, "In the past few days I have had the urge to use my mouth and lips instead of my penis for a few moments before starting the actual intercourse. It increases my urge for sexual relations and it also increases my wife's urge. Dr. Kinsey, I am studying mortuary science and someday I expect to be a prominent person in the community, so this is doubly important to me. Is this an abnormal complex?"

Kinsey assured him that oral sex was widely practiced.

Others wrote seeking advice about sex change operations—in part because of wide publicity given to the visit of Christine Jorgensen to the institute in 1953. Kinsey was considerate and neutral on the subject, usually alerting writers to the substantial physical, psychological, and social problems inherent in such a drastic change, but not making any moral judgments. Others confided their worries about transvestitism, like one wife who was deeply puzzled about the behavior of her husband: "He will be 60 years old in September and for the past five years has been donning female undergarments such as bras and step-ins, hose and girdle." Kinsey found nothing to condemn in this sort of behavior either.

One of Kinsey's most interesting correspondents was Dr. Fredric Wertham, a New York psychiatrist and advocate of freer sexual expression soon to be known for his controversial book linking juvenile delinquency to crime and horror comic books (*Seduction of the Innocent*, 1954). Wertham was director of the Quaker Emergency Service Readjustment Center in New York City. This was a psychiatric clinic that provided examination and treatment for sex offenders under the jurisdiction of the Magistrate's Court of New York City. Generally, this concerned referrals of cases involving homosexual behavior. Kinsey and Wertham had met in 1948, and Wertham wrote a note of appreciation for the *Male* volume. But he urged Kinsey to become more of an activist. "I have the feeling that the small minority of psychiatrists which is deeply dissatisfied with the current injustices of official psychiatry toward indigent mental patients and sex offenders has fundamentally an ally in you." Indeed, Kinsey was an ally, but his general method of intervention was to use the evidence of behavior to overwhelm social prejudice and dissolve legal restraint, to argue the precedence of scientific measurement of behavior over custom.[34]

Kinsey also corresponded with playwright Tennessee Williams. Williams wrote in 1950 to congratulate the biologist on his work; it was "of enormous social value," he said, "to the ignorant and/or biased public."

Kinsey had become interested in Williams because he hoped to study the "erotic element in the arts." His Bloomington colleagues and he had interviewed most of the cast of two companies that had played in *A Streetcar Named Desire*. The hope was to correlate "their acting with their sexual backgrounds."[35]

On occasion, however, Kinsey used his letters to advocate openly for liberalization of scientific attitudes toward sexual behavior. When responding to a methodological inquiry from Dr. A. R. Mangus about a questionnaire study being done by Mangus, he responded sharply, "Until you understand that sex offenders are not a group apart, except in the fact that they have been apprehended by the police, usually for extraneous reasons, you cannot make any adequate interpretations from the sort of record you get out of police court files."[36]

Sometimes, Kinsey received letters based solely on his notoriety rather than on any understanding of his book. Some writers clearly had only heard of him—for example, the student who inquired after a "Columbia University bull session" to ask whether women of different religions or races responded to sex differently. Kinsey's reply was: read my book. Scores of other letters concerned masturbation, its effects and "cures." One of the relatively few personal letters that excoriated Kinsey placed masturbation as the first entry on a list of worsening sex crimes that included fornication, adultery, and finally homosexuality, for which the perpetrator would be "doomed to suffer a complete destruction of his nervous system and to suffer the tortures of hell for eternity."

Some letters simply sought reassurance. A woman from Philadelphia wrote in 1948 to ask if it was wrong to be sexually satisfied in marriage. "Am I too much in love?" she asked. "Is it bad to love as hard and as true as we do? Is it bad to love so passionately that each sexual act is as thrilling and as precious as the first?" Again, the sexologist was reassuring, but oddly so, as if he agreed with her bewilderment, interpreting her satisfaction as curious. "We do run against such cases," he noted, "and that part of the story will be told in a later [projected] volume on marriage." Other letters poured in, some asking for information about oral and anal sex, some about divorce laws, some worrying about penis size. On occasion, a writer asked for directions to the nearest gay section of his city. But each of these, however odd or inappropriate they might have seemed, Kinsey respectfully and carefully answered.

Although it is clear why many writers sought Kinsey's advice, what he made of these letters and why he answered them so diligently, not to say obsessively, may not be so obvious. One thing is certain. Some correspondents consulted him as they might an advice column writer on intimate affairs. In a decade devoted to survey analyses, questionnaires, and ask-the-expert columns about manners, religious belief, dating, and so on, all designed to interpret norms for a rapidly changing culture, this private consultation constituted a fascinating variation on the popular public form. Many of his correspondents were deeply troubled—or thought they were—while others wanted confirmation of their life choices, or information that would assure them of their normality and respectability. Indeed, much of the correspondence revolves around defining these latter two ideas and their interaction, identifying who and what was "normal," with Kinsey refusing to employ the term.

This is another way of saying that the correspondence included strong overtones of the therapeutic. But the benefits of this treatment ran in both directions. Kinsey viewed his work itself as beneficial for readers and believed—as he said many times—that reading his book and locating oneself somewhere along the neutral axis of behaviors could be reassuring and even healing. So he often cited page numbers or referred to specific tables or paraphrased conclusions he incorporated in the book. So much is obvious. But what about Kinsey himself? What did he achieve from such exchanges? The answer is suggested by his frequent request to letter writers for interviews to take their histories, as if one more revelation would confirm the variety of behaviors that Kinsey himself secretly enacted.

Kinsey's remarkable ability to ferret out sexual stories from interviewees forms the very basis of whatever validity his taxonomy of sex possesses. But there was much more involved here than hunting and gathering information. The interview encompassed two fundamental phases. First, Kinsey asserted a quick mastery over his subject generally by indicating his sympathy, professionalism, and interest. But the effect was no doubt also one of a rapid psychic invasion, given the nature of the matter and the expectations of the subject. Almost inevitably, in the next stage, he provoked the subject to reveal some element of a secret, nonconforming sexual history. In fact, as his close assistant Wardell Pomeroy recounts it, the team assumed that every person had a story to tell, "that everybody had done everything and it was only a question of remembering the details."[37] In some respects, these revelations resembled the thousands of confessional letters he received. Most important, both phases of the interview were designed to demonstrate the validity of Kinsey's belief in the universal variety of sexual behavior and the inadequacy of prevailing definitions of masculine behavior.

The energy and psychic settings of these confessions appear, in some measure at least, to have a powerful analogue in religious conversion. Pomeroy recounts a visit to Howard University in terms that could almost describe a contemporary Billy Graham crusade. "At Howard," he wrote, "the format went as usual—the lecture followed by history taking." In other words, the sermon was followed by a session in the inquiry room. But the salvation that occurred here was as much Kinsey's as anyone else's, for the stories, over and over, reaffirmed the ordinariness of his own, secret sexual life. In this respect, the therapeutic was very personal and the variety of male sexual experience he discovered and celebrated also affirmed the validity of his own sexual experimentation.

There is considerable evidence that Kinsey himself recognized the therapeutic possibilities of the interview. Although he never would have made the comparison, there is something about the meeting akin to a compressed psychoanalytic session. These are the precise terms that Pomeroy used to describe the history taking: "Time after time people would say, 'This has been one of the most therapeutic experiences I've ever had,' or 'We should be *paying* you.'" When Kinsey recounted taking his own history, he explained "that he had given it to himself just as Freud had analyzed himself"—a telling remark from someone who rejected most of Freud's conclusions about sexuality.[38]

In arranging and conducting interviews, Kinsey very jealously controlled the entire procedure, allowing only a few of his close assistants to conduct them alone, and then only after intensive training. In fact, Kinsey himself conducted a great many of the huge number of interviews upon which both volumes of his sex behavior studies are based: around 12,000 interviews were taken, with Kinsey himself responsible for over 7,000. Pomeroy remembers the "driving, driving, driving" under the lash of Kinsey's relentless purpose.[39]

If Kinsey was driven to catalogue case after case, what interior voice whispered to him to become such a collector? Apparently no one outside a small circle knew about his secret life, but on occasion hints about the propriety of interviews surfaced in public. A bit of doggerel, written in 1952, expressed this idea:

I'm a Kinsey reporter
A job that I adore.
I can ask girlies questions,
That I never dared before.[40]

Kinsey himself kept clippings of at least two published instances where young men had telephoned women claiming they belonged to the institute and asked them intimate questions about their love lives.[41] But these lurid suggestions came with the territory of any serious study of sexuality.

Kinsey's own actions and rationale are another matter. Hence we return to the beginning of this chapter, where the issue of Kinsey's own sexual practice was raised well after his death. Had Kinsey's sexual tastes and practices at the institute been known at any time during his lifetime, his work would no doubt have been immediately compromised and discredited. As it was, however, Kinsey led his researchers and their wives to create a kind of secret sexual utopia, based in part around Kinsey's homosexual, voyeuristic, and masochistic tendencies. With "scientific knowledge" the creed by which the group justified transgressing accepted morals, Kinsey's assistants formed a tight-knit and protective community around him that not only studied sexuality, but enacted many of the behaviors it discovered. While this was not known at the time, hints began to surface in later accounts by participants in biographical material published after his death. Pomeroy, one of his most loyal supporters and fellow researchers, for example, in 1982, revealed information about Kinsey's trips to centers of homosexual activity in nearby Chicago, and later to such notorious cruising spots as the Coliseum in Rome, where he interviewed young male prostitutes. In fact, while Pomeroy's biography defends Kinsey, it is clear, reading this book, that homosexuality had to be one key to assessing Kinsey's interests and influence.[42]

The James H. Jones biography of Kinsey, published in 1997 and based upon the records of the institute and interviews with staff, finally exposed in detail the extraordinary sexual exploits of Kinsey and his researchers. Sometimes unable to disguise his distaste for this experimentation, Jones recounts that Kinsey himself had sex with his male researchers, that he observed and filmed sex acts, that he encouraged his assistants to have sex with his wife and that, on occasion, he engaged in self-inflicted pain and genital mutilation. Using just the sort of psychological theories that Kinsey deplored, Jones finds an explanation for this behavior in Kinsey's tortured reaction to a traditional, rigid, and abusive upbringing. Raised in a strict Methodist household by a cold and punitive father, Kinsey found a variety of minor outlets for his energy and rebellion—music, gardening, the Boy Scouts—until he specifically contradicted the desires of his father by taking up the academic study of biology. Despite the real sympathy the author sometimes musters for Kinsey, Jones concludes that in some respects the *Male* volume, in particular, can be read as an elaborate justification for the scientist's own repressed—and secretly expressed—homosexuality.[43] If this troubled history made Kinsey a life-long advocate for sexual freedom and crusader for an end to cruel customs and repression of sexuality, the author also concludes that it probably also skewed his survey results and corrupted his figures. It may also have contributed to his decision to depict sexual behavior as a continuum rather than marked by stages or categories normal and aberrant.

In his subsequent, revisionist biography, Jonathan Gathorne-Hardy revisited Kinsey's life and reassessed some of Jones's conclusions. The narrative does not deny the sexual activities of the institute group, but construes them somewhat differently. The author argues that while Kinsey may well have ended up predominantly a homosexual, this was a gradual process and did not corrupt his research or invalidate his findings. Moreover, Gathorne-Hardy emphasizes the importance and innovations of the *Female* volume and its contributions to a profound revision in the assumptions about female sexual behavior and the physiology of the female orgasm.[44]

Neither of these contending biographies, with their concern for the accuracy of the Kinsey studies, situates the story in one of the wider frameworks where it belongs—inside American cultural history. One way to do this is to find historical parallels. The research institute resembled nothing so much as a sexual utopia and we will understand Kinsey better if we locate his work within this context. While there were a good many distinctions, in certain important respects, the institute most closely resembled the nineteenth-century sexual utopia at Oneida, New York. Organized around a strong and inspiring leader, John Humphrey Noyes, Oneida perfectionism was an experiment in a form of authoritarian-liberalism and sexual experimentation that is familiar to every student of America's real and literary utopias. Noyes, himself, encouraged loyalty and exercised all-embracing control over the sex lives of his adherents. In some respects Noyes's "complex marriage" scheme had an analogue in Kinsey's sexual practices within his community of assistants. Noyes's purpose in part was eugenics and its rationalization was the application of a scientific outlook called "stirpi-culture" to marriage and procreation. Kinsey and his staff, in their secret City on a Hill, had internalized an ethic of scientific research that they enacted in their own lives. Their purpose, like Noyes's, was reform of the outside society. In exaggerated form, they performed the secret behavior they believed to be universal and which they sought to justify by its prevalence in American society.[45]

There are further elements that suggest that Kinsey's Institute was a community that can be understood within the rich tradition of American community experiments and utopian longings. Kinsey gathered a group of married men around him for his assistants. He insisted that they purchase houses near his own. In many respects, he intervened and controlled their social, cultural, and sexual relationships. And the research community was, in fact, nestled within the concentric boundaries of two other clearly defined and special worlds: the university itself and the small community of Bloomington. Nor was Kinsey alone at Indiana in thinking about Utopia at this time. Indeed, something seemed to be in the air. One of his university colleagues and a fellow behaviorist was B. F. Skinner, who published his remarkable novel *Walden Two* also in 1948, making this year one of the high points in the history of behavioral science.[46] Although Kinsey and Skinner were acquaintances, it is difficult to pin down precise interactions. But Skinner does reveal some interesting attitudes of his own toward sexuality that mirror Kinsey's belief that early sexual intercourse is healthy. The point of the comparison is not the measure of influence, however, but the almost general rule that utopian thinkers consistently dream and scheme about altering marriage and sexual practices.

In *Walden Two*, Frazier, the docent who explains the community to the reader, describes sex this way. "Sex is no problem in itself." Boys and girls can marry as soon as they wish—at the age of fifteen or sixteen—and thereby avoid the social games, repressions, and distortions of an outside society that insists that they postpone sexual activity. By the age of twenty-three or so, with a woman's childbearing days past, she was ready to assume her role in society. Like Kinsey, Skinner was an opponent of social and moral regulation that he believed to be irrelevant, harmful, and crusted with historical debris.[47]

If Kinsey belongs in some respects to a long line of American sex reformers and communitarian experimenters, how do we assess his remarkable and contradictory presence in the 1950s? How did his work intervene in the burgeoning discussion of masculinity? There is no doubt, of course, that like Freud, Kinsey had a huge impact on the public acceptance of sex discussion and study. In some respects, for example, the modern gay liberation movement can be traced back to his efforts, and he was certainly supportive of some of its early manifestations.[48]

Kinsey's influence on such figures as Hugh Hefner, whose Bunny Empire responded directly to some of his findings, is also obvious and demonstrable. Kinsey wrote that young middle-class white men, unlike working-class youth, were more likely to fantasize about sex than enact it, practicing masturbation as their primary sexual outlet. Hefner realized that Kinsey had discovered a niche market of college boys and young adults for soft-core pornography and he established *Playboy* in part to fill it. No doubt, too, Kinsey's works contributed to a more libertarian American attitude to sexuality, although, in the short run, he was singularly ineffective in sweeping away Victorian cobwebs. In fact, his clipping file is filled with notices of efforts to stiffen penalties for sex offenses in this period. A more personal consequence of this failure was the loss of Rockefeller Foundation funding in 1954 following the publication of the *Female* volume.[49] Certainly the crackdown on homosexuals in federal employment in the early 1950s must have been deeply disheartening. In fact, Kinsey may inadvertently have contributed to this dragnet by suggesting that broad, secret homosexual behavior existed throughout society. As if to confirm this thinking, a half-serious article in his clipping file estimated the possible numbers of homosexuals in the federal government based on his findings: twenty-one congressmen and 56,787 federal workers, it estimated, would be wholly homosexual, and over 500,000 might be possible blackmail risks.[50]

To evaluate Kinsey's impact better it is useful to revisit his most vociferous critics, for they, probably better than others, engaged and understood the revolutionary ideas he advocated. Public intellectuals such as Niebuhr, Mead, and Trilling understood the implications of the attack on concepts of the normal implicit and explicit in Kinsey's approach. By refusing to categorize behavior, except as variables on a graph or in a statistical table, Kinsey had challenged a broad class of moral judgments, and the panoply of legal and social structures that depended upon them. Kinsey's transformation of "is" into "ought" revealed his moral stance. Insofar as sexuality should be recognized publicly at all, he seemed to be arguing that society should facilitate, not repress, the individual's orgasms wherever and with whomever he desired. This was a conclusion he had implied even before most of his research had been completed. In 1940 he wrote that moral attempts to control particular forms of sexual outlet are "devoid of any logic, not to say scientific justification."[51]

A different way to evaluate Kinsey's impact is to ask whether he contributed in any significant sense to the sexual revolution and the loosening of gender stereotypes identified by observers in the 1960s and 1970s. There are two possible approaches to this question. No doubt readers of his books gained confidence in finding mention of their sexual experimentation from its inclusive tables and charts. If nothing else, a reader could locate himself, identified by behavioral category in the extensive index, and then find where he belonged in the statistical profile. The eventual lessening of punitive attitudes and prohibitions during this period is certainly grounded in part on the sexologist's findings. There is also ample evidence that Kinsey had found an already existing pattern of widespread experimentation and sexual nonconformity that prevailing discussions and moral precepts denied or criminalized. In fact, he suggested, around 95 percent of American men could be considered sex criminals by their actions at one time or another during their lives. In bringing these activities forward for public scrutiny, Kinsey reinforced the adversarial stance of researcher versus moralist that has long persisted in sex research. And if the sexual revolution is as much about talk as it is behavior, then Kinsey certainly made the contemporary conversation more open to discussing actual behavior.[52]

Latter-day critics and biographers have looked at Kinsey in the context of his place in the evolution toward contemporary definitions and standards of sexuality. Their verdicts have been divided. For example, Henry L. Minton's two works on the sexual revolution in the United States judge Kinsey to be a sexual liberal because of his refusal to essentialize sexuality—because he defined it in terms of behavior. At the same time the author notes that Kinsey did not question fundamental gender arrangements in the United States. Nor did he recognize the political usefulness of essentializing homosexuality so as to deny that it represented a revocable choice. These conflicting assessments, in fact, suggest the importance of seeing the sexologist in the context of his own times, for what he did as well as did not do.[53]

There is a final attribute of Kinsey's work that moved, perhaps still unrecognized, into the discussion of masculinity in the 1950s and which operated as a defining undercurrent to his study. In some respects this is the most important element of all: his separation of contemporary standards of masculinity itself from behavior, of sex from prevailing gender norms. In other words, he challenged the defining oppositions upon which heterosexual masculinity had been based. To Kinsey and his fellow researchers, sexual behavior and socially defined attributes of masculinity were independent variables. Quite remarkably, only once in the *Male* volume does Kinsey explicitly address masculinity itself, and this occurs in the midst of a surprising passage where he pointedly rejects the Terman-Miles masculinity-femininity scale linking sexual preference to the "masculinity or femininity of the personality." Kinsey concludes that reality is just too complex for such correlations and categories. "The living world," he concluded, "is a continuum in each and every one of its aspects." As he put it in a letter to an army private requesting information about a sex change operation, "Masculinity and femininity are partly questions of anatomy and physiologic function, partly a matter of psychology and partly a question of social adjustment [culture]."

At another place in the book, Kinsey pointedly disrupts and then inverts the standard gender assumptions of the day, carrying out an astounding reversal. In this defining moment, he challenges the primal, historic myth about American masculinity itself, honed by the struggle to subdue the frontier. In this passage, Kinsey first admits that one could find the expected stereotyped affectations and fey mannerisms among urban homosexuals, but such persons constituted only a small minority of city men with homosexual outlets. But let us look at the West for a different model, he suggests, to "older males in Western rural areas." He continued, "It is a type of homosexuality which was probably common among pioneers and outdoor men in general. Today it is found among ranchmen, cattlemen, prospectors, lumbermen, and farming groups in general—among groups that are virile and physically active. These are men who have faced the rigors of nature in the wild. They live on realities and on a minimum of theory."

For them, he concluded, "sex is sex." And that is probably the most apt summary of his message.[54]

If Kinsey had set out to caricature the American frontier myth so prevalent in his day in the vast literature assessing American character, he could not have chosen a more outrageous example. If he had wanted to disrupt Terman's virile-looking, virile-behaving continuity, he could not have found a more mainstream example to undercut. But Kinsey's point was even more radical. Even if he would not have put it quite this way, he had sought to prove that science, law, religion, culture, and even common sense had conspired to disguise standards of identity and behavior that were socially constructed. Masculinity, however anyone might plausibly define it, was therefore distinct from the sexual behavior of men. As he wrote in 1950 for the *Journal of Clinical Endocrinology*, there was no demonstrable basis for a hormonal explanation for behavior and affect. The concept of a "physical stigmata" was therefore false. True, some homosexuals show what "are popularly considered to be 'effeminate' characteristics, but there are others that are physically robust and as athletically active as the most 'masculine of men.'" Thus such designations as "masculine" were heuristic constructions, and belonged within quotation marks, not as indications of sexual identity.[55] Kinsey did not challenge the reality of a cluster of traits that society defined as masculine. He performed these stereotypes himself and maintained a persona that fulfilled many of their premises. But he argued, and demonstrated in his work, that such social definitions only disguised radical variations of behavior. Everything he wrote in *Sexual Behavior of the Human Male* argued that there was a discontinuity between sex as a physical act and socially accepted notions of morality, normality, even masculinity itself. At the same time he argued that there was continuity between sex outlets. To recognize this contradiction was the beginning of momentous change. Certainly he admitted that notions of masculinity existed, but they were fluid and contingent and no predictor of what any man might do.

6

"My Answer": Billy Graham and Male Conversions

For Billy Graham, the most important Protestant evangelical of the twentieth century, there was no masculinity crisis in the 1950s, but rather, a serious problem in attracting men to his cause. If he did not exactly articulate it in these terms, the difficulty was related to the resistance of men to a religious faith that sometimes construed conversion in terms of "feminine" qualities like submission and emotion. Because he insisted upon a public indication of conversion, Graham invited men to participate in the enactment of sentiments they might well have wanted to keep private. It was his mission, therefore, to find a way to reach out to men without challenging their masculinity.[1]

Billy Graham emerged from the same American Protestant culture that shaped the other important evangelicals of the twentieth century. Like many of them, he was a white, small-town southerner, acquainted from childhood with a fundamentalist interpretation of Christianity and a literalist reading of the Bible. Cut from much the same cloth as his great, flamboyant predecessor Billy Sunday, Graham, nonetheless, grew into a different sort of leader, distinct also from the televangelists who followed him and adapted some of his techniques of proselytizing. Graham became a central figure in this tradition, but he also garnered the prestige and respect that made him one of the most admired men in America and a recognized social and cultural leader—with no whiff of sulfur or taint of corruption or excess. As religious historian Donald Meyer said with reluctant admiration in 1955, Graham was "beautifully groomed, beautifully assured, brilliant in profile," and "equipped to meet all the requirements of the American cult of happy, healthy living, popularity, and self-assurance."[2] At the same time, Graham's message was insistently serious and sometimes strident in inveighing against the moral and social corruption of American culture. If this appeared contradictory, it merely reproduced a larger historic conflict in American culture between a deep-seated optimism coated in an eschatology of pessimism: salvation bound up in a message of sin, relieved only through conversion and rebirth and strenuous self-improvement.

If Graham embodied many of the apparent contradictions of American evangelical culture, he also squarely faced the dilemmas that had dogged the great itinerant ministers of the nineteenth-century awakenings as well as the crusaders of his own day. From its beginning, evangelical culture had appealed especially to women, just as established religion tended to do, attracting a larger number and percentage of female than male converts. This situation continued to characterize modern campaigns and Graham's own surveys revealed it to be a problem of his own movement. Men proved to be harder to convert, more difficult to bring into the fold, and more likely to stray again.[3] In part because of this situation and based on his own experience of conversion, Graham was deeply concerned and careful, especially, about the use of emotional appeals in his sermons. But the persistent question of masculine conversion became a central and explicit concern faced by the Graham crusade. The message he shaped, the mode of conversion he championed, and the particular attention he paid to male redemption all aimed to resolve this problem. It always remained true, however, that despite his best efforts, Graham could not reverse the unfavorable conversion ratio of men to women.

Graham's own conversion, as he recounted it, veered through this thicket of gender problems without any clear path, and he did not resolve his religious orientation until he had determined, in a personal sense, the male-female implications of the experience. As he wrote in 1958 for a tract aimed at teenagers, his experience at the local crusade where he converted provided him with a useful model. "I sat in the rear of the building," he recounted, "watching all the strange happenings. I wasn't quite sure what would take place next. I had always thought of religion as more or less 'sissy stuff,' and that a fellow who was going to be an athlete would have no time for such things. It was all right for old men and girls, but not for real 'he-men' with red blood in their veins." But the preacher of the moment, as he remembered him, had been an extraordinary man: virile, intense, and persuasive, "a great giant of a man." And when Graham did convert, he thought of it in the context of this masculinized vision. In the same advice book, he continued, "Christ could straighten your shoulder." He could inject character into your life: "He can make you the complete man you want to be! Let him take over your life!"[4]

Yet therein lies the difficulty, close to the very heart of the conversion process itself. Despite Graham's glossary of masculine adjectives, a very different sort of discourse simultaneously existed at the core of the experience, made up of words describing submission, yielding, giving oneself over to the will of another, and marked by visible emotionalism. As one particularly hostile potential convert described it, "It's an old woman's lie!" Ordinarily such words of submission were applied—even by Graham—to gender relationships. Thus in sequential passages, he speaks of the convert as a "yielded Christian" and then, somewhat later, insists that "the wife must submit herself to husband, and husband love and honor the wife."[5] This model of cascading submission was something to which Graham and other evangelicals paid close attention. His approach was deeply personal and self-referential. Graham finally resolved the dilemma of emotions by offering up his own experience, the assertion of his own masculinity as an example. Men could cry; they knelt in prayer; they could yield to irresistible emotion; and they could emulate this experience through his example of muscular Christianity. In this respect, Graham found himself not just the leader of an enormous uprising of evangelical interest in the 1950s; he showed, by example, how a man could be born again and remain an exemplary man.[6] It was precisely this sort of contradiction that swirled around the controversial painting *The Head of Christ*, by Warner Sallman. Was the well-known image and pictorial icon masculine or feminine in countenance—was it a rugged Jesus or a sentimentalized, feminized depiction? And by analogy, was contemporary religion masculine or feminine or both, or more important, in what measure did it convey gender?[7]

Graham's masculinist orientation was certainly not unique in the twentieth century, which was awash with disparaging caricatures of feminized Victorian Protestantism. William Ashley "Billy" Sunday, whose revival Graham attended once as a boy, and who became something of a role model, spoke and acted from a perspective of heightened concern over masculinity characteristics in the early twentieth century. Born near the turn of the century, Sunday grew up in a world where men like Theodore Roosevelt publicly despised and denounced softness and effeminacy. At the heart of contemporary Protestantism there were a number of movements that sought to raise the sweat of virility through religious exercise. For example, "Muscular Christianity," the YMCA, and the Religion and Men Forward Movement all engaged in beefing up the appeal of religion to men. In the 1920s, revivalist Paul Rader of Chicago Gospel Tabernacle also appeared to speak directly to this problem. As an in-house account of his ministry asserted, Rader was winning a male audience, and "that fact is explained by the manliness of the preacher." This was a purpose that continued and grew into the 1950s and 1960s with the organization of the Fellowship of Christian Athletes (1954) and Athletes in Action (1966). Graham offered strong support for these movements.[8]

Billy Sunday pointedly addressed the problem of male conversion by holding special meetings for men only. He lambasted weakness and spiced his vocabulary with images of physical combat. On occasion, he tore off his coat and tie, shaking his fist like a prizefighter.[9] Like Graham, after him, he embodied the converted male, the Christian athlete, the soldier, the father—a kind of manly archetype. If Graham rejected some of the histrionics of this genre of performance, he certainly did not miss the message: Christianity required careful masculine cultivation and performance.

This became particularly pertinent because of the transformations of American Protestantism during the Progressive Era, a period historian William McLoughlin aptly calls the "Third Great Awakening." At the end of the nineteenth century, and through the first two decades of the twentieth, Protestants were increasingly divided over issues of theology and social service, between a burgeoning fundamentalism and modernism. An important ingredient in this division was the acceptance by a mix of lay figures like Jane Addams of a singular emphasis upon a social gospel, with its stress upon selfless service to society using the tools of modern social science. Graham's leading role in the "Fourth Awakening" after World War II continued the rejection of social science as the tool of what Sunday considered a socialized and corrupted mainline modernism. His position represented an amalgamation of fundamentalism and the innovations in emotional technology of the great nineteenth-century itinerant ministers, Charles Grandison Finney and Dwight Moody.[10]

Graham's life also richly resonates with a version of an important story that has been endlessly repeated in a variety of guises throughout American history: the conversion narrative and its consequences. Graham underwent and initiated conversions, and he understood both his own life and his ministry in terms of the accounts of this experience; this remained his goal and focus. More generally, notions of rebirth have been the critical lifeblood of American Protestantism, and, in particular, within the evangelical tradition. Likewise, the conceit of transformation has had similar echoes through the secular halls of American culture. Religious conversion may claim to be the master narrative within this tradition, but, particularly in the twentieth century, there have been other strong, competing versions of this story that coexist and sometimes intertwine with the religious model. One of these is intrinsic to an enormous literature of self-help and economic success. From Horatio Alger stories at the turn of the century through contemporary tracts on releasing the inner, successful self, this has been a major element of American culture that often depicts a conversion-like experience as the necessary first step to economic success and psychic well-being. Advertising executive Bruce Barton's conflation of this secular message with salvation in his 1920s books on the Bible and the manly Jesus only underscores an obvious connection. Another popular conversion narrative of the twentieth century depicts the physical transformation of the self, based upon a revolution wrought by diet and exercise, to release the inner, potent self. Theodore Roosevelt and Bernarr Macfadden are probably the most obvious exemplars of this chronicle of physical rebirth, although there are countless others in sports, military, and business literature.

All of these conversion narratives share a preoccupation with the male subject, whether the Christian, the businessman, or the physical culture disciple. The most noteworthy models of such transformations in American history have almost always been male: Charles Finney, Ben Franklin, Roosevelt, and scores of other heroes of personal transformation and self cultivation. Of course, there are similar narratives that focus on women, but the centrality of men to these stories of change and rebirth is essential. So much more so in religion, but with a persistent anomaly: while the story was generally told about male conversions, the actual listening congregation of the converted usually contained a majority of women.[11]

Graham's most famous religious contemporary of the 1950s, Norman Vincent Peale, of the Marble Collegiate Church in New York City, faced the same "problem" of the female predominance in his audience. As Carol George, his biographer, writes, the audience for his message of personal empowerment was "predominantly female, Protestant, and lower middle class." While Peale made sure to associate male businessmen in public with his movement, it was actually a "national congregation made up largely of women." Of course there are crucial differences between Graham and Peale, who emerged from a rather different tradition emphasizing mental healing. From the beginning, Graham and Peale cut very different figures, for Peale had grown up the unhappy son of a minister, and was wracked by extreme sensitivity and self-consciousness. He overcame these family problems through his reading and the enactment of self-help advice. Perhaps for this reason his message of positive thinking was filled with images of masculine success. In fact, he was deeply critical of what he feared was becoming an effeminized mainline American religion.[12]

In his remarkably successful advice book, *The Power of Positive Thinking* (1952), Peale, like Graham, pursued the elusive male convert. Like the self-help advisers before him, Peale brought the language and techniques of salesmanship to his Christian message. Equating a lack of self-confidence and failure with the unregenerate soul, he prescribed the acceptance of Christ and a step-by-step ascent to self-confidence as the pathway to the twin peaks of salvation and success. Quoting the language of contemporary psychology in his diagnosis of lethargy, hopelessness, and failure, Peale advised internalizing key phrases of the Bible as a kind of success mantra. As he recounted in one of the first of scores of brief conversion chronicles that made up his famous book, a man came to see him suffering from an inferiority complex. Peale gave him a Bible verse to ponder: "I can do all things through Christ which strengtheneth me." The man accepted this potent gift: "I watched him square his shoulders and walk out into the night. He seemed a pathetic figure and yet the way he carried himself as he disappeared showed that faith was already at work in his mind."[13]

If Peale's miracle cures involved the promise of success upon delivery of oneself into the powerful hands of God, these were simultaneously stories of regenerated masculinity. One story strung together with the next and the next gave the impression of a year's dose of *Reader's Digest* optimism compressed into its pages. Of the ninety or so separate narratives of exemplary cases in the book, around seventy-five were stories of men recounted in highly gendered language remarking on the requisite stiffening of resolve, growing firmness, and command that followed the religious reorientation of life. This gender partiality–of language and example—suggests that men were both the subject and the object of the author's attention. And at the heart of it all lay the narrative of Peale's own accession to the pinnacles of masculine power.

Appropriately, Peale began his advice book autobiographically. As a child he had been "painfully thin." He "longed to be hard-boiled and tough and fat," he remembered. Despite a regimen of pies, chocolate, and cod-liver oil, however, he failed to build himself up. In a nightmare Bernarr Macfadden would have recognized, he continues: "I stayed thin and lay awake nights thinking and agonizing about it." Only with age did he begin to fatten up—and then, woefully, to excess. Worse, he bore the opprobrium of being a minister's son. "I didn't want to be a preacher's son, for preachers' sons are supposed to be nice and namby-pamby. I wanted to be known as a hard-boiled fellow." To add to these imagined disadvantages, Peale suffered terrible anxiety in public performance—while other members of his family reveled in it. When asked to make a speech, "it scared me to death, even filled me with terror." But all these problems he overcame with the "simple techniques of faith taught in the Bible." So, too, could anyone with an inferiority complex release the powers that lay within himself.[14]

While Peale appeared to be addressing a diverse audience, the malady he diagnosed and the cure for it were described in male terms. Peale himself suffered teasing by his peers and shame before his elders. In analyzing these "problems," like Walter Mitty, he performed feats in daydreams of masculinity, imagining for himself a robust virility that would enable him to overcome his physical and psychological shortcomings. While the women whose stories he recounted often suffered from similar anxieties, their problems were never encountered in the public worlds of business or politics. And for them, he frequently resorted to a different set of gender stereotypes, repeating the common wisdom of the decade's suspicion of independent women, advising them not to be aggressive, nagging, or sharp-tongued. Or he suggested that they cultivate their womanly charms by frequenting "God's beauty parlor." By and large, however, the book addressed men and their problems. Its tales of achievement suggested texts and provided watchwords to follow, with rules to guide the uncertain, the nervous, and the fearful along the road to achieving power that would lead to success in business and social life.[15]

Even if Peale formulated goals that any "hard-boiled" man might appreciate, there was a divergent story in his work that obviously appealed to women. Perhaps the reason for the disproportionate audience of women—for the book and at his Marble Collegiate Church in Manhattan—lay in a different implication of his advice. Filled with discussions of surrender of the will in order to assert oneself, of an emphasis on abundance, positive thinking, faith, relaxation, and optimism—and above all a simplified Freudianism addressed to explain unhappiness and frustration—Peale spoke to those who lacked power over themselves and their situations. Because his subject was weak men and unrealized men as he had once been, it is hardly surprising that this message also resonated with women who found themselves in the same dependent position.[16] If one key to Peale's enormous popularity was his ability to address men directly and still attract a huge audience of women, there is nothing new in this technique of a layered appeal, nor revolutionary in its implications. The subject of his stories was almost always a man, and the language and address determinedly masculine. But despite this, he could not reverse the gender imbalance that had long worried American Protestants. If he understood the problem of America in the 1950s in terms of a crisis in masculinity, in the desperate need of men to assert their personalities against the unfair odds of anxiety, failure, and diffuseness, the solution he offered, to think oneself through to a positive conclusion, only partly succeeded in attracting his target public.[17]

Historian William McLoughlin has suggested that Graham, in "Peale-like" sermons, promised psychological transformation to accompany conversion. "God," Graham said, "can rid you of boredom . . . God can rid you of anxiety . . . God can rid you of loneliness."[18] Despite such words, there were fundamental differences in the approach of the minister and the evangelist. Graham shared Peale's desire to masculinize contemporary Protestantism, but he followed a course that took him in a different spiritual, emotional, and organizational direction. He never did resolve the problem of the reluctant male convert, but he pursued this quarry with intensity and ingenuity.

As one part of his broad evangelical address to America's soul, he wrote (or supervised) an advice column that contained many similarities to Peale's suggestions for using biblical passages as self-help slogans. Both men responded to a need apparent almost everywhere in American society in the postwar period: to seek advice for living in a greatly changed world. This immense audience of advice-seekers, as Kinsey had discovered, was self-segmented into specialized groups of readers and correspondents according to the type of problems they suffered and where they sought advice. Newspapers and magazines featured advice columns on religion, sex, morality, dating behavior, family guidance, fashion, diet, consumption, psychology, do-it-yourself projects, manners, and a host of other subjects. This public airing of personal problems revealed a shared curiosity and sometimes a deeper anxiety about the changing mores of the age. Billy Graham addressed the "Aspirin Age," as Peale called it, with an ambivalent message, warning simultaneously of damnation but with the promise of unproblematic and immediate salvation. This was a more traditional message, with a different emphasis than Peale's attention to the dramas of psychic transformation and feelings of well-being.

Graham's background and upbringing provide crucial suggestions for understanding his crusade for conversions. They defined him as something of an outsider from the main line of American civilization, and perhaps help explain his relentless campaigns to convert America's cities, which he saw as the centers of modernity and corruption. This position could be turned into something of an advantage, for it made Graham a stranger to the modern world he sought to rescue from its excesses. He carried with him, in other words, a sense of remoteness, a reminder of the past, both explicitly and implicitly, and the recollection of an America that seemed to be fast disappearing. Graham was also thoroughly based in a regional evangelical tradition that saw as its task the struggle against the violence and alcoholism associated with the excesses of southern masculinity. As Ted Ownby put it, evangelicals in this mode "strove to bring man closer to the temperament of women and children."[19]

This created a number of potential contradictions. Graham developed an enormously sophisticated and effective organization and an innovative approach to media technology. In this sense, he belonged within the mainstream (not just the southern wing) of the American evangelical tradition, joining Charles Grandison Finney and Dwight Moody in inheriting an ambivalent attitude toward modernizing society, embracing its techniques of communication but denouncing its ethos. At the same time, he demonstrated ways in which modern evangelicalism[20] could be a critical response to the modernization of American society and to the dilemmas posed within that new world for Christian masculinity.

William Franklin Graham was born in 1918 on a dairy farm near Charlotte, North Carolina. Descended from Scots-Irish immigrants, both his mother and father were ardent Presbyterians. Like many in the audiences he addressed later, Billy's parents also experienced a strong reaffirmation of their faith. This phenomenon of "reconversion" is a key element in the meaning of evangelical life in America and suggests an essential ingredient in Graham's later crusades. The Christian makeover, in effect, sustained a life of belief based upon multiple rededications and recommitments. Although raised in such an intense evangelical tradition, Billy was not drawn at first to the church. He preferred to play baseball and frequently read boys' novels like *Tarzan* and westerns by Zane Grey, but the religious atmosphere in the family was the air he breathed.[21]

If this represented an unexceptional beginning, Graham's life veered from the track of sports and normal boyhood preoccupations when he attended a revival preached near his home by Mordecai Ham in 1934 when Graham was only sixteen. Conversion did not occur instantly. Billy went only reluctantly the first time, sitting in the true "anxious seat" at any such gathering—in the back and beyond the reach of the potent, encouraging gaze of the audience. But repeated visits gradually convinced him. In his autobiography, Graham describes this conversion with all the ease of a much-told tale. Although he attended several meetings, he always resisted Dr. Ham's invitation to come forward. When at last he did respond, he waited through all of the verses of "Just as I Am," the popular Baptist hymn of invitation he would adopt for similar moments at his own crusades. Then another song started up, and as the last verse was beginning, he finally succumbed. Joining about three hundred other people, he went forward to declare his commitment. But this was also a very self-conscious moment, and Graham carefully monitored his reactions. He was, at first, disappointed with the experience: "My heart sank when I looked over at the lady standing next to me with tears running down her cheeks. I was not crying. I did not feel any special emotion of any kind just then. Maybe, I thought, I am not supposed to be there."[22] While he associated a cathartic, public, and emotional conversion with the woman, his own transformation would be slower, more reasoned, and less dramatic.[23]

Although Graham gradually overcame his fears that religion was "sissy stuff," his dedication did not immediately push him into the ministry. In fact, he spent several years deciding upon his career, and attended several difference colleges: Bob Jones University, then Florida Bible Institute, and finally Wheaton College in Illinois. At Wheaton, he met and married Ruth Bell, the daughter of missionaries to China.[24] And, indeed, his continuing encounter with the North and urban American may have strengthened his resolve to regenerate them—to make them more like his boyhood South.

Two conclusions can be drawn from this prolonged experience of conviction and burgeoning dedication. Because Graham placed himself and his own changing identity at the heart of his description of the conversion process, the dynamic of his individual transformation is a key to understanding his approach to the general process. Having personally experienced initial reticence and shyness, Graham often addressed his message to the man who holds back at the edge of the tent, the reluctant convert who cannot imagine himself as a converted Christian and who, Graham felt, only obscurely grasped the possibilities of the regenerated life and his salvation through it. Secondly, Graham preached the remarkable and immediate transformation for those who came forward during his crusade. Yet he knew from his own experience that this process was inherently a long and complicated one that surely extended beyond the surge of momentary feelings. Therefore, he paid particular attention to the means that aroused belief, and tried, with some success, to police the emotional content of his message and the spectacle of the crusade itself—to use both emotion and showmanship carefully.

After graduating from Wheaton College, Graham joined the Youth for Christ International in Chicago as an itinerant evangelist. This training ground for his later successes led him to travel around the United States addressing YFCI meetings. An early evaluation of the movement by religious writer, evangelist, and publisher of *Youth for Christ* Mel Larson presented a picture of activist, virile young men, who were clean-cut, normal young Americans. Speaking of the lure used to attract young people to meetings, he wrote, "The 'bait' used is often in the form of outstanding athletes, businessmen, war heroes, musicians, lawyers."[25] In discussing this movement, Larson also invoked a tone and a narrative cliché that had long characterized the American evangelical tradition. This is the story of tested faith, in which repeated obstacles to success threw a crusade or a crucial meeting into doubt. Whether it be bad weather, opposition of established churches in a city, or just the deadening pall of sin and indifference, the crusade is described as a mode of struggle, a cycle traversing hope, worry, prayer, and then, success, with the implication of enacting God's will. In Graham's own sermons and in his autobiography and interviews, this formula is repeated frequently: the threat of failure, and with God's help, the successful resolution of the problem. In fact, however, there were three parallel and simultaneous narratives operating in such parable-like historical cycles. The first is Billy Graham's conversion and exemplary success story, told and retold in sermons, autobiographical accounts, and crusade literature. Second is the larger, more diffuse success ethic, preached and then rediscovered by Americans of almost every generation from the late eighteenth century onward—an ethic that flowered in Peale's positive thinking and Graham's optimistic prospects for conversion. The third story was always incomplete, one waiting for a name and an aspirant to fulfill it: the convert himself. In this last narrative, the process of overcoming spiritual and physical obstacles is usually dramatic. Graham issued a generic invitation to the willing to join in, to inscribe his name in a movement to overcome personal anxiety, doubt, fear, shame, and reluctance through a public act of commitment.[26]

The history of the Youth for Christ International appeared to confirm the telling of the mysterious workings of such inspired success stories and conversions. Writing of the organization, Torrey Johnson, the group's founder, commented on the efforts to overcome the obstacles to beginning a radio show on Chicago's WCFL in 1944. As he wrote, "We felt led of the Holy Spirit to speak to Mr. Taylor about our problem and solicit his help. God again marvelously undertook and, through the gracious cooperation of Mr. Taylor," they got their radio station.[27] While the rhetorical strategy behind this accounting certainly has long established roots, the model used by Graham, and the organizations with which he was associated, invoked inspired history as an authentic version of the truth: indeed, putting a story in such terms, and retelling it seemed to validate its truth.[28]

This early incarnation of the YFCI displayed in unrefined chunks of raw energy many of the elements that the Graham crusades later integrated and controlled. Graham quickly became the star of the youth-centered crusade, sporting a modified version of mid-1940s teen fashions and presiding over a variety of Bible-oriented entertainments. Initially, the movement was greatly aided by media mogul William Randolph Hearst, who enlisted his more than twenty newspapers in reporting favorably on the cause. The newspaperman's helpfulness varied, but it included both favorable publicity and various sorts of in-kind contributions, such as uniforms for the San Francisco Youth for Christ band.[29]

On the basis of his considerable success with the organization, Graham was invited to assume the presidency of the fundamentalist Northwestern Schools in Minneapolis in 1947. He remained there as head until 1952, when his attention had become increasingly preoccupied with crusades. By this time, he had assembled around him a number of the men who would form his team: for example, singer George Beverly Shea. After several trips abroad, Graham turned to the conquest of Los Angeles in 1949, and it was at this crusade that he made a noticeable national success. The event was significant because, in some respects, during the 1950s, his activities may be understood as a prolonged campaign against two special and uncommon American cities: Hollywood and New York. Each of these places symbolized a distinctive center of American culture and, to Graham and many of the itinerants who preceded and followed him, they were the preeminent centers of modernity, corruption, and debased culture. While the crusades in Los Angeles and New York represented only one part of his challenge to urban America, those cities were regarded by him, and in accounts of his efforts, as the harshest badlands to be conquered. Thus, Los Angeles in 1950 ("City of Satan") and New York City in 1957 defined the parameters of his effort, its seriousness, and its various successes. Daring to assault them was to lay siege to the heart of modern American culture and all the problems it suffered.

If Los Angeles and New York represented the twin versions of Vanity Fair in Graham's pilgrimage, they also demanded a kind of sophistication that forced the evangelist to shape an attractive, authentic, and modern message out of his old-time beliefs. They challenged him to face the problems inherent everywhere in the mission itself: emotionalism, the predicament of transitory or repeated conversions, and the lopsided gender attendance at his meetings and response to his call.

Graham had explicitly rejected the exaggerated histrionics associated with Billy Sunday. Early in his career, he learned to tame his more emotional gestures, and he disdained the tears—except temporary ones—that some other evangelicals purposely provoked. But, of course, not all traces of this style of appeal disappeared from his crusades, as evidenced in July 1957 by an irate letter to *Life* magazine. A reader angrily wrote, "Billy Graham is a maudlin sentimentalist," and remarked that Graham often spoke of making a "decision for Christ." But the word "decision," the writer continued, "involves an act of the mind, while Billy Graham's entire appeal is to the emotions." Because excessive emotion was identified as feminine and associated with weakness and subservience, this was a serious and unwelcome charge.[30] It was more or less the same accusation that theologian Reinhold Niebuhr leveled against Graham in 1957 during the New York campaign, although the words were more circumspect and polite. Graham, noted the theologian, preached a religion that provoked strong emotional responses. Try to control them as he might—channel them to avoid the excesses of his forbears and contemporaries—he could not deny their prominence and utility.[31]

The problem of the transitory recommitment (often a by-product of emotionalism) was something that Graham could well understand on the basis of his own experience. When he checked his pledge card in 1934, as a "recommitment," he was underscoring an important element in the evangelical experience: rebirth or "second blessing." Having been raised in a devout family, Graham, nonetheless, underwent a newly fervent commitment to evangelical Christianity at that moment, not a transition from nonbelief to belief. In fact, in his autobiography, he describes similar moments at other points in his life. Sometimes these were public acts and at other times they were intensely private. For example, while attending Florida Bible Institute, Graham was "smitten with love" for a fellow student, Emily Cavanough. But when she refused his marriage proposal, he became despondent. In part, he confessed, this rebuff only compounded his anxiety over the larger problem of a career choice. Would he become a full-time preacher? His classmates and teachers were urging him in this direction, but he remained uncertain—as uncertain, he remarks, as he had been "standing in the sawdust shavings of Mordecai Ham's tabernacle." His decision finally came after long walks alone on a golf course at Temple Terrace. In the moonlight he struggled to articulate an answer. "Finally, one night, I got down on my knees at the edge of one of the greens. Then I prostrated myself on the dewy turf. 'Oh God,' I sobbed, 'if you want me to serve you, I will.'" When he rose, he knew that nothing physical had happened: no voices, no signs signified his conversion, just the sharp sensation of his new commitment.[32]

At this moment, Graham certainly experienced something of the emotional response he had observed enviously at his initial commitment. Yet he still managed to place this release of sensation inside a rational and abstract formulation. He had been called to the ministry, but nothing in his surroundings had reverberated to reflect this charge: not the golf course, the damp night air, or the moonlight. Indeed, he ultimately framed this experience as a choice, an affirmation, rather than as a loss of will, or as will redirected by emotion. Two other times in Florida, Graham witnessed his faith in public. The first was his second baptism by immersion, which he arranged to do before a small group of witnesses "following my conscious conversion." The next occasion was yet another baptism, this time conducted under the auspices of the Southern Baptist ministry as an ordination ceremony.[33] These multiple private and public conversions and testimonials are crucial for understanding Graham's appreciation of the ongoing process—and it was a continuing development—that he urged others to undertake during his crusades, in the advice column he initiated, and in the films produced by his organization. Graham did not believe that the sudden emotional revolution necessarily contained the essence of the religious experience. Rather he believed it must be a more complex process in which emotion played a crucial, but not the singular role.

At the same time conversion was the least understood and most criticized element of Graham's crusades in the 1950s. Established, mainline theologians and Protestant liberals questioned the permanence and efficacy of Graham's conversions, and cited large figures of recommitments from crusades, to prove their point that Graham was ineffective in reaching new audiences. In an effort to deride his impact, a 1957 editorial in the *Christian Century*, published during the initial stages of the New York crusade, represents a typical example of this argument. The writers belittled the number of conversions and deplored their lack of permanence. After one service, 706 commitment cards were received. Of the forty signers interviewed for the article, all but two were already church members. Clearly, the meeting brought almost no new adherents into the church. Indeed, the editorial called this a "bookkeeping shuffle." Worse, they charged, Graham misunderstood the process he initiated, inciting false consciousness in the crowd. Such manipulators of mass conversion exploited heightened stresses and tensions within the revival atmosphere to produce in the individual an experience of change, "which is attributed to the work of the waiting, forgiving, reconciling spirit of God." Graham led his converts to expect more from a single experience than "anyone should expect."[34]

This critique could have been made even more powerfully using Graham's own aggregate figures for several crusades. During the 1950s, his organization kept careful demographic records of its converts and the nature of their prior religious affiliations. In looking at these statistics, it becomes obvious that female converts predominated: at least 60 percent of all commitments. Of those who signed pledges, almost 90 percent knew the name of the local church with which they wished to affiliate (or were already affiliated). Sixty-five percent were regular churchgoers, and 55 percent were already "born-again." In an in-house study of the 1953 London campaign, it appeared that only 2,000 of the 38,000 signers were actually new converts.[35]

But there is little to indicate that Graham held such a simplistic understanding of the process, and certainly his own experience of multiple conversions and public confessions provided a more complex vision. The recommitment of so many souls during the crusades may have been a disappointment in one respect, but it was an essential element in the evangelical project as Graham practiced it. And, it is particularly around the concept of emotion—that dangerous feminine expression of feeling—that Graham defined his understanding of the nature of conversion and rededication. On this point he anchored his arguments about the proper place of feelings in conversion.

In a very interesting early book, *Peace with God* (1953), Graham sought to define the role of strong emotions in the conversion process. He understood them to be necessary as well as dangerous. "Falsely produced emotionalism in some revival meetings," he admitted, "has been the stumbling block to many a serious, searching soul." And yet, emotion was as important as the intellect and the will: all three shared in the process of the controlled conversion. Thus, conviction, the sense of spirit moving in the heart, could be a highly emotional trigger experience: "The Holy Spirit may use a mother's prayers, a pastor's sermon, a Christian radio program, the sight of a church steeple, or the death of a loved one to bring about this necessary conviction," he wrote. And when Christ entered the heart, "He demands that He be Lord and Master. He demands complete surrender. He demands control of your intellectual processes. He demands that your body be subject to Him and to Him alone." If this sounds vaguely like the traditional wedding vows women used to speak, to "love, honor, and obey," the patriarchal model, is indeed, an appropriate depiction of this process. Up to this point, it might seem that conversion was highly inappropriate for a man, demanding the total submission of his will.[36]

An effective response to this danger was to pass along the burdens of emotion and subservience permanently to women. Particularly in this early period, Graham stressed that men should rule the family and that wives and children should submit. With these expressions Graham did nothing more than follow traditional patriarchal views that replicated the relationship between man and God in the relationship between woman and man. As he wrote in his 1957 *Hour of Decision* tract entitled "Father," the father must be considered the human counterpart of God. "He must take over from the 'frail shoulders' of the mother." Or as he put it many times, Christ is the head of the Church, and (quoting from Ephesians 5:23), "the husband is the head of the wife."[37]

Elsewhere, Graham wrote of the necessary and active transformation of the will and the intellect as steps in the conversion process. Indeed, he believed that emotion was an accompaniment, the background of moving chords that played along to accompany the succession of stages driven by conscious choice and by God's will operating in harmony. And, if the occasion warranted it, even Graham could cry, as Mel Larson recounts. When Graham reported back to Minneapolis after one of his crusades, the "great heart of Billy Graham bared itself wide open," Larson wrote. "He broke down. Tears filled his eyes; he choked up; said a few more words; and sat down."[38]

Graham explored the conversion experience time and again, never tiring of its psychological demands, partly because it was the test of every successful crusade and a personal reaffirmation of his own transformation. He was also inspired to do so because of his concern to police any divergence from the muscular Christianity that he preached. On occasion in his column, "My Answer," he chose to confront this question openly: Was Christianity for sissies? In response to one inquiry from "a Christian" who complained that because of his religion, "the men that I work with think they have the right to make a door mat of me and walk all over me," Graham proposed two solutions. You should expect your faith to be tested, he noted. But you should also realize that one could be manly and a Christian simultaneously. "Firmly but kindly," he wrote, "you should demand their respect and consideration. Take the initiative and begin a systematic program of doing things for them that require their admiration." While the advice specifically recommended suppressing any aggressive response, it was written with a generous sprinkling of words associated with masculine success in business: firmness, respect, initiative, and systematic, among others.[39] And, perhaps most important, Graham assumed that he and his correspondent shared a belief in the importance of displaying masculinity before an audience of other men.

In another column, Graham visited the dangers of emotionalism. This was something that each Christian must understand, for feelings could cloud and confuse the nature of the conversion experience. As one column put it, "Emotion in religion is as dangerous as emotion in love." It was equally perilous in love between man and woman and between man and God. Yet emotion was also necessary. "Proper emotions are the result of a true love just as they are the result of a genuine faith in God."[40]

If such advice appears contradictory or cryptic, that is not surprising, partly because it defines emotion as subordinate and accessory, rather than the center of any relationship. Not unexpectedly, Graham's campaigns attracted a good deal of puzzled commentary on this score. As he reported in his 1957 tract, "What Is Conversion?" he had received hundreds of letters from writers who were perplexed about the experience. To clarify his stand on emotionalism, Graham wrote that there were two sorts of conversions, a "crisis conversion" on the spot and a more difficult, slow one advancing through many stages. Yet both of them involved the entire human personality, both actively and passively: will, intellect, and emotion were all affected as the convert passed through repentance and a turning away from old ways toward rebirth and regeneration. Or as he put it in a different tract, conversion "is that voluntary change in the mind of the sinner in which he turns on the one hand *from* sin and on the other hand *to* Christ."[41]

Because there could never be a last word on this theme, Graham's close associate, staff member, and the coauthor of the "Answer" column, Robert O. Ferm, returned to the subject several times, with his last contribution a 1988 book-length treatment. He looked back over the long time period stretching from the early 1950s through the mid-1980s to assess the meaning of conversions generated by the Graham crusades. His figures were based upon answers to questionnaires as well as the analysis of commitment cards and follow-up surveys of individuals. For the period 1952–1954, on the basis of eleven crusades, he found a 38 percent male to 62 percent female conversion rate. Among these pledges, the largest two groups were students and homemakers. Such early indications proved predictors of subsequent crusades, also. And he estimated that among the inquirers at meetings, anywhere from 70 to 80 percent were already church members.[42]

Having answered the question that ostensibly provoked the book, Ferm turned to emotions and the psychology of a Billy Graham conversion. In doing so, he repeated the same ambiguous message about feelings. Confronting the charge that conversions were insubstantial because they rested upon sentiment, Ferm noted that all the great itinerants in American Protestant history (George Whitefield, Jonathan Edwards, Finney, Moody, and Sunday) focused on the actual conversion experience. Likewise, critics had charged them (and Graham) with flagrant emotionalism, for conducting a performance designed to elicit an intense momentary psychological reversal. But Ferm denied this possibility, claiming that sentiments were merely incidental to conversion itself: "Thousands of those who have gone forward at Billy Graham crusades have reported that it was the Word of God itself, not the evangelistic technique of the Graham team that impelled them to a decision for Christ." To understand the process was to recognize its complexity as the person moved gradually from a mood of crisis to the beginning of rebirth through God's will.

Yet even here, Ferm used terms of dependency. To be born again was literally to experience a new infancy: "The new convert is like a baby who constantly demands milk, but is not yet ready for solid food." Or as he put it elsewhere, "conversion is the turning outward from the self to an 'other.'" Thus he saw the conversion experience moving through stages: the phases of decision and dependency, not entirely one or the other, but related and interconnected. He was, as Billy Graham was, firmly committed to the view that emotionalism was not the essence of the experience; it was only incidental. As he bluntly stated, "Intense emotions play an incidental role in the majority of conversions."[43]

In a way, Ferm was only trying to stake out a special claim for Christian evangelicals within the larger framework of the important psychological theory of conversion developed by the philosopher William James at the beginning of the twentieth century. This remarkable text established a model for conversion that remained overt or implicit in most of the modern explorations of the process. In his essay *The Varieties of Religious Experience,* James described the process as one where the individual experiences the sudden feeling of wholeness and a new unity of the personality. As James put it, this represented the flooding of the subconscious into the consciousness. After the publication of this influential text, a number of religious thinkers adopted James's categories and descriptions. In this sense, it became the exemplary text to argue for or against.[44]

Ferm recognized the similarities between Christian conversion and the psychological process that James had identified. But for the Christian, he insisted, the true conversion had to be seen as "the work of God rather than as a psychological construct." He specifically invoked James's analysis in his 1959 book on the psychology of Christian conversion—as a way to argue against its universal implications. In fact, this tract was an answer to the philosopher's notion that conversions of any sort were similar in their effects on character. Ferm, and Graham (in his introduction to the book), were attempting to rescue conversion from its psychological descriptions, to understand it as a process inspired by God, unique to Christianity, and not defined by generalized emotional events as James proposed.

In this book, Ferm also analyzed the results of questionnaires and interviews held from 1951 to 1954 around various Graham crusades. To many of the respondents, their conversion was not the only religious upheaval in their lives. But Ferm discovered an almost universal recognition of regeneration after a Graham meeting, "like a physical birth." Further, he discovered that this surrender of the self was not particularly emotional in its nature. Few respondents experienced violent or strong feelings during conversion. Most important for his answer to James's hypothesis, Ferm claimed that the Christian conversion was different from all apparently similar psychological experiences. In the case of Christianity, the crisis always included a consciousness of sin and a resultant choice to submit to the will of God. Furthermore, this new life was enduring. Indeed, only what he called "the evangelical crisis" could be permanent. The evangelical crisis was unique because it was ultimately based upon the atonement of Christ; it was God-centered.[45]

In a book published in 1958, Ferm recounted the stories of twenty conversions instigated by the Billy Graham crusades. These narratives were presented to dispel the notion that conversion was induced by the momentary emotional pressure of the crusade, or by the misinterpretation of some transitory psychological state. These were, wrote Ferm, real transformations and clearly the work of the Holy Spirit. At the same time, there is something curious in the characteristic gendering of this collection of narratives. Ferm recounted the stories of more than twelve men and about half as many women, almost the inverse proportion of male to female converts that his own figures revealed. Did he do this because men's stories were inherently more interesting in the light of their wider worldly experience? Was he merely following a convention established by other writers like Peale, for instance? Was there a more interesting variety in their religious experience? Were their conversions more significant precisely because they were less frequent and more difficult? The answer can only be surmised, but it underscored the priority the Graham crusade gave to male conversion.[46]

If male conversion had a particular significance to the Graham crusade, how he presented himself during his crusades and how he constructed a special appeal to men became even more significant. For Graham, the crusade was the central event of his ministry and despite the elaborate development of radio, television, film, and print appeals, the meeting itself with Graham appearing in person remained the predominant tool of conversion. Indeed, the crusade often reappeared as the focal point in other media formats through visual or audio reproduction or quotation.

Although any single extended crusade during the 1950s would suffice as an example, the New York City campaign of 1957 rightfully received the greatest attention, scrutiny, and commentary during the decade. Beginning in mid-May, after almost two years of careful preparation, the crusade extended through the summer, ending finally with a large rally in Times Square on September 1. From almost the beginning, the crusade was televised, and the *New York Herald-Tribune* published a daily commentary entitled "Billy Graham Says." As with other crusades, Graham assembled a host of prominent men as sponsors. In New York, this group included William Randolph Hearst, Jr., publisher Henry Luce, aviator Capt. Eddie Rickenbacker, and Norman Vincent Peale. The most prominent honored guest was Vice President Richard Nixon who appeared at a rally on July 20 in Yankee Stadium. On occasion, the campaign aimed specifically at largely male audiences. On July 10, for example, surrounded by a bevy of prominent businessmen, Graham addressed a rally on Wall Street.[47]

Graham's physical appearance was the subject of considerable commentary during the crusade, and he obviously used his good looks and masculine affect with considerable success. Time and again, journals and newspapers mentioned his appearance, focusing on his sturdy frame and flashing eyes, sometimes even speculating on his potential for a Hollywood career. Reporters also wrote against stereotype. Graham was not the hand-wringing dispenser of old-time religion with its mellifluent homilies and pleas, but a vibrant, attractive, and serious young man. *Life* magazine described him as a lean, blond, handsome figure "with the earnest, resonant voice." *Reader's Digest* almost swooned at his appearance: "He stands six feet two, is a lanky 180 pounds. His hair is sunburned blond; his eyes blue, deep set and, as a script writer would put it, 'piercing.' He walks with a spring." When asked by a *New York Post* reporter if he was ever bothered by "lovesick women or bobby soxers," he replied, no, but implied, yes. "I never talk alone with a woman," he revealed. "I always have one or two team members with me. If they write letters, I don't see them." This denial indicated a long-standing policy of Graham's to avoid any taint of scandal of the sort that bothered other evangelical movements. But it did not refute the obvious: Graham was an immensely attractive figure. No wonder that some called him "Hollywood John the Baptist" or the "Matinee Idol Revivalist."[48]

Another much-noted trait of the crusade was its efficient, businesslike organization. Sometimes, this could appear a contradictory virtue. The *Wall Street Journal* described itself as immensely impressed and featured an article calling Graham an "efficient evangelist" who united the Bible and business. Especially impressive were his staff, who in answering his huge weekly correspondence, quickly sorted letters by problem—such as "unsaved husband," "bereavement," and "baptism," and punched out a response letter on a "robot typewriter." Graham himself encouraged this media attention to his business acumen and organizational skill. When asked about his preaching, he happily adopted the language of salesmanship: "I am selling the greatest product in the world. Why should it not be promoted as well as soap?" But this was a thin line to walk because Graham simultaneously refused to take credit for his success: no worldly explanation, by itself, could explain a conversion that was truly God's work.[49]

To his critics, his appearance, his organization, and its calculations sounded a false note of prophecy and displayed more than a little hypocrisy. The religious historian William McLoughlin, Jr., characterized the evangelist as the "head of a wealthy, influential and superbly managed business organization." With his hosts of choirs, ushers, counselors, managers, and advance men, Graham, despite his denials, operated very much in the theatrical tradition of Billy Sunday. The *Christian Century* angrily noted that Graham's audience was the same superficial set that read Peale and enthused over Cecil B. DeMille's contemporary film *The Ten Commandments*. The liberal journal detected "a certain blasphemy in all this red-hot machinery and cool contrivance." Reinhold Niebuhr, writing in the same venue, dismissed Graham's as a "frontier religion."[50]

However critics responded to it, Graham's self-presentation, among its most important purposes, aimed to create an intensely masculine public persona, surrounded by the symbols of physical attractiveness, business acumen, sports, and a group of exemplary male converts. A story in *Newsweek* in May 1957 contained more than a hint of this desired masculine impression. Based on information provided by Graham's secretary, James E. Moore, the writer noted that Graham trained "like a prize fighter."

Before the campaign began, the preacher followed a regimen of hiking, golf, and study. By the eve of the campaign, he was "as hard as a rock." And necessarily so, because the physical demands of a crusade could be exhausting. Around the same theme, Graham told the *Journal-American* that "Christianity is not a religion for weaklings. We must be strong, virile, dynamic, if we are to stand. We must somehow regain the spiritual fire and fervor of our fore-fathers."[51]

Graham could explain himself in masculine terms and tout his physical robustness and businessman's virtue to reporters, but the real test was his nightly performance in which he had to negotiate the shifting emotions of the conversion process. Graham's appearance was the central feature on any given crusade evening, although the presentation featured hymn singing by visiting choirs, testimonials, introductions of special guests, and hymns sung by George Beverly Shea. Graham was the centerpiece in this well-planned theatrical production. Furthermore, because of the frequent telecasts and considerable advance preparation, audiences knew what to expect. By their presence, they chose to participate in the larger ritual revolving around conversion, even if they did not respond to the invitation themselves.

Graham's preaching was a controlled, but electric, presentation of the Gospel. The tension created by his carefully expressed but accusatory and worrying words and prophecies was almost palpable. Graham paced the stage, gripping an open Bible in his left hand and reading passages from it, often using a chopping motion with his right hand to emphasize words or phrases. He preached to the rhythm of conversion itself: first, he sternly convicted the audience and society at large of sinfulness, predicting disastrous consequences, and then, moderating his voice, offered hope and redemption. The words and intonation thus reinforced a psychological mapping of the process itself. As one observer noted, the control that Graham asserted was quite remarkable: "There are no tear-wringing stories, no death bed scenes, no hysteria-inducing endings. This—the absence of any extremes of emotion—is a fact which every objective observer notes."[52]

After setting out his text, he explicated its meaning through a catalogue of the sinful ways of the world—crime and divorce, sickness, racial animosity, juvenile delinquency, Communism, the H-bomb, death, and drunkenness. Sometimes the list varied, but the message was always the same. This was generally the largest part of the sermon. Graham was restless, energetic, full of movement, and—most important—physically aggressive in describing the sins of individuals and their consequences. But nearing the end, he changed abruptly, and the effect was electric. Suddenly he spoke softly and calmly, inviting the audience to surrender to Christ. As he said, "When I give the invitation for people to receive Christ, it will be so quiet you can hear a pin drop." In this extraordinary moment, he would open his arms and gently invite those who wished to be saved to come forward. The choir began the soft strains of the traditional hymn "Just as I Am." With lights dimmed and audience heads bowed, Graham gestured with his hands. "You come now," he called softly. "There's time for you to come. You come."[53]

This remarkable physical transformation of Graham and the shifting spirit of his message did much more than replicate the changing emotional states of the conversion process, although they were clearly intended to mirror them. Graham also managed to explore commonly accepted "male" and "female" modes of expression: rapid-fire, almost brutal argumentation, with the abrupt transition to a welcoming submission. This was nothing new added to the lexicon of itinerancy, but Graham's version of carefully controlled "male" and "female" emotions proved to be extraordinarily effective.[54] Throughout the process, Graham remained an intensely masculine figure, and recognizably so, capable of expressing soft, welcoming words without compromise to his identity. As fellow evangelist Mel Larson described him, "When the invitation time came, he again was in command. There was no sugary-voiced pleading for people to come to Christ. It was a man-to-man approach."[55]

Yet many more women than men answered his call. Despite Graham's best efforts, the problem of male conversion remained a critical one, even if, in his own self-presentation he effectively demonstrated the self-confident, masculine possibilities of the evangelical personality. In part to address this problem, he turned to other media to speak specifically to men. In 1952, for example, he published a book aimed at servicemen: *The Chance of a Life Time*. In this extended tract, he depicted the converted life of a Christian as both service and challenge, and more difficult in some respects than combat itself. Overcoming temptations required constant strength and vigilance and the choice of companions with "the striking qualities of Christian character and manliness." There was, moreover, a thin line to walk between righteousness and self-righteousness. God demanded total commitment and surrender, but then, Graham asked rhetorically, how could a man retain the respect of his fellows? This was a traditional problem, and he applied the traditional solution of a sports analogy. Avoiding temptations and bad company was tantamount to playing in the Rose Bowl game, he explained, with encouraging crowds chanting, "Hold That Line!" On the other hand, the Christian man needed to "retreat" from temptation.[56]

In fact, Graham often acknowledged how precarious the position was, for on one side lurked the despised Christian prude who sacrificed the respect of his fellows, and on the other marched the man whose heart was "on its knees all the time," but who stood straight as he exercised leadership. A final story in the serviceman's book illustrates this paradox. Graham described a man who was saved at a tent meeting and wanted to witness his conversion the next day in his office. He greatly feared the ridicule of one particular coworker, but remained determined to speak up. And so he did: "Without further delay he blurted out, 'I say, Smith, I went to the tent last night and got saved!' 'Did you, Mudditt?' replied the other. 'So did I.'"[57]

If the language called upon to relate this encounter is stilted and unrealistic—almost British in its mawkishly artificial and cool idiom—it is because Graham is trying to handle a situation that is overloaded with emotion and decidedly unmanly implications. He thus hides the danger and intimacy behind preposterous language. In its very denial, the story suggested the dangers of a compromised masculinity for the converted man. Even more difficult, Graham was obliged to redefine elements of male culture such as drunkenness and unrestrained sexuality as sin without compromising masculinity itself. And the opposite problem of effeminacy also proved to be awkward. In one of his columns, he addressed the issue squarely. A letter writer asked, "We have an effeminate in our office. He is a menace. What should we do?" Graham's answer advised a more generous definition of masculine behavior. "While I agree with you that you may have a very serious problem, I'm not in agreement with your method. There are those men who are not the rugged he-man type, but it does not mean they are necessarily immoral or to be avoided."[58]

One frequent mode of Graham's address to a masculine audience was to recount the conversion and public witness of men whose masculinity could not be doubted. In the early 1950s, for example, Graham met with notorious West Coast gambler, Mickey Cohen. In 1957, Cohen announced he would attend the New York crusade and acknowledged that through the years he had often met with Graham for prayer and Bible-reading sessions. Other celebrated converts included men such as Louis Zamperini, former Olympic star and prisoner of war; Jim Vaus, policeman and wiretap expert; and Stuart Hamblen, former cowboy crooner and racehorse owner. Indeed, the gathering of these celebrities underscored the appeal Graham directed specifically at men who might otherwise assume that conversion was a womanly act. Again and again, in his personal life, Graham presented himself as one of a special breed of men, the long-distance runner, the athlete who faced physically daunting obstacles, challenging travails, and even physical danger—all in his pursuit of converts.[59]

A striking example of this strenuous autobiographical version of Graham's life was depicted in an NBC television episode of *Project 20* telecast in 1961 and entitled "The World of Billy Graham." As is generally true for such presentations, the program centered upon a crusade, this one in Philadelphia. In part biography, partly a commentary on Graham's organization and methods, the film featured, as a centerpiece, Graham's talk to inmates in one of Pennsylvania's maximum security prisons. Addressing an assembly of men in the prison yard, Graham spoke to those who believed that followers of Christ were "sissy and weak." "I'm strong," he declared, "and I can stand for myself. I've seen men die and I want to tell you that some of those big strong guys"—and here the camera moved to the close-up of a tattoo on a prisoner's arm to underscore the dangerous venue—"are not so strong when they face death." As he said elsewhere, "All the virtues of manhood are raised to the highest in the life of one who is surrendered to Christ."[60]

Perhaps the most striking and pointed appeals for male conversion came in the form of films made by the Graham organization's Hollywood annex, the Billy Graham Evangelistic Films Company (later, World Wide Pictures). By 1957, this group had made seven feature-length movies, and employed a staff of twelve permanent members plus occasional actors and technicians hired for each individual project. The first two films established a pattern that suggested the overriding importance of male conversion and featured some of the converted cowboys of the Hollywood Christian Group that worked closely with Graham. Given the symbolic importance of western heroes in 1950s films, and American popular culture in general, this group played a significant role in Graham's outreach. Some of the group, including Roy Rogers and his wife Dale Evans, became mainstays of the organization and participated in Graham crusades. Others became players in his feature films.[61]

The first of these films, *Mr. Texas,* was released in 1951 by World Wide Feature Films. This was a movie designed primarily for viewing in churches, although in a few instances, it made its way into standard movie houses. Starring Redd Harper as "Mr. Texas" (Jim Tyler in the film), it was focused around the 1951 Fort Worth crusade. With Harper playing the lead and featuring songs by the "Sons of Pioneers, the film's cowboy credentials were impeccable. But the story was not the usual ride-around and shoot-'em-up. Instead, it explored the complex chronicle of Tyler's reluctant conversion. His sister, played by Graham convert and country music artist Cindy Walker, tries to persuade Tyler to attend the Graham crusade. He is obviously troubled by the lifestyle he leads, without peace and contentment, but he still resists her entreaties. Finally she persuades him to attend a crusade one evening, but he leaves the auditorium before the end, just as she answers Graham's invitation to come forward. At this point, the film demonstrates the follow-up of the invitation in the counseling room.

Despite her new and infectious faith, she cannot persuade Tyler to convert. He remains aloof and stiff and unwilling to listen. But when he is thrown from a horse during a rodeo and ends up in the hospital, he begins to break down. Singer Cliff Barrows visits him, and Jim begins to listen to Graham's *Hour of Decision* on the radio. There he hears Graham describe the stages of conviction, repentance, and faith. Finally, Tyler is persuaded and accepts God, confessing his sins. In the end, he sings of his new joy.

Mr. Texas debuted at the Hollywood Bowl in September 1951 during Graham's crusade in that city. In attendance were 150 members of the Hollywood Christian Group, as well as thousands who had assembled to hear Graham. It was later shown at Madison Square Garden and given a private screening for Cecil B. DeMille. As the first in a series, the film had two distinct purposes. The first was to demonstrate and justify conversion via the media: television, newspaper columns, radio, and in this case, film. Graham confidently asserted that the mass media could trigger conversions. The other purpose was to depict the process of male conversion, in this case, an unhappy, depressed cowboy. His conversion stretched over three phases: the conversion of his sister, an accident reminding him of his mortality, and his response to the appeal of Graham himself.[62]

It was probably inevitable that a contrivance using amateur actors and a relentlessly didactic plot would result in wooden performances and staged emotions. But there is an additional deadening quality that can only be attributed to Harper himself. Actually illustrating a male conversion results in a performance that is scarcely believable because the convicted cowboy is practically emotionless. He remains a male symbol but perhaps because of this, he cannot reveal his interior struggle with conflicting emotions. As a result, the film's center slips away from the hero and refocuses on Graham, the shots of his preaching, his sermon, and the invitation, as well as the radio version of the crusade. As Harper sleepwalks through his change of heart, Graham dominates the screen—as the dynamic, virile, energetic

Christian, and the most vivid embodiment of masculinity in the film, the man who would not be thrown by emotion.[63]

If *Mr. Texas* failed to provide a convincing document of male conversion—underscoring instead, perhaps, reasons why men might not convert—the Graham film company tried again with a similar format a year later, centering this time on the Houston crusade. *Oiltown, USA* returned most of the same cast of players, although here the main character is a ruthless financier who has quarreled with his daughter and refuses to see her. When the daughter is feared to be among the dead after a disastrous fire in Texas City, his heart softens and he eventually accepts Christ. But once again the most plausible male character, the star of the film, is Graham himself preaching at Rice University stadium, rather than the unconvincing portrayal of the oilman.

Two other presentations, *Souls in Conflict* (1954) and *Wiretapper* (1955), set the narrative of conversion at some distance: the first in England and the second in the crime world of Los Angeles. Of course, both retained the central event of the Billy Graham crusade. The English story interweaves three separate narratives: of an unhappy actress, a harried working-class man, and a heroic test pilot whose flights into the ether inspire thoughts of God. In some respects, the Los Angeles film was more interesting; it followed an identifiable plot whose denouement was conversion, but which along the way revealed the workings of organized crime. Loosely based upon the biography of Jim Vaus, whom Graham converted in the early 1950s, the story follows a World War II veteran into his brush with the mob as a hired wiretapper. Vaus's conversion, which abruptly ends the film, comes as something of a cinematic surprise, urged on by his patient and suffering wife, at the last moment, whereas in his autobiographic account he responds to a radio broadcast by Graham. Likewise, in the film about the English crusade, there is a none-too-successful attempt to depict conversion. In each of these narratives, the transformation is instantaneous: in the first film, the actress discovers happiness; the shrewish wife of the worker becomes cheerful and loving, persuading him to change; and the pilot finds inner peace. In the second film, Jim Vaus renounces his life of crime and bravely tells the credulous mob his inspiring conversion story.[64]

The Graham organization continued to experiment with film and in 1957 made another effort to depict male conversion, this time centered on the New York crusade in Manhattan. For this production Graham had some new celebrity recruits, including Ethel Waters, who plays the devout servant. The story follows an advertising executive's difficult conversion.

He has many problems to preoccupy him: business reversals and a son who appears to be dying. His wife attends Graham's crusade at Madison Square Garden. When she makes a public confession of her new faith to her husband and some friends, he scornfully responds with a sarcastic headline: "Adman's Wife Hits Sawdust Trail!"

But fortune now begins to turn the family around. The husband receives an important account and his son survives the ordeal of an operation—after fervent prayers by everyone. Still, the father feels dead inside. He goes to work drunk, and then slips out for more to a bar where the television set is tuned to the Billy Graham crusade. Watching Graham preach, the father finally experiences a new openness to Christ and he returns home to tell his wife of his new joy.[65]

None of these films presents a very convincing portrayal, but they are documents that suggest the importance to Graham and his organization of the need for depicting male conversion. The psychological and emotional progression pictured in these films reflects the understanding of the organization itself as to how the process worked. First, women appear far easier to convert, usually in direct response to Graham. Men, however, resist, and in a variety of ways, usually bound up in their sense of masculine pride and reticence. They gradually relent, however, generally through the example of a woman compounded by the threat of a tragic event that focuses their minds on mortality. The actual conversion does not usually take place at the Graham crusade itself, thus suggesting the difficulty of persuading men to attend. And finally, the moment of conversion (sometimes stimulated through some other medium) is so carefully controlled, with the emotion muted to a whisper, that the change is almost imperceptible. The inrushing joy and transformation are difficult to detect even if the convert actually declares his elation. In this regard, all of these films failed to illustrate their dramatic point. But in another sense they achieved their goal by depicting Graham as the model of the converted male. The crusader himself exhibited the vibrant and charismatic vision of healthy Christian manhood. His personal example answered the questions about gender that his ministry raised. He was both masculine and controlled, as well as emotional, warning of damnation, and yet gently inviting the most hardened hearts to accept Christ: to kneel in their hearts and stand straight as men before other men.

It was possible for Graham to play this role partly because the social mores and political values he espoused lay close to the mainstream of American politics. Conservative as he was on issues like family structure, gender roles, and anti-Communism, and a somewhat timid supporter of integration, Graham occupied a central place in American culture, one symbol of which was his friendship with the Eisenhowers and Nixons. This notoriety was not just the result of puffery from Hearst. Graham was a genuinely important public figure in his own right. Like Norman Vincent Peale, as well as Alfred Kinsey, he received thousands of letters asking him for advice, some of it about love and marital problems. As he told Dorothy Kilgallen for the *New York Journal-American* in 1957, "I didn't realize until I saw all those letters how much of a problem sex is to millions of people."[66] Perhaps he did not, but the Graham crusade, from almost the beginning, did recognize the gender difficulties at the center of evangelical Protestantism. Graham's view of masculinity was, if anything, unremarkable. Yet he realized that the forms of manliness with which he was most familiar could also retard the acceptance of faith. As it turned out, Graham himself proved to be the most convincing example of converted masculinity, and his personal story remained the most persuasive illustration he could relate.

7

The Ozzie Show: Learning Companionate Fatherhood

Ozzie: You're probably too young to grasp this but . . . a man's home is his castle, and the husband and father is the Master of the house. In other words, I'm the boss around here.
Ricky: I know you are, pop.
Ozzie: You do? How did you know?
Ricky: Mom *said* you were the boss . . . and what mom says, goes.
—*The Adventures of Ozzie and Harriet* radio show, 1950

Like all of the men in this study, Ozzie Nelson possessed a fictitious public figure; he was a character of the imagination known only (or best) through the images projected through his weekly radio and television programs. The real Ozzie Nelson remained an elusive private person, who attempted to establish a continuous identity between private and public life, to seem, as it were, to be the same Ozzie at home as on the production set. In this, he was aided and abetted by family members Harriet, Ricky, and David, who also played their fictitious selves on the show. As with several other characters in early television sitcoms, such as Lucille Ball, and to a lesser extent Hollywood screen stars who carefully nurtured the roles they played, these continuities between the projected self and the private person were encouraged through publicity agents, press releases, and interviews. As the *Christian Science Monitor* commented in 1953, a year after the show made its transition to television, "Those who watch the 'Adventures of Ozzie and Harriet' on the television screen or hear their voices on radio, see or hear them exactly as they are at home."[1] Widely held family virtues publicly bridged the gap between fiction and reality. Depicting the Nelsons gathered around the dinner table in gentle repartee or settling the slight misadventures of each family member through compromise, the show had already earned several awards, including the National

Association for Better Radio and Television designation Best Family Situation Comedy. In the same year, Harriet was chosen "Hollywood Mother of the Year"—an award that cited her qualities off and on the screen. Or as *Time* magazine put it, "On and off the air, the Nelsons are Mr. and Mrs. Average Family." And the penchant of Nelson for amateurism in the choice of actors and performance, including his own, only increased the impression of verisimilitude and normality.

Well after the show terminated, Ozzie carried forward this mythology in his autobiography, stressing the continuities between the normal life of his family performing before and living beyond the camera. Yet in some respects real life insistently entered the show. At its beginning in 1944 on radio, the broadcast reflected Ozzie's earlier career as bandleader with Harriet as vocalist. But the program quickly shifted away from this show business emphasis to focus on the home. The family orientation became even stronger when Ricky and David began to play themselves in the early days of the radio series. Whatever traces of Ozzie's stage occupation remained—and it was never clear on the show what he actually did when he left home—occurred offstage. Most evidence of vaudeville and music performance disappeared until they came back into focus, reborn in Ricky's later career as a rock musician.

After signing a ten-year option with the American Broadcasting Company in 1949 for a television version of their success, the Nelsons made a Hollywood film in 1951, *Here Come the Nelsons*, to promote their coming appearance in the new visual medium. The transition from one medium to another did not occur abruptly, however. For two years, between 1952 and 1954, the radio and television versions overlapped. But, gradually thereafter, the television show changed the initial premise. In the beginning, each week's misadventures were instigated by Ozzie, although the boys frequently were the subject of an episode. After 1957, however, and Ricky's initial appearance playing the guitar and singing, the show shifted again and began to emphasize the boys even more. As Ricky became a rock star, first as a cover artist doing such numbers as Fats Domino's "I'm Walkin'" and then more independent songs, the show scrambled to keep up with other changes in the boys' lives: David's marriage, for example. Eventually, the series succumbed to shifts in audience taste, and 1965–1966 became the last season of a formula that had lasted a generation.[2]

Nostalgic vision and assumptions of normality structured this account of a family whose transparent ordinariness was its major performance value. As the principal writer for most of the *Adventures* scripts, Ozzie clearly dramatized his own idealized and selective sense of the past. Growing up in Ridgefield Park near New Brunswick, New Jersey, Ozzie remembered the spot as a Brigadoon, a town inscribed in the past and lighted by his own happy memories: "It was a charming little community," he wrote, "the kind that, unfortunately, seems to have passed from the American scene." The details he invokes to describe this idyllic past include the Hackensack River with its boating, swimming, and skating, the movie and opera house, Palisades Amusement Park, and "churches of every denomination and a Boy Scout troop in every church."[3] In reality, however, even in this idealized world, Ozzie was different from most other young men. At the age of five or six, he had already become a performer, appearing in minstrel shows. This difference was accentuated when he went on to college, earning varsity letters in football. In 1929 he entered New Jersey Law School. Clearly trying out a number of professions at this time, he also organized a band with himself as the lead singer. This group resembled other popular jazz ensembles, such as Paul Whiteman and Eddie Duchin, that played on the national circuit and appeared on the radio. In 1931, he hired Harriet Hilliard to sing with the band, and then, in 1935, they married. By the mid-1930s, the Nelsons were appearing on their own variety radio show, but this format was dropped in the 1940s when the couple created their new family comedy of manners. As Peter Kaplan wrote in 1986 of the modern radio and television fathers, "They began with Ozzie." Before him, it was "all gags."[4]

In an earlier *Esquire* article, Hollywood writer Sara Davidson had explored the contrast between the fictional and real Nelsons. "Happy, happy, happy," they were portrayed on the weekly show, but actually, she writes, the family had its share of difficulties. As son David explained, the two versions of domestic reality were completely different: "totally separate. One was real and one wasn't." The character of Ozzie differed most. Instead of the awkward, kindly, and gentle universal Dad, Ozzie, the director and writer, was disciplined and driven, a dynamo of energy, activity, and a critical disciplinarian of his two sons. Unlike his bumbling television persona, the performer had always been an overachiever, earning plaudits, awards, and honors at college (including head of student council, captain of the debating team, president of his fraternity). Appropriately, he was also an avid reader of Horatio Alger success literature, an ideology that he adapted to the series.[5]

Davidson explains the discrepancy between this active personality and the gentle character Ozzie created as a bow to the necessity for the "show to be comedic." This is certainly a plausible argument, but there is undoubtedly much more in this portrayal than the inevitable easy laugh at the expense of an embarrassed authority figure. Given the consistency of tone throughout the series and Ozzie's visible hand in writing and directing, it makes sense to look deeper for the reasons that Ozzie chose to play the opposite of himself.

For many commentators, then and now, the Nelsons are the principal (perhaps the most notorious) example of the 1950s television situation comedy family. The *Ozzie and Harriet* show has generally been understood in terms of three interlocking notions: an illustration of the emerging American suburban comedy of manners; a show structured by the demands of the situation comedy genre itself; and an illustration of the conservative gender politics of postwar society. It is, certainly, all of these things. Writing (ironically) of the "ladies of the evening," Diana Meeham, for example, suggests that most situation comedy women (Lucy, Harriet, June Cleaver, et al.), portrayed the same general character—"a woman with a smile on her face and a trick up her sleeve, who is submissive yet controlling." Most were married; most worked only as housewives. And if this picture of femininity constituted nostalgia for invented memories of easier times, it was because, she wrote, of the very real and unpleasant presence of social dislocation and cold war fears.[6]

Entirely consistent with this interpretation of Ozzie's show is David Halberstam's biting assessment of the television portrayals of the 1950s. TV "dads," he wrote, headed intact families of women and children that never suffered from divorce, disease, or alcoholism. "Dads were," he summed up, "good dads, whose worst sin was that they did not know their way around the house and could not find common household objects or that they were prone to give lectures about how much tougher things had been when they were boys."[7]

But Halberstam scratches his head in puzzlement at the popularity and longevity of *The Adventures of Ozzie and Harriet*. The show reflected a typical 1950s division of labor with male prerogative always protected and enhanced, if never actually practiced or put into operation. Ideologically, he continues, it presented mundane lives to millions of unhappy or uncertain viewers about a fictional world where nothing more could be expected from each character than to play his or her circumscribed role. In the end, everything would be resolved for the best. But, he concludes, the most important element of the show remained unstated: the growing tension between the offstage Ozzie and the rock star Ricky. Benign generational differences on the television version masked Ozzie's failure to sympathize with his real-life son and the career he was creating for himself.

The result, concludes Halberstam, was a manipulative father, forcing a fictional role onto a son he did not understand. In reality the Nelsons were a "dysfunctional family."[8]

Although Halberstam writes more fluidly and dramatically than most of the critics who have followed this vein of interpretation, his tone of irony suits the purpose he shares with others: to diminish, mock, or simply reject the middle-class portraiture that framed the Nelsons' show. He does not take the program seriously except to consider what it seems to deny. Whether or not the two Nelson families were continuous—even if every member took his or her scripts to be a public relations view of reality—the whole characterization remained, he argued, unrepresentative of the ordinary American family. And that seems to be the larger point: that much of the popular culture of the 1950s simply reinforced a kind a false consciousness (mystiques of various sorts), while reality gasped for expression, sealed inside the cookie jar of middle-class virtue. In some respects this is also the point of Lynn Spigel's interesting assessment of postwar television families. In her analysis, Ozzie represents a "prime abuser of the masculine ideal." Television, she writes, disrupted and changed older social values, performing a therapeutic function for troubling problems of 1950s gender roles. In the self-conscious family dramas, the show "dramatized the artifice of gender roles in postwar life."[9]

But looking at the show through the lens of genre, this critical emphasis on the middle-class, suburban world begins to take a somewhat different shape. Giving priority to genre suggests that various forms of artistic creation, in various subcategories of novels, films, and radio and television programs, can be understood by paying attention to the informal rules of their production and the stock characters that people them. Of course, the fit between the rules of a particular genre and an individual show is never perfect. But it should be understood that these rules, arbitrary as they might seem, are markers created by repetition that make any given type identifiable and comprehensible. From such a perspective, *The Adventures of Ozzie and Harriet* was an endeavor that both helped create, and then exemplified, the situation comedy, or more precisely, the television comedy of domestic manners and its exploration of gender roles.

Situation comedies appeared early in television history, borrowing most of their premises from radio shows and films. Television was initially an instrument of domestic entertainment, aimed at the family audience, unlike other forms of culture, like film, that were at that time increasingly produced for more segmented audiences of age groups, gender, and education. On television the situation was often the family itself. In this sense, the audience could see an enhanced version of itself reflected in this genre. Reflected in the vanity mirror of broadcast, the ordinary viewing family could see the contours of its own life (just as the Nelsons did) presented through an idealized mode of drama.

Although the circumstances of television sitcoms vary widely, from the marriage of a talented but maladroit housewife and her Cuban entertainer husband (*I Love Lucy*), to a man married to a witch (*Bewitched*), to millionaire hillbillies (*The Beverly Hillbillies*), the weekly programs generally followed the same dramatic cycle: the introduction of some misunderstanding inherent in the circumstance itself; then exploration of the humorous possibilities of the resulting confusion, and finally a temporary resolution which restores the inherent disequilibrium of the original situation. Because characters and situations never changed, the formula remained basically unaltered and could continue indefinitely.[10]

The *Adventures of Ozzie and Harriet* certainly followed most of the rules of the domestic situation comedy. Each member of the family played himself or herself according to an established pattern. At the same time, the boys aged visibly, which meant that the subjects shifted in nature and emphasis. Yet Ozzie's firm artistic control over the show imposed a remarkable consistency on the production, week to week and year to year. While events centered upon evolving domestic problems based upon the aging of the boys, there was one element of the situation that never really altered: the personality of Ozzie.

But what was the essential situation for Ozzie and Harriet? It is in answer to this question that gender issues become most suggestive. Quite rightly, historians have paid considerable attention to gender types represented in situation comedies of the 1950s. Mothers who never worked, who remained at home and offstage until needed with a ready smile and a quick word of advice, who ceded, or pretended to give in, to the wise or (more likely) unwise rule of their husbands, pretty much described the benighted characters of June Cleaver and Harriet Nelson. As Gerard Jones in his perceptive book on American sitcoms writes, television shows reflected the nature of the medium itself and its commercial purposes. They portrayed a new world of suburban consumption and depicted as their subject an idealized, bland, happy family upset only by minor adjustments. The implied relationship between the watched family and the family watching was, he contends, a complex one, anchored in mainstream politics (or no politics), an ethic of consumption, and the notion that television offered a palliative to minor problems. In other words, television itself, for the family watching family drama, could be therapeutic.[11] *Ozzie and Harriet* was not the first situation comedy, representing only one of many radio programs that made the transition to early television, but it established a much-copied tone and style. There were other prototypes, such as *I Remember Mama*, which began in 1949, or show business comedies like the *George Burns and Gracie Allen Show*. But *Ozzie and Harriet* became the exemplary nuclear family show, a drama in which the very ordinariness of their world constituted the situation.

As Jones suggests, this created a situation in which Ozzie himself became a potent gender type. "With sly self-parody," he notes, "Ozzie helped American men chuckle at their retreat from heroic maleness." This, he contends, is just part of the larger exploration of masculinity in 1950s situation comedies as Ozzie, Desi Arnaz, and Ralph Kramden (of *The Honeymooners*) struggled to preserve the prerogatives and dominion they believed were their own. As Jones concludes, in many of these productions, when the domestic harmony is threatened, when a character threatens the coherence and stability of the group, the father or husband steps in to correct the situation.[12] Except—it should be said—in the case of Ozzie.

There are many ways to view the gender relations in situation comedies. For example, Mary Beth Haralovich notices that even the architecture and designated spaces inside the TV home reflected the gender roles of model parent and child. In this domestic "architecture of gender," the suburban garage took on special meaning as a particularly male preserve, with tools and other visible signs of the do-it-yourself Dad. Kitchens, on the other hand, were redesigned to contain spaces for elaborate labor-saving devices, transforming the room into a production center for Moms to prepare food and launch housework. Such gendered designations in the television blueprint even spilled over into the actual design of homes built during the decade, making them more compatible with the increased possibilities for consumption modeled by the TV family. In the end, television projected a vision of American life into the home that could easily be emulated, in part at least, in those places in society that already resembled the ideal: in neighborhoods untouched "by heterogeneity of class, race, ethnicity, and age."[13]

Given its longevity, *The Adventures of Ozzie and Harriet* must be approached in segments, divided into three periods: from the inception of the radio show to 1952 when the first television season began; the second period from 1952 to around 1957, after which some of the secondary actors left the show; and the third, when episodes more and more focused on Ricky's music career and David's college life. As Tinky Weisblatt perceptively notes, the principal continuity in the show is Ozzie himself, who neither changes much, nor matures even while his sons manage to grow up. She also quite rightly points to the problematic function of Ozzie: his discomfort at being home and his burdensome "everyman role," trying to live in a woman's domain and yet retain a strong masculine identity. As she concludes, *Ozzie, I Love Lucy,* and the *Burns and Allen Show* actually played against the grain of assumed middle-class character during the 1950s, even if most critics then, and even later, missed the subtlety.[14]

In an extensive exploration of the TV situation comedy, Nina Leibman compared television dramas and contemporary films. While her purpose was to demonstrate their similar thematic orientations, she set up some interesting definitions and categories that apply particularly to the Nelsons and similar comedies. Foremost among these ideas is the consistent focus on the family as the site of problems as well as resolutions, the centrality of the father figure in providing the narrative center, and the sudden reversal resolving a misunderstanding that has given rise to the dramatic disruption. As she writes, "For television, each weekly episode opens with the family seemingly at peace but immediately troubled by an internal or external threat." The elimination of that irritation provides an opportunity for moral instruction and the temporary restoration of order.[15]

While Leibman is genuinely perceptive in her depiction of Harriet as a stereotypical television housewife, always at the ready with a cookie tray, she misses the extent of her ironic intervention into the misadventures of the family. As for Ozzie, she portrays him as typical of television husbands, presiding over discipline and liberal child-rearing practices, discoursing on the values of male dominance in the household. She concludes that in the show there were "no discussions of what it means to be male, or what constitutes a boy's proper behavior or identity." In fact, however, this judgment appears to be a serious misreading of both radio and television versions. It may be true that in Darrell Hamamoto's scheme of father figures (ranging from gentle patriarch to bumbling pal) Ozzie lists toward bungling. But that comic incompetence has a very serious intent.[16]

Much of this critical work on the ideological grounding, genre, and gender politics of *The Adventures of Ozzie and Harriet* suggests the relevance of the series to pictures of middle-class America and, particularly, middle-class fathers in the 1950s. At the same time, to understand this centrality, it is necessary to step beyond much of this interpretation. In the first place, it is clear that the main interest of the show is not Harriet, who is present primarily to feed Ozzie enough rope to disrupt the family situation and then gently pull him back. She is the chorus of domestic virtues, a symphony of clichés who nonetheless conducts the mayhem. Ozzie is, of course, the presumed patriarch. But he spends no time at work and never brings his job or finances home except in terms of family economy: allowances, expenditures, and his rhapsodies on themes by Horatio Alger. In this sense, Ozzie is the very opposite of the inner-directed individual praised by the public intellectuals who criticized Momism, corporate peer culture, conformity, and togetherness. In fact he is more like the pitiable embodiment of the enemy. Recite the virtues of Ben Franklin though he might, he spends his life learning the values of conformity and getting along. He tries to be other-directed by adhering to the rules of inner-direction, and herein lies the comic incongruity. With no real life beyond the family, except release time spent with pals playing poker or bowling (always at Harriet's sufferance), his is entirely a domestic world. Most important, this is where he wants to be, if only he can learn how.

While the television Nelsons clearly live a lifestyle far more flush than the American norm of the 1950s and lack any serious problems, this unreality defines a dream that many men were trying to live in the postwar world. The comedy evoked by Ozzie's capers was not just a function of genre but, rather, a comic vision of a national adjustment to male domesticity and companionate marriage. The humor and confusion erupt because Ozzie cannot master the role and sometimes tries to rebel against it. Thus the "situation" defines Ozzie's efforts to find a place in a world made up of women and children. Playing along with the contradiction between patriarchy and a female-dominated domesticity, Ozzie, in his weekly encounters, learns the same lesson twice and then again: the value of compromise and the wisdom of women and children. Ozzie is a marginal man, set in a world of other-directed values, a man who protests briefly, but really only wants to warm his feet by the embers of conformity. In this respect, the *Ozzie* show explores the essential issues of the new lifestyles of affluent, middle-class American men who chose to make the home their principal commitment. In fact, each week added a page to the primer of problems inherent in that emerging world. Thus the *Ozzie* show confronted the social problems of family transformation in the 1950s and especially the unresolved tensions between possible versions of masculinity. And in its dramatic vignettes, the series deployed gender to explore many of the problems of mass culture, suburban lifestyles, and consumption that preoccupied elite commentators. In this respect, it was often a satiric commentary on the most serious public discourse of the age.

This made continuity itself one of the most important elements of the show. The family, the set, the "adventures" were remarkably consistent and repetitious. Furthermore, episodes were repeated and updated from radio to television, lending regularity—and even stasis—to the series. In fact, this consistency preserved the character types established when the radio show began. That early radio shows could easily be recast for television suggests that the frozen formula accounted at least in part for their attractiveness. Repetition, it seems, became reality, and Ozzie was reluctant to abandon a blueprint that worked.

The radio version of *The Adventures of Ozzie and Harriet* established a pattern of plot structures, subjects, and resolutions that remained typical of the program throughout the first decade or so. And even as the production focused more and more on the boys and their problems as teenagers, the original persona of each character remained constant, even as that character aged. Even when attention shifted to the boys as they grew up, Ozzie remained the usual instigator of most of the plots and his exploration of manhood the center of the show.

Ozzie played the role of keeper and dispenser of platitudes about gender, marriage, masculinity, and child rearing. On each of these subjects he had much to say and even more to learn, although the lessons never stuck. Lacking any short-term memory for such schooling, he inevitably repeats his error in the next episode. Understanding almost nothing of the real world (that is, Harriet's domestic world) in which he seeks to live as a good citizen, he discovers over and over again that patriarchy and male dominance are dysfunctional values. The only time such ideas have any relevance is when Harriet and the boys allow Ozzie to think they matter.

The plotline in countless shows repeats this comic formula. Early on, Ozzie triggers a misunderstanding and sets misrule into motion by declaring the virtues of male supremacy, the wisdom of the patriarchal past, the virtues of high culture, the platitudes of Horatio Alger, and the wisdom of a gendered division of labor in marriage, only to discover that these maxims have little practical virtue. In fact it is remarkable how many of the strident assertions about 1950s masculinity expressed by critics of conformity, mass culture, and consumption are undercut by Ozzie's willingness to explore a new masculine domesticity as he wavers between inner- and other-direction.

These gentle lessons are administered in the quiet atmosphere of a household where kindness and affection, not force and order, prevail. Listening to or watching the *Adventures* iterated the importance of proper domestic relationships and gender identities. Each show moved from harmony to disruption and then back again. If this "situation" seems unreal in the dreary world of cold war, unemployment, McCarthyism, civil rights agitation, poverty, divorce, and juvenile delinquency, it only served to enhance the importance of family relationships as an alternative to that world. It was Ozzie's genius as creator and scriptwriter for the show to understand that he could not, in fact, simply allow his family to play themselves or rehearse real family squabbles before a national audience. Instead, he reversed the nature of things, making the characters the basis for his real family, and the fictional Nelsons into an idealized and humorous version of his understanding of American aspirations. The flexibility of this format allowed the show to engage many of the contentious cultural issues of the day. Frequently this meant that masculinity was both the subject and means of exploration.

One of the consistently exploited story lines of the early programs dramatized Ozzie's penchant to ascribe masculinity to an imaginary past of gruff fathers, hard work, and patriarchy, a world of men visibly in command. In the 1945 radio presentation "The Mustache," Ozzie listens gullibly to his barber pontificate on facial hair as a symbol of power. As the story line puts it,[17] "In the old days the father of the house had a beard and mustache. With such an appearance one could hardly help but have the respect of everyone in the family. A nice little mustache would give Ozzie dignity and maturity, and make him look more commanding, possibly just a little frightening."[18] Unbeknownst to Ozzie, Harriet's mother has suggested that the family try to make Ozzie "feel he's the master of the house." Thus, when Ozzie appears in a mustache, the boys address him as "Sir." Facial hair seems to have worked a miracle. But then the experiment begins to unravel. Harriet hears of a survey indicating that 85 percent of all women find a mustache attractive, even "devastating." And the boys "respect" him so much they won't ask him to play baseball. The next evening, looking in the mirror, Ozzie discovers that he has only half a mustache. The boys then confess that they hadn't noticed it anyway. Wondering how only half of his upper lip sprouted hair, Ozzie realizes that during the night, Harriet has secretly shaved the rest in fear that it would make him too attractive.[19]

This plot turns on Ozzie's mistaken belief that traditional masculine appearance will earn him the respect he feels he deserves. Of course it does no such thing, for the boys can't even detect the mustache. It does, however, threaten to disrupt the Nelson marriage, until Harriet attacks with a safety razor, ending Ozzie's claims to traditional male prerogatives. If he wishes to please Harriet and remain a happy, domesticated husband, he will have to forego such traditional symbols of patriarchy. It is the family group itself, not some idealized past, which decides the rules of gender appearance and behavior.

In another show, "The Manicure," broadcast in the fifth radio season, Ozzie explores the possibilities of androgyny. Musing on Harriet's discussion of makeup bargains and beauty treatments, Ozzie allows his barber to do a steam shampoo, manicure, and massage. As the barber makes his pitch, he tries to masculinize what seems patently effeminate: "A lot of fellas come into the shop and they know what they'd like, but they get embarrassed (chuckles). They think a guy's a sissy if he asks for a manicure. Imagine that?" Duly persuaded, and then primped and powdered, Ozzie returns home a changed man. He declines a football game with David and hurries off to buy a new sport coat. Harriet, however, sees a completely different implication–not that he is feminized, but that he has become even more masculine. She worries that he is looking for romance elsewhere. So they both agree that he should return to being "the disheveled—the unromantic type."[20]

In a somewhat later show, Ozzie becomes preoccupied with male physique and strength. In part, he is responding to a Charles Atlas ad—the sort of commercial that filled the inside covers of contemporary men's magazines and comic books. David, thinking that this is the route to successful romance, has begun a weight-training regime in the garage (a clearly demarcated male space). David shows Ozzie the book he has purchased. Can you imagine this, he says, "This guy used to be a fifty pound weakling?" Ozzie admits that he has seen such advertisements and envies the "terrific physique." After he nearly collapses helping his neighbor Thorny carry some packages, Ozzie decides to join David in his self-improvement program. The two decide to eat "yogurt and other nauseating items," and follow a routine of intense workouts. But David and Ozzie start to drag about, and so Harriet decides to put an end to the experiment. She tells David that his father is exhausted and Ozzie that David is worn-out and listless. Each insists he wants to continue but will sacrifice for the health of the other. It turns out that both Ozzie and David have been cheating: chocolate cake and cookies have corrupted their healthy diets. Finally, both agree to stop, "if it's going to worry Mom."[21]

Once again, in establishing the norm of masculine behavior, it is Harriet who sets the parameters. David and Ozzie are seduced by two ideas, that a toned physique will attract girls (David) and that standards of maleness are represented by the likes of Charles Atlas (Ozzie). But both are wrong. The fickle girl David tried to impress decides she likes musicians, not bodybuilders, and Harriet decides for Ozzie that health food and exercise are too much for him.

If approved male appearance was often at stake in the radio show, so were masculinity's psychological, moral, and behavioral attributes.

Although Ozzie and Harriet both proclaim extreme versions of traditional male and female virtues and declare a clearly demarcated sexual division of labor in the household, both claims prove to be highly problematic. In fact, Ozzie fails miserably at almost every masculine endeavor he attempts: physical prowess, business acumen, sports, and do-it-yourself projects around the house. Especially in the early shows, up to 1952 or 1953 and the television debut, most of these gender contests concerned Harriet, as both members of the couple vied to define their roles in the family. Increasingly, as the boys become more mature and central to the show, Ozzie's contested masculinity is played out in the arena of child rearing or in direct competition with his children. Here, too, his wistful patriarchy clashes with the reality of modern family democracy, and in most cases, he himself learns the lessons of life that he pompously sought to impart to David and Ricky. As the show evolved, Ozzie's masculinity was first tested as husband, and then, as father.

One of the most extraordinary scripts from the early radio period is "The Knitting Contest," broadcast on January 2, 1949. In this test of male superiority, Ozzie challenges Harriet to a knitting contest: "What greater proof of male superiority than to beat Harriet at her own game?" reads the story line of the show. Both bend to their task of knitting a pair of socks, and the needles fly. While Ozzie's nimble stitches gather, his friends Thorny and Verne enter. As Verne says with heavy irony, "See that man? The one so seriously engrossed in the work before him. That's Ozzie Nelson, one time holder of the title 'man.' At present he is engaged in a bitter struggle . . . the struggle of a man determined to maintain his dignity and to preserve his rightful place as head of the household."[22]

Ozzie responds, "Knit one . . . pearl one."

This wry assault on Ozzie's masculinity, however, is not the point of the episode. There is no pondering whether a man should knit or not, but whether he could or should be better at it than his wife. Performing a decidedly feminine task did not cast doubts on his manhood. But, if he outperformed Harriet, that would challenge her prerogatives. Inevitably, the resolution of this drama took a surprising turn when Ricky and David convince Ozzie that winning will embarrass their mother. So that night, Ozzie sneaks downstairs and finishes Harriet's knitting. In the morning when the family gathers, they discover that both socks are finished: "Each one wanted the other to win and each finished the other's sock."[23] Harriet tearfully thanks Ozzie for his gesture and the program ends. Left unremarked, however, was Harriet's effort to save Ozzie's pride by finishing his work and trying to let him win. So the result was a tie, and domestic tranquility was restored and Ozzie could continue to believe in male superiority in the face of contrary evidence.

One of the most common plot lines stages a contest between genders where Harriet and Ozzie exchange family roles. In "Career Woman," recorded in August 1952, and rewritten for television in 1955, Harriet rebels against being a housewife. Impressed by a lecture she and Ozzie have attended about the virtues of a career, Harriet decides that her life is narrow and meaningless. Upset at the thought, Ozzie urges Harriet to follow her "husband instinct." Later, he dismisses the lecturer as a "glamorous looking gal with a lot of silly ideas about careers for women."[24]

But Harriet is unreconciled and the next morning at breakfast she laments her wasted potential. Ozzie reassures her that her real career is at home not in some office. And then, as if on cue, each family member demonstrates how he relies on her. David can't find his sweater until Harriet tells him where he put it; Ricky forgets where his lunchbox is, until Harriet deduces that he left it at school. And, when Ozzie starts to leave for work, he cannot remember his most important task for the day. Harriet reminds him to take some papers to the insurance office. As he leaves, Ozzie gives a speech on the qualities of a good businessman. He brags, "Being in the business world calls for years of special experience and background . . . a mind trained for details." Of course he has to ask Harriet to find the papers . . . and the car keys. As he leaves, Ozzie says, "Get that look off your face. One business man is enough in the family."[25]

But is it? At this point, the plot takes an expected twist. Harriet discovers that Ozzie has forgotten the papers after all and rushes to deliver them to the insurance company. The secretary greets her and asks if she will mind the phones while she gets a cup of coffee. Harriet agrees, but just then Ozzie walks in and assumes she has taken a job (although a decidedly female one). He returns home, deeply depressed, but vows not to stand in her way, "even if it means losing his own identity, and he sighs, 'Mr. Harriet Nelson.'" That evening as the family gathers for dinner, the doorbell rings. The husband of the career lecturer introduces himself as "Mr. *Pamela* St. John." "A meek, crushed little man," he complains of his unimportance compared to his wife. But Harriet quickly realizes that Ozzie has hired the man to portray his own worst nightmare. In the end, Harriet admits she never had any intention of getting a job.[26]

The 1955 television version of this plot took advantage of the plasticity of the new medium to expand on the absurdity of Ozzie's bruised masculinity. In a new dream montage, Ozzie imagines himself the new Mr. *Harriet* Nelson. Harriet becomes president of a corporation and he stands aside as "the forgotten man." When they go duck hunting together, he retrieves. Finally, he wakes during a frightening sequence about big game hunting in which he is Harriet's gun bearer.[27]

The ideology of separate gender spheres made this and similar episodes possible. Harriet is tempted by a career but reveals her satisfaction with home work. Yet the comedy also plays against this ideology. In the first half of "Career Woman," Ozzie fails by his own definition to fulfill the demands of a career. He has no talent for remembering crucial details and is lost without Harriet. In fact, he warns her that a family should have only one businessman—because he couldn't compete against her. The second half of the episode only compounds Ozzie's insecurity. Unsure of himself, he imagines that he has become an inconsequential appendage of Harriet. Only a joke, perhaps, this specter of incompetence and underlying gender equality underscores the fragility of Ozzie's identity, his dependence upon others for definition.

In the end, of course, Harriet remains a housewife by choice and Ozzie is still the businessman by default. There is no plea to change this "situation." But it is also clear, in the new world of the domestic sitcom, that Ozzie can't be an independent and self-contained breadwinner. He needs Harriet even to fulfill this erstwhile masculine role. And as demonstrated by the end of the episode, there is the humorous suggestion that she is the one who allows this division of labor to continue.

The most remarkable tale of gender reversal came in the show "Aptitudes: Male vs. Female," broadcast on radio in November 1951. In this episode, Ozzie, as usual, procrastinates about fixing things around the house, failing to repair a table and a dripping faucet. These are men's jobs, but Ozzie still finds ways to avoid doing them. When Harriet hurts her fingers trying to put up an automatic can opener, Ozzie reminds her that she shouldn't try to "tackle a man's job." Harriet seems to agree, until David brings her a book detailing home repairs with easy instructions, something she likens to following recipes in a cookbook. She is intrigued and easily fixes the can opener. Henceforth, she announces, she will undertake all the home repairs.[28]

This suits everyone but Ozzie. As he explains to neighbor, Thorny, "it is a little embarrassing to have your wife take over such obviously masculine duties." So Ozzie jumps at the suggestion that he beat Harriet at her own game. He volunteers to assume her jobs if she does his. The next scene is the inevitable sitcom nightmare. Ozzie starts to bake a chocolate cake but makes an enormous mess instead. That night, Ozzie and Harriet compare accomplishments. All of the home repairs are finished, and Harriet is waiting for a bite of Ozzie's cake. Just then the doorbell rings and a man delivers the cake ordered by Ozzie. His own effort, he admits, resulted in "a horrible sludge." But he maintains his larger point: at least "the baker who whipped up the delightful three-layer job in front of them was a man (or at least passing)." Harriet also has a confession. She repaired the can opener but hired someone for all the other tasks. At that point the doorbell rings again and Ozzie answers it. It's Joe from Joe's Fix-It Shop.[29]

"You're Joe?" gasps Ozzie in shock.

"Well," answers the woman, "my real name's Josephine, but everyone just calls me Joe. I've got a lamp here for the missus."

Ozzie's confusion is complete when Joe mentions her business partner, "Charlie." Harriet then chides him for believing that women possess no mechanical skills. "This whole thing is getting very involved and confusing," concludes Ozzie. So Harriet decides that things should return to normal: she will cook and clean and he will do the home repairs. As the show ends, Ozzie is trying to evade washing the windows.[30]

This episode of gender reversals and unexpected masquerades temporarily suspends the roles of husbands and wives. But in the end, the couple fall back into their expected characters. Along the way, they have disrupted every form of gender stability. In the end, it is women's mechanical abilities that have been validated. While Ozzie would like to believe in a strict division of labor, he is mystified by Harriet and by Joe and her partner, Charlie. To compound the problem, the audience knows that he will fail at his next handyman task.

A number of shows raised the problem of masculine emulation—of what I have elsewhere called spectator masculinity. Given the widespread contemporary fascination with historical, sports, and celebrity male roles, the series probed the comic possibilities of comparing Ozzie to one of these heroes: the average man's perilous effort to enact modern heroism. It explored practical ways for ordinary men and boys to relate to accepted models of masculinity and it provided a commentary on the operation of spectator masculinity. In "The Hero Worshippers" for the fifth radio season, Harriet persuades David and Ricky to take an interest in the great men of American history: Edison, Lincoln, and Washington. Ozzie agrees with the choice and extols their virtues. But he is embarrassed when Ricky and David ask the obvious questions: "Are you like them?" "Was Lincoln smarter than you, Pop?" "If Edison only slept two hours a night, how come you sleep ten?" "What did you ever invent, Pop?" As the show progresses, Ozzie's stature sinks further, and he desperately seeks to reinvent himself as a hero. He despondently goes to the backyard and begins to chop wood.

Then, at the suggestion of his neighbor, Thorny, he decides to act, to prove himself "an even better man than these Titans of history."[31]

The project he chooses is to build an intricate model airplane for the boys. He retreats to the garage and labors without success, but finally dumps the incomplete contraption in the boys' room: "At least let the boys know their father for what he is—a clumsy old blunderer." The next day he sadly confesses his failure to Harriet. But the boys rush in to praise the wonderful "kite" he had constructed. Even Ben Franklin hadn't done better. What's more, Ozzie chopped wood like Lincoln and worked through the night like Thomas Edison.[32]

This translation of fictional and historic manliness into domestic masculinity demonstrated how emulation might work in the modern, suburban world. Ozzie cannot hope to be the hero his sons admire in their reading, any more than the average man of the Progressive Era could be Teddy Roosevelt or Tarzan. Yet the episode demonstrates how some sort of approximation might work. Ozzie is not remotely the equal of Lincoln or Edison or Franklin. But he can be a heroic player on his own narrow stage, performing for the family and his neighbors by acting in small ways reminiscent of these great figures. Indeed, it is his having tried that measures success. Ricky and David's pride in him is mistaken, but his masculinity remains intact—despite what the audience knows of its fragility.

Another much-exploited comic exploration of gender roles poses the question of decision making in the family. Like Walter Mitty, James Thurber's beaten-down hero, Ozzie and his friends often try unsuccessfully to rebel against the gentle oligarchy of their wives. Of course Harriet understands this problem and generally allows Ozzie to believe that he is making the decisions—at least those she intends him to make. A typical example of this plot is "Husband's Night," created for the 1949–1950 season. In this episode Ozzie and neighbor Thorny try to evade attending the Woman's Club square-dance dinner, for which they have been corralled into doing the dishes. They first make a pact to refuse, but Thorny's resistance quickly collapses. Harriet then shows Ozzie the western shirt she wants him to wear, and mentions the "cute little apron" she is making for his dish duty. Alone in his protest, Ozzie tries to organize a bowling match for anyone refusing dish duty. But, "all the neighborhood husbands have been coerced into going to the Woman's Club party—except the lone wolf—the hold-out, Ozzie."[33]

The night of the party, Ozzie relents. But Harriet insists that he keep his promise to Thorny. When Thorny stops by, Ozzie lights up, thinking that his friend's bowling shoes and old slacks mean that he has found some backbone. But, Thorny explains, these are perfect clothes for square dancing. At that point Harriet enters with Ozzie's plaid shirt and a "cute little apron with 'Nellie' on it."[34] Ozzie has reached the bathos of suburban manhood.

There are a number of typical elements in this show. Both sides win: Ozzie makes his point but agrees, finally, to attend the dance. But most interesting in this particular episode is Ozzie's feminization. Not only does he wear the square-dance costume of Harriet's choice, he is perfectly happy to do the dishes sporting his new apron embossed with "Nellie." As in the knitting episode, tasks coded female become interchangeable between the genders. Thus, Ozzie's role as husband is both masculine and androgynous. If to critics of postwar gender relations this status constituted the worst effects of Momism and female tyranny, to Ozzie, it was a small price for marital peace.

This gender ambiguity repeatedly surfaced in conjunction with the cultural problems that critics in the 1950s identified as feminizing: mass culture, suburban lifestyles, and consumption. The most frequent plot device here was the handyman caper. Do-it-yourself projects in the 1950s represented the small acts of heroism performed by frontiersmen on the suburban badlands. Within the bounds of domesticity, house repairs represented the potential free range of male recreation and a place to demonstrate productive skills in a world of consumption. Success at a project might enhance self-esteem: the modern self-made man armed with a host of tools from the local hardware store, a book of instructions, and a project. One self-described expert and leader of the handyman movement made just this claim and invoked the positive virtues of frontier experience in his justification. Working on home projects, he wrote, "helps persuade us to want to share our ideas with the other fellows and persuades him to combine with ours so that we all feel we can accomplish the things and objectives we want." This was the sort of creative thinking, he continued, "which has made us the most powerful nation of all."[35]

Ozzie's satire of the handyman was relentless, in part because of the popularity of home improvement projects during the decade. Although the movement stretched back to the early 1900s, it exploded with the new postwar suburbs. As *Business Week* explained, "This is the Age of do-it-yourself." Well might they argue this point, for one contemporary account of the movement suggested that sixty million Americans were engaged in associated hobbies. While public intellectuals like David Riesman might interpret this as a form of escapism, the movement was complex, with a variety of persons engaged in its different aspects. What linked them, wrote Albert Roland in the *American Quarterly* in 1958, was the psychological effect, for its participants gain "individual identity and satisfaction they don't get from work."[36]

Handyman advice books included complex, dense guides like *The Practical Home Handyman,* which provided detailed descriptions of difficult projects and demanded "the same state of perfection in his work as is attained by most skilled tradesmen." But a far larger part of the movement is typified by the periodical *The Family Handyman,* published through the 1950s and aimed at both men and women. The aim of *Family Handyman* was to promote "togetherness." As the publisher wrote in 1957, the "new word is as important as any in Mr. Webster's big book." "Togetherness" implied a kind of vague equality, and the journal responded with some ambiguities of its own about gender equity. Thus, the magazine ran a series "Keep Your Wife in the Kitchen—and Happy," yet it frequently addressed women specifically (they constituted a large portion of the readership) and pictured them using tools in ads. Many letters to the publisher were from women seeking special advice on projects. And the publishers sporadically included a section for the "handywoman." As one woman wrote in 1953, "Your magazine is invaluable to housewives as well as husbands." Because of its large, mixed readership, the magazine tried to appeal to both men and women, even if, in most commentary on the subject in the 1950s, this was portrayed as a male realm.[37] In the end, however, *The Family Handyman* demonstrated the link between housework and work on the house and the difficulty of sorting it all out gender-wise.

This is the ambiguity that *Ozzie and Harriet* exploited. Show after show revisited the question of home repairs and Ozzie's incompetence as a handyman. For example, in a 1952 radio production entitled "The Ego Builder," Ozzie and Thorny discuss the relative strengths and weaknesses of men and women. Thorny warns Ozzie, before he can deliver his usual sermon on male superiority, that women are actually tougher physically than men. Of course, agrees Ozzie, but not emotionally, he says. Women suffer from a lack of assurance and self-confidence. Just to underscore his point, he cites frequent magazine articles directed at women's insecurities. The subsequent episode revolves around Harriet's activities as a PTA substitute delegate. Ozzie displays his own insecurities when he mistakenly assumes that Harriet has fallen for the school superintendent. But he persists in declaring that women are helpless and lack the drive to get things done. In the end, David enters to ask Ozzie where the toolbox is. "David," he replies, "tell your Mother the tool box is right where she left it last week after she fixed the lock on the backdoor."[38]

If the circulating toolbox represents elusive masculine mechanical skills, it also functioned to symbolize the ironic interchange of gender roles as its possession changed hands. In this way, the program stressed the ideal of gendered household tasks and simultaneously undercut their exclusiveness. On the rare occasions Ozzie succeeds at some improvement project, he still contrives to fail. "The Hobby" explores this comic reversal. Confident in his skills after a trip to the local hobby shop to buy a do-it-yourself kit, Ozzie offers to construct a gift for a housewarming party. He boasts to Harriet about "what a thrill it is to be able to handle tools . . . to delve into a complex mechanical problem." Of course, she wouldn't understand because "the field of mechanics is so exclusively a man's field." After failing at every project, he wanders into the attic, where he discovers an old hall tree. With the help of Ricky and David, he manages to transform it into a lamp. But their efforts cost over forty dollars—a very hefty sum for the late 1940s. And to compound the irony, when Harriet sees the contraption, she reveals that she had already bought a present, knowing full well that Ozzie would fail. It was an antique: "A hall tree that was made out of an old floor lamp."[39]

In Ozzie's rulebook of masculine platitudes, none was more important than the virtue of frugality and judicious consumption. Harriet and the boys were certainly not spendthrifts, but they often initiated the family's consumption, so Ozzie frequently took the occasion for a lecture on hard work and savings, all but invoking Horatio Alger and his success stories by name. In a late-run radio broadcast entitled "The High Cost of Living," the Nelsons explored the limits of prudent consumption. The episode focused on decisions about where to spend and how much. Harriet hopes to persuade Ozzie to treat the family to a meal at a new French restaurant. And Ozzie leaves Harriet a hint to buy him a new sports jacket by putting a clipping advertising a sale on her dresser. Suddenly, however, the quality of meals at home declines. The family is put on a strict regimen of leftovers: "practically prison fare." When faced with lamb leftovers again, Ozzie suggests that Harriet is overdoing the economizing. But, she protests, it was Ozzie's suggestion; he left the article about the high cost of living on her dresser—the other side of the sports coat ad. So Ozzie treats the family to dinner at the new restaurant. "Harriet and the boys order plain American food," but Ozzie orders a fancy French dish that turns out to be lamb stew.[40]

The lessons learned in such dramas are always wasted on Ozzie, however. In a world of rising prices, even the affluent Nelsons need to economize. But the method Ozzie initiates results in draconian spending curbs and then, when the misunderstanding is cleared up, he takes the family off to an expensive restaurant. Harriet and the boys wisely order cheaper American food, but Ozzie asks for a dish without knowing what it is. As usual, his attempt to steward the finances of the family stumbles over his own profligacy.

If the comic patriarch was unwise in negotiating the new rules of consumption and incompetent as a repairman, he also frequently misunderstood fatherhood itself. One early radio show, "Democracy in the Family," explored the new companionate notions of marriage and child rearing. In this episode, Ozzie buys four tickets to a performance of *Macbeth*, but the boys lobby to attend an all-star baseball game, in effect, pitting high culture against sports. After a conversation with neighbor Thorny, Ozzie decides that the family should make the choice: "There should be democracy in the family—everybody voting on family decisions."[41]

When Ozzie suggests this new rule, he expects to be elected president of the family council, but Harriet wins with a bribe of chocolate cake. Ozzie postpones a decision on the play and treats the boys to candy and sodas. When the vote comes, *Macbeth* wins. But Thorny raises doubts about the fairness of the victory. And Ozzie begins to change his mind about going to hear Shakespeare. He returns home to announce his change of heart. But Harriet is one step ahead, having already exchanged the *Macbeth* tickets for seats at the ball game: "She told the boys to vote for Macbeth 'cause if Ozzie had been voted down, he would have pouted and spoiled the entire evening." So, she let him think he had won, knowing that he would change his mind.[42] Thus democracy did rule the family, not formally as Ozzie anticipated, but through Harriet's clever manipulation, making Ozzie think he got his own way. In this odd reversal, patriarchy seems both illusion and reality, allowing the father to think he rules and, because of this, allowing him, in fact, to make a decision that everyone else desired.

Another radio show raised the issues of advice manuals and child-rearing practices—both important elements in the construction of the companionate family during the 1950s. Harriet worries about the pernicious effect of crime and violence in popular culture and persuades Ozzie to buy a guide on child psychology. He chooses *A Boy's Best Friend Is His Father* by Dr. Sigmund Zweiback. The book advises treating the son as a young child, relieving him of all responsibilities, and that sounds just right to Ozzie. In the meantime, Harriet purchases a competing book by Zweiback's wife, Gertrude: *A Boy's Best Friend Is His Mother*. This tome suggests increasing the responsibility given to young boys. The couple hastily compare notes and are pleased that they have both purchased books by Zweiback.

Back at home, however, each parent institutes a different regime. Ozzie treats the older David like a baby, and Harriet urges the younger Ricky to make grown-up decisions. When the boys begin to act out the absurd advice, the parents realize their mistakes and throw out the guides.[43] Ostensibly a satire of child-rearing manuals, Dr. Spock, and Freudian theory, the show made another and more subtle point. It was no accident that Ozzie chose the permissive method. Indulging and babying fit his instinctive view of child rearing, not the strict discipline he usually enunciated and certainly not the more mature advice that appealed to Harriet. In this world of domestic mismanagement, reality perpetually undercut his refrain of platitudes about strict upbringing and get-ahead values.

Throughout the whole run of the series, the ongoing American controversy about mass culture frequently found its way into the shows, sometimes even questioning the very media that communicated *Ozzie and Harriet* itself. At first, this issue centered on comic books. No doubt the growing national debate about comics and copycat crime inspired several scripts. For example, in the November 1950 episode titled "The Vicar," Ozzie tries to persuade the boys to read books, not comics. He suggests that they begin with *The Vicar of Wakefield*, a book he has been intending to start. "It's just that people are forgetting how to read," he pontificates. "Comic books, movies, radio, now television . . . it's all part of a national deterioration of mind."[44]

In the meantime, Harriet has started a crime novel called *The Corpse in the Kitchen*, but fearing Ozzie's disapproval, she places it inside the paper cover of *The Vicar of Wakefield*. When Ozzie sees the book she is reading, he praises her to the boys. At bedtime, however, he discovers her ruse and begins the real *Vicar* to set an example. Late into the night, the whole family is still poring over their chosen medium: Harriet reading her crime novel, Ozzie plowing through Goldsmith's masterpiece, and the boys enjoying *Victor Wakefield, Crime Smasher*. To escape the trap he fell into, Ozzie turns to something he actually likes, "a stirring copy of *Superboy*." As he concludes, "I guess comic books aren't too bad. They certainly teach kids bravery and courage, and the triumph of good over evil."[45]

One reason for this benign attitude toward comics was undoubtedly a brief venture licensed by the Nelsons and appearing simultaneously with the show that explored the issue. The *Ozzie and Harriet* comic book series existed for only two years, between 1949 and 1950, and generally translated premises of the radio show into a much-simplified format. Many of the plots were similar, with Harriet and Ozzie switching roles, for example, or Ozzie forced to confront the consequences of his puffed-up yarns about a difficult childhood. But the pulp series moved quickly away from the domestic focus of the radio plays, breaking the dramatic frame that accounted for the success of the show. Episodes took the family out into the country or on vacation trips. Although the first issue tried to achieve verisimilitude with the series, featuring a photograph of the Nelson family on the cover and a blurb describing the work done by Ozzie on the story lines, the series lacked the energy and wit of the radio production, and died quickly.[46] Most significant, the new medium began to break down the established domestic format, and the character of Ozzie threatened to become a figure of ridicule and folly as opposed to the carefully controlled persona of the radio series.

When the show made its move to television, most of the devices and characterizations of the successful radio series also made the transition. Broadcast for two years in conjunction with the continuing radio version, the television production recycled old scripts at first even as it experimented with the visual possibilities of the new medium. In this sense, the transition was seamless, because the Nelsons continued to play themselves. Ozzie maintained tight control over production and continued to head a team of writers that included his brother Don Nelson, Bill Davenport, Ben Gershman, and later, John Griers and Jay Sommers. On occasion, the show used story lines developed by other writers. Also, from the start, *Ozzie and Harriet* was accompanied by a judiciously placed laugh track, used sparingly when compared to the compulsive every-three-line punctuation of present-day sitcoms.

The move to television also coincided with increasing attention paid to David and Ricky. But by and large, little changed when the broadcasts began in October 1952. The opening shot was a long focus on the front of the Nelson house that then moved to a close-up of the front door. The announcer named the characters as they emerged from the door: Ozzie first, then Harriet, David, and Ricky. Despite the potential flexibility of the new medium, the initial shows took place primarily in interior sets of the dining room, the living room, and the kitchen, with occasional exterior shots, and once in awhile, Ozzie and Harriet in bed together. In fact, one early radio program adapted for television explored the issue of sharing the same bed. But the majority of episodes centered on the other shared spaces of the house.

Television also made it possible to break the natural limitation on the plausible number of different radio voices. Thus, the cast of secondary characters grew slightly. Furthermore, television allowed the occasional dream sequence or a shift to different locations. Perhaps the greatest change came in the character of Harriet. Showing her constantly with a vacuum cleaner at hand or a tray of cookies reinforced important verbal changes. While she still possessed superior knowledge and considerable guile, the show gradually abandoned the early themes of gender switching and contests of competence.

This was partially due to the visual representation of Harriet as housewife, mother, and cook, which diminished the sense of sharp verbal repartee that characterized the radio show. Nonetheless, Ozzie retained his general character, and the show continued to center on his failures to adjust to a world of women and children. The domestic sitcom certainly remained the format even if it grew fuzzy in focus.

Another dramatic change brought affluence to the Nelsons. This put Ozzie's penny-pinching into a highly charged and ironic context. While the family carefully watched expenditures and hewed to a conservative notion of consumption, there were frequent episodes where one character persuades another to purchase something: clothing, toys, even a car. The comedy continued to revolve around misdirection and misunderstandings stemming from Ozzie's unexamined and archaic values, but the Nelsons' lifestyles had clearly improved from the radio days.

Inevitably as they aged, David and Ricky became more central to the show. There were frequent episodes in which Ozzie tries to teach the boys a growing-up lesson, only to have to learn the lesson himself. The comedy of the domestic male shifted from the troubling interaction with women to the adjustment to living with children. This also meant that Ozzie increasingly interacted with controversial elements of 1950s youth culture, particularly rock 'n' roll, dancing, hotrods, and dating. As Ricky grew more important to the show as a cover singer and teen idol, more episodes centered on music. In this way, the show came full cycle, returning, in a sense, to its 1930s origins in music performance. Throughout, however, Ozzie remained the foil for the gentle reconciliation of family disputes.[47]

Most categories of episodes established in radio reappeared on television, as did the language and expression of masculinity. In "Economical Ozzie," telecast in the second season, for example, Ozzie worries about rising family expenses: Harriet's beauty parlor dates, David's trip to the carwash, and other extravagances. Ozzie decides the family can do everything themselves. He goes to the hardware store to buy supplies and spends so much that he qualifies for a special drawing. The family voices its astonishment at how much it cost Ozzie to save, but they all pledge frugality. Ozzie tries to return some of the supplies but ends up buying even more. When he returns home, Harriet enters from the hairdresser wearing a new dress. She has just spent the money she saved by not buying a new sewing machine. Then Ricky announces that the garage man is washing the car because Ozzie made such of mess of his efforts to clean it. Just then, the telephone rings and Ozzie learns he has won 25 free car washes.[48]

The irony of this episode comes from Ozzie's misplaced notion that saving money actually means not spending it. This producer ethic proves to be an inappropriate one, however, because spending, in fact, turns out to be the best way to save. As neighbor Thorny laments, "A guy tries to practice a little economy and he spends more than he saves."[49] Trying to teach the values of hard work and individual responsibility, Ozzie is confronted with the wisdom of their opposite. His lecture on frugality becomes a lesson in modern consumption. Unable to put his traditional values into operation, he joins in acknowledging Harriet's wiser recourse of buying to save. In this respect, the older values associated with traditional manhood are subverted, and Ozzie is forced to recognize the practicality of a consumption system identified with women.

One of the explicit examinations of masculinity is "The Manly Arts," which appeared in the second television season. In this episode, Ricky and David are hired by a private detective agency to watch over the delivery of some valuable items. They are confident because David is a wrestler in high school and Ricky has learned karate. But trouble looms when Ozzie tries to help out. That night Harriet worries about the boys and dreams of a fight with gangsters who try to seize the valuables. In the sequence, Ricky and David defend themselves, but Ozzie proves a failure. Harriet awakes and recounts her fears to Ozzie, who rushes off to save the boys. David, Ricky, and even Ozzie then account for themselves in a real struggle with criminals. Each possesses a different fighting skill. The show ends with the announcement that David and Ricky have performed all of their own stunts.[50] It is silent with respect to Ozzie, however.

While Ozzie's dubious masculinity is rescued in this episode, it is David and Ricky who demonstrate the greatest natural male prowess. Nothing could be more typical of the television series than this sort of situation where the wise and skillful children instruct adults, even, as in this case, in the manly arts.

Other shows repeated the comic theme of Ozzie's incompetence. In "Spring Housecleaning," broadcast in March 1955, the plot again concerns Ozzie's desire to evade his household chores. Because he injures himself slightly in a fortunate fall chasing a baseball, he has an excuse to beg off work. As he explains to Thorny, "Believe it or not, if I hadn't hurt myself I'd be doing all this heavy cleaning for Harriet right now." Later he decides to help, explaining to the boys that he would "like to do this heavy work all by myself so that I can convince your mother once and for all that I'm not a gold bricker." But, of course, he is just that—or at least circumstances make that possible—because Harriet employs professional cleaners to do the job. Thinking that the men were actually hired to clean for the neighbors, Ozzie decides to take advantage and have them clean the Nelson house for free. He snoozes contentedly on the couch as the men go to work.[51]

While this plot is entirely consistent with the radio characterization of Ozzie, it nonetheless suggests a development found in many other episodes filmed for the new medium. Ozzie's resistance to domestic masculinity becomes less a contest for control between genders and more a purely comic antic. This does not entirely exclude the social satire characteristic of the radio shows, but it does soften the bite. In fact, on television, a new form of humor developed around the issues of domestic masculinity. In a series of plots, Ozzie begins by demonstrating his laziness and evasion, his incompetence and failure to fulfill his duties as husband. But in the course of the show, he shows that he can, in fact, fix household objects, play sports, and offer sound advice to the boys, even if events usually conspire against him.

For example, in an early episode broadcast in January 1953, Ozzie brags about his basketball prowess and tries to instruct the boys in a game they already know how to play. Of course, he is rusty and the boys obviously need no help. Thorny interrupts the game and challenges Ozzie to a basketball shooting match. When Thorny sprains his ankle, Ozzie is visibly relieved. He explains that he was too exhausted to play anyway, but the real reason is undoubtedly his fear of losing. But the last camera shot after the final credits undercuts this comic portrayal, showing Ozzie shooting baskets with considerable skill.[52]

A later show explored the same contradiction between Ozzie's initial physical incompetence and his eventual demonstration of some athletic ability. In "The Trophy," an episode for the sixth television season, the Nelsons enter a family decathlon at the annual Men's Club picnic. Ozzie brags that he had once won a decathlon by himself, but he can't produce the trophy he received. The boys win various contests, Harriet enters a prize blueberry pie, and Ricky entertains. But victory depends entirely on Ozzie's contribution. He must win an obstacle race against his rival Butch Barton. The two men run neck and neck, over fences and through mud holes. At the end, they are tied, until "Harriet saves the day by shooting a stone at Ozzie's rear with a sling shot and he bolts across the finish line victorious." When the family returns home, Harriet shows Ozzie's skeptical friend, Doc, his original trophy. Doc leaves, praising Ozzie as a real champion. Then Harriet reads the scroll that accompanied the prize: "first in the wheelbarrow race, checkers, one-legged chicken-hop, pancake eating contest, and the peanut push."[53]

One particularly significant exploration of gender was "The Career Woman" repeated and revised in 1955 from the original radio show. While much of the program was borrowed directly, a new montage added an element of slapstick to the television version when Ozzie dreams of the consequences of being "Mr. *Harriet* Nelson." Another role-reversal television program turned on the desire of Harriet and several wives to join Ozzie and his pals in their poker game. Of course Ozzie objects, explaining that women can't understand the game because they insist on making illogical bets. Harriet counters that they usually win. And he retorts, "You have such devious ways of thinking." But Harriet insists, "In other words, we're smarter than men."[54] In fact, the show tests both propositions and comes to a neutral conclusion. After a scavenger hunt with the men competing against the women, the result is a tie, despite Ozzie's effort to cheat. Then the group divides to play poker, the "girls" by their own rules and the "boys" by theirs. But when Ozzie decides to kibitz with the "girls," he is stumped trying to answer an important question about the game he claims to understand.[55]

Although this, as well as other episodes, specifically raised and affirmed the issue of family democracy (the democracy of equal value for each contribution), the slapstick plot revolving around separate but equal poker games greatly diminished the result. It underscored the importance of maintaining a separate masculine culture within the family based upon a segregation of functions. Even though the plot revealed that women were as skillful and talented as men at poker, it resolved the action with the illusion that men and women had separate cultures.

In "The Honest Face" (TV season four), Ozzie seeks to demonstrate his manly skills in another archaic fashion: by judging character. He can, he boasts, determine a man's qualities from his features. "Everything a man thinks . . . everything a man does . . . it all shows up in his face. There are certain little characteristics," he explains. But when David's high school psychology class tests this proposition, the students conclude from a photograph that Ozzie is a criminal type. Nonetheless, Ozzie bravely maintains his position. To demonstrate the point, he agrees to cash a check presented by a stranger named "Jones" who knocks at the back door. It turns out, however, that Ozzie is the victim of multiple deceptions. David's teacher intended to demonstrate a different psychology lesson. He wanted the class to judge the reaction of their fathers when told they looked like criminals. In the end, Ozzie is restored in his belief that he knows an honest face when he sees one—that is, until he discovers that Mr. Jones is a real criminal. Thus in the bewildering new world of modern psychology, Ozzie's old-fashioned values cost him money and pride.[56]

As in the radio series, on television Ozzie spent considerable time preaching to his family about the virtues of elite culture, while obviously relishing popular culture. In a fascinating episode for the fifth TV season, Ozzie chides the boys for using a shortcut synopsis of famous classics instead of reading the originals. The boys protest that they will miss television and dates with girls. But Ozzie explains, "There's nothing wrong with television and movies and all, but I don't think we should give up reading—especially the classics." So Ozzie vows he will teach by example. But then he encounters an old friend who declares that he has decided to grow old gracefully; he will relinquish sports and reread the classics. Faced with this grim future, Ozzie hurries home. But, it's too late. Harriet has fixed up a quiet room in the attic where he can read undisturbed. The family then escorts him to his high-culture intellectual isolation booth.

Once in his reading den, Ozzie quickly drifts off and dreams of the consequences of his seclusion. He imagines himself a hermit living in a cave, surrounded by books. Ricky and David visit every few months, but Harriet is too busy watching television even to call. Mercifully, Ricky wakes him from this nightmare, asking if he will listen to a new record. David enters with a portable TV and Harriet carries in a tray of sandwiches. Ozzie rejoices as he is reconnected to popular culture and his family.[57]

As in many other shows, Ozzie proclaims the virtues of elite culture and old-fashioned values (Shakespeare and Horatio Alger), only to admit later that he prefers television, sports, jazz, and rock 'n' roll, identified either with the boys or sometimes with Harriet. In several cases, the episode uses a dream sequence to imagine the absurd consequences of Ozzie's inappropriate values. And the lesson he can never quite retain is that his inappropriate masquerade as a patriarch, in command of the family ship, undermines the bliss of domestic masculinity, consumption, and his love of popular culture.

By the mid-1950s the pattern of television episodes was firmly in place, even if the old satire had moderated. Harriet's previously sharply defined role was softened, and the boys emerged as Ozzie's principal comic antagonists. Still, Ozzie explored the same paradox of masculinity: a man espousing ideas he thinks he believes in while struggling to fit into a new world of women and children, youth culture, togetherness, mass media, and consumer values.[58] Ozzie never stopped trying to be handyman, good neighbor, role model for his children, and firm but loving husband on the small stage of American suburbia. The comedy emerged from his failure to adjust to the real values of that new world. Indeed, up to the end, Ozzie was allowed to think that his patriarchal values had meaning, even as each episode demonstrated their futility. Perhaps this was his profoundest commentary on the 1950s.

Using this versatile format, the program managed to explore many of the important issues emerging in the postwar world: the new household division of labor, child rearing, family democracy, changing fashions, youth culture, gender identities, the function of the past, and the culture wars over television and modern culture. Certainly this did not exhaust the serious issues of the 1950s. Yet, for all the unreality of the show and its formulaic repetitions, it provided an endlessly fascinating exploration of one man's clumsy embrace of domestic masculinity. This was not just a case of comic rebellion but a tireless effort to join the new world, to become a new sort of man within a world of changing gender assumptions. The longevity of the show suggests that it was welcome in the homes of men, women, and children who were exploring these same issues in their own lives.

8

Mendacity: Men, Lies, and *Cat on a Hot Tin Roof*

Tennessee Williams and other playwrights not far removed, who see things as through a glass of darkness, are not giving a contemporary view of anything other than their own maladjustments.
—Ashley Montagu, 1962, *Playboy* magazine

The plays, films, and televised dramas of Tennessee Williams peopled the 1950s with some of the most memorable characters of the contemporary imagination. At least six of his short plays appeared on television. From 1950 to 1964, eleven of his major dramas were transformed into Hollywood productions (with one additional screenplay based on a short story). Twelve different plays were performed on Broadway between 1950 and 1962, with many of these receiving multiple productions throughout the United States in the same years. Although Ashley Montagu, speaking in the context of the 1962 *Playboy* forum lamenting the decline of masculinity, might have seen Williams's success as a threat to American virility—as some other cultural critics did—there was no escaping the omnipresence of America's leading gay playwright.[1] In a decade when John Wayne paraded up and down the mythical American historical consciousness in at least thirty films, saddled up for a ride into heroism, Williams presented a far different approach to masculinity that, as much as Wayne's quiet westerners, fitted these ambiguous, conflicted times. And, if Williams created some of the best roles for women in American drama, he also wrote sensitive and complex roles for men. Indeed, it could be argued that he is our greatest playwright of gender issues.

Considering Williams's male characters as an emerging composition of masculinity, with emotions and affect ranging from extremes of sensitivity to raw animal power, it is obvious that his depictions represent far more than a projection of homosexual desire.[2] Indeed, his characters embody nothing less than the male continuity that Kinsey described in his sexology. Williams spoke and wrote from the edges of the mainstream and, certainly, from an uncommon experience. But this perspective from askance only enhanced the remarkable insights he was able to muster for the exploration of the forms of masculinity found in American culture and history. What remains most remarkable and appealing about these characters is variety, possibility, and suggestion—the depiction of a repertoire of behaviors—not the representation of something essential. In addition to the beauty of his language and the compelling situations he dramatized, it is probably this fluidity of characterization that attracted millions of Americans to his plays and films. He struck a chord with his audiences because he could summon up the hidden melodies—dark though they might be—playing in the background of American culture.[3]

Although Williams came to occupy the focal point of American cultural production in the 1950s—that is the axis between Hollywood and Broadway—his upbringing and lifestyle were inherently marginal and minority. One of his biographers, Donald Spoto, recalls what he knew of Williams in the 1950s before he began his project, namely, the astounding and lurid subjects of Williams's plays: sexual exploitation, cannibalism, drug addiction, homosexuality, venereal disease, and castration. This attitude is unsurprising: no doubt it was a prevailing impression of the time.[4] But Williams was much more than notorious, and far more important than the author of dark and salacious dramas. There was much more to his talent than the dramatization of scandal and family nightmares. Still the question remains: what was it about his work that touched Americans in the 1950s? And why, in particular, did his various versions of masculinity intervene so prominently in the larger American dialogue about this subject?

There are many places to look for answers. In fact, a study of all of William's major dramas would seem to be in order. Yet one particular play, written in the midst of his most creative period, in the mid-1950s—and subsequently turned into the most popular film adaptation of any of his works—reveals the power and depth of his male characterizations and something of the appeal of his drama. In *Cat on a Hot Tin Roof,* directed first on Broadway in 1955 by Elia Kazan and then released in 1958 as a film by Richard Brooks, Williams fashioned a character in Brick Pollitt, whose withdrawal into himself, in a rage of self-pity, refusing to play husband, son, brother, or father, unleashed a storm of consequences that brought each of these roles into high relief. His defiant inertia compelled every other character in the play to join him in his search for manhood, making the drama a remarkable dialogue on the possibilities of enacting masculinity in modern America.[5]

Williams's life and works were enduringly rooted in his upbringing in the South and as the member of an emotionally troubled family. Born in Columbus, Mississippi, in 1911 (although he claimed a birth date in 1914), he entered a family entangled in southern history and its mythologies. His father came from an old and established family in Tennessee, perhaps the origin of the name he assumed.[6] His mother was the daughter of an Ohio minister. The marriage was unsuccessful, becoming deeply bitter at times. The clash of their different backgrounds was compounded by profound personal differences. A sensitive, self-conscious child, Tennessee read and wrote poetry and stories. While his mother lavished love, attention, and the illusion of gentility on her children, Tennessee suffered the contempt of his father. Like so many children in similar situations, he escaped into the imagination.

As a young man, he attended the University of Missouri, but relates that he flunked out and returned home to take a job arranged for him by his father at the International Shoe Company. By the mid-1930s, he had published a few poems and was enthusiastically reading the works of modern playwrights such as Ibsen, Strindberg, and Chekhov. In 1943, his sister Rose, who was tortured by psychological disorders, underwent a lobotomy, which ended her psychotic episodes, but forever erased her personality. And all the while, Tennessee was struggling to understand his own sexuality in a world with very little sympathy for his homosexuality.[7]

After several years of degrading jobs and literary rejections, Williams won a playwriting contest held by the Group Theatre in New York City in 1939, an accomplishment that opened doors for him to the most significant venues of New York theater culture. Even more important, he attracted the attention of two crucial allies: Elia Kazan, then a young director, and Audrey Wood, a literary agent, both of whom played essential roles in his successes during the 1950s. If this achievement did not bring him immediate success—and Williams always lived in real or imagined precariousness—it was the beginning of his most productive period and initiated a series of associations that served him well.[8]

It is easy, and reductive, to look for explanations of his art in Williams's troubled family life or to dwell on the closeted sexuality in his plays. These were certainly present. No doubt, several characters are based upon himself, his mother, father, sister, and close acquaintances. It is plausible to see, as some have done, his male and female characters as warring figments of his own psyche, isolated portions of an unstable whole. There is more than one play in which Williams skirts the issue of homosexuality and the consequences of exposure—again, elements relevant to his life. Yet this sort of analysis goes no further in his case than for other writers who project themselves and their autobiographical concerns onto the stage. What matters is the flesh-and-blood speech of his characters, not their resemblance to persons living or dead. As he put it in a 1957 interview with *Newsweek* magazine, "Often I'm asked if my pessimism, my characters, my violent scenes are not a reflection of the chaos of our world." Well, they are not," he answered in response to his own question. "I may write about troubled people, but I write from my own tensions. For me this is a form of therapy."[9] This sort of self-analytical remark came easily to writers because it had become more acceptable in the 1950s to open up one's psychological interior than to express unpopular or dissenting political and social opinions. But, in fact, no playwright could wish to achieve genuine therapy from his works if those same anxieties and compulsions were the people of his creative world. No danger in this case, however: Williams did not resolve the tensions of his early family life or integrate his divided soul. Instead, he dramatized his deepest emotions and anxieties in ways that made him the most important playwright of his era. As his Broadway collaborator and director Kazan put it in an interview, "He has a positive genius for dealing with subject matter that is on everyone's mind and part of everyone's experience, but which has not been dealt with by other writers." "Audiences," Kazan continued, "instinctively feel Williams is writing about their real problems—personal, social, whatever."[10]

By the time he composed *Cat on a Hot Tin Roof*, Williams had reached the height of his popularity, and major works poured forth in rapid succession onto the Broadway stage and then from Hollywood. However, in translating works from stage to celluloid, the film industry insisted upon revisions that softened some of the language and opened the production beyond the four walls of the theater. Most important, films expurgated any direct mention of homosexuality. But the busy Censorship Board, established by the Motion Picture Producers Association of America and headed by Joseph Breen, was ultimately unsuccessful in completely excising controversial material. The palpable void created by specific and limited cuts of language and plot lines still echoed the original script in meaningful silences and ellipses and inapt plot contrivances. This was certainly true of *Cat on a Hot Tin Roof*, which retained much of its original character despite serious changes and rearrangement; and critics at the time frequently commented on the continuity. At the same time, the plays themselves did not represent pure Williams, nor did the movies represent some clumsy collective corruption. The history of both play and screen product suggests that authorship was far more complex than this. While Williams is certainly the author of his plays, he repeatedly rewrote them on the advice of his director and literary agent. This is particularly true of *Cat on a Hot Tin Roof*, where Kazan persuaded Williams to compose a new final act for the Broadway production. These changes were so drastic, and Williams had so many second thoughts about them, that he published the original version in order to indicate his preference for it. As for the Hollywood production of *Cat,* which was based on the Broadway version, Williams disliked it intensely, despite its remarkable box office and critical success. In fact, he claimed the play to be his favorite but judged the film to be "jazzed up." This was all the more critical because, as Williams believed, "Films are more lasting than play productions." So he generally tried to retain "as much artistic control as possible in all film contracts."[11]

The challenge in writing *Cat* was to depict the complex motives of his male characters. In various versions of the play and in multiple rewrites of crucial scenes, Williams struggled to depict various forms of love between men. If this was a task he never quite succeeded in completing, his explorations provide a remarkable perspective on the performances of contemporary masculinity. There were actually four completed versions of *Cat,* beginning with a short story, "Three Players of a Summer Game," published in 1951 in the *New Yorker*. Many of the elements of the play can be found in this slight sketch, most important among them the two main characters, Margaret and Brick. The plot also foreshadows the play, although it contains elements that were eventually dropped; for example, the description of Brick possessing a "fiery thatch of hair." In the story, Brick is a heavy drinker and filled with self-loathing and disgust. He has lost his self-respect and broadly hints that his manhood is compromised. His wife, Margaret, has even taken over management of his plantation—and his life.[12] There are other elements in the story that Williams reworked into the play—such as Brick's adolescent athletic antics[13]—but when the Broadway drama appeared two years later, it was greatly changed. It had become the compelling story of a family trapped in one long day of incredibly cruel disclosures.

Among the most significant new elements Williams provided was a complex reason for Brick's alcoholic retreat, as well as the motivation for Margaret's—now Maggie—triumph over him. The new characters and setting greatly intensified and reworked these themes. In the end, Williams had created one of the masterpieces of the American stage and a haunting deconstruction of the modes of masculinity. He also initiated a creative process set in perpetual motion, with a plot that continued to evolve and change because of its resistance to resolution to a precise statement. Neither of the two published versions of the play, nor even the film, could end satisfactorily, because the actions—the inaction, really—of the main character never could be fully explained. At the same time, this irresolution and uncertainty threw light back on the issues Williams sought to explore. His hesitation to tie up all the loose ends allowed him to measure and contemplate the widespread uncertainties about gender that gave undeniable fascination to the play. As actor Karl Malden, who played Mitch in Williams's *Streetcar* put it, "I don't think Tennessee wants to end! I think Tennessee would like to go on and on and on."[14] In a sense, that is precisely what he did for *Cat*, working and reworking the two crucial, revelatory scenes of the play in an effort to find the words to capture the relations between men that drove the play.

Writing the play was a complex process, and Williams's own accounting of its inspiration and purposes suggest his multiple intentions. His complicated explanation, in turn, provides material for a number of interpretations of the final result. Inevitably, these are contradictory because they are based on the different endings written for the work. Williams himself multiplied the possibilities by indicating different sources of his inspiration. In his memoirs, he wrote that in *Cat*, he "reached beyond myself, in the second act, to a kind of crude eloquence of expression in Big Daddy [Brick Pollitt's father] that I have managed to give no other character of my creation." This would suggest, in some measure, that Big Daddy is the center of the play, as in many respects, he is. But in a letter to friend and confidant, Donald Windham, Williams proposed a different emphasis. He had long desired to write about death, he said, but had not yet dared to: "Of course, it only became explicit, something I finally learned to deal with directly, in 'Big Daddy' in 'Cat.'"[15]

One important model of Williams's conception appears to be classical drama, and, in particular, the practice of compressing the action of the play into real time. Williams achieved something of the symmetry and density, the control and rigor of drama exemplified by the French playwright Racine, for example. But at the same time, the limitations of real time exacerbated the fundamental problem of composition, which is the degree of change the character Brick could plausibly undergo in a few hours. Too abrupt a transformation would destroy verisimilitude. The compacted plot also amplified the importance, the memory, and the consequence of events that took place before the fateful day of the play. Given the complexity and obscurity of Brick's motivations for refusing sex with his wife, it is almost impossible to imagine a complete reconciliation between him and Maggie in so short a time. The problem was only compounded as the drama evolved, first in Williams's original, then in the Broadway production, and then in the film. In each of these subsequent versions, the reconciliation becomes more overt and explicit, and therefore harder to believe, even if, in the different aesthetics of movies, abrupt changes are anticipated and even necessary. In Williams's preferred first version, the play ends in obvious ambiguity, with no—or perhaps several—plausible interpretations.[16]

Quite clearly, another inspiration for the play is Williams's knowledge of the South, compounded with his own family history. The set for *Cat* is, in effect, a southern plantation, or rather, Maggie and Brick's bedroom within the house. Like many of Williams's dramas, the situation is alien to mainstream American life, as far from the reality of the 1950s suburb and of small-town main street as possible. This lush and exotic world, with its deeply accented speech and heavy atmosphere, immediately conjured a special place in American imaginative literature, where the audience expected ordinary rules to be suspended in favor of dramatic ones. Audiences anticipated that Williams's plays would contain heightened emotion, poetic speech, and larger-than-life personalities, played in the damp and electric atmosphere of the South. This exoticism granted Williams license to push beyond the normal boundaries surrounding issues like gender. Because of this, *Cat* could almost unconsciously invoke characteristic elements from other examples of southern literature. As Nancy Tischler writes of the ambiguous gender roles in the play, "This reversal of sex roles finds its way into the play, as does the victory of the strong woman. This is not a new idea for southern literature or for Williams. The faintly feminine male are characters used by Faulkner and Margaret Mitchell."[17]

Just how Williams's family was depicted in the play is also something that the playwright tried to explain. In an interview in 1967, Rip Torn, who served as the understudy to Ben Gazarra (Brick Pollitt in the original Broadway production), recounted what Tennessee told him about the origins of the story. He said that *Cat* was based on the relationship he had experienced with his father and the fact that he had never really made peace with his father. His father had always bullied him "and then, of course, the father was rarely there.... And the play in the real sense was, I think, a poetic apology for both of them: father and son who couldn't get together." Elements of this explanation may be true, although, of course, the play was much more.[18]

Williams worked for several years to shape a play from the unfinished stuff of his short story. The first version was quite abbreviated. As he wrote to agent Audrey Wood in April 1954, enclosing a draft for her to read, this was "the play that threw me into such a terrible state of depression last summer in Europe." He warned that it was overwritten and, at the same time, incomplete: "But I do think," he explained, "it has a terrible sort of truthfulness about it, and the tightest structure of anything I have done. And a terrifyingly strong curtain." Wood expressed her enthusiasm for the play, as she had when he discussed it earlier with her, but she encouraged Williams to lengthen it. It already had, she wrote, "sufficient conflict to make it a solid piece of theater for a full evening." It would not work, she advised, to plan it as half of a pair of pieces as Williams had originally suggested.[19]

This exchange indicates two important points about the playwright. One was the feeling of "terrible truth" that Williams aimed to capture. The second was the resistance he would always show to expanding the story beyond the kernel of his initial idea. In some respects, getting this play into the shape where it could be produced proved as challenging as extracting a confession, as Williams wrote and rewrote the dialogue for two key scenes. As he wrote to Wood in September of the same year, he believed that *Cat,* as conceived, was now finished and complete. Its three short acts were now entirely sufficient. "I would hate to lose the tightness," he said in justification, "that simplicity, by somehow forcing it into a more extended form simply to satisfy a convention of theatre."[20]

Williams's reluctance to extend the play matched (and was no doubt related to) his reluctance to resolve the story around which all of the action revolves—what he called the "issue" of the drama. The play takes place entirely inside the bedroom of Brick and Maggie Pollitt. Brick hobbles about on a crutch, because of a broken leg he suffered when trying to run hurdles, a drunken effort to relive his earlier athletic triumphs. But his real injuries go far deeper than this symbolic wounding. He refuses to make love to his wife and resists her through a fog of alcohol, waiting to hear the mental click that shuts the door to the outside world. His reasons revolve around a half-told, twice-told, but never fully completed story. Brick's once close friend, Skipper, confessed to him, after a failed attempt to seduce Maggie—that his affection for Brick went further than ordinary friendship should. In revulsion, Brick rejects him, and the distraught friend dies shortly thereafter in a despair of drugs and alcohol. Brick blames Maggie . . . and himself. Intensifying the pressure on him is a desperate fight for the family inheritance. Brick's father, Big Daddy, is dying of cancer, and his brother

Gooper and wife Mae plot to snare the old man's fortune in stocks and land. Their several children, with another expected, are meant to assure Big Daddy of his continuing immortality, but he scorns the obsequious and obedient son and his fecund and avaricious wife, and favors Brick. But Brick is childless and, it seems, determined to remain so. Maggie plans otherwise: to have Brick and the fortune.

Told around the homecoming of Big Daddy from a "Northern" cancer clinic, the play moves from the forced jollity of his birthday celebration to reveal ever-darker truths about Maggie and Brick, the cupidity of Gooper and Mae, the morbid diagnosis of Big Daddy's cancer, and, finally, the reality about the relations among all the characters. As day sinks into night, the deepest truths come out. The only hope that finally emerges is, ironically, the restoration of a set of fantasies around which all of the characters can live: especially the lie Maggie tells when she announces her pregnancy to the unbelieving family.

The unresolved problem that Williams posed for the play is Brick's sexuality. If he is gay, if he understands that his relationship with Skipper had been a loving one—whatever they did or didn't do physically—then there can probably be no reconciliation with Maggie, no truth possibly to come from her fabricated pregnancy. In a way, this problematic is closest to the original version of the script. If, on the other hand, Brick is really as straight as his horror at the accusation of "unnatural" love suggests, then his initial alienation from Maggie is harder to understand, although much easier to overcome, as the film version suggests. Quite clearly, Williams struggled with this issue and, in the end, left it an open question, probably even in his own mind. Thus, when critic Walter Kerr accused Williams of evading the issue, Williams responded with another evasion: was Brick a homosexual, he asked himself rhetorically? "He probably—no, I would even say certainly—went no further in physical expression than clasping Skipper's hand across the space between their twin-beds in hotel rooms—and yet—his sexual nature was not innately normal. . . . But Brick's sexual adjustment was, and always must remain, a heterosexual one."[21] "No, yet, but": if nothing else, the tortured sequence of negatives and evasions in this paragraph sounds like an uncomfortable rebellion against the author's self-imposed censorship.

Even in the stage instructions for a crucial scene between Big Daddy and Brick that almost, but not quite, exposes the nature of Skipper's and Brick's relationship, Williams suddenly veers off onto another subject. As he explains, "Some mystery should be left in the revelation of character in a play." What Big Daddy and Brick discuss is "the inadmissible thing that

Skipper died to disavow between them. The fact that if it existed it had to be disavowed to 'keep face' in the world they lived in, may be at the heart of the 'mendacity' that Brick drinks to kill his disgust with." So, in interpreting his scene Williams writes of a feeling "if it existed"; he does not claim that it did exist. Thus he refuses to resolve the conundrum that drives the play. While it might be said that Williams could not bring himself to write openly of a gay character, in a crucial sense, motivation did not matter, for his ambiguity about the subject had other profound effects on the meaning of the play and generated the brilliant volatility of its denouement.[22]

When Elia Kazan read the first version of the play, he was enthusiastic about directing it, but strongly advised Williams to make a series of changes. He insisted that Big Daddy reappear in act 3 after the wrenching confessional scene with Brick where he learns of his deadly cancer. Kazan also wanted Brick to undergo a more palpable change, and finally, he asked Williams to make Maggie a more clearly sympathetic character. Williams agreed with the last proposal and acquiesced in the former two, writing a new third act that became the version performed on Broadway and the basis for the MGM film.[23] Acts 1 and 2 remained basically unchanged.

But in letters written while he was completing his revisions, Williams expressed his reluctance to make the changes Kazan wanted. To Audrey Wood he confessed in November 1954 that he was even considering the possibility of another director, perhaps Jose Quintero or Harold Clurman. The difficulty for him was the different meanings of the two versions he now had before him. The first, he explained, was "about a vital, strong woman dominating a weak man and achieving her will." But, he complained, wouldn't changing this make it just "another case of a woman giving a man back his manhood"—something like Robert Anderson's recent play, *Tea and Sympathy*? In the same letter, he noted that writer Christopher Isherwood loved the original version, although he, too, suggested that Williams clarify the story of Skipper. That was what he had been trying to accomplish, he noted, by rewriting three crucial scenes, between Brick and Maggie, and with Brick and Big Daddy. In effect, he was seeking an idiom to express the continuities between homosexual, heterosexual, and filial love that pervaded the play.[24]

In the end, Williams did make important changes, and these amendments suggest something crucial about the nature of his work. As critic Brenda Murphy has written, the texts of his plays were always a "compromise with the theater [over subject matter and language], a compromise that was not always made willingly, but was almost always made, for as Tennessee Williams knew well, his art would not succeed without it." In effect, then, the play became a collective endeavor based, in part, on what the presumed audience, the advice of his friends and collaborators, and, finally, what the Hollywood censors could understand and accept.[25]

While three distinct versions of these scenes remain available today—the original, the Broadway version, and the 1958 film—Williams tried out, and finally discarded, many other rewrites, suggesting the difficulty in capturing the evasive reality he sought. One problem was that changes in one portion had consequences for the last scene—and vice versa. An examination of these rejected lines suggests how diligently Williams searched for the exact measure of ambiguity in portraying the nature of Brick's relationship with Skipper and the subsequent degree of reconciliation with Maggie. For example, in act 1, Maggie confronts Brick with her version of the story about what happened and did not happen between her and Skipper. In one possibility, Maggie is given a long speech that was eventually rewritten and placed in separate scenes of the play. It begins with an unmistakable accusation of homosexuality between the two men:

Maggie: "Last night I got up and crouched beside the sofa where you sleep. I put my hand on your heart and you squirmed an' turned away and said, 'Don't Skipper, don't don't . . .'"

She then continues with a long, bitter analysis of Brick's relationship with his friend. You could never consummate it, she chides him: "You and poor Skipper were such damned conventional, Puritan Protestant middle-class helpless believers in what you were told to believe that all you could do was love and love and love, without a word or a touch to speak or relieve, just eyes that blazed with a beautiful, mute adoration, till your hearts broke with it."[26]

Undoubtedly, this version was both too explicit and too clinical, and Williams's final script, while it certainly stresses the ambiguity of the relationship between Skipper and Brick, pushes the meaning back into the hazy realm of history, like "in the Greek legends" of friendship between men, as Maggie puts it. It was a love that could never be "anything satisfying or even talked about plainly." Furious with her, Brick accuses Maggie of "naming it dirty." Maggie, out of generosity or pity or desperation, translates the relationship into something abstract and distant, while Brick can only see her interpretation as vulgar and dirty. A character obsessed and damaged by the possibilities of truth, he is also unable to accept even the illusory transformation of his shameful love into myth.[27]

In act 2, Williams tried out a number of variations in the scene between Brick and Big Daddy, where both characters together explore both the truth of Brick's love for Skipper and Big Daddy's fatal cancer. In one very early, brief version of this scene, Williams wrote instructions to himself for further revisions: "From this point till end of the scene, it is walking on thin ice, or a hot tin roof, and has to be under-written and under-played at least till tested." As if to underscore the peril, Williams reminded himself later to suggest rather than explain: "The dialogue proceeds like gingerly footsteps, with incomplete sentences, half-statements, perhaps neither of the two men quite facing each other, but Brick's eyes blazing, his detachment at last removed."[28]

Another, later version of this scene is more explicit in its implications, with Williams clearly suggesting and denying simultaneously that Brick had an "unnatural" love for Skipper. Brick recounts the moment when Maggie confronted Skipper about him. While Brick lay in a hospital bed in Cleveland mending from a fracture, Maggie "poured venom in his ear like the player Queen in Hamlet." "She told him that what we had in our hearts for each other, Skipper and me, was repressed homosexuality—that we were frustrated lovers."[29]

Despite discarding the explicit in this rendering, Williams did not really change the meaning or dynamic of this scene, even if he did make it slightly more elliptical in the play itself. But two important secondary themes emerged in this scene when it was finally performed. The first is evidence of Big Daddy's remarkable life experience and the breadth of his tolerance. The second is the emotional reformulation of the opposition between mendacity and truth. Confronting Brick with the accusation that he and Skipper were homosexuals, Big Daddy refers to himself, invoking his own experience to telescope the issue. He gently tells Brick that he understands, and that he had "knocked around in his time." He had "slept in hobo jungles and railroad Y's and flophouses." Before he can elaborate, Brick breaks in and demands to know if Big Daddy is calling him "a queer" because he knew about "queers" from his tramping life. As with much else about this scene—as well as many moments throughout the play itself—the audience is suddenly jerked back just before they might have learned the truth. It is never clear what Big Daddy actually intended in this speech. Had he participated in or just observed love between men?[30] On one issue, however, Big Daddy is unambiguous, and that is the nature of his own surrogate parents, Jack Straw and Peter Ochello, two men who owned the plantation and willed it to him. It is in their former bedroom (now belonging to Brick and Maggie) that the action takes place. As Williams instructs in his set direction, the house had not changed much since Straw and Ochello occupied it. So the "room must evoke some ghosts; it is gently and poetically haunted by a relationship that must have [again, *must have*] involved a tenderness which was uncommon."[31]

What Big Daddy attempts in his generous confession and invocation of "family" origins is to perpetuate the continuity he sees in himself and his favored heir, Brick. It is perhaps a moment of acceptance of the transgression of homosexuality, but more clearly the invocation of the return of the prodigal son. There are other elements that recall this famous Bible story, specifically the elder son who has worked in his field and revered his father and already received his portion, and the younger profligate who is unexpectedly honored when he returns home. But there was also an important difference in Williams's retelling of the story: the younger son refuses his role, either to make peace with himself or to accept his own guilt. Brick cruelly lashes out at Big Daddy with the truth about his deadly cancer. The doctors had given him only a few painful months to live: there would be no returns, happy or otherwise, of his birthday party.

But moments before this sentence is pronounced, Big Daddy has grasped at a momentary release from the mendacity that rules his life. He confesses the lie that he has always lived: "All the goddam' hypocrisy that I lived with all these forty years that we been livin' together," he says of Big Mama. "What do you know about this mendacity thing? Hell! I could write a book on it!" Now he can contemplate freedom: "*Pleasure*, pleasure with *women*!" But the truth of his impending death kills this illusion too, and the only reality that remains is mendacity itself: the living lie of his marriage until death.[32]

The original and Williams's preferred version of act 2 ends with a look into the grim future through a past full of hypocrisy. Big Daddy does not return in act 3. Instead, during that last act, Big Mama becomes a kind of substitute patriarch, and the story of the prodigal son is reenacted through her. Indeed, when she realizes the scheme of elder son Gooper and Mae to take the property away from Brick, she assumes the role of the surrogate father: "What is it Big Daddy always says when he's disgusted?" She asks. Brick responds, "Crap!" "That's right—CRAP!" she shouts. "I say CRAP too, like Big Daddy!"[33] Once again Brick is restored as the favored son and the truth needs to be repeated: that Big Daddy is dying. "Oh Brick, son of Big Daddy! Big Daddy does so love you!" she cries.

Despite the compelling tidiness and symmetry of this original version, the Broadway script, commanded by Kazan, brought Big Daddy back to witness the denouement: Maggie's lie about being pregnant. It is clear in act 2 that Big Daddy knows that Brick and Maggie sleep apart; he has witnessed his son's disgust and physical revulsion toward his wife. In the original version of act 3, when Big Mama rushes off to tell Big Daddy the good news about the coming baby, there is no indication whether he will accept this as a falsehood or not. The Broadway version, however, resolves any uncertainty. Big Daddy begins act 3 with an exit, shouting "ALL—LYIN'—DYIN'—LIARS! LIARS! LIARS!" But he reappears on stage for Maggie's announcement of the impending birth and he permits this lie to stand as well as the falsehood that Brick had bought him a birthday present. When he hears Maggie's news, he breaks in without a pause, "Gooper, I want my lawyer in the mornin'"—presumably to draw up the documents leaving his property to Brick. And then he stands and prepares to leave, to go up to the rooftop of the house to overlook his plantation—"before I give up my kingdom—twenty-eight thousand acres of the richest land this side of the Valley Nile!" Big Mama rushes after him.[34]

The Broadway version also underscores even more resolutely the ambiguous and ironic definition of mendacity that configures the play: first, it is a word of loathing, and then, gradually, it emerges as a necessary creed to live by. This contradiction becomes even stronger in the film when Big Daddy accepts the pregnancy and then plans a sentimental trip—with Big Mama in tow—around all his holdings for one last time. Thus, each of the three successive versions strengthens the centrality of the necessary falsehood, even while the lie remains as corrosive and deadly as Big Daddy's cancer. And each of these shifting characterizations forced the playwright to decide finally, how to write the last scene of the play—to what degree could he depict a sexual reconciliation between Brick and Maggie? How far would they go to make a truth from Maggie's lie? Would they transform mendacity into life?

Williams experimented with a number of final speeches until he decided on the versions that became the original and Broadway scripts. He did not, however, write or approve the ending of the film. In the original play, he emphasized Maggie's immense strength of will—indeed, even her physical strength. She removes all of Brick's liquor (his excuse for impotence?), seizes his crutch, and announces that after they make love he can have his drink back. She seems almost sad at the ease of her victory over him: "Oh, you weak people, you weak beautiful people—who give up! What you want is someone to—take hold of you. Gently, gently, with love! And—I *do* love you Brick, I *do*!" "Wouldn't it be funny if that was true?" he responds.[35]

The Broadway version differs only slightly, but the change makes Brick's acquiescence in his seduction more active. It also eliminates a brilliant and suggestive symmetry between Big Daddy and Brick. In the original, Brick's last line is actually an exact repetition of Big Daddy's reaction to Big Mamma's anguished complaint: "And I did, I did so much, I did love you!" Big Daddy responds, "Wouldn't it be funny if that was true?" In the Broadway version this repetition is gone. When Maggie announces that there will be no more liquor, she asks Brick to help her "make the lie come true." Brick responds "with growing admiration" as the stage instructions indicate. "I admire you, Maggie," he says. With this, Maggie promises to hand his life back to him "like something gold you let go of—and I can! I'm determined to do it—and nothing's more determined than a cat on a tin roof—is there?" And so Brick and Maggie, like Big Daddy and Big Mama, restore the circle of their relationships, not through a renewal of love, but in the acceptance of a life-giving falsehood.[36] In the film, the reconciliation between the two couples is even more vivid and complete.

Considering the possibilities that Williams discarded, it becomes clearer that the choices he made were the right ones, for he preserved the essential ambiguity of the play and the layered meaning of the term "mendacity." One rejected possibility, for example, deflated and flattened the ending and undercut Maggie's power. "You never loved anybody," she declares. "No," agrees Brick. Then "(faintly, as if to herself) [Maggie says] "We'll make drunk love tonight . . . (smiles suddenly). With that broken ankle you can't get away!" "Slow curtain as Brick lifts his drink, looking at her above it without much interest." In two other discarded rewrites, Williams specifically raised the issue of impotence. In one, Brick finally achieves the click when drink has made him calm. Maggie asks him where he wants his pillow, on the sofa or the bed? "Turn the light out, Maggie," he responds. "I might be impotent, Maggie," he continues. "I'm not afraid," she answers. Given his ambiguous sexuality, it might be appropriate to question whether he could make love to a woman. In another option, Williams makes Brick even more assertive. Maggie asks, "Where does this pillow go, does it go on the sofa?" "It stays on the bed," he answers. "I might be *impotent*, Maggie . . ." "That I don't fear!" she cries. "And this is my time by the calendar to conceive!" At last, he says, "(sadly, humbly, gently) 'Is it? I hope you do.'"[37]

Considering Williams's choices among various alternatives, the last words were of crucial importance in resolving (or perpetuating) the puzzle of the play. In the original, the ending reaffirmed Williams's depiction of Maggie's strength and determination. In the Broadway script, the last act strengthened the contradictory notion of truth-in-mendacity that ran through both versions. But the tone was different enough that the two might be considered different plays. At least Williams thought so. But in neither is the central ambiguity of Brick's sexuality resolved. Williams realized that one discussion with the father, no matter how shattering, could not change Brick's character so completely that he would suddenly reconcile with Maggie—or more important—silence his own demons and rekindle his physical desire. So even in the Broadway version, the ending remains ambiguous and understated.

It is clear why Williams refused any easy denouement. In one unpublished revision, he placed an explanatory paragraph at the beginning of the play, following the quotation from Dylan Thomas's poem about death—"rage, rage against the dying of the light." The lines seem to suggest a focus on Big Daddy. But the unused gloss argues something different: "The mystery of Brick is the poem of the play, not the story, which belongs more to Margaret." In effect, however, the play is about all of these characters, and it is Williams's shifting spotlight and increasing sympathy for each that releases the multiple meanings of the drama and guarantees that irresolution will prevail at the curtain.[38]

If the Broadway version, which is what most theater audiences actually saw, pushed the play toward a more resolute ending, the MGM film exploited this possibility more zealously. Although Williams had little to do with the production, and deplored the changes made, it became the most successful and widely viewed of all his film adaptations. Released in 1958, *Cat on a Hot Tin Roof* was his fifth play (including his screenplay for *Baby Doll*) to be filmed. It became the highest grossing film in that year and the tenth greatest success of all MGM films up to that point.[39]

The dilemma as well as the great advantage of any Tennessee Williams play for Hollywood producers amounted to pretty much the same thing: explicit, sometimes bawdy language and frank allusions to sex. Actress Geraldine Page remarked that this expectation was what attracted audiences and even the critics who worried about the subject matter and violent language. They protested too much, she declared: "Oh, isn't that awful! That wicked man! How can he write such a decadent thing?" "But they wouldn't miss one for the world," she added. Such feigned shock and prurient interest were the stuff of life in Hollywood. Indeed, from the very beginning, filmmakers paid close attention to the moral standards of their anticipated audiences for just such reasons, coming as close as possible to the edge of censorship and sensationalism. During the 1930s, the imposition of the film code by the Motion Picture Producers Association of America created guidelines that made this approach almost inevitable. The Breen Committee (named for Joseph Breen, its chief administrator) established clear guidelines and a process of negotiation over plots, costumes, and dialogue. Enforced by a bureaucracy of would-be censors, these rules defined acceptable language, sexual situations, moral precepts, the depiction of religion, and dress codes. The code also demanded a "Hollywood ending" for most serious dramas, in which criminals, misfits, and moral outlaws received their just punishments, and basic American institutions like the church, law enforcement agencies, and marriage and the family survived and prospered.[40]

Enforcement of these guidelines generally became a matter of negotiation among censor, producer, directors, and writers. Very often the story line or the emphasis had to be shifted to accommodate the tastes of the board. While this frequently created odd plot twists and sudden reversals of fortune, Production Code approval protected the film industry from the possibility of more draconian censorship, public condemnation, and boycott. At the same time, censorship was often only partial, limited to specific lines and words or obviously suggestive scenes, leaving intact the sometimes controversial underlying story and the original conception. The resulting film clashed internally with itself as the still-visible original idea subverted the obviously tacked-on message.

Tennessee Williams's plays and scripts were particularly susceptible to this curious process of negotiated revision. But even after the process was completed, his reputation alone guaranteed an aura of controversy. In its film review of *Cat on a Hot Tin Roof,* the *Catholic World*, for example, explained that there were "venal" reasons for the success of all the author's works: "the sensational reputation attached to Tennessee Williams plays in general and this one in particular."[41] In another case, the script for *Baby Doll* underwent a number of changes after discussions with the board, particularly over how to punish the main characters "for their transgressions—namely arson and adultery." Two of Williams's early plays were cut and transformed on their way to the movie house. *Glass Menagerie* underwent a number of changes that Williams disapproved. About these, he remarked, most were "concessions to popular tastes" based upon what he described as old-fashioned notions. *A Streetcar Named Desire*, he added, sustained only one major cut: "We couldn't mention the homosexuality [of Blanche's ex-husband] as a human problem." But by and large, "they filmed it as I had written it."[42]

Cat on a Hot Tin Roof presented a formidable challenge to the censorship process. In fact, Joseph Breen of the code board initially advised against any attempt to adapt the film. Since mention of homosexuality was forbidden, the central problem of Brick's sexual ambiguity and his relationship to Skipper had to be changed or muted. This meant, also, that Brick had to be provided with a different and plausible reason for rejecting Maggie. Richard Brooks, who directed and also wrote revisions of the script, justified his changes by declaring quite remarkably that homosexuality wasn't an essential part of the play as Williams wrote it. Much as he hated censorship, the director continued, "any kind of censorship," he practiced his own version of it in denying the obvious and in reformulating Brick's motivations. As Brooks viewed it, Brick represented "the college athletic hero who tries to remain beyond his time in his comfortable world of illusions and is afraid to lose the feeling of being loved by people." It was, he added, "a lot harder to be a real man, to work and struggle as Big Daddy does to own 28,000 acres of land." While Brick still refused to grant his sexual favors to Maggie in the film, he clearly desires her, as Brooks signals in an added scene in which Brick passionately embraces Maggie's hanging nightgown. Furthermore, by the end, Brick has become much more enthusiastic about consummating his marriage to Maggie than in either stage version.[43]

Brooks's justification for executing these changes, besides skirting potential controversy, was two-fold. As he told an interviewer later, "I never had the impression that the question of homosexuality, latent or obvious, was indispensable for the story." At another point, he noted that he had several phone conversations with Williams and that the playwright had, in fact, acquiesced in the changes the director suggested. Elsewhere, however, Brooks noted that he had little affinity for Williams and generally rejected proposals to make other films from his plays. There were phone conversations about *Cat* between the two, he noted, but their tone was not particularly "tender."[44]

Brooks also gave the strong impression that he believed he had improved the Williams work by adapting it for a movie audience. Broadway playgoers, he wrote, were trained in their expectations. But a film audience would never have believed Paul Newman, who portrayed Brick, if he refused Elizabeth Taylor (Maggie) saying, "No, darling, I'm thinking about Skipper." More to the point, Brooks's extension of the confrontation of Brick and Big Daddy made it possible for the film to end with a complete reconciliation among all the characters and a strong measure of hope for Maggie and Brick.[45] In the world of Hollywood film, it was entirely acceptable, and even expected, that a single dramatic confrontation would lead to a complete reversal of sentiment, that Brick's new understanding of his father would allow him to reconcile with Maggie. Because it was so widely practiced in the 1950s, one might give this psychological reversal a name: the principle of Hollywood catharsis. In this sense, the dramatic conventions of stage and movie house seemed to be opposites, for what was impossible in one place was inevitable according to the conventions of the other.

But there was still a problem, and even the Hollywood script underwent several changes centered on the Brick-Skipper-Maggie triangle. An initial adaptation of the play by James Poe (who received a screen credit for his work) depicted the friendship of Brick and Skipper in a long, clumsy new episode centering on their halcyon college football days. Replete with voice-over narration by Brick and then Maggie, it eliminates all elements of homosexuality and emphasizes a different and entirely implausible theme: Skipper as a substitute father figure for Brick. With Big Daddy unable to respond to his son, Skipper steps in to provide emotional support. As he tells Maggie, "Big Daddy never gave him . . . (fumbling) like—love. Like— I mean—a boost . . . Shot in the arm . . . understand?" Finally, in this sequence, Maggie confesses that she actually slept with Skipper, thereby quashing any suspicion that he might be gay. He dies from remorse and guilt over betraying his friend almost immediately after Brick rebukes him.[46]

Even as the scene breaks the continuity of the drama and destroys any semblance of subtlety, it remains most remarkable for its contorted argument against the play. In this preposterous shaggy dog story, Poe attempted to erase any suggestion of a gay relationship between Brick and Skipper, or anything like the continuum of sexual expression that Williams was exploring. But he only succeeded in proposing a leaden scene with deadly potential to sink the whole production. As it was, Richard Brooks completely reworked Poe's script, bringing it closer to Williams's original intention. Nonetheless, he retained the invention of Brick's adolescent longing for a father figure—a stock dramatic convention in the mid-1950s.[47]

Besides Brick's motivation for rejecting Maggie, the most significant change in the Hollywood script came in the scene between Brick and Big Daddy. Brooks lengthened the second act dialogue between the two and extended and embellished the theme of reconciliation—between father and son and around the awful truths hidden by mendacity. His version underscored the need to live by the illusions spun to hide those truths, but he also changed their character. The film also expanded the reconciliation between Big Daddy and Big Mama. Father and son also understand one another when Brick recognizes that he must grow up and accept his role as the prodigal son. His reestablishment of sexual relations with

Maggie promises an erotic version of the happy ending. Even Big Daddy has changed too, accepting his death sentence by cancer.[48]

Despite his contortions, Brooks did not entirely erase Williams's allusions to homosexuality. This theme is still suggested in two or three lines where Big Daddy begins to hint that Brick and Skipper had a sexual relationship. What are you suggesting, Brick demands to know: "Go on say it ... Say it!" But this possibility disappears—literally—with a clap of thunder, as if Brooks were audibly indicating the place where his production differed from the play (or was this divine censorship?). At that point, the story shifts abruptly. The new theme of Brick's failure to grow up is introduced as Brick tells Big Daddy that he only wants his love. Then the film pushes to its inevitable conclusion. Another change comes when Maggie explains to Big Daddy that she had thought about seducing Skipper, but changed her mind. Brick still hangs up the telephone on Skipper, but now the reason is a lie that Skipper has told him about the encounter. Skipper kills himself out of remorse—because of the revelation of his failure with Maggie and for his cowardice on the football field. Thus, everyone is exonerated of sexual trespass. The only casualty is believability, for now Brick's initial refusal to sleep with Maggie becomes even more astonishing.

Brooks also focused Brick's anger and disgust with lies on Big Daddy's failure to love him, to accept him completely as his son. In the confrontation scene between the two, now set in the basement, amidst the clutter of bric-a-brac bought during a Cook's tour of Europe with Big Mama, Brick describes the pain of being a son in a family where Big Daddy bought things for people, but expended no emotion or love on them. Confronting his own death, Big Daddy accepts this truth and then tells the sentimental story of his own beloved hobo father, fondly picking up a battered suitcase that was his only inheritance. This scenic descent into Hollywood sentimentality ends with the reconciliation of father and son as they stumble up the stairs in each other's arms.[49]

Although Brooks struggled mightily to smooth over the ambiguities of Williams's work in his movie script by adding a theme of antimaterialism and a kind of Freudian gloss of thwarted family love, he failed to erase the uncertainties of the play or silence Williams's inquiry into masculinity. His ending was abrupt, although certainly anticipated, and the general revolution of mood and transformation of family relations and sexual desire was too sudden to be entirely believable outside the calculations of the movie industry. Yet for all his tampering with the plot and characters, Brooks recognized and even enhanced Williams's theme of mendacity and its contradictory function in human relations. The lie remains the inevitability to live and die by. As Big Daddy demands of Brick: "Why can't you live with it? There's nothing to live with but mendacity."[50] Summarizing the purpose of his transformation of the script, Brooks defended himself: "Aside from writing the homosexuality out of Brick's character, few basic changes were made in the play." But on both counts, this statement has to be challenged. Homosexuality still hovers in Big Daddy's brief insinuation—and in the larger problem of the plausibility of Brick's sexual reticence. And much of the dialogue was altered, with new lines added and scenes moved or spliced together so that the life-giving prevarication of Maggie's pregnancy becomes an even more powerful message.[51]

Considering all of these versions as a single oeuvre, what did *Cat on a Hot Tin Roof* say about American masculinity? What elements of Williams's vision entered the mainstream dialogue in American popular culture? It should be stressed that few Americans saw the first version of the play where Williams presented the clearest suggestion of a troubled, gay character. As the emphasis shifted in the Broadway version, and then moved again in the film, the paradoxical message about mendacity grew ever stronger. Nonetheless, the question of homosexuality and its relationship to heterosexuality remained a palpable undercurrent. In fact, New York drama critics, when the play opened in 1955, chided Williams for failing to confront the issue honestly. Walter Kerr, in the *New York Herald-Tribune,* was among the most aggressive critics to charge that Williams had created a "play of evasion: evasion on the part of its principal characters, evasion perhaps on the part of its playwright." Other New York critics, such as John Chapman, seconded this point. In his notice for the *Daily News*, he wondered whether Williams had not lost control of his material. "I felt frustrated myself," confessed the critic, "I felt that some heart or point or purpose was missing." And he offhandedly referred to Brick as the "queer" son. Richard Watts, Jr., in the *New York Post* found the same fault, even citing Kerr's review. "Either purposefully or unconsciously," he declared, "Mr. Williams has obscured the final truth of the character, just as he has given the play an ending that is ambiguous." Of course, there were some who just evaded the meaning of the play completely. Eleanor Roosevelt, for example, blithely wrote in her column after the opening that it was a play about the "difficulty of communication between people."[52]

Reviews of the film were less likely to evoke the homosexual theme—after all, it had been heavily censored—but some writers still emphasized its presence, perhaps because they knew of the original story or had seen the play. Paul V. Beckley, in the *New York Herald-Tribune* in September

1958, noted that "the homosexual theme is handled very softly," but that it was, nonetheless, present and to be accounted for. The *New York Times* marked the presence of this theme by its practical absence, noting that Brick's motivation "had to be cut for the screen." As the *New York Post* noted, the film retained practically all of the elements of Williams's play except "the suggestion of a homosexual relationship." Whatever they saw in the actual content of the film, the Broadway play was often referenced by critics as a starting place for their comments, thus reinjecting the issue into the film and thereby conflating the different versions.[53]

In this manner, the complexities and nuances of Williams's characterization of Brick lost something of their subtlety in translation but still remained present. Reviewers, when they discussed the play and the film, explained away the contradictions of motivation. It was no secret to many of them, and presumably not to most of the audience for the play and the film, that *Cat on a Hot Tin Roof* was "about" a homosexual character—whatever Williams's own protestations to the contrary. At the same time, to understand the play and the film in such terms is to miss much of its larger meaning and to fail to grasp the extraordinary drama underlying its creation.

Latter-day critics have repeated some of these points about the reticent sexuality, although their interests in Williams vary considerably. There has been considerable commentary on the relationship between characters in plays such as *Cat* and the author's family: his father, mother, sister, and brother. Some critics remove this to a more abstract relationship, as embodying and personifying contradictory elements of the author's own psyche.[54] Other critics have read the play as a discourse about sensitivity versus brute realism, a theme found frequently in other Williams works, when characters find themselves, for one reason or another, unable to confront the awful truths about themselves or their world, and so retreat into illusion. Others have found in Brick intimations of Williams's own personal concern for the compromises necessary for him to be heard, to be a playwright in a world where he had to accede to mendacity. Williams's own words about the play underscore this possible interpretation in his unfailing admiration for Maggie. She is a strong and determined creature, "taking hold of and gaining supremacy over and committing to her own purpose a broken, irresolute man."[55]

To fellow playwright Arthur Miller, *Cat on a Hot Tin Roof* represented a brilliant failure to follow through on the theme of materialism and greed to its resolution—issues that were paramount for him, although not for Williams. Miller believed that Brick's sexual reticence created a diversion from his failure to reject the profoundly flawed materialism represented by Big Daddy. But even in the film, which pushed this theme harder, the story draws back from such a radically different conclusion. The empire in the Mississippi Delta, in the end, will pass safely into the hands of Brick and Maggie. Miller's critique is thus pertinent to all the versions of the story. As he wrote, what the play required was an extension beyond the narrow boundaries of self: "The viewpoint of the adolescent is not enough," he wrote. Of course there are more generous versions of this motif, but Miller's point about the opposition in the play between materialism and a kind of outsider's poetic vision is suggestive. And not for the first time does a Williams male character find himself in the company of that popular, emerging typology of the 1950s that Miller alluded to—the alienated youth. This omnipresent character was becoming a stereotype of films and books that aimed at generating social criticism through the eyes of younger victims of an oppressive society. Miller may have been delivering a critique that missed the central point of the play, but he was not wrong to link Williams with this developing character in 1950s cinematic drama. In fact, actor James Dean's various film personifications and the literary adolescent Holden Caulfield (*Catcher in the Rye*, 1951) bear a generic resemblance to Brick Pollitt in their disgust with pretense and artifice.[56]

The assertion that Brick somehow embodies modern alienated youth—while clearly not Williams's primary intent—in its focus on Brick's refusal to accept adult responsibilities emphasizes the element that survived in all of the versions of *Cat on a Hot Tin Roof*. This is Tennessee Williams's deconstruction of the meaning of masculinity itself. When understood in terms of the related theme of mendacity, this exploration implies a profound engagement with the meanings attributed to modern American masculinity, and a very troubling depiction of their operation. Many critics have commented on Williams's brilliant explorations of gender—his depictions of various extremes of male and female embodiment. With men, the range of characters leads from Stanley Kowalski (*Streetcar Named Desire*, 1951) and Big Daddy—whom Williams describes as "men at the peak of their physical manhood, as coarse and direct and powerful as the primary colors." But he also sketched men in softer shades and pastels, like Brick, whose sensitivity allowed him to perceive the world with an almost paralyzing clarity.[57]

What links Brick to adolescence, although he is not really an adolescent, is his refusal to accede to the compromises and distortions of adult manhood, to dissolve ambiguity into a single stereotype. These are exactly the attributes of adulthood that seemed to alienate rebellious youth in the 1950s, although Brick clearly sees them from a different perspective. In a certain sense, it is irrelevant—as Williams undoubtedly understood—whether or not Brick actually slept with Skipper, whether his disgust and self-loathing comes mostly from his betrayal of his friend or from his love for him. It is the angle of vision that matters, not so much what put him there, that makes the play an extraordinarily powerful drama about the performance of gender.

In *Cat on a Hot Tin Roof,* Brick refuses all of the possible male roles he is asked to perform and, in so doing, exposes each to dramatic deconstruction. Each, he finds, is defined by mendacity—by the lie that makes them both intolerable and necessary at the same time. All the events of the play confirm this message. And so the drama becomes an extended commentary on the performance of masculinity. As afternoon falls into the night of the play, Brick refuses, in turn, every solicitation by the other characters to "be a man." Each refusal is etched with betrayal, and before the denouement of the drama, he has (explicitly in Williams's alternative sketches) become impotent—the loss of even the physical attributes of male gender. In the course of the evening, he refuses to play the son (to father and mother), husband (to Maggie), father (to the child he refuses to sire), brother (to Gooper), and even uncle (to the "No-Neck monsters," the obnoxious children of Gooper and Mae). When pushed by Big Daddy to reveal the secret of his relationship to Skipper, he confesses his betrayal of friendship and hints at his inability even to perform "unnatural love." Immobilized by disgust at the lies surrounding and defining each of these possibilities, he seeks escape in the thought-erasing solace of alcohol, where the "click" he awaits is a signal of the closing down of all sensations from the world around him. The moment of truth—or rather self-knowledge—occurs in the scene with Big Daddy where, between them, they echo each other's detestation of mendacity and the lies that have surrounded their existence. No matter which format, play or film, this crucial scene expresses the mutual understanding that Big Daddy and Brick achieve. Life is a lie; and the terrible irony is that mendacity is the only way to live it. Each character, thereafter, accepts the lies that make it possible to continue. Big Daddy (depending on the version) accepts the cloying, sentimental love of Big Mama and is reconciled to dying, surrounded by a family most of whom he despises. Brick allows Maggie's lie that she is pregnant to go undenied. And, again, depending on the version, more or less enthusiastically he begins to accept the role as her restored lover to make it come true.[58]

In this regard, the exact ending does not matter, nor indeed does Brick's purported homosexuality. The larger significance of the play is disclosed in Williams's commentary on the meaning of masculinity itself and its fragile dependence upon how we choose to perform it. This is a comedy of domestic manners of the most searing sort. By refusing to be a man, Brick brings all the facets of manhood into question. By exposing each as a role to be played, as a charade to enact, he rejects their essentialist verities. At the same time, in finally embracing mendacity, Brick achieves greater self-knowledge, and the possibility of acting out his role of being a man.[59] Williams's play thus unmasks the meaning of manhood by asserting, in his strongest language, that it is a truth based upon a lie. He resolves the devastating inertia of this insight by declaring the need to live nonetheless with that painful reality. Like the player of his own play, Williams suggests that masculinity itself is a role, a creation of the imagination, played to an audience of others. In his own life, lived at the very margins, Williams had earned the perspective to make this judgment. And this final resolution of the puzzle went straight to the heart of contemporary masculinity: it was everything and it was nothing.

9

The Gender of High Culture

A highbrow is a man who has found something more interesting than women.
—Edgar Wallace

The most striking fact about American consumption is that it is dominated less by a class than by the tastes, fantasies and standards of the American woman.
—Max Lerner

The mass culture debate of the 1950s generated a host of fears and recriminations about the creeping feminization of American society. Almost every position in this broad discussion, at one time or another, invoked the ultimate slur that the other side was contributing to the emasculation of American culture. Often put on the defensive, intellectuals strove to respond to the accusation that elite culture, or high culture as they preferred to call it, was a province of the effete scholar. Giving as good as they got, they alleged in their countercharge that popular culture or mass culture was weak, soft, and feminine. In contrast, modernism was a hard-edged, virile endeavor. Politicians like Sen. Joseph McCarthy on the other side scorned the intellectual as a "pink," implying treason to country as well as gender—and newspapers slyly identified public intellectuals as "egg-heads," in the mistaken belief that baldness indicated a lack of male hormones. As novelist Louis Bromfield maliciously defined the term in 1952, the egghead was "a person of specious intellectual pretensions." He was "over-emotional and feminine in reactions to any problem. Supercilious and surfeited with conceit and contempt for the experience of more sound and able men." This was such a popularly used epithet that it even gained a pseudomedical definition. As the psychologist Iago Galdston wrote in 1956, the egghead "is likely to suffer from *ejaculation praecox*, and from the precipitous and periodic loss of virility."[1]

For many intellectuals, a subsidiary element in this discussion of cultural manhood focused on suburbia and its contribution to softening masculinity. To many observers, suburbia was not merely a place, but a pernicious new culture marked by conformity and effeminacy, awash in consumerism and ruled by the unchecked power of women and Moms. Many important intellectuals participated in this debate, including well-known figures such as Dwight Macdonald, William H. Whyte, and Vance Packard. A lesser known, but equally interesting, figure was Auguste C. Spectorsky, writer, producer, amateur sociologist, and, after 1956, associate editor of *Playboy* magazine, who fashioned a striking response to the controversy implicit in the sexualization of American culture. Not only did he pretend to describe the character of the new suburban environment in a popular (but derivative) book, he also participated in what may have been the most outlandish effort of the age to virilize highbrow culture.

The mass culture dispute that blazed brightly in the mid-1950s and refracted through Spectorsky's work had old origins as well as an immigrant pedigree descended from contemporary European social theories. It had appeared in nascent form in America in the nineteenth century with the development of popular fiction, and even earlier in eighteenth-century England, with the condemnation by elite writers of the "Grub Street Scribblers." Alexis de Tocqueville had also mused about the peculiar nature of American popular arts. With the development of mass culture in its various new formats around the end of the nineteenth century and the sacralization of elite forms of culture at the same time, divisions between types of cultural production, their contents, and their audiences began to provoke serious theories of cultural difference.[2] Essayists, novelists, sociologists, and psychologists speculated about two important issues. One centered on the implications of a culture divided into distinct categories: highbrow and lowbrow, elite and mass, and popular and folk. The second assessed the social effects of culture, specifically, the presumed negative influences of mass culture. Theories claiming to measure the deeply destructive effects of mass culture became especially important around World War II in reaction to the rise of totalitarian propaganda in Germany and the Soviet Union. These theories shared points of similarity with notions that had become particularly important during the 1930s about the effects of mass culture on the quality of culture and the psychology and behavior of children. Obviously, it was not just the distaste of intellectuals for vulgar fiction, the Book-of-the-Month-Club fare, comic books, television, and debased journalism that determined the discussion. There was also a large chorus of critics who, for religious or moral reasons, denounced the spread of cheap goods and vulgar ideas.[3]

At the same time, elite writers had to face the disturbing accusation that their isolation from mainstream American culture, their European orientation, their occasional radical politics, and their sometimes complex artistic creations raised serious questions about their gender identity. This allegation lay just beneath the surface in the charge that *elite* writing meant *effete* writing. As Malcolm Cowley noted in *Exile's Return*, his famous account of American expatriate writers of the 1920s, such periodicals as the *Saturday Evening Post* gleefully pictured elite writers as underendowed with talent and masculinity, and uncertain in their patriotism.[4] The accusation remained common throughout the 1950s. As Eugene Burdick wrote in 1955 for the series the "Plight of the American Intellectual," intellectuals had lost power and influence, retreating to nurse their "anomie" in the university. The stereotype of the intellectual as Communist was, he noted, "not entirely inaccurate." Today, he concluded, the alienated intellectual in America was "cut off from the actionist, masculine, object-oriented, creative part of society."[5] Literary biographer Leo Gurko found this charge ceaselessly depicted in films and short stories. In popular culture, the intellectual "is impotent[;] the practical man, significantly virile." Books, libraries, and museums appeared as places for emasculating performances, while "trucks on long night rides over lonely highways, lend themselves *per se* to the rich full existence."[6]

Both opponents and proponents of mass culture and elite culture wrapped their arguments around an assumed gender dichotomy of culture. Almost all of them used a vocabulary of gender invective, with a deep antifemale cultural bias and a scurrilous assessment of the role of women in culture. As in other areas of American culture, "womanly" or "feminine" were sometimes code words for submissive, soft, flighty, emotional, and consumerist, while "masculine" implied productive, inventive, creative, action-oriented, and tough-minded. All sides appeared to agree that the most damaging accusation a critic could wear in his holster was the charge that the other side betrayed its gender.

Suburban lifestyles were also seen as contributing to the feminization of American society and the weakening of cultural fitness. Were these insidious places not the prime setting for the enactment of rituals of emasculation: togetherness, domesticity, and mindless consumption—the refuge of weak men like Ozzie Nelson? Once again, this was not a new idea. Lewis Mumford, one of the most widely known critics of modern cities and suburbs, wrote as early as 1921 that suburbs represented a negation of urban virtue. In wandering fecklessly from home to office, he concluded, the commuter presented a spectacle "more humiliating than a man without a country; he is a man without a city."[7]

During the 1950s, the critique of suburbia appeared in scores of critical assessments of American culture. Sociological studies turned a jaundiced eye toward the new towns crowding around cities like a suffocating tourniquet, squeezing the life from American culture. The most famous of these studies was written by William H. Whyte, editor of *Fortune* magazine. *The Organization Man*, published in 1956, is one of the sharpest and most exhaustive critiques of the age, and unsurprisingly it sparked numerous competitors and imitators. Taking the planned community of Park Forest, Illinois, as one pole and the new model business organization as the other, Whyte described an interlocking domestic and business culture in which the values of belonging and consensus reflected and reinforced each other. Although Whyte was careful about his judgments, he did not hide a tone of immense disdain.[8]

Like much of the critical sociology of the 1950s (including *The Lonely Crowd*), *The Organization Man* was conservative in its interpretation of American civilization but probably perceived by most who read it as a radical critique. Upon the foundation of individualist values, Whyte built an analysis that deplored the current direction of American civilization. The author called attention to new rules of business organization which he interpreted as a distressing transformation of the American spirit. He warned that a new collectivist ideology of compromise and bureaucratic manipulation was replacing the ages-old individualism and entrepreneurship of American enterprise. Men were now expected to subordinate themselves to the will and ideology of the group. Imprisoned in "the brotherhood" of a new order, men had lost the power to resist conformity, to act as individuals. Knowledge itself had been appropriated by the system. Whereas it was once possible to trust the resources of a liberal education, even the universities had now dedicated themselves to teaching life adjustment techniques and social engineering. The pernicious symbol of this transformation of manipulation into academic enterprise was the personality test, developed and administered to judge the ability of the individual to get along in the group and to recognize the virtues of consensus—doubly insidious because it was developed by academic sociologists and psychologists to administer to corporate employees.[9]

Whyte found abundant evidence of this new ethic in the daily life of Park Forest, with its rampant kaffeeklatsches, its hostility to the intellect and individualism, and its social code of "participation." Organized around the courtyard, this new domain of blandness seemed permanent. "The values of Park Forest," he wrote, "one gets the feeling, are harbingers of the way it's going to be." Promising happiness, the suburb delivered, instead, a life-denying lifestyle that emphasized the well-rounded man with "plenty of time with the kids," "some good hobbies," and, perhaps, sometime in the future, "a bit of reading and music."[10]

Literary culture, particularly popular novels, reflected the same worrying pattern. Since 1900, he wrote, "the vision of life presented in popular fare has been one in which conflict has slowly been giving way to adjustment." This inclination was notably prominent in Sloan Wilson's contemporary popular novel *The Man in the Gray Flannel Suit*. In this story of family and business, the lead character, Tom Rath, is compelled to choose between an ambitious career in business and familial happiness. He chooses the latter, saying, "I've been through one war. Maybe another one's coming [alluding to the cold war]. If one is, I want to be able to get the most out of the years I've got left. I want to get ahead as far as I possibly can without sacrificing my entire personal life."[11] That such a passage could be imagined to indicate debased values speaks loudly of the ethical premises of 1950s popular sociology like Whyte's.

Although Whyte's rhetoric was not overtly gendered, except in its characteristic focus on men, it fell into the familiar masculine-feminine division that typified much of the antisuburban literature. The conflation of emasculation with suburban lifestyles was also a major theme of John Keats's popular novel *The Crack in the Picture Window*, published the year following *The Organization Man*. Where Whyte had been circumspect and guarded, Keats was explicit and heavy-handed, inventing allegorical suburban figures whose names alone spelled the deplorable quality of their moral lives. The main character is John Drone, who lives with his family in a fictitious Washington, D.C., suburb. His neighbors are "the Amiables" and "the Fecunds." Condemned to an existence of monotonous shoddiness, Drone, like millions of veterans, has bought into the promise of suburbia, but he can discover no individual, meaningful existence there. Instead, there is only the illusory world of television, do-it-yourself projects, and endless boredom. Keats's study gives the impression of sophistication, erudition, and close analysis even if these qualities are festooned with moral barbs. Not that it was difficult to find a considerable contemporary literature in psychology and sociology that confirmed his judgments. Experts seemed to agree that the new suburban world was noteworthy primarily for its destructive influences. In addition to ennui, aside from inferior and substandard housing, beyond conformity, loomed the apparition of the feminized society, replete with a "frustrated matriarchy" whose only remedy for boredom was to lead the family on a consumer treasure hunt. Left to their own devices and granted immense power through their control of domesticity, such women (such "Moms") were raising a generation of passive males who would never cut loose from the apron strings of their possessive mothers. When we "huddle together," Keats grimly warned, we will end up "breeding swarms of drones [or Drones]."[12]

Novelist and sexologist John McPartland, in his best selling *No Down Payment*, published in 1958, assembled all of the elements of this bleak vision and put the individual faces on sociological analysis. In his book, he recounted the stories of several couples living in the Sunrise Hills suburban development outside San Francisco. As in other dramatizations of suburban sociology, his couples enacted their ennui in casual and thoughtless sex. The hero and heroine, Jean and David Martin, are an up-and-coming couple, but Jean worries about David's masculinity. Talking to a friend, she repeats (and personalizes) one of the clichés of the genre in a cascade of invective. Men are becoming like women, she insists, "All this do-it-yourself stuff, that's like housework for men." And nine out of ten of their careers could easily be filled by women, she continues: "Look at their jobs—salesmen, clerks, accountants, desk jobs." They even looked feminine. They "wear bright colors, show off more. They go on diets as much as women do." And girls were growing larger, stronger, more like men. In an ultimate insult, she refers to him as "a *Ladies Home Journal* kind of husband."

If McPartland's dramatic denouement was extreme and mechanistic, it nonetheless suggested that a real man might yet emerge from his ranch house to do battle with the suburban ethic. The way out of the nightmare of the novel is sudden, and the deus ex machina is David's stiffened masculinity. At work, he imposes an automated system on an unwilling client; he exposes his superior for a weak and inefficient manager; and he beats up the neighbor who has raped his wife. If too many tumblers suddenly fall into place to unlock this new virility, the point McPartland made was a compelling and familiar one: business and domestic life were reflections of each other and men needed to win back control of both.[13]

Such critiques of suburbia reinforced the related debate over the effects of mass culture on American society. As David Riesman wrote in his 1958 essay, "The Suburban Sadness," Whyte, Eric Fromm, and Paul Goodman were accurate in their various depictions of the growing alienation and anomie of the suburban world. Using such words as "trivial" and "dehumanized" to describe the culture of the new suburban man, Riesman drew a similar conclusion. The "vicarious socialization of Americans into experiences of consumption they are about to have," he wrote, was dependent upon the mass media that, in ads, features, and other formats, extolled the suburban way of life and elevated its inhabitants into "the idols of consumption." Yet he hoped that Americans might eventually discover some new model of life, and for this, they required planners and prophets with a different dream, perhaps, one suspects, critics like him.[14]

The mass culture syndrome, to which this alleged suburban blight was a contributing factor, occupied a central place in the intellectual history of the 1950s and contributed appreciably to reinforcing a gendered conception of American culture and its ills. If this division into masculine and feminine seems strange to the modern reader, it nonetheless emerged in sharp detail as sociological studies swept forlorn searchlights across American society. Now conformity, now affluence, then suburbanization and consumerism, one after the other–and sometimes all together—these elements of culture stirred considerable anxiety. It was as if gender identity had become a practical tool of analysis in the evaluation of the most important and controversial elements of modern society. Unmistakably, moral critique now inhabited (if it were ever absent) the heart of social science.[15]

The word "mass" in mass culture came to have multiple applications, in part because it was often paired with some other word as a means of calling attention to repetitious, industrial qualities. None of these terms (mass culture, mass society, mass man, mass action) denoted anything very positive; sometimes they indicated considerable anxiety.[16] But "mass" was not just a synonym for "ominous." It did not just mean mediocrity. It was more toxic stuff implying manipulation, brainwashing, and the triumph of consumer values, all of which represented the destruction of a man's "privacy and integrity," as George B. Leonard, Jr., put it in his quirky jeremiad about disappearing masculinity for *Look* magazine in 1956.[17]

The exact origins of the 1950s version of the mass culture debate are difficult to pinpoint. In the 1920s, critic Van Wyck Brooks originated the terms "highbrow" and "lowbrow" (recalling Homo sapiens and Neanderthals), but the moralizing of cultural class divisions was itself far older. Undoubtedly the proximate cause was the full-blown appearance of modern mass culture, particularly films and, later, television, with the many objections raised to their real and imagined social effects.[18]

The 1950s version of this struggle between the lettered and the masses was vociferously argued by New York intellectuals and by those in the academy whom they influenced. Furthermore, influential European refugee intellectuals, including Theodor Adorno and Herbert Marcuse, wrote important analyses of mass culture that proved to be a fount of ideas in the discussion. Other leading figures were critic Clement Greenberg, Dwight Macdonald, and the editors and contributors to the *Partisan Review*. This small, but influential New York journal published one of the initial documents on the issue: a major, ongoing symposium in 1952 immodestly entitled "Our Country and Our Culture." Toward the end of the decade, Bernard Rosenberg and David Manning White published another symposium that was even more consistently critical of popular culture featuring many of the same contributors.[19]

The European contribution to this evaluation of the popular came in echoes of a conversation that began in the mid-nineteenth century in France, Germany, and England, which then became insistent and fully elaborated in the 1930s and the 1940s with the rise of Nazism. The relationship between mass culture and totalitarianism was a link that Jürgen Habermas, Theodor Adorno, and Max Horkheimer sought to demonstrate, and that some American intellectuals more cautiously repeated. In his fine study of this intellectual history, Andreas Huyssen detects a persistent undertow in the discussion: the fear of being engulfed in feminine weakness. Tracing this sentiment back to the influential works of Gustave Le Bon on crowd psychology in the late nineteenth century, he notes that modernist rejections of mass culture revealed a "persistent gendering as feminine of that which is devalued." Translated into American terminology, this reinforced the cultural oppositions of individualism versus collectivism, high versus low, interior versus exterior, character over personality, and inner-direction versus other-direction.[20]

That the "thinking and talking" classes seriously entertained this argument was apparent everywhere in the 1950s, but nowhere so consistently as in the writings and utterances of public intellectuals. As Lionel Trilling, one of the most astute observers of the times, warned, "We are in the full tide of those desperate perceptions of our life," which "haunt and control our minds with visions of losses worse than existence—losses of civilization, personality, humanness."[21]

But intellectual hostility to mass culture could serve the politics of both left and right, liberal as well as conservative. In fact, tracing the political implications of this attitude is complicated by the unsteady and shifting biographies of the critics who articulated these positions. Consider the difficulty in sorting out the political implications of H. L. Mencken's acid essays on American culture in the 1920s or 1930s or the strident attack of Bernard Iddings Bell in *Crowd Culture*, his updated version of Le Bon's older jeremiad, *The Crowd*. Bell warned of rising collectivism and of the vulgarity in Mickey Spillane detective novels, the "rubbish" and "garbage" of popular culture. In the end, he proposed a renewal of culture, embellished by a vital religious movement, and an education "rescued from those who now 'emasculate' it."[22]

Long a political gadfly and practicing film critic, former editor of the *Partisan Review* and, in the 1960s, a movie critic for *Esquire* magazine and staff writer for the *New Yorker*, Dwight Macdonald brought together several traditions of writing about mass culture to create a memorable class analysis of American civilization. He believed he could identify three principal divisions: mass culture, high culture, and something new, middlebrow culture, which represented a sum of the lesser parts of the other two. Macdonald characterized mass culture as an instrument of domination and a device of political corruption. When mass culture borrowed ideas, forms, and images from high culture, it debased them with lowbrow content and sentimentality. This new scourge could be seen everywhere in the 1950s: in films, the culture of youth, and the sentimental worship of Mom. The dismal result was a pernicious cultural androgyny. Given the current direction of civilization, he wrote, "Peter Pan might be a better symbol of America than Uncle Sam." In his lurid description there seemed no clear way out. But one thing was certain. The opposition between creative and corrupt culture followed a gendered fault line: action versus passivity, production versus consumption, work versus easy pleasure, and intellect against sentiment.[23]

Five years after the first *Partisan Review* symposium on the subject, Bernard Rosenberg and David Manning White published a sampler of recent articles written by "excoriators" and "defenders" of mass culture. The two editors took opposing positions. Rosenberg argued that mass culture threatened "man's autonomy." At its worst, it "threatens not merely to cretinize our taste, but to brutalize our senses while paving the way to totalitarianism." White was much more generous, declaring his suspicion of elite condemnations of anything but the avant-garde. He declared that he remained optimistic about the health of American letters despite its pervasive vulgarity.[24]

While the charges leveled against mass culture (it had only a few visible defenders) ranged from political distortion to the suppression of artistic freedom, the terms of argument did not stray from certain key points. Mass culture was seductive; it rendered audiences passive; it lacked energy, complication, and intelligence. Frankfurt school intellectual Theodor Adorno, in his essay on television, argued that the result of the division was an irresponsible, popular attack on intellectuals that opened a huge gulf between them and the rest of America. In the popular mind, the artist was an aesthete, a weakling, a sissy. Ordinary opinion identified the "artist with the homosexual," he wrote, and respected only the "man of action."[25]

Beyond this, the mass culture argument had nowhere to go except into repetition, since censorship was impossible; boycott an unreality; and education apparently ineffective. But it did not die quickly. Ink continued to be spilled, tracts written, and conferences convened. In 1959, for example, Norman Jacobs published the proceedings from a symposium at New York's Tamiment Institute held in June of that year. Not unexpectedly, many of the participants were familiar troopers in this war of words. Philosopher Hannah Arendt and sociologist, psychologist, and legal scholar Ernst Van den Haag rehearsed the criticism that mass culture threatened genuine creation. Writer Randall Jarrell could not have been more blunt: "True works of art," he said, "are more and more produced away from, in opposition to society." Stanley Edgar Hyman cast his worries in the familiar mold of gender. Films, he wrote, currently had a "more pervasive homosexual imagery." To historian Oscar Handlin, the whole twentieth century illustrated an era of missed chances. Following the 1890s, authentic popular culture had become separate from mass culture. The result had been decades of confusion and irrelevant dispute. He deplored the separation of men of ideas from mass audiences. "Thus there is passing a great opportunity," he wrote, "for conversation between those who have something to say and the audience who no longer know whether they would like to listen to what there is to be said." Patrick Hazard turned this argument into an accusation against intellectuals. Their "snobbish attitude" had only made the crisis worse.[26]

The last significant meeting on the perils of mass culture appeared in the 1961 volume entitled *Mass Culture Revisited*. As the title suggested, the volume was repetitious, with almost a tone of resignation. Still, the stakes remained high: "our manhood," as Rosenberg put it. And there were new examples of dreadful mass culture added to the tab: fresh outrages on television, in advertising, and popular music. But the arguments changed little. As Paul Lazarsfeld explained, "Debates about mass culture have a tantalizing way of ending in a draw." And so this phase of discussion wound down, not with a decisive conclusion but with echoes and duplication.[27]

If the misery of mass culture proved a disturbing threat to American letters and a challenge to the masculine cast of culture, there was an even worse possibility. The scandal of homoeroticism lay across the body of American letters. In 1948, Leslie Fiedler published an essay that soon became notorious, entitled "Come Back to the Raft Ag'in, Huck Honey," in the *Partisan Review*. The young critic wrote that at the center of the newly emerging canon of American male authors (Cooper, Melville, and Twain, for example) was a homoerotic relationship between a white man—or a boy—and a dark-skinned other. Fiedler suggested that this ideal of pure male friendship and love represented an escape from responsibility, marriage, and maturity—homosocial if not homosexual. It was, he added, the essential character of the frontier experience.

Fiedler later asserted that he had been misunderstood to suggest that this implied a sexual relationship. But the misstep to that interpretation was really only a short stumble. When he reiterated his thesis in 1960 in the survey *Love and Death in the American Novel*, he restated the same point in a somewhat circumspect way. The "tie between male and male is not only considered innocent, it is taken for the very symbol of innocence itself." Of all things American writers appeared to fear most, he announced, maturity, symbolized by marriage, headed the list. But Fiedler's adaptation of Freudianism to literary interpretation had further implications even if he did not assert them. For Freud, the evasion of maturity was, at its core, a form of narcissism—the stunted development that in popularized versions of his psychology was taken to be a significant cause of homosexuality.[28]

Considered together, the proliferation of suburbs and mass culture and consumption, threatened elites, and homoerotic traditions exacerbated the sense of masculinity crisis in the conversation of 1950s intellectuals. The language of invidious gender comparisons had staked a commodious tent on the campgrounds of American literary life. Was there a way to escape this cultural predicament and resolve the masculinity crisis simultaneously? Could elite culture be restored to its rightful place as a model of intellect and manliness? Writer, editor, and amateur sociologist Auguste Comte Spectorsky confidently believed that he knew the way through this tangled forest, through a Northwest Passage to rejuvenated American masculinity. He found this way through *Playboy* magazine, with its forced marriage of sophistication and soft-core pornography. As he saw it, Hugh Hefner's celebration of sex outside marriage, sophisticated consumption, and visual titillation provided a platform on which elite writers could once again stand as men, members of a virile and creative band. Even consumption could be rescued from the hands of women by associating it with good taste and seduction. As associate editor of the publication from 1956 until his death in 1972, he strove to do exactly that, using high fees to attract leading American male writers to a readership drawn to the magazine by a format of sophisticated advertising and mild pornography. Of course, this was an already proven format. *Esquire* magazine had thrived since the 1930s on just such a mixture of sexual and literary sophistication. *Esquire* would undergo rejuvenation in the late 1950s and 1960s that proffered a parallel, although slightly different vision of the activist intellectual life in its praise of the "uncommon" man.[29] But it was the founder Hugh Hefner's genius to recognize that this formula could be pushed further and modified for a new and younger audience. In celebrating the young bachelor lifestyle, he exploited one of Kinsey's discoveries: that American men were already engaged in considerable sexual activity before and outside marriage. Kinsey had effectively identified a waiting market of middle-class college boys and young unmarried men whose active fantasy life was an important form of sexual behavior and a retail opportunity. More than that, Hefner sometimes referred to the Kinsey volumes as his Bible. In college, he wrote a term paper on the Kinsey reports and often invoked the sexologist in asserting his philosophy. And eventually, the Playboy Foundation helped support another study of American sexuality, the survey by Virginia Johnson and William Masters.[30] Meanwhile, Hefner hired Spectorsky to find the writers; he would furnish the lifestyle, the "philosophy," and the girls.[31]

As theologian Harvey Cox wrote in 1961, *Playboy* supplied its readers with exactly what they seemed to want: "a total image of what it means to be a man." Although he rejected the *Playboy* philosophy that Hefner and Spectorsky had fashioned, particularly for transforming sex into recreation and partners into objects, Cox believed that the journal spoke directly to "the male identity crisis." Except that for him, its resolution remained inadequate and expressed a "fear to be one's self."[32]

Auguste Comte Spectorsky was born to American parents in Paris in 1910 and received his Christian name in honor of the pioneer French philosopher and sociologist. His mother was an opera singer, and his father an educator. When the family returned to the United States, his father became a "dollar-a-year" volunteer with the U.S. government during World War I. Auguste attended the Ethical Culture School and Columbia Grammar School in New York City. In 1929, he went to Hollywood for a year to work with Columbia Pictures but returned to attend New York University, from which he graduated in 1934. After he sold a piece to the *New Yorker*, the magazine took him on as an editorial assistant. In 1941, he became literary editor of the *Chicago Sun* as well as a contributor to journals such as *Cosmopolitan* and *Harper's Bazaar*. For two years after 1946, he served as associate eastern story editor for Twentieth Century Fox pictures, a position that enabled him to purchase stories for conversion into films (for example, *Gentleman's Agreement*). From 1948 to 1951, he worked on several journals owned by Street and Smith Publishers. Then, in 1952, he moved to NBC Television and the *Home Show* as a writer. At the same time, he served as editor for the sophisticated *Park East* magazine.[33] If this peripatetic career described a man who ricocheted between editing and creative writing without any defining success at either, Spectorsky's multiple jobs and career paths zigzagged around the center of New York's sophisticated journalistic and popular culture industries, putting him in a advantageous position to exploit these contacts as an editor.

His published reflections upon this world of commercial New York culture earned him the reputation as an astute observer. The result was the offer to come to Chicago to become editorial director of the new *Playboy* magazine. He accepted and moved his family to the Midwest, where his wife joined him as personnel director of the publication. Over the next several years, he became vice president of the magazine, director of the Playboy Press, and a member of the board of directors of Playboy Enterprises. Taken together, this accretion of titles and responsibilities describes a man with considerable power over the intellectual content of the magazine. As his son Brook explained in a later interview, "Dad was in charge of all editorial content in *Playboy* and helped with the "Playboy" philosophy."[34]

The invitation to move to Chicago came shortly after Spectorsky had published his minor best seller, *The Exurbanites*. This exploration of American suburban life floated in the far orbit of academic sociology, although it reflected the formulas of other, more serious critical works. For a very short moment, however, it temporarily occupied the epicenter of the semiscientific literature on American society and its changing mores that fascinated the 1950s. It was a minor part of the literature of exposé, despair, and emulation about the new postwar suburbs that contributed numerous fiction and nonfiction best sellers to American letters in the 1950s. Like William Whyte's *Organization Man*, John Keats's *Crack in the Picture Window*, and, of course, Riesman's *Lonely Crowd*, *The Exurbanites* also shared some of the perspectives of fictional accounts of the phenomenon such as *Mr. Blandings Builds His Dream House* and *The*

Man in the Gray Flannel Suit. Spectorsky's book floated in this orbit between sociology and fiction.[35]

Spectorsky first began his literary engagement with suburbia in fiction, publishing three separate stories about the same middle-class family in *Colliers'*, *Cosmopolitan*, and *Park East*. He hoped that these pieces might become the basis of a television series: "I think they would be ideal TV characters," he wrote, "and the recent growth of suburban living seems to me to make them timely as well as interesting." Although the series found no immediate backers, Spectorsky continued to believe the suburbs were a fertile field for a literary harvest. Writing under the pseudonym Paul Wallace, he published a humorous but probing article on long-distance commuters: "The Darien-Westport Axis." Reaction to this piece convinced him that his best opportunity lay in sociological, not fictional, representation. At first he considered dividing his work into four articles for publication in *Coronet* magazine. But later that year, he signed a contract to do a book with J. B. Lippincott.[36]

The project, tentatively titled *The New York Commuter*, promised to expose something new in American sociological typology, the "big-city commuter," as he initially identified this new species whose habitat lay beyond the middle-class suburb. Denizens of Westchester, Fairfield, and Rockland counties around New York City, these new men were not normal suburbanites, if that meant residents of Queens or the Bronx or Levittown. They were a recent appearance that lived well beyond the city and whose professions were typically those of the "symbol manipulator"—advertisers and cultural impresarios: in short, the midwives of the new consumer culture. They produced, created, and sold nothing tangible, but emulated the styles of men who did. As a class that lived vicariously off others, they occupied a precarious and ambiguous place. Spectorsky gave a typical example: a Madison Avenue advertising executive who believed he and his family typified the American dream. Except, of course, that the fantasy was false and better understood as the personification of Thorstein Veblen's theory of conspicuous consumption. In his prospectus for the book, Spectorsky promised to reveal the lifestyles of this group, their psychological makeup, their patterns of consumption, their conversations, and their economic problems. It would be a "serious but light-heartedly written investigation of just what the hell this amazing business is all about." He also promised a delicate touch. No one would be offended by his observations; yet he would reveal the hidden tyranny of train schedules and the congenital pretense that trapped these men in a world of symbols they had themselves designed.[37]

Typical of so much of this literature of observant-participant sociojournalism, everything hung upon definitions, and the salability of the project was greatly enhanced by the title—the choice of the right word. Spectorsky found exactly this name in the "Exurbanites," a term that enlivened the thesis and helped push the book briefly onto the best-seller list in 1955. Of course, more than a title is involved in creating a best-selling book; lively writing and Spectorsky's genial identification with his subjects helped enormously. "Exurbia is," he wrote to his editor at Lippincott, "really a pretty wonderful place." Getting the tone just right was his aim. Superficiality could be a danger. And the light touch could be too light. At the same time, "the grave sociological approach is out of place." It would be best, he felt, to emulate "Russell Lynes' approach" rather than the heavy "David Riesman school." His editor agreed, but warned of the pitfall of "off-the-top-of-the-headedness."[38]

It is apparent from the research material he collected for the book that Spectorsky was combining facts and figures drawn from train timetables, surveys of real estate and consumption patterns, and articles written about suburbs with his own observations, stories related to him by exurbanite residents, and his experience in the publishing and advertising world. In some cases, the histories he chronicled were based upon real, individual experiences; in others, they were probably imagined incidents. What in another context he called "intuitive sociology" was an apt description for his own method: a study based upon the accepted folkways of upper echelon suburbs and tales told by symbol makers—research, in other words, plus common knowledge. The concept also built upon the growing importance of the advertising man as the Everyman of 1950s business culture, hero and villain of movies, novels, and sociological studies.[39]

When it appeared, few reviewers noticed how close to fiction this book came. In one of the original articles Spectorsky sketched, this tendency was vividly clear. In his outline for "Suburbia Must Face Its Sexual Problem," he noted, "This piece would necessarily be pseudonymous and should have the authority of a medical by-line." My own "spotty research," he continued, had "made it abundantly clear that there *is* a typically suburban syndrome of sexual maladjustment and unhappiness." Two other pseudonymous articles, "I Hate Commuting" and "I Love Commuting," would argue the pros and cons of suburban life, he proposed. "Both points of view would be, as has been said, presented in subjective form, but the material contained in them would be the truth. Not only the truth, but the same truth—just seen from opposite sides."[40]

If these preliminary sketches and notes reveal something of Spectorsky's eclectic working methods, the final book, when it appeared, was a good deal more complex than this suggests. At the same time, *The Exurbanites* probably achieved its brief success because the air was rife with articles, books, short stories, and novels that depicted America's temporary fascination with this species of middle-class life and habitat. Spectorsky's work also had the advantage of lively prose and keen observation. But it primarily extended the "truth" that most readers already knew, or assumed they knew, about the illusions and failures of suburban life.

The Exurbanites attracted considerable momentary attention and gained generally favorable reviews when it appeared in 1955. Like similar exposés, it bowed toward the swelling critique of suburban life and assumed the contemporary discontent with mass culture. To Spectorsky, the typical exurbanite lived in the far-flung suburbs of New York City, attached to the city by the commuter-rail line. He (the author is only marginally interested in depicting female exurbanites) was characteristically an advertising executive, a man living by manipulating words and illusions. Exploiting the anxieties of his age in his ad copy, he believed himself above the rat race of the city, but this proved to be a delusion. Indeed, his existence replicated his profession, "which is itself so rootless, so insecure, so transitory." To avoid facing this reality, some men turned to alcohol to slow down the pace of life. But almost all of them lived beyond their means, seduced into surrounding themselves with the objects and consumer items that they had converted with their own words into symbols of desire. Even their dreams of escape were a disguised extension of their own lifestyles, embodied in a desire to move even further out from the city. But the nightmare of the rat race could not be quelled by "barbiturates, gin, or sheer fatigue."[41]

If Spectorsky had maintained this bleak tone throughout, the book might have sunk with the ballast of relentlessly discouraging stereotypes. But, as he promised, there was also a light touch offered to an audience that had come to expect an ambiguous view toward the suburbs. Sociologist C. Wright Mills, in his appreciation of the book, recognized this nonacademic tone, calling it a representative of the newly invented "sociological documentary." By this he meant a book based on personal experience, but "combined with social imagination." Such works, he wrote, had virtues that were lacking in novels or academic sociology. But, while Mills was enthusiastic and generous, even suggesting that this was the best work on American culture he had come across in several years, he made a curious admission when he located *The Exurbanites* between fiction and social science. In fact, he had said more than he perhaps intended, for one might argue that much of the critical literature about the suburbs in the 1950s lay exactly in this no-man's-land between fantasy and nonfiction.[42]

Clifton Fadiman's long essay on the book for *Holiday* magazine reiterated the work's links to fiction. He suggested that Spectorsky's observations were confirmed by a spate of recent novels, of which *The Man in the Gray Flannel Suit* was probably the best example. Of course, he admitted, there were many men who lived in "exurbia" without experiencing the anxieties of Spectorsky's conformist examples. In fact, Fadiman hoped that the unpleasant elements of exurbia would eventually diminish, if only because suburbia represented the newest, most energetic outpost of American society. Although it might seem absurd to think this way, he wrote, the man in the gray flannel suit was the modern equivalent of Daniel Boone—bringer of civilization to a new frontier.[43]

The Exurbanites drifted around the bottom of the best-seller list for thirteen weeks in 1955, although in the environs of New York City it attracted considerable notice in popular culture, including the vogue of the word "exurbanites." As a publicity stunt, for example, the Biltmore Hotel invented an "Exurbanite Cocktail" (vodka on the rocks) and set aside a special phone booth reserved for exurbanites. In Darien, Connecticut, a real estate ad for a pricey property urged, "Be an 'Exurbanite!'"[44]

Spectorsky hoped to bank this success by transforming his story into other more lucrative popular media. One ambition was to sell the exurbanite idea to Broadway for a musical revue. Spectorsky's literary agent worked through 1956 and 1957 to find a suitable writer and producer for the property. It became clear, however, that the idea had sparked little interest. As his agent wrote in 1957 with the discouraging news, "It is not an obvious musical, and I think we should go to our market very carefully."[45]

The book did, however, receive a radio play adaptation in 1956 for *CBS Radio Workshop*. Significantly, the broadcast emphasized only one facet of the study: the nightmare lives of New York's dream merchants. The program portrayed the advertising executives and publishers as curiosities in American society. They were the authors of sophistication, the inventors of fashion and fad: "It is these people here in the New York exurbs who, heaven save us, set the styles, mold the fashions, and populate the dreams for the rest of the country." Yet their own lives were a wild caricature of the seductive dreams they imagined, only more so because distorted by status competition, debt, and fatigue. Ironically, their example shattered the "dream" they sold to other Americans as well as to themselves.[46]

Spectorsky's version of suburbia, mass culture, and consumption followed the common wisdom of the 1950s, although his writing was less critical than some other examples. Nor did he view the sophistication of the exurbanite automatically as a challenge to American manhood—even if men themselves had become conformist and anxious symbol workers. But he did worry deeply and expressed himself angrily about the supposed effeminacy of American culture and the female dominance of literature, particularly popular literature: the sissy republic of American writers.

This fixation emerged full-blown in a book project tentatively called *The American Male* that he proposed to McGraw-Hill in 1956. In notes to himself and the patches of research he collected—plus initial chapter sketches—there emerged a very distressed and anxious diagnosis of contemporary American manhood. He was particularly concerned about an area of culture he called "The Limp-Wristed Acts." "Get confirming material from the *Partisan Review* on homosexuality in the arts," he reminded himself at one point. The problem, he worried, was the increasing visibility of homosexuality in culture, accompanied by an unfortunate change in American men over the previous twenty years. In part, he mused, this was probably due to the vanishing "male-female differentiation in all but psychology." And he approvingly quoted Bernard DeVoto's gender-bending aphorism: "What every career woman needs is a good wife."[47]

Built into his book prospectus on American men was a refinement of several of his ideas borrowed from *The Exurbanites*, especially for a chapter entitled "The Abominable Snow-job Men." Such symbol manipulators were bohemians, exurbanites, and hidden persuaders. All of them worked in this unreal world of selling ideas because the field of letters was closed to real men. Because, he noted, the "arts are homosexual; talents of the normal are frustrated and channeled into commercialism." Normal men were also beleaguered by a distorted femininity and Momism. To some degree, Spectorsky was reflecting on his reading of women's magazines, but his anger was deeper and more personal. "Maybe," he wrote in a private harangue, "it's their fault for wanting suffrage, careers, to be nubile film stars, to be portrayed as sweethearts, to be shown as flat-stomached, etc.—whereas their natural role, the one that should be touted and glorified and mass communicated—and is not—is MOTHER."[48]

After signing with McGraw-Hill to produce the book, Spectorsky hired Douglas More, an expert on market research and adolescence, to suggest readings and themes. The two apparently shared the same vision (and joke) about the contemporary plight of American men. As More wrote slyly when he delivered some of his notes, "The following materials may be of interest to you in developing broad themes for the projected volume Homo Americanus (pun intended)." Much of the report was a list of standard sociological works, many of them in categories such as suburbanization, inner- and other-direction, conformism, mass culture, and so on. Indeed, the list read like a guide to the culture wars of the 1950s and the critical sociology that energized them.

By early 1957, McGraw-Hill began to press Spectorsky to deliver the manuscript. But he never did complete this or several of the other projects he initiated, such as *The Exurbanite Cook Book, The American Way of Divorce, The American Way of Marriage*, and *The Communicators*. He did not abandon these ideas, however. Many of them, particularly those lamenting the precarious state of the American writer, appeared in the 1962 *Playboy* symposium "The Womanization of America." And they resurfaced especially in his literary correspondence with writer Philip Wylie.[49]

Spectorsky found an ideal platform to expound his vision of American culture—what men lacked, how elite culture had been feminized, and his critical notions about advertising, sophistication, and exurbia—in the move to Hugh Hefner's *Playboy* magazine in 1956. Spectorsky traveled to Chicago in 1956 to take control of the editorial and literary content of the immensely popular new publication. In this niche, he found a means to redefine male readers as "whole men." "Each issue of *Playboy*," he wrote, "is a tacit statement to them that they are responsive to fine fiction and to pretty girls; to Lucullan dining and drinking and to serious articles and interviews that bear directly or philosophically on today's serious issues; to sports cars and classical music, jazz, fashion, the struggle for civil rights, bachelor high-life, and the world of business and finance." In fact, Spectorsky sought nothing less than to remasculinize American literature and consumerism through the juxtaposition of good writing with pictures of nude women and sophisticated advertising. If Hefner's vision was to embellish and sell sex by surrounding it with the trappings of high culture, Spectorsky's emphasis went the other way around, seeking to reinvent sophisticated culture itself by bracketing it with heterosexual desire. As he wrote somewhat later to Philip Wylie, defending *Playboy*'s sexual vision, "PLAYBOY is frankly and openly frisky and romantic— as opposed to the prurient morbidity and pious pornography which characterize the bulk of mass media who regularly associate sex with vice, crime, sin and the exposé."[50]

Spectorsky also found a means to diminish the cultural problems aggravated by mass culture and suburbia. "It was common to hear social pundits [in many respects the author had been one of them] bemoaning the advent of mass men. A funny thing happened to these sociologists on their way to conclusions: they lost their way." The dreary future predicted for mass society did not materialize, he wrote, and culture itself, through fragmentation and specialization, broke down the "surface homogeneity." Undoubtedly, in his mind, *Playboy* was an important component of this healthy disintegration.[51]

Spectorsky also found a podium from which to preach his literary tastes. Instructing one of his fiction writers, he laid down guidelines for the sort of literature that *Playboy* would publish and what it would reject. "What we don't like at all . . . are castration-defeat-doom stories. God knows it's a womanized world and a neurotic one and a castrating one, but just as surely we get literally hundreds of 'fine' stories a month which are intricate embroidery on the motto: The Sensitive Misfit is a More Interesting Man and a worthier topic than The Man Who Fulfils His Masculine Destiny. See the *New Yorker* for Christ's sake." What we don't want, he sums up, is a mutilated Hemingway hero, but a real man "who deals with the world instead of cringing and having high-tone failures."[52]

In this way, Spectorsky proposed to intervene in the gendered debate about 1950s culture by restoring the old house of virility with a stylish new decor. He welcomed the new world of consumerism and suburbia. As he put it bluntly, "If mankind can achieve the happy state of being creatively virile, intellectually fecund, artistically prolific—and still enjoy spray deodorants, outdoor barbecues, five foot shelves [of must-read books], *Life* magazine, two-tone cars, etc.—I'll go along with those."[53] That is, sophistication plus a nude centerfold could cover the sins of gender-compromising consumption.

Playboy and the masculine variant it represented pulsed with sparks of energy in Spectorsky's otherwise dark universe. Reviewing *The Decline of the American Male* by the editors of *Look* magazine in 1958, he pretty much agreed with their grim assessment of conformity and impotence. But, in some respects, he wrote, they exaggerated. In a passage he marked on the original manuscript of the review, "P.B. [*Playboy*] attitude," he concluded, "There are millions of frisky, happy, iconoclastic men in America [with] girls and wives whose life goal is not the emasculation of the opposite sex."[54]

In his history of the *Playboy* enterprise, Russell Miller suggests that Spectorsky was suspicious, if not contemptuous, of Hefner, his tastes in culture, and his bizarre lifestyle. He notes that "the people Hefner thought were glamorous, Spectorsky thought were tedious." Perhaps true, but Spectorsky certainly shared Hefner's vision of gender and sophistication sufficiently to fill the magazine with articles and stories about masculinity, and to print examples of what he believed represented a new virile literature. The two worked closely in a number of instances to shape the intellectual content of the magazine.[55] This included a heavy dose of Hemingway himself, and articles about Hemingway, stories by Ray Bradbury and Nelson Algren, as well as by Vladimir Nabokov. Whatever Spectorsky's private misgivings about the "Old Man," he used Hemingway (the manly Hemingway) to advertise the magazine's commitment to masculinity. The "Playbill" introducing the September 1956 issue, for example, proclaimed that Hemingway "stands out like a rugged oak in a field of delicate pansies (pun intended). Our literature has become a morass of incense and butterflies and Spanish Moss, of précieuse style and hyperfine imagery: There is no god but Tennessee [Williams] and Truman [Capote] is his prophet."[56]

For all its vaunted self-confidence in the bachelor lifestyle and its promotion of sophisticated consumption, however, *Playboy* returned to this issue of troubled masculinity many times and stressed time and again its commitment to a virilized high culture. If this repetition did not necessarily display uncertainty, it did suggest that the magazine felt it must teach its young audience not to fear for their gender identity if they consumed sophisticated products and read elite literature. In the same promotional piece on Hemingway, Spectorsky looked back to Paris in the 1920s. In those exuberant days, *The Boulevardier*, "a sort of Parisian *Playboy*," had published a number of great American writers: Sinclair Lewis, F. Scott Fitzgerald, and, of course, Hemingway.[57] *Playboy* aspired to carve out a similar place in sophisticated American culture.

If Spectorsky intended to make *Playboy* a kind of American *Boulevardier*, perhaps this accounts for the journal's inordinate editorial attention to French culture as a model for virile male refinement. The magazine featured articles on French food and films, with frequent reprints of ribald French medieval stories and photos of Brigitte Bardot. It even printed a very badly received serialized and decidedly minor novel by Françoise Sagan, *The Wonderful Clouds*. Sometimes, Spectorsky used his French connection in a curious way. In the "Playbill" column discussing the monthly fare, he used some very tortured logic to argue that a story by Anthony Boucher was an exemplary piece for men. It was odd, he noted, that the words "science" and "fiction" were both feminine in French, but that the combination "science fiction" in the same language was masculine. That settled the issue: "We've always felt this exciting brand of storytelling was particularly masculine in slant."[58]

Yet, for all this, a fundamental malaise about masculinity in American civilization did not disappear from *Playboy*, and Spectorsky revisited the issue periodically in his correspondence with, and by publishing articles solicited from, his friend Philip Wylie. Their letters reveal a long-standing discussion of gender issues and demonstrate Spectorsky's continued faith in *Playboy* magazine as a healthy antidote to the insipid manhood of the 1950s. The two writers had been literary friends for many years, with Spectorsky an admirer and reviewer of Wylie's early works. Wylie also had much to praise about *The Exurbanites*, comparing the book to Sinclair Lewis's *Main Street* in importance. His enthusiasm even ran to an advertising blurb for the book. When Spectorsky moved to Chicago, it became possible for him to promote his friend as a contributor to the magazine. Consequently, Wylie became one of the regulars among others such as Ian Fleming, Ray Bradbury, and J. Paul Getty.[59]

On a number of occasions, Spectorsky and/or Hefner solicited pieces from Wylie, allowing him enormous scope and suggesting scores of topics: the point being that it was Wylie, the writer, they sought and his caustic perspective on any one of a number of subjects. For example, in May 1956, shortly after Spectorsky was installed as editor, he wrote to Wylie asking for "a polemic." He made the writer two promises: substantial fees and the willingness to "print stuff that no family magazine would touch." In the same letter, he suggested that Wylie expand a thought from *Generation of Vipers* to the effect that all cosmetic ads addressed women asking, "Are you a good lay?" Could he expand the notion and give it "really a good ride?" Hefner reinforced the request, writing in August to solicit Wylie, and giving him the choice of almost any topic, but attaching a broad list of suggestions for consideration. The author complied, and "The Abdicating Male" appeared in November 1956 as an updated diatribe against "Momism" but with a catalog of new complaints. Wylie charged that men had given up control over consumption to women. The result, he continued, was an extraordinary corruption of taste. Men in gray flannel suits invented advertising copy aimed at insecure, libidinous women who were semihysterical and so anxious about their identities that they could be persuaded to buy anything that promised success in attracting a man. Wylie's solution was to persuade admen to go straight and masculinize their copy, to stop compulsively selling to women.[60]

In early 1957, Spectorsky asked for another work, a real "pro-masculine blast-off." What *Playboy* wanted, he continued, was "a bang-up, furious, documented, Wylie-type blast on how America has become a matriarchy in which women's tastes, desires, standards, mystiques, needs, etc., dominate our world." This should not be just a repeat of the author's earlier work, but something about how "our literature, movies, automatic transmissions, retail stores, daytime TV, furniture design, building design, vacation areas (with the exception of some hunting and fishing resorts which are still un-femmed up), restaurants (again with some last-ditch sanctuaries being the exception to prove the rule) and cocktail lounges, etc., are all aimed at pleasing, not upright, masculine, erect, dynamic males, but the charming, soft and cuddly cobras who have taken the world right out from under our noses."[61]

Wylie's response was a bitter attack on American women. In "The Womanization of America," published in September 1958, he began with a directory of the domains where women now dominated: culture, style, consumption, sex, and marriage. Soon, he wrote sarcastically, "I expect to see a farmer riding in a pastel tractor and wearing a matching playsuit." The "she-tyranny" of culture had created an emasculated majority who denied the authority of their own brains, intellect, and sexuality. Women had demanded power and gotten it. But at the same time they had relinquished none of the "privileges of the pedestal." The result was rampant cultural effeminacy. No wonder men thought that art was sissy and reading was uninteresting at best. If the downhill course of civilization could be traced back to the assault of women on the doors of speakeasies thirty years earlier, the final offensive would be against contemporary all-male clubs, he predicted.[62]

Wylie's portrait of a woman sufficiently impressed Spectorsky and others on the magazine to inspire a symposium in 1962 to discuss the phenomenon of "Womanization." The magazine invited a team of "experts" on masculinity to examine Wylie's depiction of culture. It included novelist Norman Mailer, editors Herbert Mayes of *McCall's* and Alexander King of *Life* magazine, public relations expert Edward Bernays, motivation expert Ernst Dichter, anthropologist Ashley Montagu, psychologist Theodor Reik, and comedian Mort Sahl. The host was Paul Krassner, editor of the *Realist* magazine, publisher of Mailer and Joseph Heller, and a brilliant satirist.[63] In recorded telephone interviews, Krassner worked through the indictments that Wylie had outlined. First, he placed before each expert the charge that women were the focus of consumption and mass culture—and longer lived at that. The result, his script suggested, was the "upswinging of homosexuality and sex obliterating aspects of togetherness." Was woman being masculinized faster than men were being feminized, he asked? These blustery indictments provoked a variety of responses, although no real agreement. But *Playboy*'s interlocutor doggedly persisted along these same lines: didn't the female desire for equality really hide a furtive seizure of power? There was no mistaking the purpose of this prodding. The magazine was trying to solicit commentary about the misery of modern gender relations and the oppression of men. What was the source of this malevolent assault on men? Krassner finally asked. Was it penis envy?

From this point, the discussion leaped to explore worries over homosexual influence "in fashion, in arts and letters, in government, in society at large"—an influence also attributed to masculinized women. Was there any hope to escape from all of these intersecting problems of feminization, mass culture, and the abdication of male power and control? *Playboy* chose to answer its own questions. The solution was to be found in the new philosophy of masculinity articulated in the magazine itself: the substitution of sophistication for the frontier in forming character, the consumption of products guided by refined men, and the careful husbandry of a new, pliant femininity. "There is a new spirit on the land," declared the journal, "evident among our own readership, which would suggest that the younger, urban people of this country are coming to a new awareness of both masculinity and femininity. That is, the men are increasingly aware that one can be masculine without being hairy-chested and muscular; the women, that one can be intelligent and sensitive—witty and wise—and at the same time completely feminine."[64] This was, of course, anything but the old picture of Hemingway soldiering after big game. Indeed, it suggested a fundamental compromise, one that made the best of the contemporary world of mass consumption, provided that it reasserted the control of men.

Shortly after the symposium, Spectorsky went back to the well and pulled one more article from Wylie. Notes from an editorial meeting at the magazine, and sent to Wylie, listed a variety of topics just suited to his venomous pen: recreationism, the cult of youth, the nice-guy syndrome, and almost anything, since "this curmudgeon Wylie hates everything, particularly everything American, as you know," wrote one editorial assistant. In particular, both Wylie and Spectorsky liked one suggestion: an exposé of working women. As Spectorsky smoldered in August 1962, "We would really like a no-holds-barred tearing apart of this miserable humanoid who calls herself woman. Having worked for Street & Smith

The Gender of High Culture   213

Publications, I speak with considerable feeling about these chromium-plated, castrating, driven, vicious, unhappy, destructive, asexual or antisexual, devouring, insatiable, incalculably destructive . . ."[65] Wylie again complied, this time, with "The Career Woman," published in January 1963.

This over-the-top diatribe against working women declared the age to be one of "cowed men and bullish women." What most threatened men was the invasion of legions of career women, entering the professions, management—all levels of work—but particularly middle-class work. They had transformed fashion and the media from these new positions of power, and worked to change and revolutionize, if need be, to "cripple manhood and masculinity." This "she-pox" could be compared to the Hun, the Gestapo, the antisexual prude. She was responsible for the distortions of fashion and the prevalent antiintellectualism of American culture. Most men did not realize, he yelped, "that they—not women—were once the arbiters of style, beauty, and design, that they had the authentic genius and genuine taste, that they possessed the true discernment and intellectual sensitivity of our species." In alliance with the housewife, career women formed a deadly phalanx that controlled and corrupted every element of American culture by dominating business as well as the home. They had betrayed their true, intended role to be the sexual companion of man. The only solution [the *Playboy* solution] was to restore women as love objects, celebrating the sexuality of "luscious womanhood."[66]

For this short moment, right up to the publication of the Betty Friedan's work on feminism in 1963 and the beginnings of the modern woman's movement, it seemed, at least to Wylie and Spectorsky, that a simple assertion of masculinity in culture could conjure the new man into being and resolve some of the worrisome cultural problems that vexed critics throughout the 1950s. It could virilize high culture and erase the aura of homosexuality that surrounded it. This was an expectation Spectorsky brought to the magazine (certainly supported by Hefner), and reinforced and punctuated in periodic articles from Wylie. But, as some astute observers recognized, there was a price to be paid for this "philosophy." There was an inherent risk in this answer to the purported masculinity crisis of the 1950s: that this message only resounded with the cultural bravado of the bachelor, the college boy, and the late adolescent—and consequently a wildly exaggerated sense of imperiled masculinity.[67] In Spectorsky's hands, this message was delivered in such a rush of anger and emotion that he seemed not to recognize that the issue was beginning to lose its gravity by the early 1960s or, ultimately, that he had already made important compromises. The mystery of

Momism was about to be unmasked as the *Feminine Mystique*. And Spectorsky's own vision of masculinity had already given up much of the contested terrain of modern consumption, suburbia, and mass culture as each of these elements reappeared through the back door of sophistication.

10

Getting Used to Women: Perspectives on Masculinity Crisis

In 1950 the Bureau of the Census released statistics showing that women outnumbered men in the population for the first time in American history. The typical state of demographic proportion, compared to most European societies, had thus finally been reached. According to the census, the inexorable march of this transition had turned westward and southward out of New England from an early moment in the history of the Republic, finally reaching a point where almost every state in the Union matched this profile. Some, like Arizona, would have to wait as late as 1970, but in the end the process was inevitable. Thus concluded a unique phase of American society—the long history of male majority. Sixty years before, Frederick Jackson Turner had spoken of the 1890 census as "the closing of a great historic movement" in his famous essay on the frontier in American history. Thirty years after that, historians and sociologists celebrated the 1920 demarcation of a shift from a rural to an urban majority. But no poet of demographic exceptionalism stepped forth to muse on the symbolism of this last finding, or to speculate about its significance for American history. Of course, David Riesman had suggested, also in 1950, that the lonely men of his age had assumed a new, other-directed character reflecting changes in production, work, and lifestyles, based upon a slowing population growth. But Riesman paid no more attention than anyone else to the attainment of a female majority in the United States.

No "demographic thesis" emerged from the 1950 census in the way that the "Frontier Thesis" sprang from 1890, or the manifold interpretations assessing the rural-urban population crossover of 1920 that poured forth from historians, political scientists, and sociologists. A few observers did suggest that there would now be more women available for marriage in the coming decades. But 1950 represents a more profound, symbolic turning point than this potential for marriage, just as 1890 meant more than the physical end of the frontier. Looking back across the expanding wave of changed gender ratios, American history appears to have repeated the same process time and again: in one place after another from east to west, until it finally concluded shortly after World War II. Initial settlement dominated by men was followed by community building centered on the increasing number and influence of women and the domestic and cultural institutions associated with their lives and needs. Certainly, this pattern can be suggested only as a general experience, for the European settlement of the United States varied enormously by group, national background, religion, region, ethnicity, race, and time period. Still, the overall configuration persisted: initial male preponderance—a homosocial world—that eventually and everywhere gave way to a female majority.[1]

The contemporary critic who came closest to recognizing this process was probably Leslie Fiedler, whose writings on the American literary canon depicted male evasion and comradeship—an adolescent escapism at the heart of some of America's greatest male writing that seemed to derive from a desire to flee the society of women for the company of men—in other words, to reverse the process and restore the (natural) state of American "innocence." But Fiedler was interested in explaining the peculiar nature of these relationships as a literary project—the innocent flight of men to the frontier and the racial implications of that experience in the encounter with a dark-skinned other—not the larger historical process of accommodating to domesticity and the presence of women. The critic sought to explain the frequency of literary types like Huck Finn, Ishmael, Tarzan, and Pathfinder—boys and men who fled civilization and the company of women—to regress to the safety and irresponsibility of an imaginary boyhood. What he did not attend to was the opposite phenomenon, the reinvention and recreation of domesticity as the converging lines of settlement filled the spaces of the United States.

Built into Turner's brilliant metaphor of the frontier as America's Mediterranean Sea, demanding of its explorers and colonists a "practical, inventive turn of mind quick to find expedients; that masterful grasp of material things" was the force he identified that energized individuals and self-reliance. To Turner, it was the repetitive demand for these qualities that sustained the unique American political and social character. Quite rightly, this visionary thesis has been revised and complicated with a very different picture of the settlement of the American frontier emanating from many directions and engaging different cultures and ethnicities. Yet there is a fundamental truth to Turner's overall notion of a repetitive experience, the iteration of social and political reinvention, which characterized the European conquest, settlement, and integration of the West into the national system. To his emphasis upon the proliferation of political democracy and market capitalism, however, must be added the transformation of settlements and outposts into communities. The growing presence of women suggests the thickening of social and cultural institutions and new patterns of consumption and, most of all, a change in the relations between genders. As much as the idea of the receding frontier, this recreation of domesticity should be considered a defining mark of the American experience.[2]

From this perspective, much of American history can be seen broadly as the domestication of the American landscape with recurring controversies over the roles and prerogatives of the men and women who settled it. Indeed, some elements of the physical landscape like the frontier itself have sometimes been imagined as gendered zones. It may well be that in those recurring moments that American historians have identified as "male panics" the unfolding history of this politics of domesticity constitutes a significant ingredient.

There was at least a dim perception of this historical cycle in the prevailing lament, the repetitious chorus of complaints by observers in the 1950s, that women were intruding into male institutions and feminizing American life. In part, this may have reflected difficulties in adjustment to civilian life after the experience of mostly male society of the military. But intellectuals poured worry and woe over evidence of America's growing culture of domesticity. One form of this censure appeared as a large and disturbing literature about imperiled masculinity, another in the sociology of the self-aggrandizing power of Momism. The major institutions of the day, the very forces in the economy and society that were leading cultural change at such a revolutionary clip, seemed most responsible for this situation, and women appeared to be on the forefront of them all. From personnel work and new managerial techniques and personality tests in business, to mass culture, suburbanization, and consumerism, the emerging lifestyle of Americans seemed to be "togetherness" and passivity, marked by the increasing feminization of culture. To one significant group of critical observers, led by David Riesman, some new form of autonomy or individualism seemed a possible remedy. To others like Billy Graham and Alfred Kinsey this crisis scarcely existed as such. Their interest in masculinity had very different purposes.

The reason I have chosen 1963 as the approximate end to this book—and as the end of the 1950s—rests upon the appearance of one final restatement, a brilliant summary of all of these arguments hostile to domesticity. Yet this work simultaneously subverted their conclusions and deprived them of their overt significance as it refocused attention on America's new female majority. This was Betty Friedan's *The Feminine Mystique*, a remarkable and hugely influential work that first repeated these cultural and sociological criticisms of domesticity, but only to sabotage their arguments, turning them upside down to plead for the liberation of women from cultural stereotypes. Surprisingly, there was little in Friedan's work that contradicted the premises of mainline 1950s social anxiety about the feminization of American culture. She repeated attacks on "togetherness," suburban culture, consumption, and mass culture—even conjuring up the phantasmagorias of Momism and homosexuality, but shifting the meaning.

Men, she wrote, had been terribly wounded by contemporary distortions of culture and beleaguered by confusing gender roles. Following Erik Erikson, she sketched an identity crisis of alarming proportions. "More and more young men in America today," she warned, "suffer an identity crisis for want of any image of man worth pursuing, for want of a purpose that truly realizes their human abilities." Later she invoked Momism to explain the widely noted collaboration of a few American prisoners with their captors during the Korean War. As she noted, "the apathetic, dependent, infantile, purposeless being, who seems so shockingly nonhuman when remarked as the emerging character of the new American man, is strangely reminiscent of the familiar 'feminine' personality as defined by the mystique." Further evidence, she noted, was the "ominous" growth of homosexuality that also seemed to be the consequence of predatory, frustrated mothers, even billboarding Tennessee Williams as the sign of troubled gender definitions.[3]

For Friedan, of course, none of this was really the central issue; it was only symptomatic of the larger, unarticulated problem. Her argument was: if you wished to have real men, you must first free women from the cultural bondage of the "mystique" that imprisoned their abilities, controlled their emotions, and distorted their femininity. The tenacity of the notion of a male crisis even within a tract for women's liberation is a striking confirmation of the centrality of this form of criticism in the 1950s.[4] Except that here it is made to argue against itself.

As the preceding chapters have demonstrated, however, not everyone responded to the presumed male crisis and feminization of American institutions in the same way, even if gender was a highly potent language widely used to explore the dramatic changes and problems of the era. Upon closer examination, the mainstream is clearly made up of cross currents. After all, opportunity is another way of describing a crisis, and there were many men during the 1950s who did not feel a threat to their masculinity in the growth of new domestic arrangements—in companionate marriages, in the suburbs, in male domestic work like do-it-yourself projects or in corporations where cooperation, not competition, defined the daily rules. Nor is it true that all men viewed their masculinity as compromised by increasing consumerism or other-directed institutions. It should be reiterated that much of this sentiment of crisis in American institutions was confined to its likely effects on middle-class, white, urban or suburban men.

In fact, there were many responses relating to questions about masculinity in the 1950s. The struggle to define masculinity individually and culturally was always a complex endeavor. Not all responses included angry attacks on women or the withdrawal into some imaginary all-male retreat. Not everyone worried about homosexuality, although the issue was never very far from anxieties about overly strong, masculinized women. In this sense, a feminized culture seemed to link both homosexual men and women who strayed from their roles as mother and helpmate. In response, men like Auguste Spectorsky worried out loud about how to remasculinize American culture, particularly its literature. He chose an extreme way to accomplish this aim—a pornographic setting for the jewel of high culture. But even he, finally, made a truce with mass consumption and suburbia—even if he renamed them sophistication and exurbia. It is also true that David Riesman reenvisioned American history as the evolution of character typologies that exhibited what in the 1950s assumed the qualities usually ascribed to feminine "otherness," but he ultimately believed he could see the emergence of an autonomous orientation that would combine the best of inner- and other-direction, proposing, in a sense, an androgynous compromise. For Alfred Kinsey, masculinity was not an issue at all. He assumed that it had little, if anything, to do with male sexual behavior—his real interest. Kinsey believed that he had discovered a sexual revolution in behavior that challenged any definition of male essentialism, and he took every opportunity to proclaim the virtues of a behavioral understanding of sexuality. Despite his secret sexual encounters, the message he delivered to the American public was that social norms and expectations had little to do with what men really did. What mattered to him was the continuity of all male conduct, the continuum of orgasms and outlets, that redefined normality as anything appearing anywhere on an inclusive behavioral chart.

Others, like Tennessee Williams, projected compelling male characters onto center stage. But as Williams did so, he seemed to be saying that these roles were, above all, performances about masculinity, not the revelation of something innate or historically constant. This was not merely attributable to his sexual orientation, but, more to the point, because his sexual perspective allowed him this viewpoint. Sometimes the playwright even let the audience see all of the props and cues of his gender creations, as in the remarkable deconstruction of Brick Pollitt in *Cat on a Hot Tin Roof.*

The oddly real but fictitious character of Ozzie Nelson was also a player of masculinity on the grand stage of popular culture, although in front of radio microphones and television cameras. Ozzie was a comic figure who tried valiantly but vainly to understand the new rules of domesticity—who wanted nothing more than to perform competently as a modern father and husband. He was no individualist rebel or social critic, but the comic variant of America's new domestic masculinity. His weekly failures were abundant and their causes varied, but one problem almost always preceded all others. Ozzie stumbled; he failed to learn because the ages-old patriarchal values he invoked were dysfunctional guidelines in the modern world. He wanted to be an up-to-date dad; consequently his weekly escapades poignantly highlighted what that new fatherhood might look like—even if he could never achieve it.

There is, finally, Billy Graham, for whom masculinity was a positive virtue, never questioned, and always clear in its personal significance. Yet for the movement he led, it remained a serious and historic concern, a problem even, affecting the universal appeal of his message. Because of the skewed gender demographics of evangelical Christianity, and the resistance of men to conversion, he sought to invent new ways to attract these hardest-to-reach of hard-hearted sinners. To succeed, he carefully modulated "male" and "female" conventions in his crusades and in his films. Yet in the end, he had only himself as his own best example of evangelical manhood, a living example that resisted dramatization.

Do these examples exhaust the possibilities of the 1950s? Surely not. They represent only six stories in a public dialogue of stunning complexity. Yet they begin to suggest that the "masculinity crisis" of this—and perhaps of any—age, if it existed at all,—was an extraordinarily intricate affair. In this decade, the notion of imperiled manhood was further complicated because of its association with a powerful cultural criticism that disparaged the new mass society of postwar America. The critique often used the terminology of masculinity crisis as a language to describe the symptoms of what seemed most objectionable about the new society. Thus the entire discussion invoked serious questions about the past and future of

American individualism—just as Turner's famous essay did for the 1890s six decades earlier.

Still, for many men there was no crisis at all. They happily moved to the suburbs, consumed from the cornucopia of new products around them, and delighted in the new mass culture without registering worry about their masculinity. They enjoyed companionship with their wives and children. They understood modern masculinity as quite other than a calamity, even if they experienced the challenge of redefining themselves. They could find a variety of confirming figures in public life and popular culture to emulate. Because of their example, we can see this historic phase of getting used to women as offering an opportunity for a new fluidity in gender roles, for new forms of self-expression, not the sorry end of individualism or a chilling menace to American manhood.

So, is the point merely the discovery of complexity? Is it enough to say that even the mainstream of opinion about the dominant sector of American society—white, middle-class men—is more complicated than first imagined? Surely this is an important conclusion because it suggests the need to revise accepted ideas about male identity crises in the 1950s and at other times. It makes it far more difficult to invoke such concepts as hegemony when the mainstream itself appears to be conflicted and contradictory. But this suggests something else about historical change. Quite clearly, the remarkable transformations in gender relations that began to appear in the 1960s in the guise of sexual liberation and feminism have their origins in the various expressions of the 1950s decade. By recognizing the existence of these roots, we can understand that the causes of change are continuously operating even when we do not, at first, recognize them. So, too, in a more general sense, is it apparent that changing domestic relations are central to the narrative of American history.

Did the issues once defined as causing a "male crisis" somehow disappear after the 1950s? Did the woman's movement resolve the contentious and complex issues of gender that lay at the heart of the trouble? Unfortunately, nothing could be farther from this happy end of history. For all the heady proclamations of individual liberty and self-fulfillment in the 1960s, there has been no escaping from the powerful grasp of the long-term forces in American culture and history. Instead, there are just changes and new challenges. If anything, issues of gender and the employment of the language of gender to understand cultural problems continue to define American civilization. Many of the experiences that worried the generation of the 1950s persist today, although they are not now generally conflated with the postwar consumer and mass culture revolutions. But to define oneself as a man or woman is no easier or more obvious or self-evident than before. Many of the same sorts of conflicting images that challenged middle-class males persist in new forms. From "smack-down" wrestlers who perform the bully, the tyrant, the coward, and the cheat for teenage boys, from the exploration of sophisticated gay culture on television and in magazines, to the endless reinvention of television comedy series featuring ill-mannered husbands and sons (as if to equate vulgarity and masculinity), from Civil War enactments to the celebration (yet again) of the exploits of Teddy Roosevelt, from the "abs" obsession of men's magazines and the lionization of bulky pro football players to admiration for fatherly political figures, the choices for "spectator masculinity" as well as practical emulation are legion. Many of the contradictions of the 1950s exist . . . and more.

So, too, have there been moments since the 1950s when male crisis preoccupied commentators on American civilization. There is no doubt that change in many arenas has provoked such reconsiderations of the appropriate terms of masculinity. If anything, shifts in gender relationships have once again been a primary cause of male uncertainty. In some cases, men have organized politically, to express their solidarity and to effect change in the face of enormous shifts in marriage, child rearing, the new visibility of diverse sexual orientations, work environments, and culture. As in the 1950s, the focus has been on gender and both the relationship between men and women and questions of masculinity.

One explanation for this cycle has been the prevalence of war in American culture and the interaction between combat and ideals of masculinity. As Joshua Goldstein argues in *War and Gender*, "the pervasiveness of war in history has influenced gender profoundly." Thus he argues that the period immediately after World War II was characterized by a "John Wayne syndrome" when men were expected to be tough, unemotional, and competitive. Looking at his own age he applied the same analysis to explaining the masculinity enunciated by psychologist Robert Bly when he appealed to the metaphoric "warrior" in modern American men.[5]

Bly established therapeutic men's gatherings, inspired by his best-selling commentary on masculinity, *Iron John*, published in 1990. Bly's psychomythological presentation began with a vision of the history of male character picked up from the stereotypes of the 1950s. That decade, he wrote, provided a "model of manhood," where fathers worked hard for their families and admired discipline and hard work. The 1960s and 1970s, he continued, introduced the "soft male," in response to the woman's movement and the traumas suffered during the war in Viet Nam. Yet, neither of these reflexes proved adequate to men's needs, and thus contemporary men expressed grief and sorrow at the absence of something they could not identify. What they lacked, he concluded, was the energy and power of the "Wild Man," a repressed self, an identity revealed in Greek mythology and primitive tribal initiation rites. Passed on to sons by their fathers and grandfathers and tribal elders, these forms and modes of manhood, these traditions, had vanished, leaving contemporary men impoverished and lacking a complete repertoire of male identity. Bly's book was widely read, but more important were the gatherings of men he organized. During weekend encampments in the woods, men sought to reenact these rites, to relate wisdom across generations through the recounting of myth and poetry and beating of drums, and, it was hoped, to promote the release of the inner masculine self. Thus, wounded fathers and sons and brothers could mutually restore the bonds of wisdom and comradeship in the safe environment of a carefully guided performance.[6] Central to his compelling vision was the insight that men had ignored the most immediate models of masculinity: their fathers. This critique of spectator masculinity undoubtedly appealed to those men for whom the emulation of distant models and celebrities offered no practical or meaningful example.

If Bly's description of masculinity and its performance seemed to be a direct answer to the changing gender roles of contemporary women, there were, nonetheless, strong elements carried over from the 1950s. Combining Freud and Jung with an anthropologized poetics of male initiation ceremonies, Bly warned of an immature, incomplete, and incoherent masculinity that, for all its emphasis on contemporary issues echoed more than a faint resemblance to the feminized 1950s male victim of suburbia, consumption, and Momism.[7]

Beyond mythopoetics, but also informed by the elaboration of an important male foundational narrative, were the Promise Keepers, an energetic and important group of evangelical Christian men that emerged in the 1990s. Founded by University of Colorado football coach Bill McCartney, the national organization held rallies in sports stadiums across the country but primarily in the Midwest and the South. The promise to keep was the pledge of each man to uphold his God-given masculine prerogatives and responsibilities, to return to his family with a clear sense of his role as father. This meant reasserting himself against wives who had assumed too much power and children who had strayed and misbehaved. The national importance of the movement peaked in 1997 with a large rally in Washington D.C. on the federal mall—a witness to the power of an idea and an affirmation of the underlying Christian tradition as a guide to sort out the problems of contemporary life. Although the movement continued to attract large gatherings into the late 1990s, it, too, rose and fell with the cycle of the decade's concern over issues of masculinity.[8]

A third major public enactment of the rituals of a troubled masculinity during the 1990s was Louis Farrakhan's Million Man March on Washington, D.C. in 1995. Like the Promise Keepers, Farrakhan's Nation of Islam followers performed their gender grievances in the center ring of American political protest, reenacting, in a sense, the multiple protests and marches and celebrations that had come to characterize American civic rituals after the civil rights and antiwar demonstrations of the 1960s. Although it would be wrong to ascribe universal acceptance of minister Farrakhan's particular political and cultural agendas to everyone who gathered that day, it is clear that once more issues of gender acted as the subject matter and expressive language for the articulation of deep political, economic, and cultural concerns of an important group of men.

The issues linking these and countless other public discussions of manhood clearly reached deeply, not just into questions about masculinity, but into prevailing spiritual, social, economic, and cultural questions. Perhaps Andrew Kimbrell, in his book *The Masculine Mystique*, had all of these movements in mind when he concluded that "Over the years I have learned that there is something terribly wrong in the lives of most men. Whatever age, political persuasion, race, or creed these men share a common condition. They feel bewildered, out of control, numbed, angered, and under attack."[9] The complex structure of ideas, the emphases that prevailed in these movements, once again suggest the importance of gender as a principal means to understand a historical moment. It must seem that, once again, Americans were faced with an unacceptable and unworkable definition of masculinity, once again confronting a "masculinity crisis." Before deciding that the 1990s movements represent the beginning of another conservative affirmation of patriarchal values for a society whose men yearn for instruction in traditional ways, it would be well to recall the complexity that we have discovered in the 1950s, the many differing voices that can be found in a period that seemed even more resolutely conservative and conformist. Was the 1990s the age of Robert Bly's Wild Men and the Promise Keepers, or was it the domestic world of the neighborly Fred Rogers? Or have we just got the question wrong again?

Notes

Chapter 1

1. Correspondence sent, July 10, 1948, to Kinsey. Papers of Alfred C. Kinsey, Kinsey Institute for Research in Sex, Gender, and Reproduction, Inc., Indiana University, Bloomington, Indiana. Hereafter cited as Kinsey MSS. Quotations courtesy of the Kinsey Institute.

2. Garry Wills, *John Wayne's America* (New York: Simon & Schuster, 1997); Paul Goodman, *Growing Up Absurd: Problems of Youth in the Organized System* (New York: Random House, 1960).

3. Carol Cohn, "Sex and Death in the Rational World of Defense Intellectuals," *Signs* 12 (Summer 1987): 687–718. See also David K. Johnson, *The Lavender Scare: The Cold War Persecution of Gays and Lesbians in the Federal Government* (Chicago: University of Chicago Press, 2004), 2–9.

4. See Michael Davidson, *Guys Like Us: Citing Masculinity in Cold War Poetics* (Chicago: University of Chicago Press, 2004), 1–27.

5. Dwight Macdonald, "A Theory of Mass Culture," *Diogenes* 3 (Summer 1953): 1–17; see also Thorstein Veblen, *Theory of the Leisure Class* (1899; New Brunswick: Transaction Publishers, 1992), 232.

6. Victoria de Grazia, *The Sex of Things: Gender and Consumption in Historical Perspective* (Berkeley: University of California Press, 1996), 1, 15, passim.

7. Lizabeth Cohen, *A Consumers' Republic: The Politics of Mass Consumption in Postwar America* (New York: Alfred A. Knopf, 2003). Cohen's larger argument is about the effort to democratize American society through consumption. See also Gary Cross, *An All-Consuming Century: Why Commercialism Won in Modern America* (New York: Columbia University Press, 2000), 2–9; and Mary Louise Roberts, "Gender, Consumption, and Commodity Culture," *American Historical Review* 103 (June 1998): 817–44.

8. Joshua S. Goldstein, *War and Gender: How Gender Shapes the War System and Vice Versa* (Cambridge, UK: Cambridge University Press, 2001).

9. C. Wright Mills, *Power, Politics and People* (New York: Oxford U. Press, 1962), 611. See also Irving Howe, "This Age of Conformity," in William Phillips and Philip Rahv, eds., *The Partisan Review Anthology* (New York: Holt, Rinehart and Winston, 1962),

145. The term "public intellectual" was not used in the 1950s; that is a later sobriquet. But there is an immense literature on the role of intellectuals in society during that decade. See Richard Posner, *Public Intellectuals: A Study of Decline* (Cambridge: Harvard University Press, 2001).

10. Richard Hofstadter, *Anti-intellectualism in American Life* (New York: Alfred A. Knopf, 1963), 418.

11. Robert J. Corben, *Homosexuality in Cold War America: Resistance and the Crisis of Masculinity* (Durham: Duke University Press, 1997), 7. Corben argues that domestic masculinity was promoted by the government through subsidized suburban developments. A survey completed at the end of the 1950s asked about reasons for moving to the suburbs. Most of the answers suggested that opportunities to enjoy the companionate family and new leisure lifestyles were a primary motivation. Based on questionnaires asked of suburban Chicagoans (with an equal number of male and female respondents), the survey purported to find that "conjugal familism" (the nuclear family) by and large motivated the move to the suburbs, rather than reasons of career or consumership. See Wendell Bell, "Social Choice, Life Styles, and Suburban Residence," in *The Suburban Community*, ed. William Mann Dobriner (New York: Putnam, 1958), 239.

12. John Kasson extends this story of aggressive compensation for feelings of inadequate masculinity to a discussion of a simultaneous new emphasis on the body. Focusing on Harry Houdini, Eugen Sandow, and the mythical Tarzan, he wrote that the white male body became a symbol of the peril and promise of masculine redemption in a time of doubts and anxieties about work, industrialism, and race. John Kasson, *Houdini, Tarzan, and the Perfect Man: The White Male Body and the Challenge of Modernity in America* (New York: Hill and Wang, 2001).

13. The "companionate family" is a modern term, popularized by Ben Lindsey in *The Companionate Family* (New York: Boni and Liveright, 1927). It was a suggested family relationship that promoted more democracy and equality between partners and an end to patriarchy. Despite the stress on separate and distinct and traditional gender roles during the 1950s, the more democratic ideal of sharing decisions about child rearing and consumption, as well as mutual satisfaction in sexual life, was also prevalent.

Chapter 2

1. R. W. Connell, *Masculinities* (Cambridge, UK: Policy Press, 1995), 71. Connell considers at length the meaning of gender and proposes, essentially, that it is one element of the way in which social practice is ordered.

2. See Bruce Traister, "Academic Viagra: The Rise of American Masculinity Studies," *American Quarterly* 52 (June 2000): 276 and passim. Traister argues that the studies in this field are based upon two larger assertions: one of abiding crisis and the second based upon Judith Butler's notion of gender as contingent and performative.

3. David D. Gilmore, *Manhood in the Making: Cultural Concepts of Masculinity* (New Haven: Yale University Press, 1990), 223–24.

4. E. Anthony Rotundo, *American Manhood: Transformations in Masculinity from the Revolution to the Modern Era* (New York: Basic Books, 1993). It is possible to detect echoes of David Riesman's exposition of three historic characters in these categories (tradition directed, inner directed, and other directed).

5. John D'Emilio and Estelle Freedman, *Intimate Matters: A History of Sexuality in America* (Chicago: University of Chicago Press, 1997), vi, 226, 233–34. This notion is given a very full treatment in George Chauncey, *Gay New York: Gender, Urban Culture, and the Making of the Gay Male World, 1890–1940* (New York: Basic Books, 1994).

6. Ibid. 274, 194–234.

7. See, for example, Barbara Melosh, ed., *Gender and American History since 1890* (London: Routledge, 1993). In this very useful collection of essays, Melosh stresses several points that structure much of modern gender studies: (1) the untenability of essentialism in defining gender; (2) the interconnectedness and mutuality of gender definitions; and (3) the importance of discourse and language in establishing the meanings of gender. This collection also treats the sexual revolution, as well as the prior Victorian era, with considerable subtlety. See also Mark C. Carnes and Clyde Griffin, eds., *Meanings for Manhood* (Chicago: University of Chicago Press, 1990).

8. D'Emilio and Freedman, *Intimate Matters*, 325.

9. Peter G. Filene, *Him/Her Self: Gender Identities in Modern America*, 3rd ed. (Baltimore: Johns Hopkins, 1998).

10. Michael Kimmel, *Manhood in America: A Cultural History* (New York: Free Press, 1996), 334, passim.

11. Tom Pendergast, *Creating the Modern Man* (Columbia: University of Missouri Press, 2000), 166.

12. Robert Griswold, *Fatherhood in America: A History* (New York: Basic Books, 1993), 187.

13. Roger Horrocks, *Masculinity in Crisis: Myths, Fantasies, and Realities* (London: Macmillan Press, 1994), 33, passim.

14. In a recent article, Andrew Heinze identifies Warren Susman as the author of the seminal essay on the transition in American society from character to personality. Heinze's persuasive commentary suggests that Susman seriously exaggerated the shift in the 1890s and that the tradition of "character" remained a strong element in twentieth-century culture. Andrew Heinze, "Schizophrenia Americana: Aliens and Alienists, and the 'Personality Shift' of Twentieth-Century Culture," *American Quarterly* 55 (June 2003): 227–56.

15. John Higham, "The Reorientation of American Culture in the 1890s," *Writing American History: Essays on Modern Scholarship* (Bloomington: Indiana University Press, 1970), 73–102.

16. David Savran, *Taking It Like a Man: White Masculinity, Masochism, and Contemporary American Culture* (Princeton: Princeton University Press, 1998), 5.

17. Savran's work, unlike engagements with more elite groups, tries to uncover the sources of white, lower-middle-class male dissatisfaction. Two other works find similar relationships between modern cultural depictions of masculinity, marginality, and

violence. David T. Courtwright, *Violent Land: Single Men and Social Disorder from the Frontier to the Inner City* (Cambridge: Harvard University Press, 1996); and Steven Cohan and Ina Rae Hark, *Screening the Male: Exploring Masculinities in Hollywood Cinema* (New York: Routledge, 1993).

18. Mark C. Carnes, *Secret Ritual and Manhood in Victorian America* (New Haven: Yale University Press, 1989), 14, 151, passim.

19. Kevin White, *The First Sexual Revolution: The Emergence of Male Heterosexuality in Modern America* (New York: New York University Press, 1993), 146.

20. Gail Bederman, *Manliness and Civilization: A Cultural History of Gender and Race in the United States, 1880–1917* (Chicago: University of Chicago Press, 1995). Bederman also includes an interesting discussion of Ida Wells and Charlotte Perkins Gilman.

21. John Taliaferro, *Tarzan Forever: The Life of Edgar Rice Burroughs, Creator of Tarzan* (New York: Scribner, 1999).

22. George L. Mosse, *The Image of Man: The Creation of Modern Masculinity* (New York: Oxford, 1996), 78, 90, 98–107. Mosse argues that the ingredient of racism made German masculinity different from identities in the remainder of Europe.

23. R. Marie Griffith, "Apostles of Abstinence: Fasting and Masculinity during the Progressive Era," *American Quarterly* 52 (December 2000): 599–638. See also Judy Hilkey, *Character Is Capital: Success Manuals and Manhood in Gilded Age America* (Chapel Hill: University of North Carolina Press, 1997), 144, passim. The anxious dietary advice of Sylvester Graham is a good example of this tendency in the nineteenth century.

24. Jeffrey P. Hartover, "The Boy Scouts and the Validation of Masculinity," in *The American Man*, ed. Elizabeth H. Pleck and Joseph H. Pleck (Englewood Cliffs: Prentice-Hall, 1980), 287.

25. Kim Townsend, *Manhood at Harvard: William James and Others* (New York: W. W. Norton, 1996).

26. Margaret Marsh, "Suburban Men and Masculine Domesticity, 1870–1915," *American Quarterly* 40 (June 1988): 165–86.

27. Mary Chapman and Glenn Hendler, eds., "Introduction," *Sentimental Men: Masculinity and the Politics of Affect in American Culture* (Berkeley: University of California Press, 1999), 9. This interesting collection challenges the perceptions of 1950s critics like Leslie Fiedler, R. W. B. Lewis, and, earlier, F. O. Matthiessen, and, later, Ann Douglas, all of whom disparaged sentimentality in writers, seeing it as a feminine, and therefore, less significant characteristic.

28. Gerald N. Izenberg, *Modernism and Masculinity* (Chicago: University of Chicago Press, 2000). While this is a study of European turn-of-the-century culture, its findings are suggestive for American society. Izenberg suggests that the Frankfurt school of intellectuals was crucial in defining a change in production and business organization as key to touching off feelings of anxiety and alienation. Given the importance of these intellectuals to American sociology in articulating a similar interpretation during the 1950s, this is an important insight.

29. K. A. Cuordileone, "Politics in an Age of Anxiety: Cold War Political Culture and the Crisis of American Masculinity, 1949–1960," *Journal of American History* 87 (September 2000): 515–43.

30. Some historians depict the 1930s as the second modern masculinity crisis.

31. Barbara Ehrenreich, *The Hearts of Men: American Dreams and the Flight from Commitment* (New York: Anchor, 1983); and Elaine Tyler May, *Homeward Bound: American Families in the Cold War Era* (New York: Basic Books, 1988). See also Susan Faludi, *Stiffed: The Betrayal of the American Man* (New York: William Morrow, 1999), 36, 448, passim. Susan Faludi's best seller forcefully argued that men in the 1950s were promised a meaningful mission in society, the possibility of mastery, and progress—in effect, a kind of social contract. What happened, however, was a betrayal, broken promises, and an "ornamental masculinity." See also Lary May, ed., *Recasting America: Culture and Politics in the Age of Cold War* (Chicago: University of Chicago Press, 1989); and Elaine Tyler May, "Explosive Issues; Sex, Women, and the Bomb," in *Changing Images of the Family*, ed. Virginia Tufte and Barbara Myerhoff (New Haven: Yale University Press, 1979). It has also been asserted with some justice that the 1950s religious revival, anti-Communism, and fervent ideology of the nuclear family provided a basis for the rise of the New Right in the 1950s. Lisa McGirr, *Suburban Warriors: The Origins of the New American Right* (Princeton: Princeton University Press, 2001).

32. David Halberstam, *The Fifties* (New York: Villard Books, 1993).

33. Joanne Meyerowitz, ed., *Not June Cleaver* (Philadelphia: Temple University Press, 1994); and Joel Foreman, ed., *The Other Fifties: Interrogating Midcentury American Icons* (Urbana: University of Illinois Press, 1997). See esp. David Shamway, "Watching Elvis: The Male Rock Star as Object of the Gaze," in *Other Fifties*, 124–43.

34. Steven Cohan, *Masked Men: Masculinity and the Movies in the Fifties* (Bloomington: Indiana University Press, 1997). See also Thomas Weyr, *Reaching for Paradise: The Playboy Vision of America* (New York: New York Times Books, 1978).

35. Robert J. Corber, *Homosexuality in Cold War America: Resistance and the Crisis of Masculinity* (Charlotte: Duke University Press, 1997).

36. Jonathan Ned Katz, *The Invention of Heterosexuality* (New York: Dutton, 1995), 14–77, passim.

37. Neil Gabler, *Life, the Movie* (New York: Knopf, 1998). This fascinating book is particularly interesting on the historical origins of fabricated images and ideas about contemporary life.

38. James Thurber, "The Secret Life of Walter Mitty," *New Yorker,* March 18, 1939. According to Burton Bernstein, Thurber's biographer, the story represented a distillation of Thurber people and themes. In a letter to Mrs. Robert Blake in 1961, for example, Thurber wrote, "The original of Walter Mitty is every other man I have ever known." Burton Bernstein, *Thurber: A Biography* (New York: Dodd, Mead, 1975), 311. The story was made into a film (1947), an opera, and a Broadway musical, although perhaps the original was too slight and polished to be expanded. During World War II there were even Walter Mitty clubs in the Pacific and Atlantic theaters and warplanes named after the main character.

Chapter 3

1. File: "The Lonely Crowd: Miscellaneous," HUG, fp 99.16, box 41; David Riesman to Professor N. Henro Pronko, February 28, 1978; File: "The Lonely Crowd: Correspondence," HUG, fp 99.16, box 40; all in the Papers of David Riesman, Harvard University Archives, Pusey Library. Quotations courtesy of the Harvard University Archives. Permission to publish granted by Mr. Michael Riesman. Hereafter cited as Riesman MSS.

2. Jonathan Yardley, "Reconsideration: The Lonely Crowd," *New Republic*, March 4, 1972, 27.

3. "Preface to the Lonely Crowd, French Edition," 2, in file, "The Lonely Crowd: Miscellaneous," HUG fp 99.16, box 41, Riesman MSS.

4. Eugene Davidson to Riesman, May 22, 1950, "Correspondence and Other Papers: Subjects and Organizations" in file, "Yale Press: Lonely Crowd," HUG fp 99.16, box 41, Riesman MSS.

5. Riesman to David J. Gray, May 1, 1963, 2, in file, "The Lonely Crowd: Correspondence," 1, HUG fp 99.16, box 40; David Riesman to Mrs. D. M. Pratt, March 2, 1957, in file, "Continuities Volume: The Lonely Crowd," HUG fp 99.16, box 39, both at Riesman MSS. Eric Larabee, "David Riesman and His Readers," in *Culture and Social Character: The Work of David Riesman*, ed. Seymour Martin Lipset and Leo Lowenthal (Glencoe: The Free Press, 1961), 413.

6. Robert Blevins to Riesman, no date; and Mrs. Jack F. Young to Riesman, February 18, 1952; File: "The Lonely Crowd: Correspondence," 1, HUG fp 99.16, box 39, both at Riesman MSS.

7. William E. Osgood to David Riesman, May 11, 1956, in file, "The Lonely Crowd: Correspondence," 2, HUG fp 99.16, box 40, Riesman MSS.

8. Riesman to L. H. Grunebaum, July 1, 1953, in file, "The Lonely Crowd: Correspondence," 2, HUG fp 99.16, box 40, Riesman MSS.

9. David Riesman, "On Discovering and Teaching Sociology: A Memoir," *Annual Review of Sociology* 14 (1988): 2; and David Barboza, "An Interview with David Riesman," *Partisan Review* 61 (Fall 1994): 574–91.

10. Riesman, "On Discovering and Teaching Sociology," 7.

11. Ibid., passim.

12. Bruno Bettelheim, "Review of *Lonely Crowd*" (clipping), *University of Chicago* magazine, March 1951, in file, "The Lonely Crowd: Correspondence," 1, HUG fp 99.16, box 40, Riesman MSS.

13. Michael McGiffert, "Selected Writings on American National Character," *American Quarterly* 15 (Summer Supplement, 1963): 271–88.

14. David Riesman, "Innocence of *The Lonely Crowd*," *Society* 27 (January/February 1990): 78. David Riesman to Andrew Hacker, July 15, 1958, in file, "General Correspondence with Individuals, 1951–1964," HUG 99.8, box 21, Riesman MSS.

15. John Higham in his essay "The Cult of the 'American Consensus,'" in *Commentary* 27 (February 1959): 93–100, argued that the vogue of de Tocqueville indicated a turn to conservatism among American historians. Moreover, he suggested that the emphasis

upon psychological tensions rather than basic opposition between distinct groups reinforced this conservative bent.

16. William Graebner, *The Age of Doubt: American Thought and Culture in the 1940s* (Boston: Twayne, 1991), 76–77; Margaret Mead, "Anthropologist and Historian: Their Common Problems," *American Quarterly* 3 (Spring 1951): 9. See also Robert E. Spiller and Eric Larabee, *American Perspectives: The National Self-Image in the Twentieth Century* (Cambridge: Harvard University Press, 1961).

17. Henry Steele Commager, *The American Mind: An Interpretation of American Thought and Character since the 1880's* (New Haven: Yale University Press, 1950). Commager had worked with the Office of War Information and the U.S. Army. A few of the other titles in this genre are: Arthur Meier Schlesinger, *What Then Is the American, This New Man*? (1943); Henry Nash Smith, *Virgin Land: The American West as Symbol and Myth* (1950); Max Lerner, *America as a Civilization* (1957); Elting E. Morison, ed., *The American Style* (1958); Leo Marx, *The Machine in the Garden: Technology and the Pastoral Ideal in America* (1964), and so on. The list is, in fact, enormous. See also David E. Stannard, "American Historians and the Idea of National Character: Some Problems and Prospects," *American Quarterly* 28 (May 1971): 202–20. Like many of the authors dealing with American character, Commager probably only had men in mind when he analyzed American society. For example, in his index there are three citations to "American character and women" and none (specifically) to men, suggesting that only these three applied to women and the rest to men. See also David Riesman, "The Study of National Character: Some Observations on the American Case," *Harvard Library Bulletin* 13 (Winter 1959), 5–24.

18. Tremain McDowell, *American Studies* (Minneapolis: University of Minnesota Press, 1948); and Rupert Wilkinson, *The Pursuit of American Character* (New York: Harper and Row, 1988), 4–16.

19. Martin Jay, *The Dialectical Imagination: A History of the Frankfurt School and the Institute of Social Research, 1923–1950* (Boston: Little Brown, 1973), 88–131, 217.

20. Erich Fromm, *Escape from Freedom* (New York: Holt, Rinehart and Winston, 1941), 284, passim.

21. Margaret Mead to Riesman, 19 October 1949, 1, in file, "Margaret Mead," HUG fp 99.16, box 31; and David Riesman to Sol [?], February 13, 1958, regarding Margaret Mead, in file, "Correspondence with Specific Individuals," HUG 99.12, box 31; both at Riesman MSS. In one short section of *Lonely Crowd*, Riesman recounted a class experiment using social character types described by Mead's student Ruth Benedict. Students almost universally saw similarities between contemporary American character and the Kwakiutl Indians, whereas, he claimed, most modern Americans resembled the more "other directed" Pueblos he described to them. Riesman, *The Lonely Crowd*, 271–82. See Margaret Mead, "Anthropologist and Historian: Their Common Problems," *American Quarterly* 3 (Spring 1951): 8–9.

22. David Riesman, "File 136 Lecture, Tocqueville," February 1, 1962, in file, "Materials Relating to Courses Taught at Harvard, 1958–1980," HUG 99.62, box 17; see also Riesman to Andrew Hacker, July 15, 1958, in file, "1951–1964: General

Correspondence with Individuals," box 21, HUG 99.8; both at Riesman MSS. David Riesman, "Psychological Types and National Character: An Informal Commentary," *American Quarterly* 5 (Winter 1953): 343.

23. Riesman, "Psychological Types," 342–43. Riesman, "Study of National Character," 10.

24. Riesman et al., "In Search of Political Apathy," Seminar report, April 27, 1948, in file, "Bernard Lecture [and Others]," HUG 99.57, box 2, Riesman MSS.

25. "Character Types and Political Apathy: Some Revisions," May 26, 1948, 1–5, in file, "Manuscript Draft, ca. 1948–1949; Chapter 5: Character Types and Political Apathy," HUG fp 99.55, box 13, Riesman MSS.

26. Ibid., 10–11.

27. Ibid., 11–14.

28. Ibid., 16–20. Riesman to Reuel Denney, 8 March 1949, 1, in file, "Reuel Denney," HUG fp 99.12, box 6, Riesman MSS.

29. David Riesman, "The Individual in a World of Power," 26, March 12, 1949, in file, "Manuscript Draft, ca. 1948–1949," HUG 99.55, box 13, Riesman MSS. Another intermediate version of the study appeared in outline form in the summer of 1948.

30. Riesman, *Lonely Crowd*, 373.

31. Dennis Wrong [1954?], in file, "Lectures, Notes, Lonely Crowd Review," HUG fp 99.57, box 2, Riesman MSS. See also Riesman, "The Saving Remnant," in *The Character of Americans: A Book of Readings*, ed. Michael McGiffert (Homewood, IL: Dorsey Press, 1964), 346. This collection contains an extensive bibliography of character studies.

32. Riesman, *Lonely Crowd*, xlviii; and Riesman, "Psychological Types," 334.

33. Reuel Denney and David Riesman, "Leisure in Industrial America," in *Creating an Industrial Civilization*, ed. Eugene Staley (New York: Hark and Bros., 1952), 278.

34. David Potter, *People of Plenty: Economic Abundance and the American Character* (Chicago: University of Chicago Press, 1954), xiv–68. For a view of Western history that emphasizes distinct groups, rather than a universal frontier experience, see also Peggy Pascoe, "Western Women at the Cultural Crossroads," in *Trails: Toward a New Western History*, ed. Patricia N. Limerick et al. (Lawrence: University of Kansas Press, 1991), 40–58.

35. David Potter, "American Women and the American Character," *Stetson University Bulletin* 62 (January 1962): 1–6. See also Glenda Riley, *The Female Frontier: A Comparative View of Women on the Prairie and the Plains* (Lawrence: University of Kansas, 1988).

36. Potter, "American Women," 11.

37. David Riesman, "Some Continuities and Discontinuities in the Education of Women," John Dewey Memorial Lecture, Bennington College, June 7, 1956.

38. David Riesman, "American Character in the Twentieth Century," *Annals of the American Academy of Political and Social Science* 370 (March 1967): 36–47; David Riesman, "Innocence of *The Lonely Crowd*," *Society* 35 (1998); and David Riesman, "Comments on 'Dennis Wrong: *The Lonely Crowd* Revisited,'" *Sociological Forum* 7, no. 12 (1992): 392.

39. Matthew Reed, "A Universe Two Stories Deep" (Ph.D. diss., Rutgers University, 1997), 1–77. This important essay discusses Riesman's masculine bias and the influence of Fromm and Freud on his thinking.

40. David Riesman and Nathan Glazer, *Faces in the Crowd: Individual Studies in Character and Politics* (New Haven: Yale University Press, 1952), 564, passim.

41. David Riesman, "Psychological Types," 330–31.

42. David Riesman, *Thorstein Veblen: A Critical Interpretation* (New York: Charles Scribner's Sons, 1953), 2, 18, 41, passim.

43. Ibid., 42. Erik Fromm's enormously popular *Art of Loving* published in 1956 made the sexual division of characteristics the basis of his analysis. The masculine character was known by qualities of "penetration, guidance, activity, discipline and adventurousness; the feminine character by the qualities of productive receptiveness, protection, realism, endurance, motherliness." Fromm, *Art of Loving* (New York: Harper, 1956), 36.

44. On the connection between gender and consumption, see Mary Louise Roberts, "Gender, Consumption, and Commodity Culture," *American Historical Review* 103 (June 1998): 817–44.

45. Riesman, *The Lonely Crowd*, 108–9.

46. Riesman, *The Lonely Crowd*, 64, 130–47; U.S. Bureau of the Census, *Historical Statistics of the United States: Colonial Times to 1970* (Washington, DC: U.S. Government Printing Office, 1975), 1:141.

47. In his collection of essays, Riesman cites an unpublished paper, "Male and Female in *The Lonely Crowd*" by Walter Weisskopf, which argues that "the spread among men of empathy and 'other-direction' is part of a protest against the 'maleness' of large-scale industrial society, with its abstraction and artificiality"; Riesman, *Abundance for What?* (Garden City: Doubleday, 1964), 332. See also Angel Kwolek-Folland, *Engendering Business: Men and Women in the Corporate Office, 1870–1930* (Baltimore: Johns Hopkins University Press, 1994), 75. Kwolek-Folland argues that gender relations for men entered a period of crisis when women entered the corporate office.

48. Richard Hofstadter, "Comment," in Morison, ed., *American Style*, 354–55.

49. William H. Whyte, *The Organization Man* (New York: Simon and Schuster, 1956).

50. David Riesman, "The Suburban Sadness," in *The Suburban Community*, ed. William M. Dobriner (New York: G. P. Putnam's Sons, 1958), 375, 380, passim; and "The Suburban Dislocation," in Riesman, *Abundance for What?* 252. There is a curious echo of this in today's depiction of "soccer moms" driving their SUVs—the twenty-first-century version of the station wagon.

51. John Hewitt, *Dilemmas of the American Self* (Philadelphia: Temple University Press, 1989). This excellent essay discusses the 1950s conversation on conformity and the reception of Riesman's work. See also Seymour Martin Lipset, "A Changing American Character?" in *Culture and Social Character: The Work of David Riesman Reconsidered*, ed. Seymour Martin Lipset (Glencoe: Free Press, 1961), 272. See also Alan Wolfe, *Marginalized in the Middle* (Chicago: University of Chicago Press, 1996). Wolfe speaks of the Golden Age of social criticism, referring to the 1950s and Riesman's work.

52. Lipset, *Culture and Social Character*, 164.

53. "The People," *Time* 64 (September 27, 1954): 22–25. Will Herberg, "Riesman's Lonely Man," *Commonweal* 60 (September 3, 1954): 538–40.

54. Potter, *People of Plenty*; and Carl N. Degler, "The Sociologist as Historian: Riesman's *The Lonely Crowd*," *American Quarterly* 15 (Winter 1963), 484–97.

55. Theodore Levitt, "The Lonely Crowd and the Economic Man," *Quarterly Journal of Economics* 70 (February 1956): 95–116.

56. David Riesman to Max [?], December 23, 1957, in file, "Correspondence with Specific Individuals: McKitrick, Eric, Before 1960," HUG 99.12, box 31; Richard Hofstadter to Riesman, April 20, 1951, in file, "Lonely Crowd: Correspondence," 1, HUG fp 99.16, box 39; and Reuel Denney, January 23, 1968 to Riesman, in file, "The Lonely Crowd," HUG 99.16, box 39; all at Riesman MSS.

57. Eugene Lunn, in a very interesting discussion of *The Lonely Crowd*, emphasizes Riesman's intent to explore the positive potential in other-direction, mass culture, and consumption. There is certainly strong evidence for this in the work, even if most readers did not come away with that impression. Interestingly, Lunn also misreads Riesman in a not uncommon way. His article consistently refers to "outer-direction," not, as Riesman wrote it, "other-direction." Eugene Lunn, "Beyond 'Mass Culture': The Lonely Crowd, the Uses of Literacy, and the Postwar Era," *Theory and Society* 19 (February 1990): 63–86. See p. 65 for example.

58. E. Digby Baltzell, "The American Aristocrat and Other-Direction," in Lipset, ed., *Culture and Social Character*, 268; Cushing Strout, "A Note on Degler, Riesman, and Tocqueville," *American Quarterly* 16 (Spring 1964): 102.

59. Riesman, *Lonely Crowd*, 367, 362–66. In some respects this is the most difficult and least compelling portion of the book. In effect, it calls for the professionalization of leisure and consumption.

60. David Riesman, "The Lonely Crowd: Twenty Years After," *Encounter* 33 (October 1969): 36.

61. Kenneth Kennistan to Riesman, January 3, 1969, in file, "The Lonely Crowd," HUG fp 99.16, box 39, Riesman MSS.

Chapter 4

1. Arthur M. Schlesinger, Jr., *Kennedy or Nixon: Does It Make Any Difference?* (New York: Macmillan, 1960), 4–17. Schlesinger deployed Riesman's notions of "other-direction" to characterize Nixon's weakness, calling him a "lonely man."

2. Arthur M. Schlesinger, Jr., "The Crisis of American Masculinity," in *The Politics of Hope* (Boston: Houghton Mifflin, 1963), 237–46.

3. Ibid., 244.

4. Joseph H. Peck, M.D., *All About Men* (Englewood Cliffs: Prentice-Hall, 1958), 41.

5. Carl C. Seltzer, "The Relationship between the Masculine Component and Personality," in *Personality in Nature, Society, and Culture*, ed. Clyde Kluckhohn and Henry A. Murray (London: Jonathan Cape, 1949), 85, 91, 95.

6. Elizabeth Lunbeck, *The Psychiatric Persuasion: Knowledge, Gender, and Power in Modern America* (Princeton: Princeton University Press, 1994); Joseph H. Pleck, *The Myth of Masculinity* (Cambridge: MIT Press, 1981), 158. See also Abram Kardiner, *Sex and Morality* (London: Routledge, 1955), 188, passim.

7. Commenting on gender categories during the 1950s, historian Stephen Whitfield argues that they were "sharply circumscribed." Nevertheless, he finds that the tensions around gender were not debilitating. Both "hard" and "soft masculinity" could be reconciled in pursuit of the goal of higher living standards, he writes. See Stephen J. Whitfield, "Sex and the Single Decade," *American Literary History* 12 (Winter 2000): 771–79.

8. Richard Gehman, "Toupees, Girdles, and Sun Lamps," *Cosmopolitan* 142 (May 1957): 39–43. Gehman might have concluded that the flight was just like home.

9. In "Wake Up, America!" Wright enunciated in 1940 political aphorisms worthy of Rand's flat-footed prose. "The only safe-guard Democracy can ever have," he asserted, for example, "is a free, morally enlightened, fearless minority." See Frank Lloyd Wright, *Collected Writings*, vol. 4, *1939–1949*, ed. Brooks Pfeiffer (New York: Rizzoli, 1994), 40.

10. Ayn Rand, *The Fountainhead* (1943; New York: Scribner Classics, 2000), 220, 724. Stacey Olster has a very interesting commentary on Rand in "Something Old, Something New, Something Borrowed, Something (Red, White) and Blue," in *The Other Fifties: Interrogating Midcentury American Icons*, ed. Joel Foreman (Urbana: University of Illinois Press, 1997), 292–96.

11. Philip Wylie, *Generation of Vipers* (1942; New York: Rinehart & Co., 1955), 50, 61, 98ff.

12. James Truslow Adams, *The American: The Making of a New Man* (New York: Scribner's Sons, 1943), 373.

13. Leland Stowe, "What's Wrong with American Women?" *Reader's Digest*, November 1949, 49–51.

14. Ramona Barth, "What's Wrong with American Men," ibid., 24.

15. Russell Lynes, *A Surfeit of Honey* (New York: Harper & Brothers, 1957), 5.

16. Dorothy Barclay, "Trousered Mothers and Dishwashing Dads," *New York Times Magazine*, April 28, 1957, 48.

17. Margaret Mead, "American Man in a Woman's World," *New York Times Magazine*, February 10, 1957, 11, 22–23. See also, Mead, *Male and Female: A Study of the Sexes in a Changing World* (New York: W. Morrow, 1949), 291.

18. Helen Meyer Hacker, "The New Burdens of Masculinity," *Marriage and Family Living* 19 (August 1957): 229. Hacker also invoked homosexuality as a symptom of male maladjustment.

19. Erik Erikson, *Childhood and Society* (New York: W. W. Norton, 1950), 282, 254.

20. See Philip Cushman, *Constructing the Self and Constructing America: A Cultural History of Psychotherapy* (Reading, Mass.: Addison-Wesley, 1995). Cushing emphasizes that psychology in the 1950s was deeply influenced by psychoanalysis and celebrated youth, consumption, and the liberation of the inner self. Emily Rosenberg finds strong elements of continuity between the theme of male crisis in the family and culture and

the predicaments of American foreign policy. See Emily Rosenberg, "'Foreign Affairs': World War II: Connecting Sexual and International Politics," *Diplomatic History* 18 (Winter 1994): 59–70.

21. William H. Whyte, Jr., *The Organization Man* (New York: Simon and Schuster, 1956), 3. Whyte's use of "taking vows" suggested that commitment to the corporation relinquished sexual identity.

22. Editors of *Look* magazine, *The Decline of the American Male* (New York: Random House, 1958), 3. This is a reprint of their successful magazine symposium of the same name.

23. J. Robert Moskin, "Why Do Women Dominate Him?" in ibid., 3–24. This is the same series and book in which Schlesinger's article appeared.

24. Edward A. Strecker, *Their Mothers' Sons: The Psychiatrist Examines an American Problem* (1946; Philadelphia: J. B. Lippincott, 1951).

25. Quoted by Amory Clark in "His Sex Habits," *Cosmopolitan* 142 (May 1957): 32.

26. Paul Goodman, *Growing Up Absurd: Problems of Youth in the Organized System* (New York: Random House, 1960), 14.

27. Robert J. Corber, *Homosexuality in Cold War America: Resistance and the Crisis of Masculinity* (Durham: Duke University Press, 1997).

28. Joanne Meyerowitz, *How Sex Changed: A History of Transsexuality in the United States* (Cambridge: Harvard University Press, 2002).

29. Talcott Parsons, Robert F. Bales, et al., *Family, Socialization, and the Interaction Process* (Glencoe: Free Press, 1955), 103–4.

30. For a discussion of the extent and depth of the sexual revolution in the 1950s, see Beth Bailey, *Sex in the Heartland* (Cambridge: Harvard University Press, 1999).

31. Thomas Weyr, *Reaching for Paradise: The Playboy Vision of America* (New York: New York Times, 1978), xvi–ii. See also David Allyn, *Make Love, Not War: The Sexual Revolution; An Unfettered History* (Boston: Little, Brown, 2000).

32. Harvey Cox, "*Playboy*'s Doctrine of the Male," *Christianity and Crisis* 21 (April 17, 1961).

33. Amran Scheinfeld, "The American Male," *Cosmopolitan* 142 (May 1957): 23–25.

34. Lemuel C. McGee, M.D. "The Suicidal Cult of 'Manliness,'" *Today's Health* 35 (January 1957): 28–30. McGee published books on urology and industrial medicine.

35. Hannah Lees, "Our Men are Killing Themselves," *Saturday Evening Post* 228 (January 28, 1956): 114.

36. Otis L. Wiese, "Live the Life of McCall's," *McCall's* 81 (May 1954): 27.

Chapter 5

1. Judith A. Reisman, *Kinsey: Crimes and Consequences; The Red Queen and the Grand Scheme* (Arlington, Va.: Institute for Media Education, 1998). This wildly irresponsible and baffling book charges Kinsey with countless sex crimes and invidious influences, even linking his work to Nazi experiments. Nonetheless, it contains some interesting information about the reaction to Kinsey. And it is true that Kinsey used material in his research contributed by pedophiles. The children's material in the Kinsey volumes was

derived largely from the extensive diary of an anonymous man who had frequent sex with minors. Kinsey also did interviews with children. In 1953, the Reece Committee of the House of Representatives began a series of hostile investigations of foundations. One target was the Rockefeller Foundation and its funding of Kinsey. See James H. Jones, *Alfred C. Kinsey, a Public/Private Life* (New York: W. W. Norton, 1997), 752.

2. The Jones biography is largely responsible for revealing this material. It is ironic that Jones uses the language of psychoanalysis (something Kinsey firmly rejected) to explain the sexologist's behavior. Jones, *Kinsey*, 4.

3. Paul Robinson, *The Modernization of Sex: Havelock Ellis, Alfred Kinsey, William Masters, and Virginia Johnson* (New York: Harper and Row, 1976), 11, 68. See, for example, George W. Henry, *Sex Variants: A Study of Homosexual Patterns* (New York: P. B. Hoeber, 1941).

4. Regina Markett Morantz, "The Scientist as Sex Crusader: Alfred Kinsey and American Culture," *American Quarterly* 29, Special Issue (Winter 1977).

5. This stress on the normal and abnormal facilitated a link with Christian theology as some writers invoked the support of Freud as corroborating the norm of sex expressed only within a loving, sanctified marriage. See W. Norman Pittenger, *The Christian View of Sexual Behavior* (Greenwich, Conn.: Seabury Press, 1954). On Freudianism in America, see Eli Zaretsky, *Secrets of the Soul: A Social and Cultural History of Psychoanalysis* (New York: Alfred A. Knopf, 2004).

6. Carl C. Seltzer, "The Relationship between the Masculine Component and Personality," in *Personality in Nature, Society, and Culture*, ed. Clyde Kluckhohn and Henry A. Murray (London: Jonathan Cape, 1949), 84–96; and Lewis M. Terman and Catharine Cox Miles, *Sex and Personality: Studies in Masculinity and Femininity* (1936; New York: Russell and Russell, 1968). Both of these publications implied that strong masculine characteristics implied performance.

7. Terman and Miles, *Sex and Personality,* 121.

8. Bernarr Macfadden, *Man's Sex Life* (New York: Macfadden Book Co., 1935); Robert Ernst, *Weakness Is a Crime: The Life of Bernarr Macfadden* (Syracuse: Syracuse University Press, 1991). Macfadden corresponded with Kinsey, and Kinsey was aware of his books. Kinsey's clipping file includes an item indicating that the U.S. Naval Academy expelled men who had been found masturbating.

9. Robinson, *Modernization of Sex*. This is an excellent introduction to the history of modern sexology and Alfred Kinsey's place in it. Robinson pays close attention to attitudes toward homosexuality as a marker to distinguish Kinsey from Freud and Ellis.

10. Elizabeth Lunbeck argues that by the 1920s in the United States, the concept of normality had come to be part of the psychiatric field. Lunbeck, *The Psychiatric Persuasion: Knowledge, Gender, and Power in Modern America* (Princeton: Princeton University Press, 1994), 306.

11. See Morantz, "Scientist as Sex Crusader," 563–89, for a reliable reading of Kinsey's career and influence.

12. Alfred C. Kinsey, *The Gall Wasp Genus Cynips: A Study in the Origin of Species* (Bloomington: Indiana University Studies, 1930). His next volume he entitled, *The*

Origin of Higher Categories in Cynips (Bloomington: Indiana University Press, 1936), perhaps in unconscious reference to Darwin's volume on higher animals. Kinsey's biology textbook depicted the theory of evolution at a time when this was controversial, and throughout his work, the entomologist expresses admiration for Darwin.

13. Sophie D. Aberle and George W. Corner, *Twenty-Five Years of Sex Research: History of the National Research Council Committee for Research in Problems of Sex, 1922–1947* (Philadelphia: W. B. Saunders Co., 1953), 64, 101.

14. Jonathan Gathorne-Hardy, *Sex the Measure of All Things: A Life of Alfred C. Kinsey* (Bloomington: University of Indiana Press, 1998), 269–71. This is the second of the exhaustive, contending recent biographies of Kinsey. Both Jones and Gathorne-Hardy based their writing on a large store of documents from the Kinsey Institute as well as interviews with participants in the research projects. They recount a private life and a laboratory culture which, had they been known at the time, would have immediately discredited Kinsey's work. Both biographies tell a similar story but with very different interpretations. Jones, while admiring the work of the institute, portrays Kinsey as a homosexual masochist bent upon normalizing his troubling behavior. Gathorne-Hardy, using the same materials and new interviews with principal figures around Kinsey, acknowledges Kinsey's unorthodox behavior but defends the objectivity of his work.

15. Alfred C. Kinsey, Wardell B. Pomeroy, and Clyde E. Martin, *Sexual Behavior in the Human Male* (1948; reprint, Bloomington: Indiana University Press, 1998).

16. Ibid., 17.

17. Ibid., 34.

18. Ibid., 197.

19. Ibid., 638, 488–93.

20. Leon Gutterman, "Our Film Folk," *National Jewish Ledger*, June 23, 1950.

21. See Wardell Pomeroy, *Dr. Kinsey and the Institute for Sex Research,* 2nd ed. (New Haven: Yale University Press, 1982), for the reception to Kinsey's work. See also "I.U. Man's Sex Study Wins Acclaim," Gallup Poll, *Indianapolis Star*, March 21, 1948. About 57 percent of Americans believed that Kinsey's information was socially beneficial. For Kinsey as a symbol of sex, see Lawrence Lariar, *A Photographic Reaction to the Kinsey Report* (New York: Cartwrite Publishing, 1953). This book showed the "shocked" photographic "reaction" of women to the *Female* volume published in 1953.

22. Gathorne-Hardy, *Sex the Measure*, 310–11. Regina Mackell Morantz provides an excellent and careful accounting of Kinsey and the reaction to his work. It is puzzling, however, that she concludes that he was a sexual conservative. See Morantz, "Scientist as Sex Crusader," 563–89.

23. These objections were even raised in the largely favorable symposium published in 1948 devoted to the report. See Albert Deutsche, ed., *Sex Habits of American Men: A Symposium on the Kinsey Report* (New York: Prentice-Hall, 1948), esp. Robert P. Knight, "Psychiatric Issues in the Kinsey Report." See also Jack Kerouac *On the Road* (New York: Penguin, 1957), 122.

24. Wardell Pomeroy, Carol C. Flax, and Connie Christine Wheeler, *Taking a Sex History: Interviewing and Recording* (New York: Macmillan, 1982), 8.

25. Lewis Terman, "Kinsey's 'Sexual Behavior in the Human Male': Some Comments and Criticisms," *Psychological Bulletin* 45 (September 1948): 443–59, esp. 455, 458–59. See also Donald Porter Geddes and Enid Curie, *About the Kinsey Report: Observations by Experts on 'Sexual Behavior in the Human Male'* (New York: New American Library, 1948).

26. W. Allen Wallis, "Statistics of the Kinsey Report," *Journal of the American Statistical Association* 44 (December 1949): 463–84.

27. "Must We Change Our Sex Standards?" *Reader's Digest*, June and September 1941, Kinsey Clipping File, Papers of Alfred C. Kinsey, Kinsey Institute for Research in Sex, Gender, and Reproduction, Inc., Indiana University, Bloomington, Indiana. Hereafter cited as Kinsey MSS. Kinsey and editor Oursler had a substantial correspondence. At one point, despite his critical attitude, Oursler asked if he might excerpt part of the forthcoming volume on women for his magazine.

28. "Sheehy Attacks Kinsey Report," *Washington Post*, November 14, 1948. The National Council of Catholic Women denounced the report in September 1948; Kinsey Clipping File, Kinsey MSS.

29. "Report of a Meeting of the American Social Hygiene Association," *New York Herald-Tribune*, April 4, 1948; Geoffrey Gorer, "Justification by Numbers," *American Scholar* 17 (July 1948): 280; and Dorothy Thompson, "Some Observations on a Sensational Book," *Ladies Home Journal* (May 1948).

30. Lionel Trilling, "The Kinsey Report," in *The Liberal Imagination: Essays on Literature and Society* (London: Secker and Warburg, 1951), 223–42. This essay first appeared in 1948 in the *Partisan Review*.

31. Lionel Trilling, "Freud and Literature," in *Liberal Imagination*, 34. This essay was published in 1947. See also "The Kinsey Report," 235.

32. Perhaps the most substantial success of the two Kinsey studies was the influence of his findings on the American Law Institute's "Model Penal Code," developed in 1955 with funds from Rockefeller. This code argued that behavior that did not injure others should be decriminalized. Herbert Wechsler's "The Challenge of a Model Penal Code," published in the *Harvard Law Review* in 1952, explored ways in which Kinsey's data might be incorporated into a model code. This article became one of the most heavily cited articles in the history of legal journals. *Harvard Law Review* 65 (May 1952): 1097–1133. Kinsey's own clipping file contains his statement that several state legislatures were revising their laws using his material or in direct consultation with the institute. "Kinsey Says Book on Sex Acts Is Leading to Revision of Laws," Clipping File, Kinsey MSS; see also Robinson, *Modernization of Sex*, for an excellent account of Kinsey's influence.

33. In this section, dealing with correspondence to Kinsey, I have eliminated specific citations in the footnotes so as to obscure the names.

34. Fredric Wertham to Alfred Kinsey, April 10, 1948, New York, Kinsey MSS.

35. Tennessee Williams to Alfred Kinsey, January 18, 1950; and Alfred Kinsey to Tennessee Williams, January 14, 1950. Kinsey MSS.

36. Alfred Kinsey to Dr. A. R. Mangus, Bloomington, Indiana, May 20, 1952, Kinsey MSS.

37. Pomeroy, *Kinsey*, 124.

38. Ibid., 108–9.

39. Ibid., 101. Pomeroy estimates that he and Kinsey took about 85 percent of the total histories completed at the time of Kinsey's death in 1956. See John Bancroft, "Kinsey: A 50th Anniversary Symposium," in *Sexualities* 1 (February 1998): 88.

40. *Best's Life Insurance News*, June 1952, Kinsey Clipping File, Kinsey MSS.

41. "False Kinsey 'Aides' Phone Women, Request Sex Data," *Buffalo Courier Express*, September 4, 1951, Kinsey Clipping File, Kinsey MSS.

42. Pomeroy, *Kinsey*, 63, 425.

43. Jones, *Kinsey*.

44. Gathorne-Hardy, *Measure*.

45. Lawrence Foster, introduction, *Free Love in Utopia: John Humphrey Noyes and the Origins of the Oneida Community* (Urbana: University of Illinois Press, 2001); and Robert S. Fogarty, *Desire and Duty at Oneida* (Bloomington: Indiana University Press, 2000).

46. Gathorne-Hardy, *Measure*, 39. Gathorne-Hardy speculates that Kinsey got his behaviorism from John Watson and especially Skinner. But, of course, there is a difference. While Watson and Skinner were attempting to understand the origins of behavior with the purpose of social control, Kinsey sought to measure behavior to eliminate social control. The author also stresses Kinsey's displaced Methodist evangelism. *Measure*, 311.

47. B. F. Skinner, *Walden Two* (New York: Macmillan, 1948), 108–9. Jones briefly explores the concept of utopia in describing the Kinsey Institute. Jones, *Kinsey*, 603. Another publishing event of 1948 was Norman Mailer's *Naked and the Dead*.

48. Henry L. Minton, *Departing from Deviance: A History of Homosexual Rights and Emancipatory Science in America* (Chicago: University of Chicago Press, 2002), 182–203. Minton argues that Kinsey was a social conservative because he did not understand the value of a "homosexual identity." Minton, "The Making of Sexual and Scientific Revolutions," *Contemporary Psychology* 41 (October 1996): 977. See also "Kinsey: A 50th Anniversary Symposium," 83–106. Several of the authors in this reevaluation make similar points about Kinsey, specifically citing his "masculinism."

49. Jones, *Kinsey*, 627–32. "Charter for Gestapo," *Washington Daily News*, February 4, 1951, recounts a proposed crime bill by James C. Davies (House) and Howard W. Smith (Senate) that would have greatly increased penalties for sex crimes. Kinsey MSS. Robert Yerkes, who was crucial to Kinsey's support in the Committee, had long tried to get the investigator to explore only "normal" sexuality. Jones, *Kinsey*, 440.

50. Miriam Grace Reuman, "American Sexual Character in the Age of Kinsey, 1946–64" (Ph.D. diss., Brown University, 1998), 32–34, 389, Kinsey Clipping File, Kinsey MSS.

51. Cornelia V. Christenson, *Kinsey: A Biography* (Bloomington: Indiana University press, 1971), 211, quoted from a speech, "A Scientist's Responsibility in Sex Instruction," to the National Association of Biology Teachers, December 1940.

52. See David Allyn, *Make Love Not War: The Sexual Revolution, an Unfettered History* (New York: Routledge, 2001). Allyn dates the revolution to the birth control pill, topless bikinis, pornography, and other such changes. See also, John Heidney, *What Wild Ecstasy: The Rise and Fall of the Sexual Revolution* (New York: Simon and Schuster, 1997). He argues for the importance of Kinsey to the sexual revolution and the centrality of changing the depictions and discussions of sexuality.

53. Henry L. Minton, "The Making of Sexual and Scientific Revolutions," *Contemporary Psychology* 41 (October 1996): 977; and Minton, *Departing from Deviance*, 168; see also Regina Morantz, "The Scientist as Sex Crusader: Alfred C. Kinsey and American Culture," *American Quarterly* 29 (Winter 1977): 589. Kinsey's position as a behaviorist, as well as his own bisexuality, probably influenced his stance on the nature of homosexuality.

54. Kinsey, *Sexual Behavior in the Human Male*, 638–39, 457.

55. Alfred Kinsey, "Homosexuality: Criteria for a Hormonal Explanation of the Homosexual," *Journal of Clinical Endocrinology* 1, no. 5 (May 1950): 427.

Chapter 6

1. Billy Graham, *How to be Born Again* (Waco, TX: Word Books, 1977), 168. In this tract, Graham lists the four steps of conversion: recognize God, repent, receive Christ, and confess faith in public.

2. Donald Meyer, "Billy Graham and Success," *New Republic* 133 (August 22, 1955): 9. Billy Sunday was, incidentally, a midwesterner.

3. Leon J. Podles, *The Church Impotent: The Feminization of Christianity* (Dallas: Spence Publishing, 1999), 11, passim. Podles traces this "problem" back to the Puritan Cotton Mather. Podles quotes Terman to the effect that men interested in religion do not have a masculine affect. See also Ann Douglas, *The Feminization of American Culture* (1977; New York: Farrar, Straus, Giroux, 1998), 13, 74–124. Douglas writes of the role of sentimental culture and its impact on American Protestants.

4. Billy Graham, *Billy Graham Talks to Teenagers* (Wheaton: Miracle Books, 1958), 10–11, 35.

5. See L. R. Scarborough, *The Tears of Jesus; The Central Passion of the Gospel* (1922; Grand Rapids: Baker Book House, 1967), 48. After saying this, the resisting man cries out and falls into the arms of the preacher. These were widely read sermons in evangelical circles. See also, Graham, *Talks to Teenagers*, 24–25.

6. Not everyone was persuaded by this argument. When Graham visited President Truman for a private meeting, reporters and photographers were not invited in. So they asked Graham to recount the meeting. Graham and several of his aides knelt on the White House lawn to demonstrate the stance of prayer that he and the president had assumed. Truman was furious, no doubt because this offended his touchy male pride.

7. Sallman first drew his famous sketch in 1924 for the cover of a religious periodical and reproduced it hundreds of times for illustrated talks. He recounted the inspiration of a leader of the Moody Bible Institute: "Make Him a real man." David Morgan,

Icons of American Protestantism: The Art of Warner Sallman (New Haven: Yale University Press, 1996).

8. Tony Ladd and James A. Mathisen, *Muscular Christianity: Evangelical Protestants and the Development of American Sport* (Grand Rapids: Baker Books, 1999). The quotation is from Tona J. Hangen, *Redeeming the Dial: Radio, Religion, and Popular Culture in America* (Chapel Hill: University of North Carolina Press, 2002), 41

9. Robert F. Martin, "Billy Sunday and Christian Manliness," *Historian* 58 (Summer 1996): 811–27.

10. William G. McLoughlin, Jr., *Billy Graham: Revivalist in a Secular Age* (New York: Ronald Press, 1960), 10–24.

11. James Craig Holte, *The Conversion Experience in America: A Sourcebook on Religious Conversion Autobiography* (New York: Greenwood, 1992), xii. Holte includes the conversion stories of Finney, Jim Bakker, Jerry Falwell, and Pat Robertson, but not Graham. He proposes that the conversion narrative is a fundamental aspect of autobiographical writing in America. See also Joe Edward Barnhart and Mary Ann Barnhart, *The New Birth: A Naturalistic View of Religious Conversion* (Mercer, Ga.: Mercer University Press, 1981).

12. Carol George, *God's Salesman: Norman Vincent Peale and the Power of Positive Thinking* (New York: Oxford, 1993), viii, 9–10, 26–31. Peale also shared Graham's political perspective and admiration for Richard Nixon.

13. Norman Vincent Peale, *The Power of Positive Thinking* (1952; New York: Fawcett Columbine, 1956), xiii, 2.

14. Peale, *Power*, 4–5.

15. Ibid., 46, 91–92.

16. Peale reported that he had twelve psychiatrists on the staff of the Marble Collegiate Church at 5th Avenue and 29th Street in New York. George, *God's Salesman*, 105.

17. Donald Meyer, *The Positive Thinkers*, 262–70, on the popularization of Freudian thinking among figures such as Peale.

18. McLoughlin, *Billy Graham*, 136–37.

19. Ted Ownby, *Subduing Satan: Religion, Recreation and Manhood in the Rural South, 1865–1920* (Chapel Hill: University of North Carolina Press, 1990), 14.

20. Christian Smith makes the argument that Graham was a "neo-evangelical" who believed that the fundamentalists were too parochial and pessimistic to engage the world as he wished to. Smith et al., *American Evangelicalism: Embattled and Thriving* (Chicago: University of Chicago Press, 1998), 10–12, 20.

21. William Martin, *A Prophet with Honor: The Billy Graham Story* (New York: William Morrow, 1991), 55–74.

22. Billy Graham, *Just as I Am: The Autobiography of Billy Graham* (San Francisco: Harper, 1997), 29. This title quotes the title of the Baptist hymn.

23. Just as I am, without one plea,
But that Thy blood was shed for me.
And that Thou bidst me come to Thee,
O Lamb of God, I come, I come.

24. Martin, *Prophet with Honor*, 55–74.

25. Mel Larson, *Youth for Christ* (Grand Rapids: Zondervan, 1947), 114. Larsen also noted the masculine characteristics of prominent American Evangelicals; 100–105.

26. Graham, *Just as I Am*, 275.

27. Herbert John Taylor had been a successful businessman, president of Club Aluminum Products, and international president of Rotary.

28. Torrey M. Johnson and Robert Cook, *Reaching Youth for Christ* (Chicago: Moody Press, 1944), 18. This tract contains numerous examples of divine intervention in men's lives.

29. Larry Eskridge, "'One Way': Billy Graham, the Jesus Generation, and the Idea of an Evangelical Youth Culture," *Church History* 67 (March 1998): 85; and Larson, *Youth for Christ*, 72.

30. Katherine Anderson to *Life* magazine 43 (July 22, 1957): 17.

31. Reinhold Niebuhr, "After Comment, the Deluge," *Christian Century* 74 (September 4, 1957): 1034.

32. Graham, *Just as I Am*, 51–53.

33. Ibid., 56–57.

34. "Mass Conversions," *Christian Century* 74 (May 29, 1957): 677–79. Unspoken in this critique was the charge that Graham disrupted mainline churches.

35. McLoughlin, *Billy Graham*, 182–95.

36. Billy Graham, *Peace with God* (Garden City, N.J.: Doubleday, 1953), 117–18.

37. Billy Graham, "Father," *Hour of Decision Tracts*, 1957, 2; Papers of Billy Graham, Wheaton College, Wheaton, Ill. Hereafter cited as Graham MSS. Graham often paraphrased this Bible verse. See, for example, "the wife is to submit to the husband"; Graham, *Talks to Teenagers*, 25. See also the discussion of gender relations among evangelicals in Sally Gallagher, *Evangelical Identity and Gendered Family Life* (New Brunswick, N.J.: Rutgers University Press, 2003). Gallagher argues that evangelical belief in the biblical basis of "headship" by husbands in the family is a "nonnegotiable, God-given spiritual hierarchy established in creation" (84).

38. Mel Larson in *Revival in Our Time*, by Billy Graham et al. (Wheaton, Ill.: Van Kampen Press, 1950), 25.

39. "My Answer: Questions and Answers," file 10, box 8, collection 19, Robert O. Ferm Papers, Billy Graham Center, Wheaton College. Hereafter cited as Ferm MSS. It is unclear whether Graham was the actual author of these words, although they were published under his name. That hardly matters, because Graham, for the purposes of this essay, has to be seen as the sum of his public attributes.

40. "My Answer," file 9, box 8, Ferm MSS.

41. "What Is Conversion?" 1957; "Christian Conversion," *Hour of Decision Tracts*, 1959, 4, Graham MSS.

42. Robert O. Ferm with Caroline M. Whiting, *Billy Graham: Do the Conversions Last?* (Minneapolis: World Wide Publications, 1988), 20–25, passim.

43. Ibid., 14, 40–45, passim.

44. A number of works by Christian theologians adopted James's descriptions and categories of the conversion experience. Among the most interesting of these was

Harold Begbie's *Twice-Born Men: A Clinic in Regeneration* (New York: Fleming H. Revell, 1909). Begbie explored the efforts of the Salvation Army to convert the toughest men in the worst parts of London and describes their success in making religion relevant to the most virile but debauched men.

45. Ferm, *Billy Graham*, 14–15. See also, Robert O. Ferm, *The Psychology of Christian Conversion* (Westwood, N.J.: Fleming Revell, 1959). Ferm uses Begbie's work on conversions as one of his starting points.

46. Robert O. Ferm, *Persuaded to Live: Conversion Stories from the Billy Graham Crusades* (Westwood, N.J.: Fleming Revell Co., 1958). Begbie also describes a preponderance of male conversions.

47. *Life* magazine 42 (May 27, 1957): 21, Billy Graham Clipping File, Graham MSS.

48. Stanley High, "Billy Graham: The Personal Story of the Man," *Reader's Digest* (May 1957): 18, 71; Hope MacLeod, *New York Post*, May 12, 1957.

49. "Efficient Evangelist: Billy Graham Unites the Bible, Business Methods as He Starts New York Crusade," *Wall Street Journal*, May 10, 1957; *New York Times*, March 4, 1957.

50. William G. McLoughlin, Jr., "In Business with the Lord," *Nation*, May 11, 1957, 4–3, 404; Reinhold Niebuhr, "Graham in the Garden," *Christian Century*, May 15, 1957; Graham Clipping File, Graham MSS.

51. "Billy Graham's 'Invasion,'" *Newsweek*, May 20, 1957, 67; Billy Graham, "What's Wrong with American Morals," *American Weekly: Journal-American*, May 12, 1957, 27; Graham Clipping File, Graham MSS.

52. Stanley High, "Billy Graham," 66.

53. Stanley Rowland, Jr., "As Billy Graham Sees His Role," *New York Times Magazine*, April 21, 1957. Rowland stressed the transformation of Graham's affect in the midst of his sermon.

54. Wayne Bond, "The Rhetoric of Billy Graham: A Description, Analysis, and Evaluation" (Ph.D. diss., Southern Illinois University, 1973), University Microfilms, 121–34. Bond analyzes the nature of Graham's rhetorical appeal to very different audiences simultaneously. He stresses the enormous tension created by Graham which was released through the invitation. My own analysis of Graham is based on viewing television records of his New York crusade located at the Billy Graham Center, Wheaton, Ill.

55. Quoted in Joel Carpenter, ed., *Billy Graham: The Early Billy Graham Sermon and Revival Accounts* (1947; New York: Garland, 1988), 23.

56. Billy Graham, *The Chance of a Life Time: Helps for Servicemen* (Grand Rapids, Mich.: Zondervan Publishing, 1952), 11–13. See also Ladd and Mathisen, *Muscular Christianity*, on the interaction of sport and religion.

57. Graham, *Chance of a Life Time*, 38.

58. File 10, box 8, Ferm MSS.

59. "Mickey Cohen and Billy Graham Pray and Read Bible Together," *Youth for Christ Magazine*, Clipping File, Graham MSS. A number of Hollywood converts joined the Hollywood Christian Group.

60. "The World of Billy Graham," *Project 20*, NBC, 1961, in Motion Picture Collection, Library of Congress. Elsewhere, Graham paid considerable attention to male converts, including criminals; Billy Graham, *How to Be Born Again* (Waco: World Books, 1977). See also Billy Graham, *My Answer* (Garden City: Doubleday, 1960), 45.

61. James Edwin Orr, *The Inside Story of the Hollywood Christian Group* (Grand Rapids, Mich.: Zondervan Publishing House, 1955).

62. Walker and Redd were converted at a service held by Graham for the Hollywood Christian Group. Afterward, both wrote Christian cowboy songs.

63. *Mr. Texas* (World Wide Pictures, 1951); Graham MSS.

64. *Souls in Conflict* (World Wide Pictures, 1954). This film featured (incongruously) a sermon by All-American football star Don Moomaw. *Wiretapper* (World Wide Pictures, 1955) was based on *Why I Quit Syndicated Crime*, by James A. Vaus, Jr.

65. *The Heart is a Rebel* (World Wide Films, 1957), Graham MSS. Another film in 1960, *Shadow of the Boomerang*, revisited cowboy culture, but this time featuring an American transplanted to the Australian Outback. Once again the plot revolves around the conversion of the hard-hearted hero—this time softened by a despised Aboriginal boy who dies saving the cowboy's life *and* soul.

66. *Journal-American* 19 (May 1957). A look at some of the letters sent to the Graham organization confirm that writers were deeply concerned with issues of love, sex, homosexuality, and abortion—in other words, all of the issues that writers asked Kinsey about. See boxes 8–9, Ferm MSS. See also, Graham, *Just as I Am*, 165.

Chapter 7

1. Hazel Hitchcock Fox, "Four on TV Stairs Together," *Christian Science Monitor*, October 8, 1953. Cecelia Tichi suggests that television became the standard by which the non-TV world was perceived. The Nelson's experience would seem, literally, to exemplify this theory. Tichi, *Electronic Hearth: Creating an American Television Culture* (New York: Oxford, 1991), 37.

2. Ozzie Nelson, *Ozzie* (Englewood Cliffs: Prentice-Hall, 1973), 196.

3. Ibid., 10–11.

4. Peter W. Kaplan, "Dads Who Know Best," *Esquire* 105 (June 1986): 167.

5. Sara Davidson, "The Happy, Happy, Happy Nelsons," *Esquire* 75 (June 1971): 99, 101.

6. Diana M. Meeham, *Ladies of the Evening: Women Characters of Prime-Time Television* (Metuchen, N.J.: Scarecrow Press, 1983), 119, 125. See also Elaine May, *Homeward Bound: American Families in the Cold War* (New York: Basic Books, 1988).

7. David Halberstam, *The Fifties* (New York: Villard Books, 1993), 509.

8. Ibid., 510–20.

9. Lynn Spigel, *Make Room for TV: Television and the Family Ideal in Postwar America* (Chicago: University of Chicago Press, 1992), 65, 174.

10. Horace Newcomb, *TV: The Most Popular Art* (Garden City, N.Y.: Anchor Press, 1974), 10–34. Based on his reading of Marshall McLuhan, John Cawelti, and others, Newcomb outlines the various formats of situation comedies and their functions.

11. Gerard Jones, *"Honey, I'm Home!" Sitcoms: Selling the American Dream* (New York: St. Martin's Press, 1992), 35, 37.

12. Jones, *"Honey, I'm Home!"* 94, 12, 4. This is more or less true, with some characters, such as Ralph Kramden of *The Honeymooners*, clearly contributing more chaos than order to the family.

13. Mary Beth Haralovich, "Sitcoms and Suburbs: Positioning the 1950s Homemaker," *Quarterly Review of Film and Video* 11 (1989): 62–69, 74, 80. See also Shelly Nickles, "More is Better: Mass Consumption, Gender, and Class Identity in Postwar America," *American Quarterly* 54 (December 2002): 581–622. Nickles discusses the way in which consumer objects of the 1950s eventually began to reflect the tastes of working-class women. This fascinating account amends the uncomplicated narrative of middle-class dominance of the era's taste and consumption.

14. Tinky Weisblatt, "Will the Real George and Gracie and Ozzie and Harriet and Desi and Lucy Please Stand Up? The Functions of Popular Biography in 1950s Television" (Ph.D. diss., University of Texas at Austin, 1991), 104–8, 119. This dissertation is primarily concerned with comparing the biographies with the TV roles of stars who played themselves.

15. Nina Leibman, *Living Room Lectures: The Fifties Family in Films and Television* (Austin: University of Texas Press, 1995), 19.

16. Ibid., 182; Darrell Y. Hamamoto, *Nervous Laughter: Television Situation Comedy and Liberal Democratic Ideology* (New York: Praeger, 1989).

17. The story-line version of the script is a four- or five-page summary of the action that suggests how the episode is to be played and what issues are involved. These suggest what Nelson had in mind as the central focus and the ironic turn of each show.

18. "The Mustache: The Adventures of Ozzie and Harriet," radio season 4, book 30, show 28, story lines box 66, pp. 79–81. Ozzie and Harriet Manuscripts, Division of Rare Books and Special Collections, American Heritage Center, University of Wyoming, Laramie, Wyo.; hereafter cited as Nelson MSS. Quotations by permission of the American Heritage Center.

19. Ibid., 80–81. This script is played with no hint of a Freudian interpretation.

20. "The Manicure," radio season 5, show 2, book 62, scripts box 76, pp. 49, 65; and book 34, story lines box 69, p. 3, Nelson MSS.

21. "Physical Fitness," radio season 7, show 7, book 52, story lines box 73, pp. 14–15, Nelson MSS.

22. "The Knitting Contest," radio season 5, show 14, book 36, story lines box 69, pp. 32–33; and revised script, scripts box 69, p. 18; Nelson MSS.

23. "Knitting Contest," story line, p. 32.

24. "Career Woman," radio season 3, book 72, scripts box 78, pp. 79, 81, Nelson MSS.

25. Ibid., 83–85.

26. "Career Woman," radio season 3, show 7, book 18, story lines box 66, p. 17, Nelson MSS.

27. "Career Woman," television season 3, show 22, book 11, story lines box 89, p. 47, Nelson MSS.

28. "Aptitudes: Male vs. Female," radio season 8, show 7, book 63, story lines box 76, pp. 14–15, Nelson MSS. See also "The Alternate," broadcast in March 1954.

29. "Aptitudes," 14–15.

30. "Aptitudes," radio season 8, show 7, book 63, scripts box 76, pp. 34–36, Nelson MSS.

31. "The Hero Worshippers," radio season 5, show 15, book 36, story lines box 69, pp. 33–34, Nelson MSS. See also "Man and Superman," radio season 5, show 30, story lines box 69, pp. 33–34, Nelson MSS.

32. Ibid.

33. "Husband's Night," radio season 6, show 4, book 43, story lines box 71, p. 9, Nelson MSS.

34. Ibid., 11.

35. A. E. Salmons to the editor, *Family Handyman* 1 (Winter 1951): 10.

36. Carolyn M. Goldstein, *Do It Yourself Home Improvement in 20th Century America* (New York: Princeton Architectural Press and National Building Museum, 1998), 11–34; Albert Roland, "Do-it-Yourself: A Walden for the Millions?" *American Quarterly* 10 (Summer 1958): 154–61.

37. Stacey Maney, *The Practical Home Handyman* (New York: Greystone Press, 1945), 13; "Shop Talk with the Publisher," *Family Handyman* 6 (January–February 1957): 15; "How to Keep Your Wife in the Kitchen—and Happy!" *Family Handyman* 2 (December 1952–January 1953); Steven M. Gelber, "Do-it-Yourself and Constructing, Repairing, and Maintaining Domestic Masculinity," *American Quarterly* 49 (1997): 66–112. Gelber argues that do-it-yourself was a badge of masculinity in the 1950s.

38. "The Ego Builder," radio season 8, show 26, book 68, story lines box 76, p. 33. See also "The Hobby," radio season 3, show 5, book 26, scripts box 67, p. 144, Nelson MSS.

39. "The Hobby," radio season 3, show 5, book 17, story lines box 66, pp. 12–13, Nelson MSS.

40. "The High Cost of Living," radio season 8, show 5, book 63, story lines box 76, pp. 9–11, Nelson MSS.

41. "Democracy in the Family," radio season 4, show 41, book 33, story lines box 66, p. 114, Nelson MSS.

42. Ibid, 116.

43. "A Boy's Best Friend," radio season 3, show 8, book 18, story lines box 66, pp. 20–22, Nelson MSS. "Don't Spare the Rod," broadcast in May 1949, also explored family discipline. Ozzie appears to endorse corporal punishment in an interview with a reporter. Several misunderstandings later, it is clear what the confusion was: Ozzie was talking about fishing rods.

44. "The Vicar," radio season 7, show 10, book 53, scripts box 74, p. 42, Nelson MSS.

45. Ibid., story lines box 73, pp. 21–22, Nelson MSS. A similar opposition between high and low culture appeared in the radio show late in the ninth season, "The Comic Books." Once again Ozzie worries about comic books only to praise them in the end. See also "The Vicar," scripts, p. 68.

46. *Ozzie and Harriet*, DC Comics, nos. 1–4, 1949–1950. National Comics Publications.

47. Nina Leibman remarks on some of the changes from radio to a TV format. Leibman, *Living Room Lectures*, 9. See also Ella Taylor, *Prime-Time Families: Television Culture in Postwar America* (Berkeley: University of California Press, 1989), 24–25.

48. "Economical Ozzie," television season 2, show 38, book 6, story lines box 86, pp. 1–4, Nelson MSS.

49. Ibid., scripts box 87, p. 134, Nelson MSS.

50. "The Manly Arts," television video, 1954, Motion Picture Collection, Library of Congress.

51. "Spring Housecleaning," television season 3, show 27, book 12, scripts box 89, pp. 9, 17; and story lines box 89, pp. 62–65, Nelson MSS.

52. "The Basketball Player," broadcast January 9, 1953, Motion Picture and Television Collection, Library of Congress.

53. "The Trophy," television season 6, show 14, book 29, story lines box 92, pp. 37–39, Nelson MSS. Another show broadcast in the same year, "The Fourteen Mile Hike," presented a similar comic reversal questioning Ozzie's athletic abilities.

54. "The Scavenger Hunt," television season 6, show 24, book 31, scripts box 93, p. 69, Nelson MSS.

55. Ibid., 98–99; and ibid., story lines box 92, pp. 66–68, Nelson MSS. Another role-reversal episode was broadcast in 1957 in "The Editor." In this episode, Harriet becomes editor of the *Woman's Club Journal*. When Ozzie tries to interfere, boasting of his talent as a reporter, he fails.

56. "The Honest Face," television season 4, show 31, book 18, scripts box 90, p. 71; and story lines box 89, pp. 53–55, Nelson MSS.

57. "The Reading Room," television season 5, show 21, book 23, scripts box 91, p. 6; and story lines box 90, pp. 55–57, Nelson MSS.

58. For an example of the emerging prominence of the boys, see "David and the Men's Club," television season 6, book 30, scripts box 93, Nelson MSS. In this show, a contest between women's and men's values, pitched as a struggle between the Men's Club and the Women's Club, is resolved by the younger generation, represented by David.

Chapter 8

1. Williams did not openly admit his homosexuality until an interview in 1970 on television with David Frost. See "Playboy Interview: Tennessee Williams," *Playboy* 20 (April 1973): 74.

2. See Kimball King, "The Rebirth of Orpheus Descending," in *Critical Essays on Tennessee Williams*, ed. Robert A. Martin (New York: Simon and Schuster, 1997), 140. King argues that Williams counterbalanced two predominant sorts of masculine images in his plays: "the rough, boorish Stanley Kowalski and the sensitive misunderstood victim like homosexual Sebastian" from *Suddenly Last Summer*. Reading across his work, this may appear to be true, yet many of his characters occupy a distinct middle ground.

3. John M. Clum, *Still Acting Gay: Male Homosexuality in Modern Drama* (New York: St. Martin's, 2000), 132. Clum writes of Williams as a playwright active in "the era of John Wayne." See also Robert A. Martin, introduction to *Critical Essays*, 12, on the importance of Williams for post–World War II audiences and their mood of dispossession in a materialistic world.

4. Donald Spoto, *The Kindness of Strangers: The Life of Tennessee Williams* (New York: Da Capo Press, 1997), xv.

5. R. Barton Palmer, "Hollywood in Crisis: Tennessee Williams and the Evolution of the Adult Film," in *The Cambridge Companion to Tennessee Williams*, ed. Matthew C. Roudané (Cambridge: Cambridge University Press, 1997), 221, 231. Palmer suggests that Williams popularized a new kind of vulnerable and desirable masculinity.

6. There are several possible explanations for this nickname given by Lyle Leverich in his biography, *Tom: The Unknown Tennessee Williams* (New York: Crown Publishers, 1995), 274–75.

7. Spoto, *Kindness*, 4–66. Leverich, *Tom*, 224–25. Tennessee Williams, *Memoirs* (New York: Doubleday, 1975), 11–48.

8. David Halberstam, *The Fifties* (New York: Villard Books, 1993), 255–61.

9. "The Playwright," *Newsweek*, April 1, 1957, 81.

10. William Baer, ed., *Elia Kazan Interviews* (Jackson: University of Mississippi Press, 2000), 16.

11. "Playboy Interview," 82. Williams to Audrey Wood, August 5, 1954, file 55.6, box 55, in Papers of Tennessee Williams, Harry Ransom Humanities Research Center, University of Texas at Austin. Hereafter cited as TW MSS. All quotations from this collection and from the University of Delaware Library are quoted with permission from the Georges Borchardt Agency.

12. Williams, "Three Players of a Summer's Game," in *Tennessee Williams: Collected Stories*, ed. Gore Vidal (New York: New Directions, 1985), 303–26. Spoto, *Kindness*, 176.

13. In the short story, Brick has injured himself running over a wicket, not jumping hurdles, as in the film. In addition, the theme of Brick's affair with a doctor's widow is dropped.

14. Quoted in Mike Steen, *A Look at Tennessee Williams* (New York: Hawthorne Books, 1969), 5.

15. Williams, *Memoirs*, 168; and Donald Windham, *Tennessee Williams' Letters to Donald Windham, 1940–1965* (New York: Holt, Rinehart and Winston, 1977), 302–3.

16. Albert E. Kalson, "A Source for 'Cat on a Hot Tin Roof,'" in *Tennessee Williams Newsletter* 2 (Fall 1980): 21–22. Kalson argues that Williams was undoubtedly aware of J. B. Priestley's 1932 *Dangerous Corner*, a play with a homosexual undercurrent about a young writer grappling with his identity and the memory of a strong bond with a now dead young man.

17. Nancy M. Tischler, "On Creating Cat," *Tennessee Williams Literary Journal* 2 (Winter 1991–1992): 9–13.

18. Interview, January 2, 1967, in Steen, *A Look at Tennessee Williams*, 211.

19. Tennessee Williams to Audrey Wood, April 1954, file 55.6, box 55; and Audrey Wood to Tennessee Williams, July 19, 1954, file 59.3, box 59, in TW MSS. An undated, but obviously early version of the play, subtitled "A Place of Stone," contains stage instructions describing Brick with "flaming red hair." It also introduces two characters, a very handsome but mentally disturbed young man named Thorgersen and his wife. "Cat on a Hot Tin Roof," RG 112, file 9, box 1, Papers of Tennessee Williams, Special Collections, University of Delaware Library. Hereafter cited as Delaware MSS.

20. Tennessee Williams to Audrey Wood, September 7, 1954, file 55.6, box 55, TW MSS.

21. Clum, *Still Acting Gay,* 131.

22. Tennessee Williams, *Cat on a Hot Tin Roof,* act 2, in *The Theatre of Tennessee Williams* (New York: New Directions Books, 1971), 98–99. In both stage versions, act 2 is essentially the same. However, I will indicate which version of act 3 is under consideration.

23. "Note of Explanation," Williams, *The Theatre of Tennessee Williams,* 151–52.

24. Tennessee Williams to Audrey Wood, November 23, 1954, file 55.6, box 55, TW MSS. In a letter to Williams from an unidentified correspondent, the issue of Brick's transformation is clearly argued in terms of his homosexuality. "I agree," wrote the correspondent, "with Gadg (Kazan) that Brick's facing the truth about his homosexuality should have consequences for him. Perhaps it reconciles him to the mendacity of living with Maggie. But if that is the case, he should have a line to say so." Kenny? To Williams, no date, file 7, box 60, TW MSS. Looking at the correspondence from Kazan about *Cat* and other plays, it becomes clear that the director also offered scores of minor changes to strengthen the interpretive meaning he wished to give to the plays.

25. Brenda Murphy, "Tennessee Williams and the Broadway Audience: The Revision of Camino Real," in *Critical Essays,* ed. Martin, 117.

26. Tennessee Williams, *Cat on a Hot Tin Roof,* "Revisions to Act I," no date, box 8.4, file 8, TW MSS.

27. Tennessee Williams, *Cat on a Hot Tin Roof,* act 1, in *The Theatre of Tennessee Williams,* 57–58. See also Mark Royden Winchell, "Come Back to the Locker Room Ag'in Brick, Honey!" *Mississippi Quarterly* 48 (Fall 1995): 701–12. Winchell argues that the play fulfills Leslie Fiedler's assertion that traditional male American heroes often privilege a chaste, homosocial relationship with another man. To suggest physical love between them is to introduce scandal, and that is what *Cat* does.

28. Tennessee Williams, *Cat on a Hot Tin Roof,* act 2, Meyerson version (named for the typing service), 2–28, file 9, RG112, box 1, Delaware MSS.

29. Williams, *Cat,* "Revisions to Act II," file 8.7, box 8, TW MSS.

30. Williams, *Cat on a Hot Tin Roof,* act 2, in *Theatre of Tennessee Williams,* 99.

31. Williams, "Notes for the Designer," *Cat on a Hot Tin Roof,* in *Theatre of Tennessee Williams,* 15.

32. Williams, *Cat on a Hot Tin Roof,* act 2, in *Theatre of Tennessee Williams,* 77, 93, 108. The prodigal son, Luke 15:11–32. Geoffrey S. Proehl argues that many American domestic dramas after World War II featured the return of a prodigal—son or husband. *Coming Home Again: American Family Drama and the Figure of the Prodigal* (Madison, N.J.: Fairleigh Dickinson University Press, 1997), 10.

33. Williams, *Cat on a Hot Tin Roof,* act 2, original version, in *Theatre of Tennessee Williams,* 156.

34. Williams, *Cat on a Hot Tin Roof,* act 3, Broadway version, in *Theatre of Tennessee Williams,* 208–9.

35. Williams, *Cat on a Hot Tin Roof,* act 3, Original version, in *Theatre of Tennessee Williams,* 165–66.

36. Williams, *Cat on a Hot Tin Roof,* act 3, Broadway version, in *Theatre of Tennessee Williams,* 215–16.

37. Tennessee Williams, "Revisions to Act III of *Cat on a Hot Tin Roof,*" file 8.9, box 8; and "*Cat* draft fragments," file 9.1, box 9, TW MSS.

38. Williams, *Cat,* "Revisions to Act III," file 8.4, box 8, TW MSS. Critic John Clum explores the accusation that Williams in some of his plays and stories assumes the moral position of the homophobic audience and contributes to this feeling by his depiction of characters. Clum argues that, in fact, Williams seems to betray a fear of exposure as well as a degree of self-hatred. See John M. Clum, "Something Cloudy, Something Clear: Homophobic Discourse in Tennessee Williams," *South Atlantic Quarterly* 88 (Winter 1989): 161–79.

39. Directed by Richard Brooks, it was originally proposed as a vehicle for Grace Kelly, but Elizabeth Taylor eventually won the role of Maggie. Paul Newman played Brick, Judith Anderson was Big Mama, and Burl Ives repeated his Broadway role as Big Daddy. The film received six Academy Award nominations, and Ives won for best supporting actor.

40. "The Motion Picture Production Code," appendix 1 in Gerald Gardner, *The Censorship Papers: Movie Censorship Letters from the Hays Office, 1934–1968* (New York: Dodd, Mead, 1987), 207–12.

41. "Cat on a Hot Tin Roof," *Catholic World* 188 (November 1958): 153–54.

42. Memo from Warner Brothers, March 24, 1952, file 60.5, box 60, TW MSS. See also Bob Thomas, "Tennessee Williams Mixed on Film Versions of Plays," June 27, 1958, clipping from scrapbook 2, TW MSS. The difficulty dealing with homosexuality in *Streetcar* foreshadows the changes made in the film of *Cat.*

43. Gardner, *Censorship Papers,* 201. Thomas Pryor, "Hollywood Cat," *New York Times,* January 5, 1958. See also William Sachsteder, "The Three Cats; A Study in Dramatic Structure," *Drama Survey* 5 (Winter 1966–1967): 252–66. This is a very astute reading of all three versions. In an unusual twist, Sachsteder argues his preference for the film version.

44. Patrick Brion, *Richard Brooks* (Paris: Chêne, 1986), 143 (my translation). See also Richard Brooks, "La Seconde Chance," *Cahiers du Cinema* (nos. 166–67), 90. It is worth noting that the MGM film *Tea and Sympathy* had encountered difficulty because of its homosexual theme.

45. Brion, *Richard Brooks,* 143. Brooks also adapted *Sweet Bird of Youth* for Hollywood.

46. James Poe, "Cat on a Hot Tin Roof," 119, script in file 10, RG 112, box 1, Delaware MSS. Poe also worked on Williams's *Summer and Smoke* (1961).

47. It can be argued that Hollywood movies, more than once, used the story of a boy's search for a father figure as a camouflage for a discussion of homosexuality. In much of the popular psychiatric literature of the day, this disrupted relationship formed the explanation for homosexuality.

48. *Cat on a Hot Tin Roof*, MGM Productions, 1958. See also R. Barton Palmer, "Hollywood in Crisis," in Roudané, ed., *Cambridge Companion*, 204–31. See also Gene Phillips, *The Films of Tennessee Williams* (Philadelphia: Art Alliance Press, 1980), 134ff.

49. Thaddeus Paige Wakefield, "The Commodification of the American Family: An Analysis of Twentieth Century American Drama" (Ph.D. diss., University of California, Riverside, 2001). Wakefield emphasizes this theme of greed in *Cat*. This introduction of the hobo father erases Williams's mysterious and probably gay surrogate fathers who leave the plantation to Big Daddy.

50. *Cat on a Hot Tin Roof*, MGM, 1958. Perhaps one reason why Williams left the end open to interpretation and revision was the closeness to his own unresolved feelings about his family. See Phillips, *Films of Tennessee Williams*, 39, 133. In *Streetcar Named Desire*, Stella chooses not to believe Blanche in the end as the only way to continue in her marriage to Stanley, another incidence of the enabling lie. See Tom Scanlan, *Family, Drama, and American Drama* (Westport: Greenwood, 1978), 162.

51. Brooks quote in Phillips, *Films of Tennessee Williams*, 147.

52. Walter Kerr, *New York Herald-Tribune*, March 25, 1955; John Chapman, *Daily News*, March 26, 1955; Richard Watts, Jr., *New York Post*, April 10, 1955. See also, George W. Crandell, *The Critical Response to Tennessee Williams* (Westport: Greenwood Press, 1996). Crandell suggests that this sort of response was widespread. Eleanor Roosevelt, "Williams' Play Well Written, Beautifully Acted—Mrs. FDR" Scrapbook 3, 1955, TW MSS.

53. Paul V. Beckley, *New York Herald-Tribune*, September 19, 1958; *New York Times*, September 21, 1958; *New York Post*, September 19, 1958. See also Paul J. Hurly, "Tennessee Williams: The Playwright as Social Critic," in Crandell, *Critical Response to Tennessee Williams*, 128, 135. Hurly argues that most critics believed the subject of the play to be homosexuality and that homosexuality is a metaphor for difference that Williams valued.

54. Mary Ann Corrigan, "Realism and Theatricalism in 'A Streetcar Named Desire,'" in Martin, *Critical Essays*, 85. See also, for example, remarks by John Simon in Crandell, *Critical Response to Tennessee Williams*, 121. He says that the character of Maggie is partly modeled after a male lover of Williams's.

55. Charles May, "Brick Pollitt as Homo Ludens: 'Three Players of a Summer Game' and 'Cat on a Hot Tin Roof,'" in *Tennessee Williams: A Tribute*, ed. Jac Thorpe (Jackson: University Press of Mississippi, 1977), 280; and Marion Price, "'Cat on a Hot Tin Roof': The Uneasy Marriage of Success and Idealism," in *Modern Drama* 38 (Fall 1995): 330, 332–33.

56. Arthur Miller, "The Shadow of the Gods," *The Theatre Essays of Arthur Miller*, ed. Robert A. Martin and Steven R. Centola (New York: DaCapo Press, 1996), 190–92. Brooks in an interview noted that he wanted Newman because of his dramatic face

and "something about his pale blue eyes." Bernard R. Kantor, Irwin R. Blacker, Anne Dramer, *Directors at Work: Interviews with American Film-Makers* (New York: Funk and Wagnalls, 1970), 26.

57. Corrigan, "Realism and Theatricalism," in Martin, ed., *Critical Essays*, 85.

58. A different emphasis on these elements leads Susan Mayberry to link illusion to the grotesque. Each character, she argues, is distorted, either physically or spiritually, except Maggie. Of all the characters, only she understands others and herself. Susan Neal Mayberry, "A Study of Illusion and the Grotesque in Tennessee Williams's 'Cat on a Hot Tin Roof,'" *Southern Studies* 22 (Fall 1983): 359–65.

59. David Savran, *Communists, Cowboys, and Queers: The Politics of Masculinity in the Work of Arthur Miller and Tennessee Williams* (Minneapolis: University of Minnesota Press, 1992), 9–10, 16, 81.

Chapter 9

1. Quoted in Richard Hofstadter, *Anti-Intellectualism in American Life* (1962; New York: Alfred Knopf, 1979), 9. Hofstadter's book makes clear the deep American popular distrust of intellectuals and elite institutions. It also suggests the degree to which this resentment lay behind the countercharge that mass culture was feminizing. See also Arthur M. Schlesinger, Jr., "The Highbrow in American Politics," *The Scene Before You: A New Approach to American Culture* (New York: Rinehart, 1955), 255–65; this work contains a very interesting discussion of the political usages of the term "egghead." Iago Galdston, MD, "Psychopathia Intellectualis," *Pacific Spectator* 10 (Spring 1956): 100.

2. Lawrence Levine, *High Brow/Low Brow: The Emergence of Cultural Hierarchy in America* (Cambridge: Harvard University Press, 1988).

3. See James Gilbert, *A Cycle of Outrage: America's Reaction to the Juvenile Delinquent in the 1950s* (New York: Oxford University Press, 1986). The alignment of forces in this discussion made for uncomfortable bedfellows. Thus, for example, the Catholic Church hierarchy and Marxist intellectuals, for very different reasons, shared a deep suspicion of Hollywood.

4. Malcolm Cowley, *Exile's Return: A Literary Odyssey of the 1920s* (New York: Viking, 1951), 53.

5. Eugene Burdick, "The Estrangement of the American Intellectual," in "Plight of the American Intellectual Series," *Pacific Spectator* 9 (Autumn 1955): 357, 359.

6. Leo Gurko, *Heroes, Highbrows, and the Popular Mind* (Indianapolis: Bobbs-Merrill, 1953), 41.

7. Lewis Mumford, "The Wilderness of Suburbia," *New Republic*, 28 (September 7, 1921): 44–45. This sort of analysis reappeared in the 1930s. See, for example, George A. Lundberg, Mirra Komarovsky, and Mary Alice McInery, *Leisure: A Suburban Study* (New York: Columbia University Press, 1934).

8. William H. Whyte, Jr., *The Organization Man* (New York: Simon and Schuster, 1956). Among those Whyte thanks in his preface are Herbert Gans and David Riesman.

9. Ibid., 3, 12, 23, 100, 383–93.

10. Ibid., 280, 132–33.

11. Sloan Wilson, *The Man in the Gray Flannel Suit* (New York: Simon and Schuster, 1955), 255, 277.

12. John Keats, *The Crack in the Picture Window* (Boston: Houghton, Mifflin, 1957): xii–23, 144–45, 149, 193. Keats's choice of the term "drone" is intentional in its neutered masculinity. While this genre of critique was widely accepted, there were other observers who viewed the suburbs with considerably more subtlety. See, for example, Herbert Gans, *The Levittowners: Ways of Life and Politics in a New Suburban Community* (New York: Pantheon, 1967). Gans is sharply critical of Whyte and Keats as well as others who disparage the suburbs. He found little of the conformity they claimed to discover. See also Carol A. O'Connor, "Sorting Out the Suburbs: Patterns of Land Use, Class, and Culture," *American Quarterly* 37 (1985).

13. John McPartland, *No Down Payment* (New York: Simon and Schuster, 1957), 88, 233. See also McPartland, *Sex in Our Changing World* (New York: Rinehart, 1947).

14. David Riesman, "The Suburban Sadness," in *The Suburban Community*, ed. William M. Dobriner (New York: G. P. Putnam's, 1958), 390, 402. He is speaking of Percival and Paul Goodman's *Communitas: Means of Livelihood and Ways of Life* (Chicago: University of Chicago Press, 1947).

15. Barbara Ehrenreich, *Fear of Falling: The Inner Life of the Middle Class* (New York: Pantheon, 1989), 4–40.

16. For a critique of the world of "mass" see William Kornhauser, *The Politics of Mass Society* (Glencoe: Free Press, 1959).

17. George B. Leonard, Jr., "The American Male: Why Is He Afraid to Be Different?" in *Look: The Decline of the American Male*, by the Editors of *Look* (New York: Random House, 1958), 26–48. See also David Savran, *Taking It Like a Man: White Masculinity, Masochism, and Contemporary American Culture* (Princeton: Princeton University Press, 1998). This book includes an important discussion of masculinity and perceptions of it in the 1950s. Savran is particularly interested in the Beats and other marginal and oppositional thinkers in challenging older ideas about masculinity.

18. Leo Gurko credits Brooks with inventing this terminology. See *Heroes, High Brows, and the Popular Mind*, 310.

19. Bernard Rosenberg and David Manning White, *Mass Culture: The Popular Arts in America* (Glencoe: Free Press, 1957).

20. Andreas Huyssen, *After the Great Divide: Modernism, Mass Culture, Postmodernism* (Bloomington: Indiana University Press, 1986), iv, 16–17.

21. Lionel Trilling, "Art and Culture," *The Liberal Imagination: Essays on Literature and Society* (Garden City: Doubleday, 1953): 260. See also, Thomas Bender, "Lionel Trilling and American Civilization," *American Quarterly* 42 (June 1990): 324–47.

22. Bernard Iddings Bell, *Crowd Culture: An Examination of the American Way of Life* (New York: Harpers, 1952), 15–17, 92, 109.

23. Dwight Macdonald, "A Theory of Mass Culture," *Diogenes* 1 (Summer 1953): 10. Macdonald approvingly quotes Paul Lazarsfeld and Leo Lowenthal in their important 1942 essay, "Radio Research," on the distinction between the "idols of production" and

the "idols of consumption." On Macdonald, see Michael Wrezin, *A Rebel in Defense of Tradition: The Life and Politics of Dwight Macdonald* (New York: Basic Books, 1994).

24. Rosenberg and White, *Mass Culture*, 9, 5–45.

25. T. W. Adorno, "Television and the Patterns of Mass Culture," in Rosenberg and White, *Mass Culture*, 486.

26. Jarrell and Handlin in Norman Jacobs, ed., *Culture for the Millions: Mass Media in Modern Society* (Princeton: D. Van Nostrand, 1959), intro. by Paul Lazarsfeld, 108, 128, 66, 69–70. See also Ralf Ross and Ernest van den Haag, *The Fabric of Society: An Introduction to the Social Sciences* (New York: Harcourt, Brace, 1957). Much of this book is an exploration of the destructive effects of mass culture on society. The authors condemn the 100 Great Books movement, do-it-yourself hobbies, and Norman Vincent Peale. Their patron saints were de Tocqueville and Ortega y Gasset, whose 1930 book *The Revolt of the Masses* made a considerable stir among American intellectuals.

27. Paul Lazarsfeld in *Mass Culture Revisited*, ed. Bernard Rosenberg and David Manning White (New York: Van Nostrand, Reinhold, 1971): viii, 3. Many of the entries were reprinted from *Daedalus* in 1960.

28. Leslie Fiedler, *Love and Death in the American Novel* (1960; Normal, Ill.: Dalkey Archive Press, 1967), vi, 350, 338.

29. *Esquire* bolstered its credentials by attracting Dwight Macdonald to be its film critic and featured writers such as Arthur Schlesinger, Jr.

30. Thomas Weyr, *Reaching for Paradise: The Playboy Vision of America* (New York: New York Times, 1978), 197, 216.

31. Barbara Ehrenreich, *The Hearts of Men: American Desires and the Flight from Commitment* (New York: Anchor, 1983): 44–49 on Kinsey and Hefner. See also Andrew Ross, *No Respect: Intellectuals and Popular Culture* (New York: Routledge, 1989), 173.

32. Harvey Cox, "*Playboy*'s Doctrine of Male," *Christianity and Crisis* 21 (April 17, 1961): 56–58, 60. Cox noted that the magazine's readership dropped sharply among men over the age of thirty.

33. "A. C. Spectorsky," in *Current Biography* (New York: H. W. Wilson, 1960), 394.

34. Kim Wendel, "WKYC's Rocketing Ratings No Surprise to Spectorsky," *Sun Newspapers*, August 27, 1998.

35. Eric Hodgins, *Mr. Blandings Builds His Dream House* (New York: Simon and Schuster, 1946); and Wilson, *Man in the Gray Flannel Suit*.

36. A. C. Spectorsky to Phyllis Jackson at Music Corporation of America, July 8, 1954, "Correspondence," box 1, Auguste Comte Spectorsky Manuscripts, American Heritage Center, University of Wyoming, Laramie. Hereafter cited as Spectorsky MSS. Quotations by permission of the American Heritage Center. See also "Writer to do Definitive Study on New York City Commuter," *News from Lippincott*, 1954, Biographical file, Spectorsky MSS.

37. "New York Commuter," proposal, file folders: "Research Materials: *The Exurbanites*," box 12, Spectorsky MSS.

38. Spectorsky to Tay Hohoff at Lippincott, December 20, 1954; and Hohoff to Spectorsky, January 31, 1955, "Correspondence," box 1, Spectorsky MSS.

Spectorsky was speaking of Russell Lynes, author of *The Taste-Makers* (New York: Harper, 1949). Lynes had contributed one of the opening salvos in the culture wars of the 1950s with an article "Highbrow, Lowbrow, Middlebrow" in *Harper's* magazine in 1949.

39. Spectorsky to Hohoff, no date, no place, in file, "Research Materials: *The Exurbanites*," box 12; and "Mens Sana in Corporate Suburbia," review prepared for *Suburbia Today*, in file, "*Suburbia Today*," box 5. See also Notes: "Research Material: *The Exurbanites*," box 12, Spectorsky MSS.

40. Spectorsky, "Article Suggestion: Suburbia Must Face Its Sexual Problem," "I Hate Commuting," and "I Love Commuting," in file, "Commuting Article Idea," box 3, Spectorsky MSS.

41. Auguste Comte Spectorsky, *The Exurbanites* (Philadelphia: J. B. Lippincott, 1955), 12.

42. C. Wright Mills, "The Exurbanites," one of two reviews published simultaneously by the *Saturday Review of Literature*. The other was written by John Haverstick, who emphasized Spectorsky's concern about conformity in the suburbs. See *Saturday Review of Literature* 38 (October 29, 1955): 11–12.

43. Clifton Fadiman, "Party of One," *Holiday* 18 (November 1955): 6, 8, 9. Fadiman wrote to Spectorsky that he greatly admired his book for its ability to present sociology clearly: "the opposite of Riesman, who should be muzzled, or at least forced to learn English." Clifton Fadiman to Spectorsky, August 1, 1955, "Correspondence, June–December 1955," box 2, Spectorsky MSS.

44. *Time*, November 7, 1955, "Periodicals, Publicity, Scrapbook of *Exurbanites*," oversized box 9, Spectorsky MSS.

45. Claire S. Degener to Spectorsky, April 15, 1957, "Correspondence, 1957"; Lyne Auston to Spectorsky, August 29, 1956, "Correspondence, 1956"; and memo of Spectorsky to PA, PJ, and VC re: musical, January 29, 1956, box 2, Spectorsky MSS. Spectorsky contacted Alan Jay Lerner, among others, about the project.

46. Pruitt speaking, "The Exurbanites," *CBS Radio Workshop* script, adapted by Charles Monroe and broadcast, Friday, March 30, 1956, on CNYT. Eric Severeid was the narrator. File, "CBS Radio, Correspondence, 1956," box 2, Spectorsky MSS.

47. Spectorsky, in file, "American Male: Notes, 1956ff," box 3, p. 1, Spectorsky MSS.

48. Ibid., 3.

49. Douglas M. More to Spectorsky, November 15, 1956, "Correspondence, 1956," box 2. See also "Book Ideas," in file, "Book and Article Ideas," box 3, Spectorsky MSS. Spectorsky did, however, publish several more books, mostly on sports and nature. Spectorsky had actually reviewed much of the literature that More recommended, including books by Russell Lynes, John Keats, Vance Packard, and others.

50. Auguste Spectorsky, "How to Keep a Magazine Young," speech to the American Business Press Association, Harriman, N.Y., October 28, 1968, in file, "Speeches," box 10, Spectorsky MSS. Spectorsky to Philip Wylie, December 7, 1961, in folder 2, "Spectorsky," The Papers of Philip Wylie, box 211, Department of Rare Books and Special Collections, Princeton University Library. Hereafter cited as Wylie MSS. See also

Richard Keller Simon, *Trash Culture: Popular Culture and the Great Tradition* (Berkeley: University of California Press, 1999), 102–13.

51. Spectorsky, "Publishing in a Permissive Society," to the International Federation of the Periodical Press, London, May 6, 1971, in file, "Speeches," box 10, Spectorsky MSS. Spectorsky reviewed John Keats's *Crack in the Picture Window* in 1957 and, while he agreed with the gloomy analysis, he disagreed with the author's solution. File, "ETC Reviews," box 4, Spectorsky MSS.

52. Spectorsky to unknown correspondent, in file, "American Male: Notes," probably 1956 or 1957, box 3, pp. 1–3, Spectorsky MSS.

53. Spectorsky to Warren Allen Smith, no date, in file, "No Dates/Partial Dates," box 2, Spectorsky MSS. Robie Macauley, brought on as literary editor of *Playboy* in 1966, credits Spectorsky with the creation of the magazine's intellectual content.

54. "The Decline of the American Male," typescript of a review, file folder, "*New York Times* Reviews," box 4, Spectorsky MSS.

55. Russell Miller, *Bunny: The Real Story of Playboy* (New York: Holt, Rinehart and Winston, 1984): 99–100, 139. In internal memos, Hefner and Spectorsky discuss the merits of some of Wylie's proposals and drafts, for example. See Wylie correspondence, which included items forwarded from Spectorsky; Wylie MSS.

56. "Playbill," *Playboy* 3 (September 1956): 3–4.

57. Ibid.

58. This column is not signed, but Spectorsky is undoubtedly the source of the linguistic information. "Playbill," *Playboy* 5 (May 1958).

59. On Wylie, see Truman Frederich Keefer, *Philip Wylie* (Boston: Twayne Publishers, 1977).

60. Spectorsky to Wylie, May 28, 1956; Wylie to Spectorsky, June 9, 1956; Spectorsky to Wylie, June 22, 1956; Hefner to Wylie, August 8, 1956; all in box 211, Wylie MSS. Philip Wylie, "The Abdicating Male," *Playboy* 3 (November 1956). Spectorsky had sent Wylie the galleys of *The Exurbanites* for comment and suggestions.

61. Spectorsky to Wylie, January 25, 1957, folder 2, "Spectorsky," box 211, Wylie MSS.

62. Philip Wylie, "The Womanization of America," *Playboy* 5 (September 1958).

63. Krassner had also worked at *Mad Magazine* and often wrote for *Playboy*. He was noted for his interviews and notorious later for his role in founding the Yippies, an anarchist/humorist, political-cultural movement.

64. "The Playboy Panel: The Womanization of America," *Playboy* 9 (June 1962). Before Wylie participated in the panel, he and Spectorsky had considerable correspondence about the magazine. At one point Wylie accused it of being "a major exponent of disease." What he meant was that it teased rather than offering an account of real sex. In part, he derived this notion from the Playboy clubs, where he discovered that the "Bunnies" were not allowed to date any of the customers.

65. Spectorsky to Wylie, June 11, 1962; and memorandum to JK from F DeB, August 16, 1962, file 2, "Spectorsky," box 211, Wylie MSS.

66. Philip Wylie, "The Career Woman," *Playboy* 10 (January 1963). A cartoon figure over the title of the article depicts a skeleton dressed for business.

67. "Playboy and the Preachers," *Columbia Journalism Review* (Spring 1966): 32–35. Harvey Cox, in particular, pursued this point. Note also that the median age of readers in 1958 was twenty-five. Twenty-two percent were college students and 74 percent were under 35. "Meet the Playboy Reader," *Playboy* 5 (April 1958): 63.

Chapter 10

1. The population disparity in the United States is largely the result of differential immigration. See "Population by Sex and Race, 1790–1970," in *Historical Statistics of the United States, Colonial Times to 1970, Part 1* (Washington, D.C.: U.S. Government Printing Office, 1975), 14. The crossover from male to female majority occurred in the following places in the indicated years: Massachusetts and Connecticut, 1790; New York, 1860 (this majority shifted back and forth due to huge numbers of male immigrants); South Carolina, 1830; North Carolina, 1840; Illinois, Iowa, Texas, and California, 1950; and Utah, 1960. The 1906 census reveals a comparable and probably related ratio of religious communicants by region and this, too, seems to reflect (as a snapshot) the relationship between female population increase and the growth of religious membership when they entered a male-dominated area.

2. Frederick Jackson Turner, "The Significance of the Frontier in American History [1893]," in *Rereading Frederick Jackson Turner*, ed. John Mack Faraghan (New York: Henry Holt, 1997), 31–60.

3. Betty Friedan, *The Feminine Mystique* (New York: Norton, 1963), 79, 286, 272–74.

4. David Horowitz, *Betty Friedan and the Making of the Feminine Mystique: The American Left, the Cold War, and Modern Feminism* (Amherst: University of Massachusetts Press, 1998).

5. Joshua S. Goldstein, *War and Gender: How Gender Shapes the War System and Vice Versa* (Cambridge, UK: Cambridge University Press, 2001), 2, 286.

6. Robert Bly, *Iron John: A Book about Men* (Reading, Mass.: Addison-Wesley, 1990), 1–25, passim.

7. Andrew Kimbrell, *The Masculine Mystique: The Politics of Masculinity* (New York: Ballantine Books, 1995), 140–43.

8. Susan Faludi, *Stiffed: The Betrayal of the American Man* (New York: William Morrow, 1999), 300–301.

9. Kimbrell, *The Masculine Mystique*, xii.

Index

Adams, Henry, 22
Adams, James Truslow, 70
Addams, Jane, 79
Adorno, Theodor, 196, 198. *See also* Frankfurt school
Adventures of Ozzie and Harriet, The, 12, 135
    episodes of, 145–52
    interpretations of, 138–40
    origins of, 136–37
    radio and TV versions of, 144, 148–49, 157–58, 160, 161
    and spectator masculinity, 150–51
    See also Nelson, Harriet; Nelson, Ozzie
African Americans. *See* race
Alger, Horatio, 110, 137, 143, 144, 154, 162
Algren, Nelson, 209
All About Men (Peck), 64
American, The (Adams), 70
American character, study of, 39–43, 46, 51–52, 58–59, 231n17. *See also* Riesman, David; Tocqueville, Alexis de
"American Character in the 20th Century" (Riesman), 52
American Library Association, 37
American Manhood (Rotundo), 17
American Mind, The (Commager), 40
American People (Mead and Gorer), 40
American Quarterly (journal), 39, 41, 43, 153
American studies, 40–41

Anderson, Robert, 173
And Keep Your Powder Dry (Mead), 40
Angell, Norman, 91
"Apostles of Abstinence" (Griffith), 26–27
Arendt, Hannah, 198
Arnaz, Desi, 141
Athletes in Action, 109
Atlas, Charles, 146

Baby and Child Care (Spock), 82
Baby Doll (Williams), 179, 180
Backus, Jim, 76
Baldwin, James, 75
Ball, Lucille, 135
Baltzell, E. Digby, 60
Bardot, Brigitte, 209
Barrows, Cliff, 131
Barth, Ramona, 70
Barton, Bruce, 110
Beats, 7
Beckley, Paul V., 184
Bederman, Gail, 25
Bell, Bernard Iddings, 197
Bell, Ruth, 115
Benedict, Ruth, 43
Bernays, Edward, 211
Bettelheim, Bruno, 39
Beverly Hillbillies, The (TV show), 140
Bewitched (TV show), 140
Bly, Robert, 222–23, 224

Boone, Daniel, 205
Boucher, Anthony, 209
Boy Scouts of America, 83, 99, 137
Bradbury, Ray, 209, 210
Brandeis, Louis, 38
Brando, Marlon, 8
Breen, Joseph, 167, 179–80
Bromfield, Louis, 189
Brooks, Richard, 165, 181, 182, 183–84
Brooks, Van Wyck, 28, 195
Burdick, Eugene, 191
Burroughs, Edgar Rice, 25–26

Capote, Truman, 209
Carnes, Mark, 24
Catcher in the Rye (Salinger), 186
Catholic Family Life Conference, 75
Cat on a Hot Tin Roof (Williams) 12, 62, 164–88
    censorship of, 180
    early version of, 168
    ending of, 178–79
    film version of, 179–85
    on mendacity, 176–78
    revision of, 167–68, 173–75
    See also Williams, Tennessee
Cavanagh, John, 75
Cavanough, Emily, 118
census, 1950, 215–16
Center for the Study of Leisure, 56
Chance of a Life Time (Graham), 128–29
Chapman, John, 184
Chapman, Mary, 28
Chekhov, Anton, 166
Childhood and Society (Erikson), 72–73
Child Study Association of America, 70
Clurman, Harold, 173
Cohan, Steven, 30
Cohen, Lizabeth, 5
Cohen, Mickey, 129
cold war, 6, 29, 40, 43, 91, 138, 144, 193
comic books, 156–57
Commager, Henry Steele, 40

Committee on National Policy, 38, 43
Connell, R. W., 15
consumption, 10, 12, 80, 202, 217
    gendered as feminine, 4–5, 36, 66, 74, 152, 195, 196, 211
    and historiography of masculinity, 17
    and late nineteenth-century masculinity, 20
    masculinized in *Playboy,* 78, 207–8, 212
    on *The Adventures of Ozzie and Harriet,* 140, 143–44, 154–55, 158–59, 162
    See also mass culture; suburbia
Cooper, Gary, 8
Cooper, James Fenimore, 28, 63, 199
Corber, Robert J., 30, 75, 226n11
Cowley, Malcolm, 191
Cox, Harvey, 78, 200
Crack in the Picture Window, The (Keats), 193–94, 201
"Crisis of American Masculinity" (Schlesinger), 62–63
Crockett, Davy, 8, 50
Cross, Gary, 5
Crowd, The (Le Bon), 197

Darwin, Charles, 85
Davenport, Bill, 157
Dean, James, 8, 186
Decline of the American Male, The, 208
Degeneration (Nordau), 23
Degler, Carl, 58
De Grazia, Victoria, 5
D'Emilio, John, 18
DeMille, Cecil B., 126, 131
Democracy in America (Tocqueville), 39–40. *See also* American character; Tocqueville, Alexis de
Denney, Reuel, 38, 46, 59
DeVoto, Bernard, 206
Dewey, Edward Hook, 27
Dichter, Ernst, 211

Dickinson, Robert L., 82
Domino, Fats, 136
DuBois, W. E. B., 28
Duchin, Eddie, 137

Edison, Thomas, 150, 151
Edwards, Jonathan, 123
Ehrenreich, Barbara, 29
Eisenhower, Dwight, 3, 134
Elkins, Stanley, 59
Ellis, Havelock, 82
Erikson, Erik, 44, 72–73, 218
Escape from Freedom (Fromm),
    41–42. *See also* Riesman, David
evangelical culture, 107–8, 114, 116
    and emotion, 118–23
    See also Graham, Billy
Evans, Dale, 130
Exile's Return (Cowley), 191
Exurbanites, The (Spectorsky),
    60, 210
    origins of, 201–2
    popular reaction to, 205
    reviews of, 204–5
    title of, 203
    See also *Playboy*

Faces in the Crowd (Riesman, Glazer),
    38, 52. *See also* Riesman, David
Fadiman, Clifton, 205
family. *See* marriage
*Family, Socialization, and Interaction
    Process* (Parsons et al.), 77
Family Handyman, The, 153. *See also*
    Handyman movement
Farrakhan, Louis, 224
Fatherhood in America (Griswold), 20
Faulkner, William, 170
Fellowship of Christian Athletes, 109
Feminine Mystique, The (Friedan),
    214, 218
Ferm, Robert, 122–25
Fiedler, Leslie, 199, 216
Filene, Peter, 19

film
    censorship in, 179–80
    Graham's use of, 130–33
    the Nelsons and, 136
    portrayals of masculinity in, 8,
        32–33, 76
    and spectatorship masculinity, 30–31
    Tennessee Williams on, 168
    See also *Cat on a Hot Tin Roof*
        (Williams)
Finney, Charles Grandison, 109, 110,
    114, 123
First Sexual Revolution, The (White), 25
Fitzgerald, F. Scott, 209
Fleming, Ian, 210
Foreman, Joel, 30
Fountainhead, The (Rand), 67–68
Frankfurter, Felix, 38
Frankfurt school, 41–42, 47, 60, 228n28.
    See also Marxism
Franklin, Ben, 110, 143, 151
Freedman, Estelle, 18
Freud, Sigmund, 199, 223
    influence on Fromm and Riesman,
        38, 42, 43
    influence on Wylie, 69
    and Kinsey, 88, 98, 101
    in 1950s popular culture, 82
    See also psychology
Friedan, Betty, 7, 213, 218
Fromm, Erich, 194
    Escape from Freedom, 41–42
    relationship with and influence
        on Riesman, 38, 40, 41–42, 44,
        46, 50, 56, 233n43

Gabler, Neil, 30
Galdston, Iago, 189
Gall Wasp Genus Cynips, The
    (Kinsey), 85
Gathorne-Hardy, Jonathan, 100,
    238n14, 240n46
Gazarra, Ben, 170
Gehman, Richard, 65–66

Generation of Vipers (Wylie), 10, 68–72, 210. *See also* Momism
Gentlemen's Agreement (film), 201
George, Carol, 110
George Burns and Gracie Allen Show, The (TV show), 141, 142
Gershman, Ben, 157
Getty, J. Paul, 210
Gilmore, David, 17
Ginsberg, Allen, 75
Glass Menagerie, The (Williams), 180
Glazer, Nathan, 38, 46, 52
Goldstein, Joshua, 222
Goodman, Paul, 1, 56, 75, 194
Gorer, Geoffrey, 40, 43, 74, 91
Graham, Billy, 11–12, 106–34, 217, 220
    advice column of, 113, 121–22
    background of, 106–7, 114–17
    conversion of, 107, 109–10, 114–15
    conversions by, 121–25
    criticism of, 118–19
    and evangelical culture, 107, 109–10
    films of, 130–33
    and Kinsey, 91, 98
    masculinity of, 125–26
    and "muscular Christianity," 107–8, 121
    1957 New York Crusade of, 125–27
    and Norman Vincent Peale, 110–13
    preaching of, 127–28
    See also evangelical culture
Greenberg, Clement, 196
Grey, Zane, 114
Griers, John, 157
Griffith, R. Marie, 26–27
Griswold, Robert, 20, 21
Growing Up Absurd (Goodman), 75
Gurko, Leo, 191

Habermas, Jürgen, 196
Hacker, Andrew, 40
Hacker, Helen Meyer, 71
Halberstam, David, 29, 138–39
Hall, G. Stanley, 9, 23, 25

Ham, Mordecai, 114–15, 118
Hamamoto, Darrell, 142
Hamblen, Stuart, 129
Handlin, Oscar, 198
Handyman movement, 152–54, 194, 219
Haralovich, Mary Beth, 141
Harper, Redd, 130
Hartover, Jeffrey, 27
Hayworth, Rita, 88
Hazard, Patrick, 198
Head of Christ (Sallman), 108
Hearst, William Randolph, 117, 134
Hearst, William Randolph Jr., 125
Hearts of Men, The (Ehrenreich), 29
Hefner, Hugh, 13, 77–78, 101–2, 209, 213
    philosophy of, 199–200
Heller, Joseph, 211
Hemingway, Ernest, 208, 209, 212
Hendler, Glenn, 28
Herberg, Will, 58
Here Come the Nelsons (film), 136
Higham, John, 22–24
Hitchcock, Alfred, 82
Hitler, Adolf, 75
Hofstadter, Richard, 6, 56, 59
Homeward Bound (May), 29
homosexuality, 26, 212
    in American literature, 199, 206
    gay liberation movement, 101
    and Kinsey's sexual practices, 99–100
    Kinsey's study of, 85, 86–87, 89, 94–95, 104
    laws against, 84, 86
    and Momism, 67, 69, 74–77
    1950s fear of, 3, 18, 21, 29, 30, 32, 65, 91, 102, 218–19
    popular conception of, 198
    in *Rebel Without a Cause,* 76
    Schlesinger on, 62
    and social construction of gender, 15, 18, 25, 103
    and Tennessee Williams, 165, 166–67, 172–76, 180–81, 182–85

Homosexuality in Cold War America
    (Corber), 30, 75
Honeymooners, The (TV show), 141
Hoover, J. Edgar, 91
Horkheimer, Max, 196. *See also* Frankfurt
    school
Horney, Karen, 38, 50
Horrocks, Roger, 21
Hour of Decision (Graham), 121, 131
Howe, Irving, 6
Hudson, Rock, 8
Huyssen, Andres, 196
Hyman, Stanley Edgar, 198

Ibsen, Henrik, 166
I Love Lucy (TV show), 140, 142
Intimate Matters (D'Emilio and
    Freedman), 18
Invention of Heterosexuality, The
    (Katz), 30
I Remember Mama (TV show), 141
Iron John (Bly), 222–23
Izenberg, Gerald, 28

Jacobs, Norman, 198
James, William
    on the conversion experience,
        123–24
    and Progressive Era masculinity, 9,
        22, 23, 27
Jarrell, Randall, 198
Johnson, Lyndon, 62
Johnson, Torrey, 116
Johnson, Virginia, 200
Jones, Gerard, 140–41
Jones, James H., 99–100, 237n2,
    238n14
Jorgensen, Christine, 62, 76, 95
Jung, Carl, 69, 223
juvenile delinquency, 1, 21, 145
    Graham on, 127
    and Momism, 67, 74–75
    in *Rebel Without a Cause,* 76
    See also mass culture

Kaplan, Peter, 137
Kardiner, Abram, 65
Katz, Jonathan, 30
Kaye, Danny, 88
Kazan, Elia, 165, 166, 167, 168,
    173, 176
Keats, John, 193–94, 201
Kenistan, Kenneth, 61
Kennedy, John, 4, 31, 62, 63
Kerouac, Jack, 75, 89
Kerr, Walter, 172, 184
Kilgallen, Dorothy, 134
Kimbrell, Andrew, 224
Kimmel, Michael, 19
King, Alexander, 211
Kinsey, Alfred, 11, 77, 81–105, 113,
    134, 165, 200, 217, 219
    correspondence with readers,
        1, 93–97
    definition of masculinity, 103–4
    definition of sex, 86
    impact of, 102–4
    sexual habits of, 81, 98–101
    See also sex; *Sexual Behavior in the
        Human Male*
Klineberg, Otto, 71
Kraft-Ebbing, Richard Freiherr
    von, 82
Krassner, Paul, 211–12

Larabee, Eric, 36
Larson, Mel, 116, 121, 128
Lazarsfeld, Paul, 198
Le Bon, Gustave, 196, 197
Lees, Hannah, 79
Leibman, Nina, 142
Leonard, George, 195
Lerner, Max, 189
Levitt, Theodore, 59
Lewis, Sinclair, 209, 210
Liberace, 8, 69
Lincoln, Abraham, 150, 151
Lindbergh, Charles, 19
Lipset, Seymour Martin, 57

Lonely Crowd, The (Riesman), 6, 9–10, 34–61, 192, 201
    and American history, 49–50
    on the autonomous personality, 60
    character typologies, 35–37, 44–45, 49–50
    genesis of, 39–43
    misunderstanding of, 35–36
    reaction to, 36–37, 48, 57
    title of, 34
Love and Death in the American Novel (Fiedler), 199
Lowell, James, 28
Luce, Henry, 125
Lunbeck, Elizabeth, 64–65
Lynd, Helen, 39
Lynd, Robert, 39
Lynes, Russell, 70, 203

Macbeth (Shakespeare), 105
Macdonald, Dwight, 4, 8, 68, 190, 196, 197
Macfadden, Bernarr, 27, 84, 110, 111, 237n8
Mailer, Norman, 18, 211
Main Street (Lewis), 210
Malden, Karl, 169
Man in the Gray Flannel Suit, The (Wilson), 193, 201–2, 205
Mangus, R. A., 96
Manhood in America (Kimmel), 19
Manhood at Harvard (Townsend), 27–28
Manhood in the Making (Gilmore), 17
Manliness and Civilization (Bederman), 25
Marcuse, Herbert, 196
marriage, 15, 47
    companionate, 12, 19, 20–21, 28, 30, 219, 226n13
    Graham on, 121
    Kinsey on, 87
    and the Nelsons, 143–44, 155–56
    sex in, 82
    on television, 138–39, 141
Marsh, Margaret, 28

Marxism, 41–42, 43, 47, 60. *See also* Frankfurt school; mass culture
Masculine Mystique, The (Kimbrell), 224
masculinity
    at end of nineteenth century, 9, 16–17, 22–25
    essentialist view of, 83
    and evangelical culture, 107–10
    historiography of, 17–30
    Kinsey's definition of, 84–85, 103–4
    and "male panic," 2–3, 7–8, 11, 13, 16–17, 23, 28, 32–33, 67, 79–80, 213–14, 217, 220–24
    Ozzie Nelson and, 145–46, 159
    as pathology, 21
    Potter on, 50–51
    Rand on, 68
    Riesman on, 47
    social construction of, 15–16, 22
    spectatorship masculinity, 23–24, 26, 30–32, 150–51, 222
    on television, 141
    and the therapeutic culture, 65
Masculinity in Crisis (Horrocks), 21
mass culture, 8, 10, 12, 24, 32, 59, 78, 204
    and Frankfurt school, 41–42, 196, 198
    and gender anxiety, 4–5, 152, 189, 194–99, 211, 217
    history of debate over, 190–91
    Macdonald's analysis of, 197
    and the Nelsons, 143–44, 156–57, 162
    and public intellectuals, 6–7, 63
    Riesman on, 34, 35–36, 43–44, 45–46, 48–49, 54, 61
    role in the construction of gender, 15–16
    See also consumption; masculinity; suburbia
Mass Culture Revisited, 198
Masters, William, 200
May, Elaine Tyler, 29
Mayes, Herbert, 211
McCarthy, Joseph, 69, 189

McCartney, Bill, 223
McGee, Lemuel, 79
McGiffert, Michael, 39
McKittrick, Eric, 59
McLoughlin, William, 109, 113, 126
McPartland, John, 194
Mead, Margaret, 50, 58, 74
    on feminism, 51
    influence on Riesman, 35, 40, 42–43, 231n21
    on Kinsey, 91, 102
    on Momism, 71
    on sexuality, 82
Meeham, Diana, 138
Melville, Herman, 28, 199
men. See masculinity
Mencken, H. L., 197
Meyer, Donald, 106
Meyerowitz, Joanne, 30
Miles, Catherine Cox, 83, 103
Mill, John Stuart, 45
Miller, Arthur, 185
Miller, Russell, 209
Mills, C. Wright, 6, 35, 204–5
Minton, Henry C., 103
Mitchell, Margaret, 170
Modernism and Masculinity (Izenberg), 28
Momism, 7, 67, 71–75, 77, 143, 152, 190, 197, 217–18
    and "bossism," 72–73
    Keats on, 194
    Spectorsky on, 206
    Whyte on, 68–70, 210–11
    See also women; Wylie, Philip
Montagu, Ashley, 164, 211
Moody, Dwight, 109, 114, 123
Moore, James E., 126
More, Douglas, 207
Moskin, J. Robert, 74
Mosse, George L., 26
Motion Picture Producers Association of America, 167, 179–80. See also Breen, Joseph; film

Mr. Blandings Builds His Dream House (film), 201
Mr. Texas (film), 130–32
Mumford, Lewis, 191–92
Murphy, Brenda, 173
Mussolini, Benito, 75

Nabokov, Vladimir, 209
National Council of Catholic Women, 91
National Research Council, 83, 85
Nation of Islam, 224
Nelson, David, 135–63 passim
    attitude toward Ozzie, 147, 151, 154
    masculinity of, 159, 162
Nelson, Don, 157
Nelson, Harriet, 135–63 passim
    music career of, 136, 137
    radio show of, 136
    and struggle over gender roles, 146–53
    See also *Adventures of Ozzie and Harriet, The*
Nelson, Ozzie, 12, 135–63, 220
    background of, 137
    and consumption, 154–55
    and fatherhood, 155
    and mass culture, 156–58, 162
    music career of, 136
    as other-directed, 142–44
    See also *Adventures of Ozzie and Harriet, The*
Nelson, Ricky, 135–63 passim
    attitude toward Ozzie, 151
    music of, 136, 138, 146, 147
    masculinity of, 159
Neoconservatism
    and Riesman, 57–58
Newman, Paul, 181
Niebuhr, Reinhold, 35
    on Billy Graham, 118, 126
    on Kinsey, 91, 102
Nixon, Richard, 62, 125, 134
No Down Payment (McPartland), 194

Nordau, Max, 23
Not June Cleaver (Meyerowitz), 30
Noyes, John Humphrey, 100

Oiltown, USA (film), 132
Oneida colony, 100
On the Road (Kerouac), 89
Organization Man, The (Whyte), 6, 56, 60, 73, 192–93, 201
Other Fifties, The (Foreman), 30
Oursler, Fulton, 91
Ownby, Ted, 114
Ozzie and Harriet (comic books), 156–57

Packard, Vance, 6, 35, 190
Page, Geraldine, 179
Parsons, Talcott, 38, 77
Peace with God (Graham), 120–21
Peale, Norman Vincent, 125
    compared to Billy Graham, 110–13, 124, 126, 134
    on Kinsey, 91
Peck, Joseph, 64
Pendergast, Tom, 20
People of Plenty (Potter), 58
Pierson, George Wilson, 39
Playboy (magazine), 13, 18, 30, 164, 190, 199–200, 207–14
    conception of sexuality, 77–78
    and Kinsey, 102
    literary ambitions of, 208
    philosophy of, 207
    symposium on masculinity of, 207, 211–12
    See also Hefner, Hugh; Spectorsky, Auguste Comte
Pleck, Joseph, 65
Poe, James, 182
Pomeroy, Wardell, 89, 97–98, 99
Potter, David, 50–51, 58
Power of Positive Thinking, The (Peale), 111–13
Practical Home Handyman, The (magazine), 153

Presley, Elvis, 8
Princess of Mars, A (Burroughs), 26
Promise Keepers, 223–24
psychology
    and contemporary masculinity, 223
    at end of nineteenth century, 23, 27
    Fromm and, 42–43
    and homosexuality, 199
    influence on Riesman, 37–39, 46, 49, 53, 60
    and Momism, 72–74
    and the Nelsons, 155–56, 161–62
    and religion, 111, 123–24
    and sex, 82, 92
    and Tennessee Williams, 167
    the therapeutic model of culture, 65
    See also Freud, Sigmund
public intellectuals, 9, 11, 14, 41, 47, 57, 60, 143
    and mass culture debate, 5–7, 34–35, 54, 217
    See also consumption; mass culture; Riesman, David; suburbia

Quintero, Jose, 173

race, 3–4, 16, 25–26, 33
Racine, Jean, 169
Rader, Paul, 108–9
Rand, Ayn, 67–68, 71
Rebel Without a Cause (film), 76
Reich, William, 82
Reik, Theodore, 211
"Relationship between the Masculine Component and Personality, The" (Seltzer), 64, 83
Religion and Men Forward Movement, 108
"Reorientation of American Culture, The" (Higham), 22–24
Rickenbacker, Eddie, 125

Riesman, David, 34–61, 62, 66, 74, 152, 194–95, 201, 203, 215, 217, 219
  on American character, 41, 52
  background of, 37–39
  on gender, 51–56
  and historiography, 58–59
  and neoconservatism, 57
  political apathy project of, 43–44
  as public intellectual, 47
  and religion, 37
Robinson, Jackie, 91
Rogers, Fred, 224
Rogers, Roy, 130
Roland, Albert, 153
Roosevelt, Eleanor, 184
Roosevelt, Theodore, 222
  and Christianity, 108, 110
  and Progressive Era masculinity, 9, 22, 23, 25, 27, 28, 31
Rosenberg, Bernard, 196, 197–98
Rotundo, E. Anthony, 17

Sagan, Francoise, 209
Sahl, Mort, 211
Sallman, Warner, 108
Sartre, Jean-Paul, 45
"Saving Remnant, The" (Riesman), 48
Savran, David, 24, 227–28n17
Scheinfeld, Amram, 78
Schlesinger, Arthur Jr., 29, 62–63
"Secret Life of Walter Mitty, The" (Thurber), 31, 112, 229n38
Seduction of the Innocent (Wertham), 95
Seltzer, Carl, 64, 83
sex
  in *Cat on a Hot Tin Roof,* 170, 177–78, 179–80
  and concept of "normality," 86–92, 96–97
  and gender, 83
  Graham on, 134
  Kinsey's definition of, 86
  laws regulating, 83–84
  and masculinity, 11
  and *Playboy,* 199–200
  sexual revolution of 1960s, 77, 103–4, 227n7
  sexual utopia of Kinsey, 100–101
  See also Kinsey, Alfred
Sex and Personality (Miles and Terman), 83
Sexual Behavior in the Human Female (Kinsey), 87, 100, 102
Sexual Behavior in the Human Male (Kinsey), 81–105
  reaction to, 85–86, 88–92
  sampling and interviewing methods in, 89–90, 97–98
Sexual Revolution, The (Reich), 82
Shakespeare, William, 70, 155, 162
Shea, George Beverly, 117, 127
Sheehy, Monsignor Maurice S., 91
Skinner, B. F., 38, 101
Sommers, Jay, 157
Souls in Conflict (film), 132
Spectorsky, Auguste Comte, 13, 78, 190, 199–200, 219
  articles by, 203
  background of, 200–201
  career of, 201–2
  relationship with Hefner, 209
  relationship with Wylie, 210, 213
  See also Exurbanites, The
Spectorsky, Brook, 201
Spigel, Lynn, 139
Spock, Benjamin, 82
Spoto, Donald, 165
Stalin, Joseph, 75
Stockman, Steve, 81
Strecker, Edward A., 74
Streetcar Named Desire, A (Williams), 96, 169, 180, 186
Strindberg, August, 166
Strout, Cushing, 60
suburbia, 59
  as feminizing, 4, 162, 190, 191–94, 199–200, 223

suburbia (*continued*)
   Spectorsky on, 201–4, 208
   on television, 138, 140
   Whyte on, 56–57, 192–93
   See also consumption; mass culture; public intellectuals
Sullivan, Harry Stack, 38
Sunday, Billy, 108–9, 118, 123, 126
Susman, Warren, 72

Taking It Like a Man (Savran), 24
Tarzan, 25, 31, 32, 114
Taylor, Elizabeth, 181
Tea and Sympathy (Anderson), 62, 173
Ten Commandments, The (film), 126
Terman, Lewis
   criticism of Kinsey, 90
   masculinity-femininity scale of, 103, 104
   works of, 82, 83
Their Mothers' Sons (Strecker), 74
Theory of the Leisure Class (Veblen), 5, 53
Thomas, Dylan, 179
Thompson, Dorothy, 91–92
Thurber, James, 31, 69, 151
Tischler, Nancy, 170
Tocqueville, Alexis de, 190, 230n15
   influence on American studies, 38, 39–40, 43
   Riesman and, 45, 47, 57, 58
   See also American studies
Tocqueville and Democracy in America (Pierson), 39
Tolstoy, Leo, 45
Torn, Rip, 170
Townsend, Kim, 27–28
Transsexuality, 76, 95
Trilling, Lionel, 92, 102, 196
Turner, Frederick Jackson, 22, 47, 49–50, 215, 216–17, 221
Twain, Mark, 199

Van den Haag, Ernst, 198
Varieties of Religious Experience, The (James), 123–24
Vaus, Jim, 129, 132
Veblen, Thorstein, 4–5, 47, 53–54, 202
Vicar of Wakefield, The (Goldsmith), 156
Vidal, Gore, 75
Virginian, The (Wister), 23

Walden Two (Skinner), 101
Walker, Cindy, 131
Wallace, Edgar, 189
Wallis, W. Allen, 90
War and Gender (Goldstein), 222
Washington, George, 150
Waters, Ethel, 132
Watson, John, 38
Watts, Richard Jr., 184
Wayne, John, 1, 8, 33, 164, 222
Weber, Max, 38, 47
Weisblatt, Tinky, 141
Wertham, Fredric, 95
West, Mae, 88
White, David Manning, 196, 197–98
White, Kevin, 25
Whitefield, George, 123
Whiteman, Paul, 137
Whyte, William H., 6, 34, 56, 57, 201
   and Momism, 73, 190, 192–93, 194
Wiese, Chris, 79
Williams, Rose, 166
Williams, Tennessee, 12, 33, 63, 75, 164–88, 209, 218, 219–20
   background of, 166–67
   and Kinsey, 95–96
   on masculinity, 186–88
   sexuality of, 164–67, 181
   See also *Cat on a Hot Tin Roof*
Wills, Gary, 1
Wilson, Sloan, 193
Windham, David, 169
Wiretapper, 132
Wister, Owen, 23, 27

women
    debate over femininity, 2
    and feminist movements, 16, 217–18, 221
    as "handymen," 153
    journalistic condemnation of, 10, 32, 70–73, 210–13
    as majority, 215–16
    1920s "New Woman," 19
    as other-directed, 51, 55–56
    as religious converts, 111–12
    Riesman on, 51–55
    on television, 138
    See also marriage; Momism
Wonderful Clouds, The (Sagan), 209

Wood, Audrey, 166, 171, 173
Wright, Frank Lloyd, 67
Wrong, Dennis, 48
Wylie, Philip, 10, 13
    articles for *Playboy*, 210–13
    on Momism, 68–70, 71, 74, 79, 207–8
    See also Momism

Yerkes, Robert, 82
Young Men's Christian Association (YMCA), 108
Youth for Christ International, 115–17

Zamperini, Louis, 129